Kingsley Amis, who was born in South London in 1922, was educated at the City of London School and St John's College, Oxford. At one time he was a university lecturer, a keen reader of science fiction and a jazz enthusiast. His novels include *Lucky Jim* (1954), *Take A Girl Like You* (1960), *One Fat Englishman* (1963), *The Anti-Death League* (1966), *The Riverside Villas Murder* (1973), *Ending Up* (1974), *The Alteration* (1976, winner of the John W. Campbell Memorial Award), *Jake's Thing* (1978), *Russian Hide-and-Seek* (1980), *Stanley and the Women* (1984), *The Old Devils* (1986, winner of the Booker Prize), *Difficulties with Girls* (1988) and *The Folks that Live on the Hill* (1990). Among his other publications are *New Maps of Hell*, a survey of science fiction (1960), *The James Bond Dossier* (1965), *Colonel Sun*, a James Bond adventure (1968, under the pseudonym of Robert Markham), *Rudyard Kipling and his World* (1975) and *The Golden Age of Science Fiction* (1981). He published his *Collected Poems* in 1979 and his *Collected Short Stories* in 1980 (revised edition 1987), as well as a work of non-fiction, *Memoirs*, in 1991. Many of his books are published by Penguin. He has written ephemerally on politics, education, language, films, television, restaurants and drink. Kingsley Amis was awarded the CBE in 1981 and received a knighthood in 1990.

KINGSLEY AMIS

———

THE AMIS COLLECTION

SELECTED NON-FICTION
1954–1990

WITH AN INTRODUCTION BY
JOHN MCDERMOTT

PENGUIN BOOKS

PENGUIN BOOKS

Published by the Penguin Group
Penguin Books Ltd, 27 Wrights Lane, London W8 5TZ, England
Penguin Books USA Inc., 375 Hudson Street, New York, New York 10014, USA
Penguin Books Australia Ltd, Ringwood, Victoria, Australia
Penguin Books Canada Ltd, 10 Alcorn Avenue, Toronto, Ontario, Canada M4V 3B2
Penguin Books (NZ) Ltd, 182–190 Wairau Road, Auckland 10, New Zealand

Penguin Books Ltd, Registered Offices: Harmondsworth, Middlesex, England

First published by Hutchinson, an imprint of the Random Century Group, 1990
Published in Penguin Books 1991
1 3 5 7 9 10 8 6 4 2

This collection copyright © Kingsley Amis, 1990
'The Anti-Sex, Croquet-Playing, Statistic-Snubbing, Boyle-Baiting, Black Fascist Paper'
copyright © Kingsley Amis and Robert Conquest, 1969
'A Short Educational Dictionary' copyright © Kingsley Amis and Robert Conquest, 1970
'ILEA Confidential' copyright © Kingsley Amis and Robert Conquest, 1975
All rights reserved

The moral right of the author has been asserted

Printed in England by Clays Ltd, St Ives plc

Except in the United States of America, this book is sold subject
to the condition that it shall not, by way of trade or otherwise, be lent,
re-sold, hired out, or otherwise circulated without the publisher's
prior consent in any form of binding or cover other than that in
which it is published and without a similar condition including this
condition being imposed on the subsequent purchaser

Contents

PART THREE
ANTHOLOGIES

Preface

Some of the pieces reprinted here have been shortened, to avoid where possible going over the same ground twice or otherwise trying the reader's patience. A few have been lengthened, to incorporate later information. But, much as I should have liked to here and there, I have nowhere materially altered what I first wrote, though I have corrected a few stylistic errors.

KINGSLEY AMIS
London
May 1990

Introduction

The earliest of these pieces appeared in 1954, the year of *Lucky Jim*, and the most recent in 1990, the year of *The Folks That Live on the Hill*, Kingsley Amis's twentieth novel. Over that period his reputation has gone through ups and downs that have seen him successively hailed and derided as subversively philistine, scorned as a socialist turncoat who voted Tory and turned pornographer, and finally acknowledged (albeit through gritted teeth for some) as among the handful of most considerable novelists now writing. This looks ominously like a career with 'early', 'middle' and 'late' periods, terms uncomfortably in keeping with the sort of artist-as-man-apart pretentiousness which Amis himself has always been prompt to mock, not least because such posturing is usually a mark of the second-rate rather than of excellence.

Those who object to his novels generally do so for one of a number of related reasons. The first is that he writes *so much*: clearly no one who is so productive, so busy, can be serious as an *artist*. A second depends upon irrelevant ideological criteria to damn him either because the novels are expressions of the author's unacceptable private views (and therefore not very good novels) or because, although the novels do all the requisite things in terms of laughter and tears, their author is known to hold heterodox views, and the novels are no good for that reason. If fresh evidence were needed to establish that this is often the case, the publicity that followed publication of *The Folks That Live on the Hill* supplies it abundantly. For example, one (generally sympathetic) commentator described Amis as a 'charming curmudgeon with appalling views'; a woman reviewer observed that 'you don't have to be a woman to dislike [the novel]—but it helps'. Whether admiringly or otherwise, the parallel most frequently drawn is with Evelyn Waugh, though recognition of the writer's skill is not often as frankly conceded as in this example: 'Amis has come to occupy the Evelyn Waugh Chair of Savage Indignation. Like Waugh, he is splendid with prejudice, rich in bracing dislikes. Also like Waugh, he is a consummate writer of sentences, a mordant practitioner of perfected English prose.'

However we characterise the successive phases of his development as a novelist, there is a consistency about the prominence that Amis's views have always enjoyed. This has generally been based on the idea of his 'having it in for highbrows' (as another recent review puts it). It is a loaded way of saying that he opposes whatever vitiates the genuine purposes of writing and the proper commerce between writer and reader — be it the log-rolling of an influential clique, new-fangled notions of theory which occupy rival academics in taking in each other's washing, or the operations of subsidy.

It is difficult to see in what genuine sense the term 'philistine' can justly be applied to a career-long commitment to (as he puts it) 'writing novels within the main English-language tradition. That is, trying to tell interesting stories about understandable characters in a reasonably straightforward style, no tricks, no experimental tomfoolery'. In the early days, the alleged philistinism was a matter of seeing heroes such as Jim Dixon, John Lewis (*That Uncertain Feeling*) and Garnet Bowen (*I Like It Here*) as storm-troops of a social revolution committed to dingy mediocrity and hatred of art. More tellingly, Amis used his position as a critic (from 1953 he reviewed regularly for the *Spectator*) to debunk the central documents of post-Bloomsbury, post-modernist culture, along with their proponents; as Harry Ritchie has written, 'this necessarily seemed like an attack on a class because his target was a socially homogeneous group, even a caste, reinforced by networks of family ties no less than school ones. A *Who's Who*? entry reading Eton-Balliol *New Statesman-Horizon-Sunday Times* is actually Connolly's but is faithful to the type. The corps of English gentlemen-of-letters — Cyril Connolly and Raymond Mortimer (*Sunday Times* reviewers), John Lehmann (editor of the *London Magazine*), Stephen Spender (joint editor of *Encounter*), Philip Toynbee (principal reviewer of the *Observer*) and Alan Pryce-Jones (editor of the *Times Literary Supplement*) — occupied the high ground of literary influence. They constituted a mandarin class that Toynbee himself described as "younger members of, or immediate and grateful heirs to, the Bloomsbury Group", united in professing a high-minded devotion to Art with a capital A, in particular to the modernist work of the "School of Paris".'

Not many of these people were to any serious extent original writers on their own account, but what they held up for admiration in their journalism was a version of the avant-garde and of modernism that seemed outmoded as well as uninteresting. This was the real issue, a concern that literature should connect with recognisable human affairs and not with other literature and should do so in a language accessible to readers, but it unavoidably became entangled with issues of class, setting the philistine against the high-falutin', the plain man against the mandarin.

In December 1953 the *Sunday Times* thought its two leading reviewers sufficiently important to warrant profiles: Connolly prescribed despair and angst as necessary virtues for the modern writer, whilst Mortimer boasted of his collection of Sèvres porcelain, and described the dining-room of his Bloomsbury flat which he had decorated with French newspapers. When *Lucky Jim* came out a few weeks later, its mocking picture of arty dilettantism should have seemed feeble by comparison with the real thing. The tactics of opposition to belletristic posturing produced in the novels heroes who were provincial heterosexual beer-drinkers, who liked England, rather than metropolitan, pansified claret-bibbers, who liked it *there*. In the reviews it produced a willingness to deflate the pretensions of angst (as in Colin Wilson's *The Outsider*) and to displace such shibboleths as *Beowulf, Paradise Lost* and *The Faerie Queene* because of their lack of human interest. At the same time Amis recognised a wider sense of culture that could embrace jazz and science fiction as well as 'filthy Mozart'.

Such an emphasis also marks the gap between Amis and another source of opposition to the London mandarins. Leavis and his apostles had their own campaign against literary dilettantism in the name of high moral seriousness. That this could so often show itself as high moral fuss, and get it so wrong as to elevate such a fraud as D. H. Lawrence at the expense of a genuine moralist (who could write) such as Fielding, led Amis to conclude that Leavis (who once called him a 'pornographer') and *Scrutiny* 'have, on balance, done more harm than good to literature and its study'. Part of the point of *I Like It Here*—in my view, at least—is that there is *Great Tradition* phoniness as well as the mandarin variety.

These attempts to insist on human concerns and rational procedures as the central business of literature have been consistent from the 1953 mocking of W. R. Rodgers and Edith Sitwell, with all the other attacks on overblown neo-Romanticism. Consistent too has been the pleasure Amis takes in simple annoyance of his opponents. Yet the whirligig of time brings in his revenges, and from opposing those who treated literature as too exclusive a domain Amis has now done an about-face on the same plot of ground. He now attacks those who sell it cheap, displacing literary qualities with paraphrase.

In the process Amis has developed, as well as acquired, a public personality: the radical intellectual of the Fifties deplored by the Establishment now dismisses socialism, bemoans a decline in educational standards, denounces the Arts Council, pornography, attitudes to public service, American literature, contemporary music. There has been a long sequence of spectacular rows conducted through the correspondence columns of various journals and newspapers—on the right of reply to misrepresentation, American involvement in Vietnam, Yevtushenko's candidature for the Oxford Poetry Chair, and the current state of British education, among others.

The best description of the line Amis takes is the one he gives himself in talking of Chesterton, whom he resembles in some essential ways much more than he resembles Waugh: 'What is simple, generally agreed, old and obvious is not only more likely to be true than what is complex, original, new and subtle, but much more interesting as well—a prescription calculated to alienate almost any type of progressive thinker.' As these collected pieces make clear, he is an interesting, as well as a vigorous, polemicist, and his role as a good hater is performed with great wit added to the gusto. What partly irritates those who don't like him is that the old devil seems to have all the best jokes.

But the very success with which the early and late *personae*—philistine, vulgarian, fat-cat and reactionary elitist—passed into public currency has persistently stood between some readers and a proper appreciation of the novels, which by some critical *petitio principii* have been too easily read as glosses on the journalism and even as autobiography. So one reviewer of his most recent novel (dedicated to the last-surviving mandarin, Peter Quennell) speaks of its 'merits as a handbook for philistines, snobs and sexists', while another, calling him a 'reactionary misogynist', begins with the proposition that 'by now we might assume that the name of Kingsley Amis stands either as a sufficient recommendation or a sufficient warning'. Whatever may be the sense of that as regards views expressed in the novels, one tires of asking 'what about the novels as novels, then?'

Actually, the misogynist business—and *cf.* xenophobe, homophobe, etc—is an interesting case in point since it is so impressively obvious that he does what more ideologically trendy writers have not yet dared to do: he treats women the same as men, criticising their vices as well as celebrating their virtues. There is not only Margaret Peel but Christine; and if there is one character who embodies the decent virtues that Amis desiderates it is Jenny Bunn, in both her incarnations (rather than Patrick Standish in both his), who will doubtless age into a version of the equally decent and ill-treated Rhiannon Weaver. It is his co-sexers who generally get a rough ride in the novels, the heterosexual ones especially; there are enough types such as Roger Micheldene, Bernard Bastable and Alan Weaver to constitute a new fictional model—the hero-as-shit.

One reason why Amis is convincing as a novelist is that his characters, nice or nasty, are rendered so fully; no major character is ever entirely one or the other—he is too clever a tactician for that. And readers who should know better, being writers themselves, persist in not reading fiction as fiction. Thus D. J. Enright, discussing *Take A Girl Like You* (1960), speaks of the inclusion of Beethoven in a cricket team of bad men as a sign of Amis's, not Patrick Standish's, delight in sneering: filthy Beethoven, this time. Writing of Philip Roth many years ago, Amis asked, 'Could we have a modest return to fiction as fiction?'

To make this plea is not to deny an important connection between novels and the worlds they describe. Amis's novels are effective in part because of the faithfulness with which they capture the recognisable surface of everyday experience. Amis has often been acute and accurate in capturing the flavour and texture of the periods he is writing about, most notably through their language, which he mimics uncannily well (no contemporary writer produces such sharply rendered dialogue—for once the allusion to Waugh has some point). From *Lucky Jim* onwards there are in effect 'state of England' novels so rich in their evocation of social detail and movements of contemporary feeling that receptive readers of differing views may find in them illustrative instances of what most strikes them about contemporary society.

On a number of occasions Amis has said that his subject is the permanent things in human nature: 'I could reel you off a list as long as your arm, beginning with ambition, sexual desire, vainglory, foolishness . . . the dress in which these abstractions are clothed must be contemporary . . . but it's not the job of the novelist to represent the scene in any sense. He may turn out to be doing that, if he's any good'. As his poem 'A Bookshop Idyll' puts it

> *From somewhere in this (as in any) matter*
> *A moral beckons*

and the moral is drawn out in another poem, 'The Huge Artifice', as well as all over the novels.

The Amis Collection brings together a large number of non-fiction pieces that cover thirty-odd years of literary history as well as a range of social and personal issues. Many of them were printed first in the *Spectator* or the *Observer*, titles that indicate the stance of a writer who stands back for an appraisal of real and made-up people, and knows the difference between them.

I acknowledge the help given me by Harry Ritchie's work on Kingsley Amis in the preparation of this introduction.

JOHN McDERMOTT
Wigan
June 1990

PART ONE
Writing

Real and Made-up People

All fiction is autobiographical in the sense that its writer cannot truly invent anyone or anything, can only edit his experience, and cannot, poor fellow, represent ideas that have never entered his head. Let us at once discard this trifling and tautological sense, and notice the plain distinction between action based on what the writer has made up and that based on what has actually happened to him. The distinction is not always sharp, but in practice we usually know where we are. Treatment of character is the surest guide.

The second kind of writer only arrived on the scene about 1900. We are told that Dickens put something of his father into Mr Micawber, but he is not writing about his father. Maggie Tulliver is rather the same sort of person as George Eliot, but the latter is not writing about herself in *The Mill on the Floss*, nor about what actually happened to her, and Dorothea Brooke is not to any interesting extent the same sort of person as she. (Mr Casaubon may look like a different case, one I will return to.) Then D. H. Lawrence started writing about himself, people he knew and what there was of what had actually happened to him, and his knowing or unknowing heirs are all around us today. They have raised the ghosts of long-dead Philistines who thought the poet a liar and history the only truth, and Katherine Mansfield is called 'the most autobiographical of writers' in unadorned commendation (admittedly on television).

This is not a polemical piece; we have plenty of room for two, or two dozen, kinds of novelist. But the autobiographical kind works under severe limitations. The writer whose direct experience gives him one satisfactory novel (as opposed to a short or a very short story) in fifty years is very lucky. The rest of the time, thinness, repetitiousness, poverty of incident, scarcity of character supervene. If, in life, his marriage breaks down, he takes off with somebody else, has difficulties with her and with his children and finally returns home, or stays away, he has little hope, even with the aid of a fictitious charwoman or taxi-driver here and there, of writing about that experience and those people and coming through with a novel. As my friend George MacBeth put it to me the other day, such a novelist is simply not doing enough.

The writer who makes things up is on the face of it much freer. I make things up, make my characters up, not out of superior virtue but through something deeper than conscious choice. I did once, out of laziness or sagging imagination, try to put real people on paper and produced what is by common consent my worst novel, *I Like It Here*. There were fictitious characters and incidents in it too, and it is only those that I dare to allow to cross my conscious mind nowadays. Real people are interesting enough, but everybody is what he does, and to portray a man doing what he actually did do means holding up the whole show while he does it. By what is either a paradox or a truism, the closer the likeness of the real interesting person, the less interesting he will be in the novel.

I learnt my lesson in the course of setting out to repeat my mistake. Old Jock MacDonald, I thought (the name and all details are changed)—here is somebody so unconsciously funny that I must 'put him into a book'. But I liked Jock and could not offend him; so he became Welsh instead of Scotch, an architect instead of a stockbroker, a bachelor instead of a married man. And then, as the plot took shape, I needed Jock to do things he not only had not actually done, but never would have done, so there was very little left of him in the result. Later Jock told me he had particularly enjoyed the portrayal of that Welsh architect fellow. Had he seen? Had he not seen? Most likely he had seen without knowing he had seen.

So where, since those days, do those characters come from? Me, in the first instance. All my heroes, and other principal figures, have a great deal of me in them. No doubt the heroes, at least, show some family likeness, but I am not writing about different, or similar, bits of me. Nor, incidentally, am I writing about me mixed up, as camouflage or for fun, with some real person. 'Who were you getting at in that television chap in your last one? Robin Frost? David Day?' Nobody; I made him up.

But to resume: even intelligent readers, even those who might consciously reject the concept of fiction as experience with style sauce, much overestimate the degree of identification between author and central character. I treasure the memory of being introduced to the amiable Marghanita Laski not long after the publication of my first novel, *Lucky Jim*. On hearing my name, she looked at me and about her in something not far from panic. She was wondering which I would do first: pour my pint of bitter over her or assault her sexually. To this day, on hearing that I was born in South London, people will murmur that they always thought I was a Yorkshireman; Jim in fact came from Lancashire, but only a close reading shows that.

Either origin would have done to produce the distancing that, through that deep instinct, I felt I needed: he must not come from anywhere near London, teach English, be married, admire Mozart, be much too law-abiding—or cowardly—to appear drunk on the lecture platform or hijack a professor's taxi, as in my own case. And, again incidentally, to polish up my non-autobiographical claims, the whole

4

basic situation of that novel was clear in my mind before I ever thought of teaching at a university, let alone had started to do so.

Yes, but there is still some sort of identification: all my heroes start from me and in a sense stay with me, even when there are half a dozen of them occupying the same book, as in *The Anti-Death League*. This bond is at least as strong when the protagonist is unpleasant. Roger Micheldene of *One Fat Englishman* is, at least in intention, unlike me in various radical ways, starting with his gluttony about food, a substance my own gluttonies do not touch (curries excepted). I strongly disapprove of nearly everything Roger is and does, and yet the critic who wrote, 'I can't help feeling that the author likes the character', had seen the truth, not that it is a very surprising one. We all like people we disapprove of: one of the injustices of life that at the same time help to make it bearable. And it is doubly hard to dislike one's child. That worn and sentimentalising metaphor does still give a hint of the strength of the attachment in question.

The novelist's heroes, or central characters, are clearly meant to do more than just go round being close or distant relatives of him. As between him and them in the first place, they are vehicles of his self-criticism—an important function of poetry too. By that very act of distancing, by projecting himself into an entity that is part of himself and yet not himself, he may be able to see more clearly, and judge more harshly, his own weaknesses and follies; and, since he must know that no failings are unique, he may be helped to acquire tolerance for them in others. In the second place, if the novel comes off at all, the reader will perhaps accompany the writer in some parallel process of self-discovery.

But that is still not enough; in an age that increasingly likes to view art as occupational therapy for the artist, it may even be too much. What about the character working in the novel? For me, the novel works on the character, at any rate rough-hews the character. It is not the case that a fully-formed hero goes stalking about in search of situations in which he can be effectively arrogant or incompetent or spiteful or pathetic or even decent, though he may very likely fall as if by chance into a couple of such in the course of being written about. The central situation comes first in every sense.

Here I must be unabashedly personal to show what I mean. *Lucky Jim* originally quickened in the womb of time when I spent a few minutes in the senior common-room of a provincial university (not Swansea). I thought at once, 'Christ, somebody ought to do something about *this*'. What followed can most easily, and accurately, be put in note form. University shags. Provincial. Probably keen on culture. Crappy culture. Fellow who doesn't fit in. Seems anti-culture. Non-U. Non-Oxbridge. Beer. Girls. Can't say what he really thinks. Boss trouble. Given chores. Disasters. Boring boss (a) so boring girl (b). Nice girl comes but someone else's property. Whose? etc.

This may be too articulate or logical and in the wrong order here and there, but not in the wrong order overall. Those who remember the novel will see that a large amount of Jim's character is already there, stated or implied, and reflection may suggest that even what could seem quite accidental quirks of behaviour are logical extensions of that same character. The various faces Jim makes to himself, for instance, are the covert protests and tension-reducers of a man in enemy territory without effective allies. Not that I saw them as that when I first thought of them; it took a critic to point the connection out to me. So much of all this takes place at some non-conscious level that almost any account of it must be riddled with unintended rationalisations and false links.

Jim, and *Jim*, took literally years to emerge even half-formed from those depths. Not practice but good fortune saw to it that, on one later occasion, the situation-cum-character complex appeared in a twinkling. I was in search of a taxi in Tottenham Court Road, saw one with its light on, hailed it, saw that a small brown man nearer it had done the same, cursed, was astonished when it passed the brown man and stopped at my side. I got in without demur, but a voice not my own was saying at top volume in my head, 'Turn round and go back and pick up that other chap, you racialist!' So was born Sir Roy Vandervane of *Girl, 20*, and his randy girlfriend who would have to be there to give the incident an edge, and his views, and the fix he would be in and what he would do, and, somehow or other, the knowledge that he would be hero but not narrator.

I suspect that the 'creation' of minor characters is subject to the same kind of process, though with them there is often a sense of wider choice, or the illusion of it. Here, the novelist may well start from a real person, as George Eliot may have started Mr Casaubon from Mark Pattison. But then he became Mr Casaubon, because he had to do things Mark Pattison did not do. I read (parts of) the recent long correspondence in the *Times Literary Supplement* about whether or not Pattison 'was meant to be'—or even 'was' Casaubon—or the other way round—with incredulity. Even if it were a real question, any answer could have been of no more literary interest than some supposed identification of Shakespeare's Dark Lady. George Eliot *made up* Casaubon, and Pattison, to compare great things with small, went the way of Jock MacDonald.

One last run of personal examples: about halfway through writing *I Want It Now*, I found I needed a character who was rich, boring, revolting, rude, egotistical, stupid and a figure of fun, needed him for a vital turn in the plot: to compete almost successfully with the hero as a suitor of the heroine. He (Student Mansfield by name) was already there, had been hanging about the place for dozens of pages, passing himself off as a mere illustration of the awful kind of people who surrounded the heroine. A little later, I found I needed another character for another vital turn in the plot: to assist in the public humiliation of the heroine's mother. He (Bill Hamer by name) had been about the place even longer, pretending to be no more than an illustration of the awful kind of people who surrounded the hero. In each case, nothing had to be trimmed from the figure as he had already taken shape, and very little added.

A third character in that novel, an even more minor character, on the scene for a mere ten pages altogether, is my favourite in anything I have written, George Parrot by name. Trying to regard each as a real person, I am fonder of James Churchill in *The Anti-Death League*, see Brian Leonard in that same book as a much more decent man, would far rather have a drink (no more, thank you) with Patrick Standish of *Take a Girl Like You*. But George, who is as unreal a person as any of the others is or started as, remains my favourite because, in making him up, I thought I was for once cutting quite free of the demands of the plot. All he had to do, I thought, was be rich, disclose some information and make his car available at a crucial point.

So it seemed I tried to make George, got to the end of making George, a fool at first sight but formidable very soon thereafter, chivalrous, vengeful, sensitive, cynical, hot-tempered, snobbish, naïve, distrustful, intelligent, lazy and acutely aware of linguistic niceties. Not, of course, that I had compiled any sort of list of traits and ticked them off as each was supposedly realised; George simply turned out to be such a person. But did he? After I had quite done with him, I saw that he had to be everything he was, except perhaps linguistically aware; at that point, ordinary, authorial fears of being unentertaining may have taken over, though I doubt it. I probably value George because, longer than anyone else, he kept me in the dark about what he was doing in my book.

It does rather look as though the freedom I attributed to the non-autobiographical novelist is indeed illusory. But, if he is confined, he is at least confined by something outside the narrow twists and turns of his own real existence. How that something comes into being I have very little idea. The process may be neither grand nor significant but it is rather mysterious.

Times Literary Supplement, 27 July 1973

7

How to Get Your Novel Published

No writer can be altogether whole-hearted in resenting unsolicited mail. However boring, however outrageous the demands made on him by strangers or (worse, because harder to resist) acquaintances, at least it is him they are bothering; it is his philosophy of life, his favourable response to some merit-free forthcoming volume, his signed photograph, his money that is being requisitioned and not, or not only, Margaret Drabble's. But this consideration vanishes into thin air when it comes to the postal item most likely to get our man running amuck with an axe or blinding himself: another uninvited unpublished typescript. Before we go any further, do not, reader, send me your novel (especially that), your poems, your essays for my comments and assistance. For one thing, it will do you no good.

Let me explain why. The warmth of my emotion at being saddled with the rubbish might surprise some people but, I think, few writers. They (writers as a class) guard their free time as jealously as their working-time, and if free time is to be invaded by work of any sort there must be no sense of obligation about it. On top of that, the unhappy recipient may think he sees a cheerful implication that he sits about the place week after week waiting for something to turn up, like a one-parent-family saga dropped out of the blue. More plausibly he will sense utter indifference to his own concerns, and inexorable self-promotion. That sort of single-mindedness is a most useful, perhaps even necessary, quality in a young aspirant, but it lacks charm at the receiving end.

One notes also the important principle that there must be something a bit funny about a fellow who sends his creations to be read and criticised by a complete stranger. To my knowledge, no writer I respect has ever done it. The practice ceases to be objectionable if the thing arrives naked, without any pleas or queries attached, and I tolerate those persons who doggedly go on just sending me their publications year after year, though they would do at least as well to send them straight to my second-hand bookseller.

Anyway, in the normal course of events the man with the manuscript is likely to be in about the worst frame of mind possible when, if ever, he glances through what he has been sent. In fact he probably will do this sooner or later, not quite having the heart to send it back unread, unwilling to destroy it not through any scruple but for fear of some gruesome revenge—anyone mad enough to have sent it in the first place must be generally unsafe. And then . . . Suppose, against all the odds, just suppose there actually seems to be something to be said for it, what happens after that?

At this point I will unveil my latest case, the one that finally supplied the adrenalin to launch this article. Somebody I will call Arbuckle writes from SW7 enclosing three chapters of a novel, the remainder to follow if I ask for them. Now most petitioners of this type kick off in panegyrical style, more or less thanking me for having given them a reason to go on living, the idea presumably being to get me so fuddled with flattery that I will do anything they ask. Nothing so crude for Arbuckle. He merely and baldly states that he and I have the same birthday and went to the same college, then wonders if he might trespass on this coincidence (eh?) to ask if I would be kind enough to, etc. The punch comes at the end of the second paragraph. Perhaps I would advise him how best to go about getting his novel published. Others have put it a little differently but what they all mean is, *fucking* get it published. (And needless to say without the offer of a commission or any anti-life notions of that kind. And usually, as in Arbuckle's case, without return postage either.)

A great many people outside the literary world or on its fringes imagine that the whole thing is run on patronage, on old-boy networks and words dropped in the right quarter. I thought that myself once. Some bits actually are rather like that, bits of the little-magazine scene, for instance. But commercial publishing is not, could not be. The only way of getting a novel (say) published is to have written one that a publisher likes because he reckons he will do well with it. To identify novels in that category he looks with sufficient care at each one sent to him. The idea that he would somehow look harder or more benevolently in response to a nod from me, or anyone else, is moonshine. I think I can tell good novels from bad. He thinks he can tell profitable novels from flops. What he thinks goes.

Not that he will ignore my nod altogether. There are various degrees of nod. In the Arbuckle case I could send him (Arbuckle) an enthusiastic letter which he would then physically or metaphorically attach to his typescript on its questing journey round the various publishers. If more strongly moved I could send my own publisher an enthusiastic letter or even pay him an enthusiastic personal visit. None of this would make any difference to the novel's chances of acceptance. This is rather obviously not quite accurate. In some ways a publisher works like a committee, and clearly, in the event of a split about the publishableness of Arbuckle, any intervention, even a word in the club, on Arbuckle's side by an author of any standing would strengthen the pro-Arbuckle faction in the firm. The effect of such intervention would depend on the standing of the author, his closeness to the publisher, etc, but I cannot think it would ever be large. However much he might respect my opinion, any publisher would have to make up his own mind on his own principles. All he might do is move the thing up the queue, read it not more carefully but sooner. Some of the chronically unpublished will find this a hard lesson to learn. Obviously lack of influence is more dignified than lack of talent.

So you see, sending me your novel will do you no good, no decisive good anyway. But of course you, the kind of person who without turning a hair sends his novel to a private individual he has never met, will never read these lines, selectively blinded by the same mysterious power that protects trendies and illiterates from seeing articles about 'hopefully' and 'disinterested'. I will therefore address myself to another you, the kind of person who can face trying to get his novel published under his own steam. I have already told you that there is only one method—writing a publishable novel. But there is an accelerator, a way of speeding the progress of that publishable novel to a publisher who will publish it.

Realise that not all publishers publish all kinds of books or even all kinds of novels. They have their specialities and preferences. So avoid things like approaching in the first place the Oxford University Press with your piece of hardish porn. More specifically, go to the public library and look through the contemporary novels until you find one or more that seem to you to be of the same general kind as your novel, note the publisher(s) and proceed from there. (I owe this suggestion to the incomparable Pat Kavanagh.) Type page 1 afresh for each submission, keep your covering letter as brief as possible and trust in God.

I suppose you might find no novels that you think resemble yours. In that case you might be a genius. And in *that* case you might well run into difficulty getting published. But if you are merely bloody good you will have no trouble. And thereafter (Christ) you will have the world at your feet.

Times Literary Supplement, 2 October 1981

Hints for Scribblers

The Writer's Handbook 1988, edited by Barry Turner, Macmillan

This impressively-sized book is presumably meant not for any or every writer but for the beginner. 'So You Want to be an Author?' says or asks the heading of the first section, and in a bright sub-literate style it offers general and particular advice on how to get published, most of it unfortunately superfluous or insufficient or both at once.

Rather in the spirit of those educationists who encourage you by relating how badly Sir Winston Churchill did at Harrow, the compilers begin with stories of early difficulties famously overcome. If Frederick Forsyth, for instance, had lost heart after four (four!) rejection slips, we should never have had *The Day of the Jackal*, so *keep trying*, everybody. It might have been more useful all round to state that no one without enough self-will and resilience for ten has any business even to contemplate a literary career.

So how do you find a publisher? Well, first of all you ask chaps who already have one. Or you seek out publishers who are growing and looking for new blood. 'Admittedly, these characters are not always easy to spot'—certainly not from the list in this handbook. But you will broadly be able to find out which firms publish which sorts of book, and can save time by not sending your monograph on cattlefeed to people who are interested only in fiction, maps and DIY. If you happen to have written something on tatting or acid rain, go to Dryad Books (an imprint of B. T. Batsford Ltd).

Further guidance is patchy in the extreme. The entry on Jonathan Cape lists twenty of their recent titles, very helpful if they mean anything to you; that on Century Hutchinson has none, though it supplies a detailed breakdown by category; that on Cassell has neither. The compilers have depended throughout on what they were told in response to their inquiries, not on their own observations or conclusions, except for some gossip on the doings of trendy figures in the publishing world. This is like putting a Good Food manual together from information supplied by restaurateurs and head waiters.

Patchiness runs riot in the long sections (120 pages in all) on newspapers and magazines, aimed rather shakily at the budding freelance. Dates of founding are often given; not always. A journal's politics are usually given; not always—not, for example, those of the *Daily Mirror*, though I can see a special reason for that. On the *Sunday Post* of Glasgow, with a circulation that beats the London *Sunday Times*, there is virtually nothing bar a couple of editorial names—far less than could be gleaned by looking through an edition for five minutes. But it may be useful to learn that the *News of the World* (circulation 4,954,416) 'thrives on the public's insatiable demand for scandal, tragedy and sex'.

A point of some general interest surfaces in that part of the preamble optimistically headed 'And so to the contract'. An account is given here of the Minimum Terms Agreement (MTA) under which a publisher promises to pay an author a certain level of advance and royalties and offers other guarantees. The favourable view of MTA taken in *The Writer's Handbook* is the standard one, and it certainly sounds a good idea. The trouble is that, like any other minimum wage deal, it creates unemployment, or at least makes it more difficult for the unemployed to find work.

Many writers when they start off (I was one) are much less interested in money than in being known. Rightly or wrongly, they think that something may happen when they achieve print, nothing can until they do. They want publication at any price, or none, and they used to be able to get it. In effect, a publisher with £500 to spend could give £100 each to five new writers and take them all on. But under MTA he must give the whole £500 to one of them and let the other four go. By protecting that one from 'exploitation', the agreement keeps the other four out of work (and also out of readers' hands). This is particularly injurious at a time when other pressures are already making it hard for untried writers to start their careers.

Like all trade-union arrangements, then, and the Writers' Guild, its chief sponsor, is a trade union, MTA favours those already in work at the expense of the unemployed. Just as typically, it favours the established employer at the expense of the struggling newcomer, whom it forces to move in large costly steps instead of small cheap ones. It amazes me that some eminent publishers are still putting off joining the scheme and bleating about fair play and special relationships with authors. They should be falling over themselves to sign.

This book also includes a discussion of the Public Lending Right whereby authors are paid a small amount, something over 1p, for every time a book of theirs is borrowed from a public library. This is an unequivocally good idea from which authors can only benefit, despite objections that the present flat-rate arrangement mostly profits those already doing well from sales. The point is fairly argued here. But nobody ever says that, however the money may be distributed, it is at present inequitably provided, by a block grant from the taxpayer instead of payments by the customer, the borrower.

The free library is a cherished national institution, but a Conservative government should be questioning its sacrosanctity. Philip Larkin, for years a public librarian, once remarked that defenders-to-the-death of free loans should take note of all the current-year registrations in library car-parks on a Saturday morning, and think again.

To refer even in passing to unpublished or struggling authors and their problems is to put oneself at some risk, so I will say here and now that any unsolicited manuscripts or typescripts sent to me will be destroyed unread. You must make your way yourself. Why you should be so set on the nearly always disappointing profession is a puzzling question.

Sunday Telegraph 1987

Report on a Fiction Prize

What a lot of novels, I thought to myself when the entries arrived, and what a lot of novelists I'd never heard of, having years ago given up reading reviews of new fiction, let alone new fiction itself, except when friends or jeer-figures were involved. Reading and assessing the books and writing about them at the offered fee has not exactly been sweated labour, but to be brutally frank I have subsidised the Arts Council a bit in so doing. I told myself it was worth it to be forced to do some catching up. (My real reason for taking on the job was that nothing beats sitting around in the daytime with a novel on your lap and—truthfully—telling yourself you're working.)

Not quite all novels, my notes say, but only two volumes of shorts—a sad reflection of mounting commercial difficulties. Further noted: some sagas or slices of working-class life—why is this theme so hard to handle, if not impossible? Not much science fiction and, of that not-much, almost none that showed the requisite familiarity with the genre. Some limp fantasy. Some historical novels replete with anachronistic idioms. Not much how-it-is stuff, reports on now London or now San Francisco. 'Straight' fiction predominated.

The honest-bore novelist writes in plain English, believing that the material on offer is interesting enough in itself; it's his (or her) bad luck to have been mistaken in this belief. The dishonest bore is afraid, perhaps even intermittently aware, of having too little to serve up to the reader as it stands, so he (or she) falls back on verbal shock tactics, dislocated syntax, unnatural epithets and other affectations of singularity. There was just as much of this sort of thing as I'd found when I first read novels in bulk, reviewing in the Fifties. I see less excuse for it now, all those years further away from the origins of shock tactics in the period of *Ulysses*. Decadence has been a long time decaying. But this is a large subject.

I exaggerated rather at the start when I professed to have abandoned new fiction; in fact I had looked at enough of it over the years to expect nothing very much from a general batch of it (as opposed to a batch of crime or espionage, where, everybody knows, some formidable talents are to be found). As it turned out I had no difficulty in putting together a short list of five, though a less short list of ten might have taxed me a little. At this point I might offer a not excessively heartfelt apology to some of the writers who failed to get a place. Judging novels is very different from reviewing them, as I've tried to show in this article. The reviewer must strive for a measure of objectivity, awarding marks for effort, finding grounds for praise in books that in the end leave him cold, telling his readers he didn't much care for this or that but they might. The judge has his responsibilities too, but he must back his taste; he can't be expected to let a valuable prize, or even a packet of toothpicks, go to something he doesn't really like.

It should also be said, of course, that what appears uncongenial must not be too readily excluded, nor the inviting too warmly embraced. I fell like a ton of bricks for a book I finally excluded from my short list, instead bestowing an honourable mention: *The Moscow Option*, by David Downing. Its main attraction for me began in its subtitle, *An Alternative Second World War*. Everything is as it was until the afternoon of 4 August 1941, when Hitler, flying west from Novy Borrisov, meets with an accident that puts him into a coma for an unpredictable time. The generals take over the direction of the war and by November, with Moscow already fallen, special units are charging across the ice to Kronstadt. But . . . Mr Downing is writing history that never happened rather than historical fiction, but within the consequent limits this is a most readable and clever tale, full of striking inventions.

Negatives are very important in estimating novels, even more so to the judge than to the reviewer. One of the best things about Muriel Spark's *Territorial Rights* is that, although set in Venice, it doesn't go on about Venice. Nothing wrong with the place, but going on about places in novels is nearly always a self-indulgence, tempting because you have the material waiting to be used up, you're eking out the narrative with it and you may impress the reader with your sensitivity. Mrs Spark doesn't care what the reader thinks of her, another good thing. And—more negatives—there's no uplift or edification here. What's offered is pure entertainment of a high order.

The characters I like best are Robert, who graduates from living off rich elderly men to blackmailing one of them and at the end is sent to train in a terrorist camp; Lina, a frightful freeloading Bulgarian girl who looks after Number One with a kind of romantic intensity; and an interfering old bag called Grace who used to be a school matron, travels 'looking lefty' in the hope of getting young people to hump her cases and says she must be off to have her lodger's supper ready and so prevent him sitting around 'like a spray of deadly nightshade waiting for someone to pick it'. The author manages to be spiteful both through and about Grace. The plot, lightly involving revelations of wartime skulduggery, is just the right size to hang the characters on.

29, Herriot Street, by John Hutton (by the way, these four are just in the order I happened to read them in), is a first novel by a writer born in 1928. That interested me, as did the absence of the smallest sign of inexperience. I was attracted too by the idea, a criminologist in about 1970 out to interview the two surviving witnesses in a murder case of 1931. (The fictional case is founded on, without closely following, the Wallace case of that year, one I've always found fascinating.) Mr Hutton shows great skill in handling the transitions between various points in the period 1913–31 and the continuing investigation in 1970. I admire that; I find that sort of work very testing.

With so much to recommend it to me, this book had clearly got to be subjected to stringent examination. This it more than survived. The four main characters are developed with constant creativeness and truth. None of them can be reduced to any short description; they just go on revealing more of themselves and one another in some surprising and some less surprising ways. The subject, a huge one rarely attempted, is how ordinary, unexciting men and women lead their lives. (It's true that one of them is a murderer and another the victim, but I imagine most of those are pretty ordinary until the last minute, a point Mr Hutton persuasively makes.) A thoroughly satisfactory job.

The inclusion here of *Winter Doves*, by David Cook, testifies to the wonderful breadth of my sympathy. If there's anything that isn't my sort of thing I should have thought it would be a story about a love affair between a middle-aged, feeble-minded man and an embittered, suicidal, not-so-young woman, set first in a mental hospital and then among London down-and-outs. But actually I was caught from the start; interested at once, soon deeply engaged. There's an earlyish episode in which the couple meet daily in the grounds in order to stand holding hands for a time, she talking, he silent because he knows he has a voice people hate. I thought that bit was touching and awful. If he doesn't let it slip, I thought to myself, he's in.

And he doesn't. Mr Cook is absorbed in his subject matter; he finds what he has to tell so absorbing and important that, to him, it has only to be set down on paper for the reader to feel the same pity and outrage as himself. This gives him an invigorating confidence; no advertisements of the author's originality or imaginativeness are needed here. It also imparts a sense of pressure, a feeling that the book had to be written, rather than that it was about time to be turning out the next one. And yet the result is a thousand miles away from any crude outpouring, everything under control, transitions deft, style neat and free of inadvertences. It demands to be read. I was very impressed.

The Other Side of the Mountain, by Christopher Hood, is set in South Wales and thereby raises an immediate difficulty. The South Welsh (never mind the North) are hard to write about. Outsiders notice noticeable externals and produce a caricature; natives turn romantic (or Gothic) and produce a fantasy. Mr Hood's narrator had an English father, lives in London, but knew the valleys as a child, Mr Hood's own position in effect if not in fact. From it he paints a picture that seems quite undistorted (which is as much as is needed) and is sparkingly clear and detailed: a village in the coal-belt, or rather a tiny industrial town that has lost its industry and less tangible things besides, though the author doesn't go on about that.

What most interests him (or what to me was his most interesting interest) is character, not quite in itself, partly as seen or heard in dialogue: how we reveal ourselves by what we say, the words we use.

I noticed particularly Glanfawr Price Evans the television Welshman, Horace the perpetually over-reacting Englishman, poor schizophrenic Kate (there are dark passages in what sets off as a bright story) and whining, ruthless, monstrous Uncle Dai. I also took to the narrator's running commentary, much more someone talking to you than what we normally understand by narrative. Mr Hood knows a lot and has thought about things; I don't know why this should make such a difference in fiction, but it does. I enjoyed every bit of it.

And now the winning entry, which emerged after much cogitation. Penelope Lively's *Treasures of Time* is one of those novels whose distinction lies all in the writing, which means that if summarised in a couple of hundred words they would sound very undistinguished, in this case like what used to be (and for all I know still is) called a women's-magazine story—not that real women's-magazine stories are anywhere near the worst kind of story. Well, the present book resembles those of the late Elizabeth Taylor in this respect, and in others too. By mentioning those others I mean a high compliment, and I fancy from internal evidence that Mrs Lively would take it for that.

Within the chapters the novel is divided into sections of varying lengths, corresponding to changes from one character's point of view to another's or a shift backwards or forwards in time; a sure instinct governs these switches. Excellent descriptions of towns, countryside and journeys between them give a strong sense that this is England as it now looks. Strongly-drawn characters: a sad girl, another Kate, one who always puts herself in the worst possible light, knows it, and can't change; Tony, a possibly-pansy TV producer not connected to much bar TV—his film about Kate's dead father, a famous archaeologist, provides the centre of the story; fearful Laura, Kate's mother, getting everything possible out of being a famous archaeologist's widow in the intervals of effortlessly and instantly putting everyone else at a disadvantage. But the most important is Tom Rider, historian, and Kate's boyfriend.

Portraying the opposite sex brings any novelist notorious problems. Experience, flair or effrontery will solve most of them, but something more than an average portion of these qualities is needed for scenes where there's nobody of one's own sex around to act as mediator, if that daring step is to be taken at all. Mrs Lively tackles Tom head on, entering and staying in his thoughts as he goes about his business, holds his own against his elders, even Laura (a surprise there), dashes up the M1 with Tony, tries to handle Kate. It's not so much that the author gets everything right as that she moves with entire freedom; in every line you can sense her restrained enjoyment of the task. An episode in which Tom shows a party of bewildered Japanese round Oxford and Oxfordshire, apart from being marvellously funny, is significantly irrelevant to the main business. (The unity of action doesn't apply to full-length novels.)

What more can I say than that I believed, I was moved, I laughed,

I was interested in it all? That last is really the most important. Oh, and the characters' names are just the names they would have had if they were real people. Not a guarantee of merit, but awkwardness in naming always means awkwardness elsewhere. No generalisations force themselves on me after my reading stint, just satisfaction at seeing that very difficult feat, telling an entertaining story in attractive language about characters whom one can see some way into and who talk in a believable and vivid way, is still occasionally being brought off.

Observer, 1979

Sacred Cows

An early Congress of the United States debated what language the new nation was to speak. English symbolised the vanquished colonial oppressor, its sole virtue being that everyone used it. As so many of us know, it won the contest, narrowly beating German. There were also votes — not many — for Ancient Greek, as the language of the first democracy, and for a Red Indian language, perhaps Massachusetts or Cree, because it was *American*.

The second of these, even more than the first, was impracticable. Indian languages are full of horrible words like *ninitutamawahw* (Cree for 'I ask him for it') and unsuited to the expression of civilised concepts. But just suppose: *if* the first Americans had gritted their teeth and decided to speak and write Cree, one of the more probable results would be that they would now have what at present, after a great deal of conscious effort, they show no signs of ever producing — a distinctively American literature. Instead, they offer a vast number of books in English that in some ways resemble what I shall have to call British literature and in other ways don't. Those other ways are likewise non-American, whether they spring from other European cultures like German or French (the latter by direct borrowing) or from non-national cultures: Jewish, Negro. No coherent tradition could emerge from all that, and without a tradition any writer is adrift, nervously self-assertive, an individualist lost in a crowd of individualists.

The earlier American writers, living in what was culturally still a British province, were the most successful, both from the artistic point of view and in producing work that differed from that of their British contemporaries without, it seems, conscious effort to that end. I am thinking of novelists like Cooper and Hawthorne and, among poets, Emily Dickinson, Longfellow and one who approached greatness, Walt Whitman. None of these sounded actually American—unless Whitman's Americanisms count as that—just, as I have said, non-British, which proved to be as far as it was safe to go.

Even at this stage, all was not well. The mock-Gothic initiative of Edgar Allan Poe luckily failed; not so Melville's *Moby Dick*. This enormous novel shows the author's will at work in places where it has no business to be: the style *shall* be individual, the scope *shall* be universal, the whole thing *shall* be profound, a masterpiece. The pursuit of the masterpiece has bedevilled American writers ever since, both 'creative' and critical. To be dead is no protection; so, for instance, Mark Twain, that innocuous romancer, has been made to ascend into profundity with *Huckleberry Finn*.

In the later Nineteenth Century and long after, Americans turned to the Old World to redress the balance of the New. Henry James de-Americanised himself by taking on those very traits—fuss about social position, art-snobbery, high-flown circuitous talk—that ordinary Americans most dislike about 'Europe'. To judge by results, Ezra Pound acquired global culture from a one-volume encyclopedia, cribs of certain foreign books and a few Latin texts with eccentric vocabularies. As Melville had done, he got himself accepted as 'great' (at any rate among people with rather novelettish ideas about greatness) by so obviously striving to be called so. Hemingway treated outdoor matters in an indoor—salon or café—style. Only Eliot had the talent, the intelligence and the nerve to transplant altogether and successfully.

Other writers (Sinclair Lewis, Steinbeck, Faulkner) portrayed America—the land and the people—as if this were an untouched subject. In practice the result was provincialism, ruralism, regionalism (Southernism), difficult positions to maintain in an advanced country except at a murderous price in self-consciousness. Like the move away from America, the move into it was a resort of writers who were forced to work out from scratch where to go, instead of having their path roughly indicated for them by their predecessors, as in Europe.

All the names I have mentioned are attached to bodies of work of some quantity and on a fairly consistent level, however low, perhaps as a result of the still-surviving British connection. By 1945 that was quite gone. 'American literature' began to be taught in universities there, the writers took on an even more embattled cultural nationalism, and the day of the temporary genius, helped on by Scott Fitzgerald, had arrived. When *The Naked and the Dead* appeared, I thought someone the size of Dickens was among us; I had not allowed for the fact that Mailer was an American. So with J. D. Salinger, who did struggle on for one more decent effort after the marvellous *Catcher in the Rye*. So with Gore Vidal, whose talent has declined precisely as his fame has grown. And so, at various points on the scale, with Irwin Shaw, Herman Wouk, Peter Matthiessen, Warren Eisler.

America takes her writers too seriously. (In New York, book *reviewers* get recognised in restaurants.) She regards them as key operators in the national heritage business and gives them too much too soon, thus magnifying their innate instability, making them both restless and complacent. The same desire to find and reward the 'great', and that characteristically innocent readiness to take the will for the deed if the will is signalled boldly enough, have elevated Nabokov and Bellow, neither of whom writes English. Nabokov, in a way peculiar to foreigners, never stops showing off his mastery of the language; his books are jewels a hundred thousand words long. Bellow is a Ukrainian-Canadian, I believe. It is painful to watch him trying to pick his way between the unidiomatic on the one hand and the affected on the other.

Common humanity precludes mention of any poets born after 1925 or so. Every nation is entitled to a few sacred domestic cows, and 'American literature' no doubt helps to boost morale on the home front. When it goes for export, when the fashionable view here is that people write better over there, rude noises are in order. Our own lot are bad enough; *they* are a bloody sight worse.

There are exceptions.

Undated

Art and Craft

The Craft of Letters in England, a symposium edited by John Lehmann, Cresset Press

The dilemma of the novel, the predicament of modern poetry, the quandary of the artist, the crisis of our culture—these topics have become as much a part of our daily reading as undersea fishing or vice in our capital city. But as long as a few people find time to turn out the necessary creative material for all these assessments and appraisals and evaluations and surveys, we cannot really complain. And the latest addition to the literature of summation is both judicious and readable, a rare combination of qualities in this field. *The Craft of Letters in*

England is designed to mark the occasion of the PEN International Congress in London, and it will certainly do that. Not only the visiting Brazilians, Swedes and Belgians, but resident Britons, too, will find it stimulating. Mr John Lehmann has chosen his panel wisely, if a little unadventurously: we have Messrs Francis Wyndham, Philip Toynbee, Roy Fuller, G. S. Fraser, T. C. Worsley, L. D. Lerner, Maurice Cranston and others writing on the novel (two essays), verse (two essays), the theatre, criticism, the literature of ideas and so on. All in all, this is an excellent compilation, with plenty of hard thought in it and plenty of material for discussion.

If I now turn at once to the game of Why-this and Why-not-that which no decent symposium can hope to evade, it is in order to get such fault-finding out of the way. Briefly, then: Why all the genuflection before the shades of Lytton Strachey and Virginia Woolf, who score more heavily in the index than anybody but Shakespeare and Mr Eliot? Agreement might possibly be wrested from me that there is more than one tenable opinion about the Bloomsbury lot, but to imply that they still influence English letters overwhelmingly, or even strongly, will strike some as misleading. Well, never mind. Although there may be a few such sins of commission, there are next to none of omission. I did look in vain for the names of Mrs Hester W. Chapman and Mrs Doris Lessing in the female novelist section. I found no reference anywhere to Mr Alexander Baron. And since Dylan Thomas got into the book in spite of the limitation implied in the last word of its title, I should have thought Messrs Gwyn Thomas and R. S. Thomas might have got in as well. But I quite see that not everyone can hope to get in, and especially that the inclusion of Wales would force the inclusion of Ireland and Scotland, which might not prove unmixed gain.

A more interesting approach to this survey might be along the lines of the points of agreement between the contributors, some of which Mr Lehmann has shrewdly extracted in his introduction. One he does not mention (it tends to be latent rather than open) is a suspicious and even hostile attitude towards universities, more notably the provincial ones. I should like, if I can, to still the fluttering hearts of the anti-academics by trying to convince them that even today seats of learning are often quite amiable places, where a good number of both staff and students can read and write, where academicism in the bad sense is hated just as much, and sometimes from a rather better-informed standpoint, compared with outside, and where lecturers in English are seldom seen fresh from the semantics laboratory in white coats wet with formalin and the precious life-blood of master-spirits.

But really it is lecturers in philosophy, rather than those in English, who draw the fire. I have noted—not of course with 'concern', just with annoyance—how non-philosophers are more and more taking it upon themselves to tell the philosopher what he ought to be doing, and using words like 'arid' and 'sterile' to label what they fancy he is doing. Soon, I suppose, they will be telling the statisticians to stop all that silly adding-up and start integrating the concept of the random sample into the needs of the modern consciousness. And already we find Mr Cranston faulting modern economists with being obscure— obscure, that is, to non-economists. Mr Cranston, again, faults modern philosophers with stylistic inelegance, with not treating their subject as a branch of literature. Now we all love style, but there seems no obligatory connection between it and philosophy or economics. The plea for more style ties up interestingly with Mr Toynbee's assertion that plainness, dependence on ordinary speech, will no longer do for the novelist, and with Mr Wyndham's assertion that it is 'refreshing to find a young writer who can be accused of preciosity'. Is it? I would not be understood as faulting Mr Cranston here, but there does seem to be a lot of sonority-hunger about, a rather shamefaced nostalgia for the old purple patch. As if in confirmation, the essays of two other contributors, Messrs Alan Pryce-Jones and Paul Bloomfield, show here and there the cloven hoof of preciosity peeping out, as they might put it, among the rich skirts of urbanity.

The real complaint against the philosopher, however, is that he sells short not on style but on system. It is indeed true, as Mr Cranston observes, that 'philosophy in England has ceased to be a substitute for religion', and of this he clearly approves, but others would not do so. Certain minds must find it galling that the philosopher no longer provides the wherewithal for a sort of ontological debauch, that beauty, truth and goodness are no longer around to provide their own special brand of unilluminating uplift. From Wittgenstein to Ayer, not one of these fellows will give you a man-sized 'belief'. And of course you must have a belief if you want to do any serious writing; Mr Eliot has gone on record to that effect. I wonder if a distinction could be made between *an ideology*, which compels formulation, and *a set of ideas*, which do not need to be formulated, or even held before the attention, to have their effect. However this may be, it seems unnecessary to do as Mr Lehmann does and upbraid the philosopher for abdicating his function of manufacturing world-views. Nobody can order philosophy about.

An elegiac note frequently enters these essays: like the ideological philosopher, the literary giant has passed from our midst. Only Mr Wyndham doubts the final truth of this, and nobody at all doubts that, if true, it represents certain loss. There is a case for arguing that it could represent gain as well. The one unifying characteristic of our giants – the Jameses, the Woolfs, the Lawrences – was the immense seriousness with which they took themselves. Indefatigable writers of prefaces to their own work, unflinchingly pretentious about themselves in their letters to friends, inflexibly determined to regard themselves at the highest possible artistic valuation throughout their huge ego-maniacal journals, they grew to be giants partly (yes, all right, not wholly) because of their readiness to explain their qualifications for the name in interestingly unusual language. After all, this was England, and Carlyle had shown them the technique, and here were plenty of potential worshippers, even more than in Carlyle's day, to write the books on them: those who take themselves seriously get taken seriously. To be spared all that for the time being, even if it means forgoing some real talent, is not total disaster. There is some ground for equanimity in looking forward to an era of minor literature.

Finally, there is a point of Mr Fraser's I should like to take up. In a most interesting essay on the poet's media—his various outlets to his audience—Mr Fraser had a good deal to say on the role of broadcasting. I agree very strongly that to write with the spoken word in mind, even if it encourages dilution, must help the poet, not of course because 'verbal music' is of the least importance, but because the spoken word requires clarity. If a poet these days is interested in having his work read or heard, as distinct from having his name noticed, he must not only be clear after inspection, he must be clear instantaneously, on one superficial reading. (I do not mean that his working must yield up its all on one such reading.) Against these considerations must be set the inevitable disadvantages of the poetry recital. Poetry has the edge on music in needing no interpreter; it seems perverse to introduce one voluntarily. And readers are still usually bad, with an uncanny power of forcing their tones on the memory. This applies just as much when the poet does the reading himself: I have to make an effort, on having a look at 'The Teasers', to forget how Professor Empson recited it. Someone ought to tell some of the ordinary men readers, too, that contrary to their evident belief they are not there to do an imitation of Henry Ainley in *Hassan*. As for what some of the women readers ought to be told—I leave it to you!

Spectator, 13 July 1956

The American View

A Sinking Island: the Modern English Writers, by Hugh Kenner, Barrie & Jenkins

It is firmly established that the focal point or centre of gravity of English-speaking culture, or something like that, has left here and come down somewhere transatlantic like New York or perhaps San

Francisco. This has been accepted for so long, not only by Americans, that when in the mid-Sixties popular music took on a British accent the phenomenon was seen as a welcome redressing of the balance. Now here comes Hugh Kenner to explain that our literature, at any rate, has been no good since the year 1895.

Dr Kenner is a veteran American critic and teacher. His Irish descent, which I infer from his surname, may help to account for a certain lack of discipline in his account of our artistic decline. No wonder we write so badly in our crowded, foggy island with its dumpy little Queen (in 1895) and endemic snobbery (traceable to 1470, when Caxton french-ified Malory's diction) and all those vandalised telephone boxes in Trafalgar Square (just the other day). Dr Kenner interrupts his attack on Philip Larkin for apparently not minding the sight of lots of dis-mantled cars out of the train window (in *The Whitsun Weddings*) to reprehend our trains in general. Well, who could put a decent poem together on a diet of BR cheese sandwiches?

What has really deflected Dr Kenner from the true path of critical rigour can be guessed from the list of his works opposite the half-title. Starting in 1948, they deal with, in order of publication, Ezra Pound, Wyndham Lewis, James Joyce, Samuel Beckett, T. S. Eliot, Pound again, Beckett again, Buckminster Fuller, Flaubert, Joyce again and then Beckett and Joyce and *Ulysses*. This is not just any old veteran; this is a veteran foot-slogger or camp-follower of the old Modernist movement, or what he calls International Modernism, the prime exam-ple of which is notoriously *Ulysses*.

As Dr Kenner says of it in his distinctive idiom, 'anyone in 1895 who'd fore-guessed a book so transcendently innovative would have expected its dictionary to be French'. And, his story goes, the British were so incensed to find 'their' language used instead for an avant-garde work like that (rather a filthy one, too) that they turned their backs on it for good—on it and on all subsequent innovative works in that vein. The unforgivable crime of the tight little islanders is that they, we, refused to follow the Irish-cum-American lead, and instead set up a 'conspiracy to pretend that Pound and Eliot never happened'.

Dr Kenner's story is, needless to say, much longer and more detailed than that and it goes back much further, to 1895 in fact. By that date three disasters had hit English letters or were on a collision course with them. First, a mass-reading public had grown up, nourished by *Tit-Bits* magazine, a popular weekly anticipating the Northcliffe daily press, and by the romances of Marie Corelli, authoress of *The Sorrows of Satan*, etc. She died in 1924, but she must have injured the youthful Kenner in some awful personal way. My goodness, he does let her have it. Anyhow, what with her and *Tit-Bits* it was no wonder the British public were pretty effectively conditioned against all forms of good writing.

The second blow came from Everyman's Library, which, together with the Copyright Act of 1911, somehow stopped any of our forefathers, and our elder contemporaries too, from reading anything published after 1870. That made us 'impervious to novelty'. And third, there was the Oscar Wilde affair, which finally burnt out any lingering traces of respect for art. Thenceforth, in British eyes, art was perverted, affected, foreign, unChristian, incomprehensible and connected with absinthe-drinking. The way was clear for Wells, Bennett, Conan Doyle and P. G. Wodehouse's Oxford doctorate in 1939.

Such is the liveliest and certainly the most original part of this book. What follows it is a series of essays on Henry James, Yeats, Ford Madox Ford and others who did less well in GB than Dr Kenner might have preferred. We hear too of D. H. Lawrence, Shaw, Virginia Woolf in discursive terms. The extent of his treatment of those born in this century fosters an earlier suspicion that we are reading a smartened-up course of academic lectures on not very many not-very-modern English writers, with a final section on The Situation Today, or Yesterday, and a unifying theme hard to fault, that bad Brit-lit is not so hot. Among those not so much as mentioned, and presumably beneath Dr Kenner's contempt, are (novelists only) J. G. Ballard, Elizabeth Bowen, William Cooper, William Golding, Henry Green, L. P. Hartley, Rosamond Lehmann, Iris Murdoch, Anthony Powell, V. S. Pritchett, Paul Scott, Alan Sillitoe, Elizabeth Taylor and Angus Wilson.

Dr Kenner is nothing if not an academic, and an American one too, which means he can call Aubrey Beardsley's sense of line and design 'irrefutable' and find it 'orienting' to remember that Samuel Johnson died only sixty-five years before J. M. Dent was born. He, Dr Kenner, reveals his nature and outlook, his whole literary position, when he characterises The Waste Land as above all 'the century's most influential poem' and a 'supremely important poem'. If you see literature as a matter of influences and importances *of course* you are going to fall for International Modernism with its innovativenesses, experiments, developments and echoes, so much more inviting to lecture on than the intractable, unclassifiable qualities of an actual work of literature. *Of course* you are going to get fed up with people who go on contentedly ignoring everything your life's work has stood for. I think you are also going to lose the right to call such people Philistines, as Dr Kenner keeps calling us, but that is by the way.

It is tempting to suggest that what you get when whole generations of poets and novelists think in this way is a lot of innovative, stylistically aware, challenging, even great works that are not really much good and no fun to read, something uncannily like American literature of the present century, in fact. What needs saying to critics and others, on both sides of the Atlantic and elsewhere, is that influencing other writers, individually or by the batch, is neither here nor there, and that in literature, as in some other spheres, importance isn't important. Only good writing is.

Sunday Telegraph, 11 September 1988

Why Are You Telling Me All This?

Reading almost any piece of writing above the emotional level of a guidebook or a public notice is like listening to someone talking to you in private, talking to you alone. However well aware you may be that the words have reached and are continuing to reach countless others, you feel, in the act of reading, I suggest, like an audience of one, that is to say in a relation of peculiar intimacy and immediacy, less intense than when in company with a real person but otherwise very much the same, and unique in being so.

Accordingly you respond to what you are being told, if it is told well enough, very much as you would in life, thrilling to the adventures, chuckling at the funny bits, feeling a touch of the tender emotions when these are appealed to. This more or less simple correspondence breaks down when what you are being told consists of a passage of explicit sexual description, or ESD.

In life, the recounting of sexual confidences by one man to another (I know there are other possible combinations) is governed by an unspoken but pretty stringent contract if they are to be admitted at all. Even in the most favourable circumstances, venturing into physical detail is in danger of producing discomfort in the hearer. This discomfort is not really shock, not at any rate the sort that old ladies are supposed to feel at being reminded, or perhaps more fully informed, of the disgusting things people get up to. It is more like embarrassment, born of uneasy speculation about what sort of fellow it can be who is prepared to tell you all this. Whether he does it to boast, to indulge his fancy, to advertise his emancipation from something or other, to shake you out of your bourgeois sedateness, etc, will hardly concern you. Nor will you take the slightest notice of any pretences he may make of increasing the store of human knowledge, affected or half-baked protestations of wonderment at the mystery of it all, or suchlike. Whereas if his theme is the horror or nastiness of it all you will already have left. Very well, let it be shock, but at his telling it, not at whatever he might or might not have done.

Try as he may, the writer of such things is seized by the same trap as his social counterpart. No matter that, by the very act of agreeing to read his tale, you have given him something of the privilege of a close friend, and that the conditions of reading make him at the same time secure from interruption and available for pondering *ad libitum*. Indeed, the fact that he well and truly has your ear only makes it worse of him. A writer has none of the real-life excuses of drunkenness, caprice, boredom. It is his considered judgement that you should be told exactly what he or what's-his-name got up to. No matter either how sincerely he thinks, or would say he thinks, that his intentions are immaculate, how loudly he protests his devotion to art, truth, love, self-understanding, the essential holiness of sex or anything else; the unbreakable connection between literature and life reduces him to the same moral level as the chap you make sure of avoiding in the pub.

It is often said that the sexual act is ludicrous to a detached observer, though opportunities to check this on the ground, so to speak, must be rare. Certainly sex is a subject very well suited for comic treatment, so much so that some accounts of sexual behaviour notoriously attract laughter against that writer's intention, and *Lady Chatterley's Lover* might be a masterpiece of unconscious humour but for the boring non-sexual bits in between. The book also provokes in full measure the irritation that is never far from the reader's mind in such cases, expressible perhaps by the grumble, 'Well, all I can say is if it was me doing it, I wouldn't be doing it like that.'

A full ESD in comic terms, if possible at all, would be a dubious venture; what little I have seen along those lines has indicated that a little goes a long way. But obviously enough the real sight of a copulating couple would to most people not be funny in the least. Most people finding themselves somehow faced with it would, from feelings I need not indicate, get out as fast as they could. A minority would stay; more practically, they would have fixed it up in the first place.

In life, that minority is a small one; among readers, not so small. These readers, voyeurs at one remove, are, of course, purposeful and responsive readers of pornography, obtaining sexual excitement from what purport to be accounts of others' behaviour. Pornography is unlike any other kind of writing. It has no analogy with the social act of talking to someone and its reader has no sense of an author; places, time, individuals and their motives and reactions and whole lives vanish too. In this sense, as in others, it is dehumanising. And it is no respecter of motives. I mean that any detailed account of copulation, however 'purely' intended, is liable to excite sexually those whom it does not revolt, bore or move to laughter. That is in the strict sense the dilemma of the explicit describer. Some writers cheerfully ignore it and may make a lot of money, for instance Harold Robbins, whose *The Story-teller* shows its very Robbins-like 'hero' writing a rape scene in a visibly worked-up state.

Well, if you don't mind your readers seeing you in that light, go ahead and run off all the ESDs you fancy; forget that there are those to whom another fellow's sexual excitement is the least engaging thing in the world. In the present context to infer its presence is to realise that you have crossed the frontiers into pornography-on-purpose. Like many frontiers this one is often hard to draw precisely, but you can tell straight away which side of it you are on.

To argue in this way is not—obviously, I hope—to interdict sex as a literary subject. The special importance of that subject, however, imposes special restraints on those setting out to deal with it. Such restraints are not constricting to a writer of any care or skill. Quite the contrary: the tension between the need to make matters clear enough and the need to do so tactfully can be turned to artistic account, like the poetic tension between metre and natural speech. In *Jude the Obscure* it is not just that Hardy succeeds in telling us all we need to know about Jude and Arabella, and Jude and Sue, without ever taking us into the bedroom; the manner of his success is part of the literary success of the novel. In Henry Newbolt's poem, 'The Viking's Song', a less familiar example, we hear how the raider's first forays were not welcome to the recipient territory. But, approaching the shore now,

> *Where once but watch-fires burned*
> *I see thy beacon shine,*
> *And know the land hath learned*
> *Desire that welcomes mine.*

Nothing could be clearer, or less explicit; and again, the poem would not just be less good if Newbolt had said, 'Darling, when I first started to . . .' etc, it would not exist at all.

The ESD-merchant's greatest disservice is not that of offending briefly and effaceably against good taste and good sense too, though he or she asks to be reminded that at a time when anything may be published there is a particular duty to be responsible. It is that the very nature of the enterprise reinforces the assumption that physical sex is the important part or the most interesting or only interesting part of sex. Life and a great deal of literature teach the importance and interest of those moments and days and whole relationships which are deeply sexual, but in which nobody even looks like touching anybody. Of course, the trouble with that sort of thing is that it can be quite difficult to write about. Breasts and buttocks are child's play.

Spectator, 23 August 1986

Writing for a TV Series

I first wrote for television in 1964: a full-length play for Granada called *A Question about Hell*. As was testified by the title and about fifty other quotations and clues, as well as most of the events, this was an adaptation of *The Duchess of Malfi*, set very roughly in the then contemporary Caribbean. I take critics into account no more than most writers, but I did think that, in this case, they might smile on me out of complacency at their own cleverness in having, against all odds, uncovered my source. I had overestimated them. Only two of them got it (a third scored an inner by naming *The White Devil*), and one of those two believed he had done a public service by having, against all odds, exposed a shabby attempt to plagiarise a great but little-known original. This has been on my chest ever since, so please forgive so early a digression.

Anyway: *A Question* was part of a series, but a short series, an anthology series linked only by a loose requirement that grim or ghastly matters should be treated of. Other limitations, inherent in television as it was and still largely is, were hardly more constricting: not too many sets, not too many speaking parts, as little film as possible. Cuts for length in the original script were agreed without trouble; I had designedly written to be pruned rather than padded. Apart from the usual satisfactions and dissatisfactions of authorship, and the weirdness of eventually seeing and hearing all those non-existent persons walking and talking, the whole business was a useful exercise in discipline, though not a very stringent one.

Stringent is high on the list of things I would call writing an episode for *Softly, Softly*. Some of the factors working for stringency are obvious: inherited 'regular' characters who must be prominently dis-played—I rather missed the second half of that one in my draft script; inherited 'regular' sets with the same sort of proviso; an inherited view (related to fact and flavour much more than anything moral or social) of how 'Task Force' police work is carried out. Various other limitations transpired at various stages. I could not choose which regular characters should appear. Fair enough. I could not have the murder I had orig-inally designed, the quota for murders in this particular run of the series having been filled. Better than fair enough, as it turned out: by a mysterious yet familiar process the prohibition improved the result. For—I suppose—economic reasons, the recording of the episode must be continuous, hence the Detective Chief Inspector could not leave the pub at the end of Scene Sixteen and be in police HQ at the start of Scene Seventeen; he must duly proceed from one part of the studio to another while somebody else did something. Unfair enough at first sight, but good for discipline.

The initial proposal having been made and promptly accepted, there was a lunchtime thrash—I mean, of course, a meeting over lunch at which some problems and possibilities were thrashed out. I left with what proved to be just the right amount of jointly-agreed synopsis in my head—about half of it (the synopsis) had been crystallised into 'The chap's a shit but he didn't do it', or perhaps the other way round—and a bundle of previous scripts under my arm. Later, more material flowed in by post, facts about the police, 'biographies' of regular characters, photographs of regular sets. It was nice to have, rather than any positive help. I was on my own.

Or I was until the draft script reading at the BBC. Thereafter, by telephone and mail, I had company enough. Having said at the one lunch, in a sudden access of modesty, that that draft must not be regarded as Holy Writ, I found myself taken at my word. The draft would make quite a nice play, but as a *Softly, Softly* episode, well . . . I asked for suggestions, detailed ones. They were detailed, all eight single-spaced folio pages of them. I incorporated the lot, one way and another. After several further exchanges, I had a script that was not only an acceptable contribution to the series, but a better play, too. I say 'I' rather than 'we' because I had written every bit of it. Not a single word was forced into anybody's mouth. A couple of days before the read-through, I was being telephoned to approve such restructurings as a change from 'Let's go', to 'Come on'.

All this was a nuisance to me, but it was both proper and necessary. At the time I often felt I was getting the Procrustes treatment; I soon saw that my reluctance to cut came chiefly from the simple fact that what I was cutting was already there, and the additions meant more work. To write for a series entails a compromise between the writer and the series, and that 'compromise' takes on its adverse tinge only insofar as the writer may feel *on reflection* that he has been pressed, in one way or another, to change what should have been left as it was. Not so here.

I hope I have not suggested that the exercise gave me no enjoyment. It gave me a great deal in several ways. Working with a group refreshes a man who normally sees, week in, week out, only the flat face of his typewriter. The actual writing of a script is a joy to a novelist who finds, as I do, dialogue relatively easy and everything else arduous. To be able, to be *expected*, to slam down:

1 INT. TASK FORCE CAR. NIGHT
(SNOW AND NESBITT.
NESBITT DRIVING)

in the knowledge that They are responsible for showing the car and the night and Snow and Nesbitt, clearly and quickly and believably and effectively, filled me with a sort of minor, malicious glee.

It is not all like that. For me, the production of a novel falls into three phases of an emotional state. 1. Before writing. Euphoria: god-like creation of beings and situations under no discernible pressure, until the dreaded onset of 2. Writing. Continuous anxiety. 3. After writing. Relief followed by depression followed by relief. A script is almost the contrary, as follows. 1. Prolonged anxiety about devising a complete, right-sized plot within set limits. 2. Euphoric rapid writing of draft from start to finish. 3 Anxiety about what They will say, followed by irritated speculation about what They will say next, fol-

lowed slowly by relief. (Touching wood, I suppose, that, in unfortunate cases, relief is replaced by resignation or apoplexy.)

Lastly, the satisfaction of doing something new—new for oneself,
of course. I believe that any proper writer ought to be able to write
anything, from an Easter Day sermon to a sheep-dip handout. He will
not want to write everything, nor would he benefit from doing so,
but contributing to a TV series is the sort of thing that keeps in good
repair what talents he may have. One or two of them might even gain
a welcome sharpening in the process.

The Listener, 19 and 26 December 1974

Caledonian Attitudes

Scotland the Brave, by Iain Hamilton, Michael Joseph

The relationship between England and the other national areas of
these islands has never been static, but there are signs that it is
starting to change quite fast. The status of London may well be on the
verge of a decline in an English as well as in a British context. The
adumbration of yet another cultural 'trend' is not to be lightly under-
taken these days, and nobody ought to want to give any established
regionalism a shot in the arm, but it does look as if anybody interested
in what is going on in the United Kingdom has a rapidly increasing
obligation to turn an occasional glance north of the Tweed and west
of the Wye, if no farther. (North of Hampstead and west of Shepherds
Bush will do for first-year students.)

These remarks may serve to introduce Mr Iain Hamilton's autobiographical account of a childhood and adolescence spent on Clydeside,
on Lanarkshire farms and at school in Renfrewshire. His portrayal of
these places and the people associated with them, of the varied and
sometimes almost self-contradictory things that Scottish romanticism
can mean, is sympathetic and illuminating, but in a vigorous and not
an inertly contemplative way: the egotisms of the introspective kind
of autobiography are sharply avoided. *Scotland the Brave* deserves a far
wider audience than the localised one it may appear superficially to
invite. And this is so not only because we should all try to keep up

with the Jocks and what they are currently thinking, but because of the book's personal qualities.

Mr Hamilton has the virtues of honesty, humility and—above all—complete absence of that affectation which bedevils so many autobiographies, especially those in which childhood is important. Ability to re-evoke a world seen through a child's eyes is not uncommon these days, and Mr Hamilton manages it as well as most, but where he particularly scores is in describing those sudden random shifts of mood everyone has experienced and never quite—never nearly in some cases—outgrows. Those dreads and loathings of nothing very special, those trance-like lassitudes, those petrifying lonely boredoms are all beautifully caught. The author knows that it is vacuity, not sensitiveness, which fastens the child's attention on what the adult does not see, and that the tears which solitude brings are most likely the accompaniment of a jaw-dislocating yawn.

Such insights are the marks of an astringency which sets off, without ever being allowed to distort, the remembered sentiment and idealism to be found in other parts of the story. But one would not wish that sentiment to be remembered only, and it is not. Although there is abundant humour here (the adolescent's discovery that there are girls about can seldom have been treated so hilariously) and abundant self-deflation, Scotland clearly remains for Mr Hamilton the most romantic place in the world. Few subjects are worthier or more of our own day than a man's love-affair with his native heath, provided the man is a man, and not a cheapjack or a rhapsodist or a professional Celt—especially that. In the present case, these provisions hold. *Scotland the Brave* shows itself in every line to be the work of a genuine human being and a genuine writer.

Spectator, 15 November 1957

Publisher at Work

Gollancz: The Story of a Publishing House, by Sheila Hodges, Gollancz

The offices of Victor Gollancz Ltd at 14 Henrietta Street in Covent Garden, very well described in Sheila Hodges's book, told you a lot about the firm and the man. When I first stepped across the threshold in 1953 I felt I was entering a banana warehouse recently and hastily fitted with second-hand partitions; indeed I half-believed I really was, the banana myth being widely current at the time and even extending to the name—Fyffes—of the erstwhile importers. It comes almost as a disappointment to find that the building has housed publishers throughout its 100–odd years of existence.

I used to think that the pervading unluxury, which was not greatly alleviated in the chairman's sanctum, served the function of the disintegrating suit you wear on visits to the taxman: it made it harder to ask for another £25 advance when they couldn't even afford lino on the stairs. More encouragingly, it suggested that all the spare cash around went into bringing the books out. This was a fair inference for what it was worth, but I see now that the essential object had been to get right away from the oak panelling, sporting-print, sherry-decanter associations of the trade. At Henrietta Street there was nowhere to put your feet up.

The secret of Victor Gollancz's success was as open a one as could be imagined; he worked. Other men caused books to be printed and sold: Victor published them. He saw himself as first and foremost an educator, reasonably enough, though some might prefer a word like 'propagandist' without its derogatory implications, or most of them. At the same time he had it quite clear in his mind that he must acquire money, fame and prestige before he could develop the political part of his list. Although he hated the label, he was a businessman of great ability, daring alike in conception and execution.

To make money it was necessary both to save and to spend it with the utmost zeal. String and packing paper that came into the office were to be kept for re-use—like the décor—far less a literal economy measure than a means of fostering the right attitude among staff. Authors got no publication parties (a lonely exception was made for Ivy Compton-Burnett) and in at least one case got no look at the menu when taken out to lunch. Book exhibitions were thought a troublesome expense. Production was plain and rigidly standardised. 'Picture' jackets were out, though here again not only cheapness was the subject; his attention once caught by the soon-familiar yellow ground, the potential buyer must be startled into interest by simple statements about the book or its author in tabloid-headline style and, often, purposely outré typography.

That same style with its tendency to prod, provoke or challenge the reader and sometimes to shout at him, reappeared in the firm's press advertising. Here Victor really spread himself, occupying whole pages of the *Observer* and *The Sunday Times* and making all his competitors look genteel, a speciality of his. It was nothing for a couple of hundred booksellers to get a telegram about a title he really wanted to push. Once, 3,000 of them were sent carefully marked cuttings of a favourable review of Daphne du Maurier's *My Cousin Rachel*, an operation carried out the day the newspaper appeared by the entire staff working in teams.

Victor backed his hunches. When he saw the Stage Society production of *Journey's End* (there seemed then little prospect of a commercial offer), he told the author, R. C. Sherriff, in the first interval that he wanted to publish it. He should not be thought of as, outside his political products, interested only in what would sell. For one who certainly had such an interest he was quite choosy, with the result that for years his crime list was the best in the land (which meant, okay, that it sold a lot). All in all, did he deserve the luck that brought him A. J. Cronin, whose wife literally took a pin to a list of publishers. The most fascinating parts of Sheila Hodges's continuously fascinating chronicle are her accounts of the firm's dealings with the authors already mentioned and with M. P. ('Purple Cloud') Shiel, Shaw, Frank Harris, Elizabeth Jenkins, Dorothy L. Sayers and George Orwell.

The last name inevitably brings up the Thirties, Spain, the Left Book Club. Whether Victor realised at the time that the club was in effect run by Stalinists is unclear; perhaps he did and didn't mind, though he said later he regretted the bits of covering-up for Stalin he had felt he had to do. But these and related matters will no doubt be fully discussed elsewhere. Perhaps I might recall not only Victor's rejection of *Animal Farm* early in 1944, a less than ideal moment to set about publishing an attack on Soviet totalitarianism, but the fact, not explored here, that he wouldn't, or at any rate didn't, publish *Homage to Catalonia*, presumably because of its accounts of the massacres carried out by the Stalinists upon their allies on the Republican side.

What happened? Orwell wrote to a friend that Victor was 'of course part of the communism racket' and had said, on hearing what Orwell had seen in Spain, that 'he probably wouldn't want the book, which was not yet even begun; I think he must have very astutely foreseen that something of the kind would happen, as when I went to Spain he drew up a contract undertaking to publish my fiction but not other books'. But Orwell was far from the pillar of truthfulness he is often taken to be; I rather doubt if he ever shot that elephant. Victor wrote of him: 'He was too desperately anxious to be honest to be really honest', thinking perhaps of his manner in conversation, though I can feel it in his work, here and there. So . . . ?

Not a note to end on. I once saw a questionnaire in which chaps named their favourite virtue: Victor's was '*unconscious* goodness'—his italics. Well, he was a bit of a rogue and a bit of a humbug and he really should have let me see that menu, but yes, he had more than a touch of the quality he admired.

Observer, 23 April 1978

Victor the Rogue and Publicist

Victor Gollancz: a Biography, by Ruth Dudley Edwards, Gollancz

Ruth Dudley Edwards is an Irishwoman who has written biographies of the Dublin rebels Patrick Pearse and James Connolly, shot by the British in 1916. These were apparently thought to qualify her to write the official Life of Victor Gollancz. In whatever frame of mind she may have come to her task, she quickly became fascinated with its subject, as she says herself and as is clear from every page (all 738 of them) of this immensely informative and readable book.

From it we learn that Victor Gollancz was born in Maida Vale, London in 1893, the youngest child of a thriving Jewish family much given to philanthropy and the arts, his mother given also to mesmerism, Ibsen, the subconscious and Herbert Spencer. Precociously at school at St Paul's, and then at New College, Oxford in the couple of years before the Great War, he came out for human dignity, universal brotherhood, feminism, pacifism, co-education, tax-reform and other new or not-so-new progressive concerns, though he approached them all from a top-drawer position. He incidentally developed a passion for opera, not least Wagnerian opera, something which in my experience points to a general readiness to be taken in by shams.

Although he made no attempt to avoid war service, Victor found himself at Repton in 1916 teaching classics and, soon enough, much else besides. He loved it, remarking years afterwards that he had remained a schoolmaster ever since—and a first-rate one, it might be added, at least as far as holding the class's attention was concerned.

Thrown out of the school for his pacifist activities, he finally turned to publishing, first with Benn Brothers Ltd, where he at once showed his lifelong capacity for hard work, for brilliance and originality in trade matters, for publicity and for rubbing people up the wrong way. By the end of 1927 he had what he had to have, his own business and unquestionable authority.

If a publisher can be called a genius, which is uncertain, Victor was one. How he operated in detail is told, as Ruth Dudley Edwards says, by Sheila Hodges in her *Victor Gollancz: The Story of a Publishing House* (1978), another absorbing book. The present work concentrates rather on the character and activities of Victor the publicist. So we follow his political progress: a professing socialist by 1931, an ardent supporter of the USSR by 1933, the originator and co-founder of the Left Book Club in 1936. From then on he ceased to be a publisher with a strong line in books about socialism and became a more or less straightforward propagandist with a strong general list.

34

The Club's monthly selections alternated between, or combined, attacks on Hitler's Germany and eulogies of Stalin's Russia and its ideology. I for one had not grasped until now the eager readiness with which Victor followed the directions of the British Communist Party in this matter among others. With its growing membership (reaching 57,000 in April 1939), monthly news-letter, occasional pamphlets, discussion groups and rallies, the Club acquired some of the look of a mass movement and was widely thought to have helped to bring the Labour Party to power in 1945. After that it soon fell away and for the last twenty years of his life Victor was thrown back on comparatively minor causes, from relief for post-war Europe to the reprieve of Adolf Eichmann.

The extent of Victor's influence on events, rather than on passing opinion, was probably slight. Like many socialists, he and his cronies were inclined to overestimate the degree to which left-wing ideas as such can ever appeal widely. But such influence as he had will strike some non-socialists as harmful on balance. It was good that he encouraged resistance to fascism, but bad that he gave it a Stalinist bias, and to me at least the United Europe Movement, not to speak of CND, were unequivocal steps in the wrong direction.

Victor Gollancz was a monster of egotism, vanity and self-delusion who was also entirely capable of disinterested generosity both moral and monetary, genuine warmth of heart and readiness to go to endless trouble on behalf of those he valued. He was mean to some of his authors and may have cheated some too, but as far as I know he was always fair with me, and like a great many others I grew fond of him, finding him at worst an engaging rogue. I suppose the engagingness might have fallen off a bit if I had been able to see the depth of his roguery.

Independent, 11 January 1987

PART TWO
Prose Writers

Under the Net

Under the Net, by Iris Murdoch, Chatto & Windus

*U*nder the Net is a winner, a thoroughly accomplished first novel. It successfully combines elements which are difficult to combine and some of which are tricky to do on their own. To start with, it is some sort of triumph for a woman writer to carry off a first-person male narrator without either implausibility or knowingness. It is hard in a different way to introduce, and give an account of, conversations with a philosophical bias and make them plausible, interesting, related to theme and character instead of just stuck in for uplift, and (what people like me will find most noteworthy) intelligible. This gets worked in with a mime-theatre, a cold-cure establishment, a gambling sequence, a pub-crawl turning into a bathe in the Thames, the kidnapping of a dog film-star, a fight in a film studio with a cast of thousands, a bit about Paris and an escape from a hospital. The important thing here is to keep the throttle open throughout without becoming self-consciously Bohemian or 'mad' or picaresque—especially that. Miss Murdoch manages all this with aplomb, as well as being funny and serious almost the whole time.

Jake Donaghue is an industrious hack-writer (not a drifter: good) who, though addicted to judo and reasoning, gets everything wrong. He mentally permutes the probable relations between his male and female acquaintances with great ingenuity and inaccuracy, and keeps it up well. One of his friends, met in the cold-cure establishment, is Hugo Belfounder, a sort of rushing-about Wittgenstein whom Jake is ill-advised enough to ask for a statement of his philosophical position. Belfounder is naturally very affronted by this demand, but replies to the extent of showing how all theorising is flight. Jake writes it up into a dialogue appropriately called *The Silencer*, from which we are given a too-short extract. Much later, it is Jake who follows the example of Wittgenstein by becoming a hospital orderly.

The shade of Wittgenstein can be detected elsewhere in the book, intermittently performing a *pas de deux* with an apparition of M. Sartre. But the result is no philosophical gallimaufry; it is a new brand of humour—never, of course, 'mere' humour. Apart from the disconcerting intrusion of a kind of 'sensitive' short story about Paris on 14 July, Miss Murdoch's control of her variegated material is completely assured. She is a distinguished novelist of a rare kind.

Spectator, 11 June 1954

Max

Conversation with Max, by S. N. Behrman, Hamish Hamilton

There are certain writers likely to tempt the critic into a kind of hypocritical generosity. One can hardly contemplate assembling a careful destructive analysis of the work of Warwick Deeping, say, or John Buchan; it would not only be not worthwhile, but also, so to speak, a shame to take the money. English vengeance wars not with the dead — at least only with the powerful, annoying, *Chatterley*-writing dead. So attention gets shifted on to presumptively interesting traits of character, on to the curious state of marital felicity enjoyed by Sorrel and his son, or that 'ambivalent' Hannay-Medina stuff in *The Three Hostages*.

There is no chance of anything like that in dealing with another author on the level of merit I have implied, Max Beerbohm. To search his writings for a key to his personality would be a barren exercise, there being nothing to unlock. Self-effacement, behind parody, behind special sorts of farce and fantasy, could hardly go farther. The only real oddities about Beerbohm are not in him or his work, but in how it ever got about in the first place that he was worth taking seriously, and in how, having got about, it still stays about. I suppose there never was much of a chance of Lord David Cecil not expressing high admiration for *Zuleika Dobson* or not saying that it distils the quintessence of Oxford; so indeed it does, I fear — of one aspect of Oxford, at any rate. It is more surprising, perhaps, to find E. M. Forster remarking of the same book not that (for instance) it draws out to a quite shameless length a gag markedly less funny than (for instance) the one about Princess Margaret and the *schadchen*, but on the contrary that it has 'a beauty unattainable by serious literature . . . it is so funny and charming, so iridescent, yet so profound'. It is even odder to note that at one time there was nearly a film version of the thing and, somewhat earlier, nearly a Gershwin musical of it—not quite, though, thank heaven. What could it be like to be reminded of *Zuleika* as often as one is of *Porgy and Bess*?

It may be charitably assumed that finally getting round to reading the book was what induced George and Ira to drop their project. No such plea, however, is available to the more familiar 'Maximilians', as—forgive me if you knew this already—Beerbohm-addicts are evidently called: compare 'Janeite', and ponder on the significance of obtruding authorial Christian names. ('Dylan' is a rather different case—or is it?) Anyway: the attribution of incomparability to Max is presumably to be connected with the notion, characteristic of Lord David's Oxford and of Bloomsbury, that style is a self-sufficient entity, to be separated at will from qualities of subject matter and capable of exhibiting a 'charm' or 'iridescence' of its own. By such means it is possible not to notice that Beerbohm had nothing to say, or nothing that we commonly distinguish as creative. A sharp critical intelligence lies behind pieces like the Henry James parody, 'The Mote in the Middle Distance', and emerges more memorably in the cartoons, the confirmed popularity of which seems justified. Only the relative sizes of some of the figures—Wilde enormously swollen, Swinburne reduced to a doll—give an archaic air; the pure, clear colours have not dated, and the penetration into character shown in drawings like that of Matthew Arnold affords a commentary of permanent interest and value, one which no arrangement of words could match.

Mr Behrman's book, doubtless through no fault of his, lets the cartoons down badly by printing too few of them, and in black-and-white, and with poor definition; I should have thought nobody who wanted to possess a book about Beerbohm would have been deterred by another ten bob or more on the price. In other respects, *Conversation with Max* is a good buy. It is very much what the title suggests—an account of a series of visits Mr Behrman made to Beerbohm's house in Rapallo between 1952 and 1956, the year of Beerbohm's death. Large portions of what was said are set out verbatim, and since I do not believe Mr Behrman would have invented or paraphrased anything, he must be possessed of either considerable talent with recording devices or total aural and visual recall. I wish I knew which, for if Mr Behrman is not a memorial prodigy then Beerbohm, prepared to chat with the utmost freedom into a tape microphone or a shorthand notebook, was equally extraordinary.

Mr Berhman, invoking the hero of *The Catcher in the Rye*, whose literary criterion, it will be remembered, was whether or not he felt like calling an author up, simply called Beerbohm up and went and saw him. Holden Caulfield is hardly, one would have thought, a very plausible figure in a Maximilian context, and one readily imagines the Bronx cheer he would have produced after reading a couple of pages of 'Maltby and Braxton', let alone *Zuleika Dobson*. But he would, I think, have at least maintained a respectful silence if forced into contact with Mr Behrman's book, which as an exercise in portraiture could hardly be bettered, keen and vivid in its reporting, pervaded by a completely unfussy and unphoney sense of period, affectionate and respectful to its subject. It is not hard to see why he immediately won Beerbohm's confidence.

To throw doubt on the basis of Beerbohm's literary reputation need involve no denial of what is, on this showing, the fact that he was in many ways an interesting, intelligent, witty man. His period, which corresponds less closely to his lifetime than that of any other figure that I can think of (1870 to 1914 is about as close as one is likely to get), was an entertaining one, and nobody who has been attracted by it will fail to get a good deal in the way of entertainment as well as understanding out of this book.

Few people today are much interested, I would guess, in figures of the calibre of Alfred Sutro, Sir Sydney Cockerell, Gordon Craig or Reginald Turner, however nice a man the last-named probably (on this account certainly) was. But there is plenty of new information, or food for thought, about Wilde, Shaw, Frank Harris, Pound, Ibsen and that notable friend of culture, the boxer Gene Tunney. On all these Beerbohm is interesting, on some finely illuminating (Trollope 'reminds us that sanity need not be Philistine'), but in nearly every case a note of coldness and disparagement emerges. Almost the only recipients of his wholehearted appreciation are Little Tich and Dan Leno, a reflection of interests which, whatever their justification in Beerbohm's own day, are likely to strike us now as fairly rarefied.

One tiny mystery, if I may minimally contradict what I said at the beginning, remains. How did Beerbohm manage to go on living in Rapallo all those years, forty-five of them? He took in the milk and he paid the rent, but what did he do all that time, what did he do — apart from decorating, illustrating, grangerising individual volumes for the benefit of individual friends, self-imposed tasks, each one stretching over several months? An obsession with failure, with setting one's aim safely low, emerges clearly from this portrait of one who never risked coming clean about himself on any but minor issues. And perhaps it is all right to leave it there, though a belated sense of justice may lead some readers to tip their hats momentarily in the direction of somebody so unfashionable as to make not a single claim to importance of any kind.

Spectator, 25 November 1960

The Poet and the Lunatics

The Man Who Was Thursday, by G. K. Chesterton

My excuse for making this a more than usually personal reappraisal is that, as it happens, *The Man Who Was Thursday* was the first grown-up novel I remember reading outside school. (*The War of the Worlds* may have preceded it, but I did not then count that as grown-up.) I had reached *Thursday* by way of the Father Brown stories, and went on from it to Chesterton's first novel, *The Napoleon of Notting Hill*. I found, as I have continued to find, that I could not happily get very much further with the rest of his fiction; though I now reflect, a generation later, that a total score of seven lasting volumes out of seventeen is rather enviable. Anyway, their author had impressed himself upon me to the extent that I can still remember how I felt at the news of his death in 1936, the first total stranger's death that meant anything to me personally.

The foregoing is not intended as just an account of boyhood sensitivity. *Thursday* is a boys' book as well as a grown-ups' book, along with *Hamlet* and *The Mill on the Floss*, and not along with *King Lear* and *Middlemarch*. The degree of overlap between the adolescent and the adult response must vary from case to case, and will remain very hard to chart while we know so little about the former. If we could find out, by some more reliable means than the adult re-reader's unreliable memory, how adolescents respond to works of literature (beyond categorising them as terrific or tripe), then we would have found out a lot about literature. However, I had better shut down this line of speculation: I can think of nobody I could trust to pursue it who would also want to.

Anyhow, a boy either gobbles a book up or throws it away. I gobbled up *The Man Who Was Thursday*. The opening caught me by the scruff: two poets discussing art and anarchism at an open-air party in a romantic setting under an extraordinary sunset. Art I knew I was for; anarchism seemed a sinister and alluring fantasy, dreamed up by the author himself from nothing or from some sliver of remote past— I may have noticed indifferently that the book was first published in 1908. Today, anarchism is something else, but lapse of time and events has done nothing to date Chesterton's insight into it: a little more of this later. What I find unchanged and wonderful is the setting and the sunset. Here, as almost throughout, the novel reveals a characteristic it shares with some—though by no means all—greater works; an irresistible power of suggestion that the extraordinary is, if not the most ordinary thing in the world, as G.K.C. might have put it, then at least almost literally round the corner. I did not know on my first readings, and do not care now, that the suburb of 'Saffron Park' stands for Bedford Park, a vanished name for the network of streets just north of Turnham Green station, probably at no time long on romantic potential. I still step, with the first sentence, into village gardens, glowing with Chinese lanterns and overhung with a heaven full of red-hot plumes. No writer has ever excelled Chesterton, that drop-out art student, in descriptions of skies and the effects of light on landscape.

After the party, the story takes an apparently more ordinary turn (more like Bulldog Drummond, I thought originally), whereby the poet who has talked against anarchism, Gabriel Syme, gets himself elected to the Central Anarchist Council, the members of which are named after the days of the week. Syme is not merely an anti-anarchist, but a member of the New Detective Corps formed expressly to fight anarchism, and carries credentials franked 'The Last Crusade'—not quite like Bulldog Drummond. The flashback account of Syme's enlistment, in a totally dark room at (so it says) Scotland Yard, deserves a quotation: Chesterton could elevate melodrama, or prose opera, to the threshold of poetry:

> 'Are you the new recruit?' asked a heavy voice.
>
> And in some strange way, though there was not the shadow of a shape in the room, Syme knew two things: first, that it came from a man of massive stature; and second, that the man had his back to him.
>
> 'Are you the new recruit?' asked the invisible chief, who seemed to have heard all about it. 'All right. You are engaged.'
>
> Syme, quite swept off his feet, made a feeble fight against this irrevocable phrase.
>
> 'I really have no experience,' he began.
>
> 'No one has any experience,' said the other, 'of the battle of Armageddon.'
>
> 'But I am really unfit—'
>
> 'You are willing, that is enough,' said the unknown.
>
> 'Well, really,' said Syme. 'I don't know any profession of which mere willingness is the final test.'
>
> 'I do,' said the other—'martyrs. I am condemning you to death. Good day.'

Hardly like Bulldog Drummond at all.

In due course, Syme meets the other members of the Council, an array of carefully described and sharply-differentiated grotesques. The chair of Friday is filled by the ancient Professor de Worms, who seems to have moved beyond decrepitude into actual corruption, so that, whenever he moves, Syme is afraid a leg or arm might fall off. Saturday is young Dr Bull, coarse and commonplace but for his black glasses: Syme thinks his eyes might be covered up because they are too frightful to be seen. But, as is fitting, the President, Sunday, outclasses them all with his unnatural bulk, such that his face, seen close to, might be too big to be possible. Melodrama again, if you like, but done with such pictorial, concrete energy and conviction that I believe every detail as firmly as I ever did, even though I now know almost by heart what is to follow.

What follows is the revelation of first Tuesday, then Friday and Saturday as co-members of the anti-anarchist constabulary, a trip to France to frustrate a bomb-throwing by Wednesday, a duel with swords, a pursuit on foot, on horses, by motor-car, a final confrontation on the seashore. The reader of this article can guess, only a little more easily than the reader of the book, what Wednesday and finally Monday, the fanatical Secretary, turn out to be: but that confrontation, in which four detectives, believing themselves to be the last champions of Christendom, turn at bay against what seems a world given over to anarchy, remains undimmed, full of fine, highly artificial rhetoric and gestures both theatrical and dignified, enough on its own to earn the novel its subtitle, 'A Nightmare'.

What Sunday turns out to be—apart, of course, from having doubled as the man in the dark room—is not foreseeable. Unfortunately it is also not quite satisfactory or even clear. Near the end, in flight from the detective posse, he turns practical joker or comic ogre, taking rides on a Zoo elephant and a balloon from the Earl's Court Exhibition. (This part is shot through with facetiousness that will make most people wriggle; as a lad I thought the fault was in me—a sadly dated reaction—or was reading too fast to notice.) Right at the end, Sunday is revealed as something like Pan, or Nature, or God. Just before his death, Chesterton disclaimed this as a pious disavowal by one who had joined the Roman Church years after the book was written. At any rate, one is finally left thrilled and baffled, peering at a half-decipherable message about life being a bewildering but good-natured and all-reconciling joke.

Boy Amis and man Amis differ most sharply over some possible defects in presentation: what the latter, in his know-all way, might describe as on-the-face-of-it unlikelihoods or impossibilities (which the former took in his stride). Thus, half the plot hangs on the detectives having given, and continuing to keep, crazy promises not to go to the police. Defence: the promises were necessary in order to get on to the Council, and to break them would have fatally dishonoured the Last Crusade. Well yes, but these are inferences, not in the book. Again, the seasons are muddled up, so that the Council breakfasts on an open balcony in Leicester Square just before a February snowstorm, and two days later the countryside near Calais is hot at seven in the morning. Here a juvenile defence works best: the open-air breakfast is fun, and the snowstorm is exciting, and every schoolboy knows (what grown-ups have forgotten) that France is much hotter than England.

But thirdly, time is hectically telescoped, so much so that, as recounted, with no pauses in conversation etc, the Channel crossing evidently takes about five minutes. Defence: the whole thing is a nightmare. This will not quite do: it is a novel as well as a nightmare, and so must observe some limitations; worse, Chesterton telescopes time in other, non-nightmarish stories. Does it matter whether he knew what he was doing, whether all these oddities are skilful nightmare adjuncts or sheer carelessness?—he certainly shows carelessness in allowing his own narrative style to infiltrate dialogue. But is the question a real question? The narrative-into-dialogue business apart, everything fits well enough into *this* story, and, more generally, writers, like other people, know what they are doing when they may seem not to know they know.

The Man Who Was Thursday is not a political novel, but it has political implications, and from this point of view the 1971 reader is better served than the 1935 reader, perhaps even the 1908 reader. Rather as Jack London foretold the rise of fascism in *The Iron Heel* (published the previous year), Chesterton foretold the shape of some of our present discontents. He saw destructive forces in our society that would be nothing but destructive, 'not trying to alter things, but to annihilate them', basing themselves in the first place on an inner anarchy that denies all the moral distinctions 'on which mere rebels base themselves'. 'The most dangerous criminal now is the entirely lawless modern philosopher.' The enemy arises not from among the people, but from the educated and well-off, those who unite intellectualism and ignorance and who are helped on their way by 'a weak worship of intellect and force'—near the knuckle, that one. Most specifically, Chesterton, or the man in the dark room, 'is certain that the scientific and artistic worlds are silently bound in a crusade against the Family and the State'. By 'silently' he can hardly have meant more than 'secretly'—if he had meant 'by an unspoken consensus' he would have been not just a remarkable prophet but a terrifying one.

All in all, I rather envy the younger self of mine who thought that the bad men in *Thursday* were anarchists, or bomb-throwers, or political assassins, chiefly because they had to be something.

New Statesman, 26 February 1971

Where Q Stands Now

Quiller-Couch: a Portrait of 'Q', by A. L. Rowse, Methuen

Not many readers of this newspaper [*Sunday Telegraph*] will be aware that Sir Arthur Quiller-Couch (generally referred to as 'Q') was a university don, critic and miscellaneous writer who in effect founded the English School at Cambridge after the First World War. Rather more will know of him as a compiler of anthologies of English verse, one or two of which have lasted to the present day. But very few of any description will make out the reason for this book. To commemorate the 125th anniversary of his birth? The forty-fourth of his death? Then to repair his reputation as a matter of some urgency?

More likely A. L. Rowse just wanted to write about his old friend and fellow-Cornishman, and the publishers, rightly confident of provoking some interest with the author's name, took on this easy-going account of a 'rather overlooked and underestimated figure', as they modestly describe Q. Dr Rowse, whose 'definitive biography', *Shakespeare the Man*, clearly a more ambitious project, is also due in the shops, writes in *Quiller-Couch* in his usual uncluttered, talkative, amiably cocksure style. Plenty of people will enjoy this book without being persuaded of many or even any of its claims about Q's achievements.

Almost the chief attraction is the regularity with which Dr Rowse lays about him at the numerous objects of his dislike and disapproval: modern Oxford, ditto taxation, football crowds, Shakespearian scholarship, black African states, verse ('uncooked' stuff), novels ('the thuggery and buggery, the mugging and drugging', etc). Now and again his obvious relish may set up a reaction in favour of his victim. He never leaves the Germans alone: however the subject may come up, he gives them a kicking for their inbred cruelty and aggression. He was vociferously taking this line at meetings in Oxford in 1941, and deeply unfashionable it was, to give him his due, at that place and time. Some of this negative spirit appears in Dr Rowse's defence of Q's writings. The latter's fiction 'did not have the vulgarity of a Maugham or the brutalism of a Hemingway'—no doubt, nor a lot else besides.

But it must be difficult to say anything very interesting about books the reader has never heard of and will never see, for Q's novels and stories are gone for good. Well, for all I know they are much talked of in Cornwall, of which we hear a great deal in these pages, too much for some Saxons and doubtless others, who regard the Cornish as an unnecessary and uninviting pseudo-nation, their last notable representative being Michael Foot. (The Rowse style is catching.)

Q had a good gift for parody, and a take-off he wrote of Praed had captivated me before I knew who Praed was, but even that, I suppose, has something donnish about it, and Dr Rowse is quite positive that Q's literary aspirations were quenched by his academic career. That career has come to seem the acme, or the nadir, of orthodoxy, making it hard to recall now that it was Q who pushed philology out of the compulsory part of the Cambridge English syllabus, introduced post-1830 literature and literary criticism, held that literature was 'a living art, to be practised as well as admired', and got F. R. Leavis taken on at Downing.

Now that the Leavis regime itself has passed into history, it is tempting to conclude that although any kind of academic study of indigenous literature is probably harmful, the Leavis kind did more general damage than the Q kind; dissatisfaction with the Bourbons need not make us like the Jacobins any better.

Q's own literary criticism looks pretty thin today. It confines itself largely to pious generalities, which while perhaps less harmful than 'creative insights' are still unenlivening. Most of it must be lightly edited lectures; he wrote them out, says Dr Rowse, which saves time in the end. His 'introduction' to a 1930 edition of Matthew Arnold's poems, given longer passages of quotation, would be just right for one of those innumerable fifty-minute hours (or a railway journey without a newspaper). But, to be fair, it does find room to say that Arnold used italics and the interjection 'Ah!' too much, which is a bloody sight more than I carried away from the average morning session in the hall of Magdalen or New College in the distant 1940s.

Where Q lives is in his anthologies, the ballads, the Victorian verse and above all of course *The Oxford Book of English Verse 1250–1900* (1901; second edition, *1250–1918*, first published 1939). This is still selling half a century later and sixteen years after the first appearance of Helen Gardner's excellent compilation, *The New Oxford Book of English Verse*, though the Oxford University Press were characteristically too coy to tell me precisely how Q is still doing. His selection remains about the best one-volume attempt to give an idea of what English verse has done in that time. Dame Helen points out that it neglects satiric, political, epistolary and didactic verse, which seems a good plan on the whole.

Even for his date, Q was a naughty editor. He tinkered with early texts; he reduced Arthur O'Shaughnessy's *Ode* ('We are the music-makers') from eight verses to three without telling anyone, and it is no real defence to say that they are the best verses and the poem is much better as mutilated. I caught him at a less well-known bit of fudging recently when I was putting together an anthology of my own. In a vague way I had long admired poem 485 in the old *Oxford Book*, a piece by Crabbe in two eight-line stanzas headed 'Late Wisdom', good vigorous stuff in the poet's best moralising vein and, for him, noticeably and unusually succinct. Just right for my purpose,

I thought. Since the title as given, though admirably appropriate, seemed unlikely to have been Crabbe's own, I set about discovering the original one. This proved to be 'Reflections' or, in full, 'Reflections upon the subject—' followed by a couplet of Claudian's about the uselessness of remorse and an English translation of the same, presumably by Crabbe himself. Q's invented title was obviously an improvement on this rigmarole, and to me worth considering at least.

What I could not quite stomach was the ruthlessly comprehensive surgery that Q, again without a word to anyone, had inflicted on Crabbe's text. 'Reflections' had been a poem of 108 lines in twelve stanzas of six, eight, ten and twelve lines. 'Late Wisdom' is made up of lines 25–8, 33–6 and 45–52 of it, the last eight forming lines 1–8 of one of the 12-line stanzas. The fact that these chunks cohere into a plausible whole says something about the original poem and about Crabbe himself, but as rightly or wrongly I dropped 'Late Wisdom' from my draft list of contents I felt I had found out a little more about Q as well, not altogether to his credit. Yet his taste, his nose for the first-rate, was impeccable. I once spent a day reading all Michael Drayton's 150-odd sonnets, on the view that anything as marvellous as the celebrated 'Since there's no help' could not be the only good one. No; Q had picked the only winner.

The old boy evidently knew a lot of people, even if a lot of them were bores like Robert Bridges or the learned but famously idle Nichol Smith. Unfortunately Dr Rowse has found no colourful stories to tell of him, but that must be the sign of a well-spent and agreeable life.

Sunday Telegraph, 10 April 1988

C. S. Lewis

C. S. Lewis: a Biography, by A. N. Wilson, Collins

C. S. (Clive Staples, known to family and friends as Jack) Lewis was the best lecturer, in more than one sense, that I have ever heard. Technically to start with: always audible, clear and articulate, by no means run-of-the-mill virtues, as his friend Tolkien for one, in dire need of speech therapy, demonstrated every week, if not twice (I have been trying for a long time to forget all about his horrible Old English classes).

Lewis, while continuously entertaining you, dictated the necessary paragraphs of authors he knew you would never find or read, gave abstracts of the less necessary, supplied references to what you could look up yourself. After an hour's enjoyment you came away with a complete account of what he had said.

I heard him in Oxford in the 1940s on medieval literature and Renaissance literature, neither of them a favourite territory of mine, but he explained them, saved me from being a mere uncomprehending tourist of those distant regions and from patronising them. As A. N. Wilson puts it well in *C. S. Lewis*, he has not, in expounding the medieval picture of the universe, 'represented (it) as "better" than the modern; but he has shown us that both are merely pictures'. He helped me to read *The Faerie Queene* with, among other insights, the simple-sounding assertion that, like his contemporaries, Spenser was always intending literally what we unthinkingly pass over as metaphor.

His writing showed the same gift of compression, as when he distinguished between good unoriginality and good originality in the animated film of *Snow White and the Seven Dwarfs*. The first was shown in the befriending of the fleeing princess by little creatures of the woods, the second in her and our first mistaking their eyes, seen in the dark, for those of dangerous monsters. Good unoriginality! I had never thought of that before. And, more shortly still, what is there left to be said for 'evaluative' literary criticism after the remark, quoted here, that it 'is always better to read Chaucer (or whoever you please) again than to read a new criticism of him'?

If I seem to have come, rather late, any nearer the book supposedly under review, it is partly because it deals at length, as it has to, with Lewis's function or career as a Christian apologist. Here it strikes me, even after trying to allow for my own agnosticism, that not only was he pursuing what he was less suited for, good at, than the interpretation of literature and its supporting ways of thought, as with the medieval writers and their Ptolemaic universe; he also revealed the less attractive sides of his nature. He was prone to an excessively bluff and breezy way with obstinate opponents or thorny points that can amount to loud-mouthed arrogance, reminding one uncomfortably that he was an Ulsterman, an Orangeman, suggesting now and then a miraculously learned and intelligent Ian Paisley.

More damaging to Lewis's cause was his tendency to approach the most delicate questions in bull-in-a-china-shop style. *The Problem of Pain*—there's an informative title for you. The fact that a merciful God had made suffering an inescapable part of human existence was, properly viewed, just a little local difficulty that a bit of common sense and tough-mindedness would soon sort out. Wilson is properly unsparing here, showing good old Jack reading the book aloud to his all-male circle over beer and whisky, polishing off hell and the justification for it in what would amount to nine pages of print. An account of his conversion to Christianity in his middle thirties would have been more interesting, but Lewis seems to have ducked it. Some shyness can be sensed behind the bullying.

He had an extraordinary and mostly unfortunate personal life. His mother died when he was nine years old and he did not get on with his father. We are told here that he had an 'emotionally stultifying' and, at Malvern, 'appalling' school life, though Wilson is rather given to that kind of thing, going on to complain about the English class system and so on. In his twenties he became part of a household that comprised a Mrs Moore (the mother of a friend killed in France in 1918), her daughter and Lewis's elder brother Warren (Warnie).

There was never any doubt about the mutual devotion of the two brothers, but just what the relationship between Lewis and Mrs Moore was and became remains unclear. Son/mother? At first, certainly. Lovers ever? Platonically attached only? First one then the other? Nobody seems to know for certain. To judge from the pedestrian style in which Wilson tells the story of those earlier years he does not much care either, though things perk up greatly when he reaches the undeniably sexual and sadly brief love and marriage, over-shadowed by illness, that came to Lewis in his late fifties.

An extraordinary life is not necessarily worth telling or hearing a great deal about. Wilson is at his best on Lewis's works, the books elucidating earlier literature, the religious pamphlets, the delightful science fiction trilogy, *Out of the Silent Planet, Perelandra* or *Voyage to Venus, That Hideous Strength*; the account of the virtues and defects of the last-named is scrupulously fair. He also of course deals at some length with *The Lion, the Witch and the Wardrobe* and the other Narnia stories written for children. These I have not read, having been an old man of twenty-eight when the first one came out, and never having much cared for kids' stuff at any age, except in comics. But plenty of children feel differently, specifically about Narnia, which has held an enduring appeal for them.

Sunday Telegraph, 18 February 1990

Bare Choirs?

Argufying, by William Empson, edited by John Haffenden, Chatto & Windus

In Oxford during the Second World War, a great many people seemed to be reading two works of criticism: *The Allegory of Love* by C. S. Lewis and *Seven Types of Ambiguity* by William Empson. Of the two, the drawback to the Lewis was that you had to read a lot of other books, medieval ones and such, to get much out of it, and Lewis himself was unglamorously teaching and examining in the Oxford English school. Empson was younger (by eight years), not a don in that sense, hardly more than an undergraduate, a Cambridge man, an expert on psychology and new stuff like that, a pioneer—we would probably have called him 'exciting' if that usage had been around then. And his book had the great merit of being sufficient to itself, with no rotten old romances and epics to wade through. There was not even an index.

I was in as deep as any; I went so far as to steal the Oxford Union library's copy of *Seven Types*, as the cognoscenti called it. (It was out of print at the time, which I suppose both aggravates and extenuates the offence.) The feeling of illumination it gave, of helping you to see things in poetry you had had no idea were there—ten different reasons why Shakespeare's 'bare ruined choirs' in Sonnet 73 was an appropriate phrase—is hard to recapture now, or even to find charitable reasons for.

The essays and reviews that make up *Argufying*, collected from the whole period 1928 to 1974, are really just like Empson's earlier writings, though of course without the show of organisation, of scientific 'rigour', in *Seven Types*, or at least in its title. As ever, he divides his time between the pursuit of general themes and theories on the one hand, and explorations of particular writers and writings on the other. In neither activity does he give this reader much to bite on.

In Empson's theoretical discussions, here as elsewhere, he raises all manner of problems and puts them down again unsolved. He wonders how well a poet should understand his own poetry, indeed what 'understand' means, how much metre, rhythm, sound itself matter, what an image is, what symbolism is, or was, and is still wondering when he changes tack or gives up until the next time the subject comes round. Though an entirely masculine figure, he 'discusses' things rather in the way some women do, not for any result or making up of minds but merely to hold the attention and give off a vague but creditable air of concern. There is none of the sense of purpose and direction that, for instance, enabled Lewis to reach the generalisation that innumerable words and expressions we now understand metaphorically were meant literally by the Elizabethans and earlier writers, a perception that reaches much further than just *The Faerie Queene*, say, and other works of that era.

Well, Empson may have been inclined to dabble and potter a bit when speculating at large, but perhaps he scored when he switched to considering individual passages. Many readers of *Seven Types* must remember arriving with relief at the little blocks of quotation among the masses of discourse. Alas, travelling hopefully can now be seen to be a good deal better. Even the immediate thrill died down as you began to wonder what you had actually learnt. Mostly it was that Empson could think of all sorts of ingenious shades and possibilities of meaning that did seem a tiny bit unlikely to have been anywhere in the poet's mind at the time. These days you might be more inclined to call most of his suggestions absurd or manifestly beside the point.

Empson's most famous critical observation, the only one I think that anybody remembers, came not in *Seven Types* but in its successor. It said of the 'Full many a flower is born to blush unseen' stanza in Gray's *Elegy* that it was a piece of political fudging, designed to help everyone go on feeling satisfied with the arrangement whereby those at the bottom of the eighteenth century social order had not much of a way of climbing up it. In the best, illuminatory style, the remark spreads over and says something true about the whole poem, though of course there are other no less true things to be said about it. The matter comes up in an article of 1947 reprinted here, but characteristically Empson leaves it in a fuzzier state than he found it.

That happens over and over again in the 600–odd pages of this collection. The longest piece is an unbelievably arid and unenlightening disquisition on *The Ancient Mariner*. It brings up all manner of rightly neglected factors—about Coleridge's first draft, about history, anthropology, anything that strikes Empson's fancy—in a performance that only leaves new difficulties in the way of fathoming that enigmatic poem. But the performance itself, the engagingly tentative, colloquial, self-deflating style, constantly tempts the reader to believe that something coherent and sensible is being imparted. It is not for nothing that Empson's favourite poet was Donne.

There are big questions looming in the background about the worth of any analytic criticism, and even about that of teaching English literature at all at the level of the university. The most I can do here is suggest that the critic who goes further than clarifying his text by glossing the hard words and explaining the references—further than the scholar, that is—does so at his and our peril. In his Oxonian way, C. S. Lewis was rather that scholarly sort of critic, and would perhaps have disclaimed the label of 'critic' altogether, writing as he once did that if we really want to improve our understanding and appreciation of any given author, it is always better to read that author again than to read a new criticism of him. Lewis perhaps overestimated the number of people who really want that.

Sunday Telegraph, 29 November 1987

The Man Who Gave Us Billy Bunter

Frank Richards: the Chap Behind the Chums, by Mary Cadogan, Viking

Only oldsters can have any direct memory of the boys' comic papers the *Gem* (published weekly 1907 to 1939) and the better-known *Magnet* (1908–40), each number of which carried a 20,000-word school story. Of all the scores of characters in which those closely-printed pages were so rich, none have taken root in the public mind but Billy Bunter, the Fat Owl of the Remove, though there may be a flicker of life left in the names of Greyfriars School, brave, decent Harry Wharton and the gimlet-eyed beak Mr Quelch, all of the *Magnet*. Everything else is gone.

Greyfriars was of course a public school, a boarding school, like St Jim's in the *Gem* and like every other school that has ever appeared in anything that could be called a school story. Readers of the two comics were well enough aware that other kinds of school existed, if only because nearly all of them attended such places, but no healthy boy ever wanted to read about his own kind of life. The attraction of the Greyfriars-St Jim's kind of life, with its Eton suits, bizarre slang, prize cups, elaborate raggings, teas round the study fire, breakings of bounds, dormitory feasts and so on, was that it was remote, more than half-way to fantasy, and yet intelligible to any schoolboy. Any English schoolboy, that is. No foreigner, no American even, could ever have made head or tail of it. Indeed it is hard to imagine a school story worth the name having been written outside what was then the Empire.

Writing at about the time when the two papers went out of production, George Orwell made this point in the course of an entertaining but characteristically fatuous attack on them as offering 'a perfectly deliberate incitement to wealth-fantasy', and equally deliberate propaganda for the political status quo. He goes on about snobbery, not such a terrible failing as all that anyway, I should have thought, and

54

present or appealed to in some form in most other kinds of fiction from fairy stories on. The Greyfriars-St Jim's stories have about as much to do with snobbery as the works of P. G. Wodehouse, with which they have far more in common than their historical overlap. The Hon. Arthur Augustus 'Gussy' D'Arcy, the dandified, inept swell of St Jim's, turned up there in 1907; Bertie Wooster first appeared about 1911. Both owe something to the 'knut' of the contemporary music-hall.

Orwell could have been forgiven for assuming that the two concurrent sagas could not in the nature of things have been the work of one man sustained over thirty years, and must have issued from a group or succession of individuals working in a common, deliberately homogenised style. To what must have been the surprise of the readers of *Horizon*, the monthly where Orwell's essay had appeared in 1940, somebody replied with the information that he was and always had been the sole author. (He added that the slang complained of derived from Chaucer and Lewis Carroll, not *Stalky & Co*, and defended the lack of sex to be found in the stories, surely unnecessarily in the case of fiction originally intended for Edwardian schoolboys and later read by many children no older than ten.)

This person was a Charles Edward St John Hamilton (1876–1961), better known by his *Magnet* pseudonym, Frank Richards (he used twenty-eight in all). He had been the sixth child of a drunken London-Scottish journalist with poetical ambitions and puritanical quirks, who denied his wife and daughters the indulgence of wearing their hair in fringes.

Although only seven years old when his father died, Richards had had plenty of time to develop a warm antipathy to him. It is as interesting as such things ever get that both Harry Wharton and his fellow-hero, Tom Merry of St Jim's, are orphans. By what must be coincidence, Bertie too lacks a visible father; not Gussy, though.

Nobody who wrote about public schools in *Magnet/Gem* manner could possibly have been anywhere near one himself, and Richards was educated at a succession of private day-schools in West London. He sold his first story at the age of seventeen for the large sum of five guineas and continued for some years to publish tales of adventure about life at sea, by which he once visited the Isle of Man, and in Canada and the American West, where he never went, though his father had thought of emigrating to Canada in the 1870s and Richards saw one of Buffalo Bill's London shows. He finally turned to school stories in 1903.

Throughout his active career Richards's writing speed was fifty words a minute or 1.5 million words a year, the equivalent of twenty full-length novels, which should take the silly grins off the faces of those of us who think 500 words in a morning is pretty good going. Nothing else about him is very remarkable. *Frank Richards* shows us that, although a most interesting phenomenon, he was and remained a most uninteresting man, something that can be said of many who make their way in the world, not by any means excluding geniuses, as the examples of Mozart and Tennyson suggest.

Greyfriars, with Billy Bunter the central figure, achieved some revival after the Second World War in various printed versions, though most notably in the 1950s with several TV series, to which Richards contributed fresh material. Gerald Campion as the Fat Owl was really quite good but, to the eye and ear of this former *Magnet* reader at least, nothing else was. From Father Brown to (once more) Bertie Wooster, television is helpless with existing material whose appeal is all in the writing. It was the style that made Richards's world.

All gone now, as I said. To one's grown-up self, Greyfriars and St Jim's are one with Nineveh and Tyre, but then they were not created for grown-ups. I suspect that children's fiction pleases its intended readers best when they sense that their elders would find it utterly beneath their notice. Where does that leave you, Beatrix Potter?

Sunday Telegraph, 30 October 1988

Afternoon World

The Acceptance World, by Anthony Powell, Heinemann

With the appearance of Mr Anthony Powell's new volume we are back again in that shapeless and yet homogeneous world which lies somewhere between the borders of commerce, politics, the arts, fashion, the gay life and the not-quite-so-gay life. The centre of its stage is occupied by an Etonian trio—Jenkins, Stringham and Templer—and a fourth component, also Etonian but solitary—Widmerpool. Around them is disposed a large intermediate group of relatives, family friends, and acquaintances made at the university or in London, and beyond these again there seem to be several hundred marginal figures: hostesses, publishers, museum officials, fellows who ran into one's first wife's uncle in Capetown in 1911, and any number of ex-boyfriends and old flames. The gyrations of these last are so complex and often so brisk that a conversation between Powell-readers is liable to turn into a competition of erudite gossip: 'Heard the latest? Dicky Umfraville has taken Anne Stepney away from Barnby. She's had quite a career since she left Charles Stringham.'—'No, no, you're muddling her up with her sister. Charles married Peggy Stepney.'

This third term in the series begun by *A Question of Upbringing* (1951) and *A Buyer's Market* (1952) introduces us to the Acceptance World, in the first place nothing more than the name given by Templer to the financial house now dignified by the presence of Widmerpool. Apart from this, however, the phrase represents 'the world in which the essential element—happiness, for example—is drawn, as it were, from an engagement to meet a bill . . . Besides, in another sense, the whole world is the Acceptance World as one approaches thirty; at least some illusions discarded'. And, it might be added, at least some desires and hopes abandoned. As regards the story, this proceeds along the lines already established, in five long episodes or sequences, each tending to be continuous in action. We have moved forward in time to the early 1930s. The first item concerns Jenkins, the narrator, having his fortune told (correctly, as it turns out) by a mysterious female connection of his Uncle Giles: a proceeding closely anticipated by an incident in Mr Powell's early novel, *Venusberg*, of which the hero, Lushington, has other points in common with Jenkins. Having moved from the Ufford Hotel, Bayswater, to the Ritz, we encounter Quiggin, a pushing literary man, who conducts throughout the book an intermittent campaign for the dislodgement of a rival and the insertion of himself as secretary to a *démodé* but still 'distinguished' novelist. Templer also appears, followed by his wife and married sister Jean, who has recently been deserted, though without utter finality, by her husband, Bob Duport. Almost involuntarily at first, but with a rapid access of sentiment and energy, Jenkins enters upon a love affair with her, and this forms the main subject of the book. Subsidiary concerns involve the glimpsing of Sillery, the don with the Nietzschean moustache, at a left-wing demonstration, a planchette session at which Karl Marx is alleged to assist, the departure of Templer's wife in an unexpected direction, and the activities of Widmerpool, who not only gets the supposedly powerful Bill Truscott flung out of his job with Donners-Brebner but also, by making an uninvited speech about his commercial experiences at a reunion dinner, causes Le Bas, his old housemaster, to drop down in a seizure. Other apparently minor incidents have a larger bearing, most notably a half-serious physical tussle at the end in which Widmerpool, the representative of egotistical ambition, defeats Stringham, the tough-skinned but cracking vessel of romantic melancholy.

Though so firmly located in the sequence which includes it, *The Acceptance World* differs from its predecessors in some elements of presentation. There is a departure from the earlier practice whereby all manner of paintings and sculptures got brought in to provide decoration and imagery, the fictitious ones so vividly that one could hardly credit not having come across Mr Deacon's *Boyhood of Cyrus*, in particular, in some municipal gallery, and the real ones with such insistence that one wondered at times whether Mr Powell might not have been intending finally to pass under review the entire corpus of Western visual art. The whole method is notably less discursive than that of the previous volume, where it seemed here and there as if a Henry James fired with enthusiasm for the question-and-answer section of *Ulysses* had stood at the author's elbow. The behaviour and feelings of Jenkins in love are described with a sharpness, almost at times an acidity, which sets him free from the curious somnambulism—not in itself at all unsympathetic—that has been apt to afflict some of Mr Powell's earlier heroes: there are traces of it in Lushington of *Venusberg*, but Atwater of *Afternoon Men* is the most typical. However, the main preoccupations and themes echo those of the two earlier volumes in this series.

The title of the complete series, *The Music of Time*, taken together with the frequent images of human life as a ritual dance performed to that music, gives some sort of key with which the vast and complicated design may be unlocked. Nobody can have failed to notice, to start with, the immense number of chance meetings by which vital episodes are set in train, and in this instalment again the main section, nearly a third of the book, contains only two purposed encounters. This theory of existence, whereby things only happen when they are somehow appropriate, when the evolutions of the human dance bring them about, is in the first place a way of doubting the validity of effort and seems indeed to be approaching the edge of quietism, a point I mean to take up later. One's second reaction is likely to be that to throw so much emphasis on the casual meeting as the mainspring of events is only possible, if it is not to degenerate into the coincidence-convention of picaresque, in cases where the characters dealt with inhabit a restricted world. This is certainly true of Mr Powell's characters, who all belong to—well, 'the ruling class' sounds a bit snappish, and not much in the way of ruling evidently gets done; while 'society' sounds a bit something else, and 'the rich' may have the effect, to be avoided if possible, of recalling Miss Nancy Mitford or Miss Angela Thirkell. Anyway, it was unerringly pointed out recently that we find nothing of the working classes in *The Music of Time*, and in addition politics are not taken very seriously—this in the 1930s. Mr Powell is not 'committed', in fact—except to an interest in human behaviour and to the duty of irony and scepticism which confronts every chronicler of an exclusive group. A glance at some contemporary talents 'committed' in other directions will not show that Mr Powell has chosen wrongly.

The theme of the human dance, to continue, is in any case not the only theme, sinking as it does at times more to the level of a *leitmotiv*. At least as important and, to some, more interesting is the generalisation about power, or living by the will, which is gradually gathering shape in these pages. Power has always interested this author: everyone in *What's Become of Waring?* wanted power, at least according to the narrator: that frightful pair in *Agents and Patients*, Maltravers and Chipchase, were pursuing it in their own way; even the farcical Zouch, the *übermensch* of *From a View to a Death*, was after the stuff. In *The Music of Time* the pattern is clearer still. Widmerpool, Quiggin and Sillery are only its most obvious embodiments, for Members, Quiggin's rival, covets literary status chiefly for the influence it brings; Barnby, the womanising painter, is interested in domination rather than sensuality; Uncle Giles, shackled and ineffectual as he is, remains the type of the entire egotist; and so on. In an age where the will to power takes ever more unexpected forms, we need someone to teach us the lesson that it can and does co-exist with grotesqueness and fatuity.

The characters on the other side in this battle are to be distinguished as not fighting in it, as drifting, acquiescing, accepting. Though much charm, most intelligence and all humour are annexed to them, their only outlet is finally the arts, inasmuch as their friendships ebb and flow with the measures of the dance, and their encounters with women place them, as does Jenkins's with Jean Duport, at the mercy of the power-seekers. It is here that their predicament takes on the aspect of quietism mentioned earlier: if effort is assertion of the will, and to assert the will is to indulge the desire for power, self-abandonment becomes their only way of staying human. Whatever alternative may be salvaged by *The Music of Time* when complete, we can at least recognise meanwhile that it is better, in all situations, to submit like Jenkins than to climb like Widmerpool. And, finally, we can think ourselves lucky to have a group of novels which, even more successfully than their author's early work, combine wit and sadness and farce and charm, which, without a hint of keening or gesticulation, are entirely serious. I would rather read Mr Powell than any other English novelist now writing.

Spectator, 13 May 1955

The Powell Country

Casanova's Chinese Restaurant, by Anthony Powell, Heinemann

With the fifth volume of Mr Anthony Powell's sequence *The Music of Time* there is a sense of having reached the close of the exposition, the opening of a development section in which some earlier themes are reworked. To be sure, as on previous occasions, there is abundant fresh material too. We see most of two figures in the professional world of music, a composer named Moreland and a critic named Maclintick, and the vicissitudes of their marriages. By a stroke of irony more overtly grim than is common with this author, Moreland's is restored to something like equilibrium by the reverberation of the collapse of Maclintick's, the final fate of whom reaches a depth of horror that reminds us how much more there is in Mr Powell than the urbanely detached (and inexhaustibly witty) chronicler of aristocratic and bohemian cavortings.

It is at a party given for Moreland that the book's other main dramatic point is to be found. The hostess is Mrs Foxe, mother of Charles Stringham, that non-writing Byron who has been slipping in and out of the life of the narrator, Nicholas Jenkins, ever since their school-days. The confluence of these three in changed circumstances leads us to remember that luncheon party in an earlier volume at which Stringham was in lazy control, amiably patronising his mother's secretary, Miss Weedon. Now, however, it is Miss Weedon, grown to the stature of Stringham's gaoler and alcohol-rationer, who dominates the proceedings, with frightful, polite ruthlessness preventing him from toddling off to a night-club with Mrs Maclintick (incidentally a wonderful portrait of peevish vivacity) and ignominiously sending him off to bed.

I single out this short but oddly disconcerting episode for a variety of reasons. In its technical aspect, the fluency with which it is incorporated into, and yet thrown into relief against, a host of other issues signifies a writer in absolute control of his material and his design, no trifling qualification when these are so large. Thematically, Miss Weedon carries the role of a new recruit, or rather a newly disclosed adherent, to that heterogeneous band of thrusters, of those that live by their will, whose incalculable assaults we have already traced in the activities of Widmerpool (that tireless machinator in the City), Sillery (the wire-pulling don), and others, and whose full complement and final significance are yet to be revealed. And, viewed as a piece of character-drawing, Miss Weedon shows that typically Powellian sense of fairness, that refusal to distort by omission or selective exaggeration, that sustained concern that the reader shall true deliverance make, which recall George Eliot—an appropriate comparison in several other ways.

Even Widmerpool, perhaps especially Widmerpool, would be less horribly funny if he were not so sinister, and he would not be a Powell character if there were not a tiny nugget of the really sinister and the joke-sinister, and a morsel of real impressiveness there too, to set against all the stuff about his overcoat and his appalling mother and the time Barbara Goring poured a whole castor of sugar over his head at the Huntercombes' dance.

One thinks too of such minor figures as General Conyers, who put Widmerpool under his own peculiar psychoanalytic microscope at the end of *At Lady Molly's*. The General, we are told through Jenkins, 'was complete master of himself in allowing no trace of ribaldry or ill-nature' to appear in his diagnosis, and this applies with redoubled force to his creator: how easy it would have been, how irresistible for almost any other novelist, not to rest content with showing the General as funny but to turn him into a figure of fun as well. The genuinely comic writer must be capable of taking everything seriously.

I hope I have said enough to show, at any rate, the seriousness with which Mr Powell's achievement is to be taken. Alongside all that splendid vitality, that high-spirited, wholly non-introverted, endlessly inquisitive melancholy, what I find most impressive in *Casanova's Chinese Restaurant*, as in the previous volumes, is the quality of its poise, unimprovable because it never sees itself as poise, giving cohesion to, but never blurring, a vast range of emotion and violent shifts in mood.

The Music of Time is in a sense, as one critic remarked, the chronicle of an 'obsolescent' world (poor old George Eliot with her obsolescent provinces, poor old Joyce with his obsolescent Dublin), and it may well prove to be the last great English novel of its kind as our society— not merely its upper crust—breaks up into something too compartmented to allow the breadth of scope, the unity-plus-diversity afforded by the group of people Mr Powell takes as his subject.

Observer, 19 June 1960

The Final Cadence

Hearing Secret Harmonies, by Anthony Powell, Heinemann

The rounding-off of a national sequence must pose special problems of selection and emphasis: which ends must be carefully tied up and which call for the most perfunctory of knots or can be left loose, how to tackle all this, while keeping two stories going at once, that of the series and that of the volume. Mr Anthony Powell brings off these difficult feats without any sign of strain. He has always been a master of the arts of transition and of persuading the reader to accept unlikelihood, to such a degree that every encounter or reminiscence or piece of news, however eccentric, seems inevitable.

The book opens after the usual vividly pictorial style in the grounds of Nicholas Jenkins' house in the country. Four new characters — at first glance a mere band of youthful hippies — are at once on the scene. If this were one of the author's pre-war novels, even one of the earlier volumes of the sequence, the quartet would have been presented chiefly for our amusement. They do amuse: one of them, a battered tart called Rusty, is a comic miniature drawn with remarkable sharpness considering that she never speaks, just hums and grins to herself a lot. But Scorpio Murtlock with his amulet and blue kaftan, high priest of a — to begin with — merely silly private cult, does much more.

Despite his 'run-of-the-mill outlandishness', Murtlock very soon reveals himself as one of that tribe who live by the will rather than by the emotions or senses. Power people of all sorts, sometimes bossing their more compliant fellows, sometimes competing with one another, are the dominant figures in *A Dance to the Music of Time*: an example from the first volume is scheming Sillery, the don (dead at not quite 100 years old in the present one). Measured in terms of results, Murtlock is the most formidable of them all. After his first appearance, he returns in the flesh only once, and that briefly, but his presence is felt throughout, and in the end he accomplishes the overthrow of Widmerpool, hitherto a power man in complete steel.

The decline and fall of Kenneth (more recently Lord) Widmerpool is the main theme of *Hearing Secret Harmonies*. Kenneth — was it that weird pre-vision sometimes granted novelists that led Mr Powell, some time before 1951, to bestow a Christian name not only appropriate to the point of unalterability (real-life Kenneths please excuse), but also awaiting trendy truncation to Ken under letters to the press in the early Seventies? Well, anyway, Ken, suspected of being a bit barmy near the end of the previous volume, goes all the way downhill in this. The various stages are precisely charted in terms both comic and horrible: it has been a distinction of this author to blend the two, but he has never before achieved so rich a mixture as here.

Soon after Murtlock has left the stage, Ken comes on, on to the television screen, actually during the News. He is being installed as a university chancellor when he falls victim' to an atrocious attack, emerging covered with what looks like blood but turns out to be red paint. Asked for his comments on the spot, he applauds the deed. This is an odious novelty. Ruminating on the affair, Jenkins naturally recalls the time when Barbara Goring poured a whole castor of sugar over Widmerpool's head at the Huntercombes' dance (*A Buyer's Market*). Then, though he may have taken a moment's private pleasure at his own humiliation, he was far from announcing that it was justified. Jenkins thinks the change is due to improved ability to cope, and I suppose he should know, but it can also be taken as an early example of that abject surrender to fashionable heresies — in this case, approval of student violence — which leads Widmerpool to his ruin.

Before that comes a significant incident at a Royal Academy banquet. Jenkins sits next to a Canon Fenneau whom we have not met before: a fine walk-on part, this, the more so in that the end is so near. Fenneau is another power man; like Widmerpool and Murtlock, he has the faculty of making those about him feel a little uncomfortable. Near the end of the evening, Widmerpool, in a red polo-sweater, appears and asks Fenneau to put him in touch with Murtlock. Fenneau advises against it, but Widmerpool insists. At the time, this is no more than faintly ominous, but in retrospect it carries the fearful implication that there is something fated, even something willed, about Widmerpool's destruction, as perhaps about all such.

Mr Powell's energy is unabated. He handles his large scenes — the dinner at which Russell Gwinnett receives an award for his book on X, Trapnel, Sebastian Cutts's wedding at Stourwater — with all the old confidence and cunning. Over the years, the style of the sequence has changed a good deal, from sometimes elaborate periods, full of suspensions and parentheses, to assemblages of short clauses, now and then rather summarily linked. (A comparison of the paint-throwing episode with the sugar-pouring episode will show what I mean.) The desire for brevity betrays Mr Powell once into what Fowler calls *legerdemain* with two senses ('if Murtlock liked sex at all, he preferred his own'), and a few participial phrases seem to hang in the air. But that is the worst I can do.

All reviewers of this continuously entertaining novel will have to declare that whatever its internal merits, those of the sequence as a whole cannot yet be measured. I duly so declare. But I will go further and say that *Hearing Secret Harmonies*, as well as being a worthy conclusion to *A Dance to the Music of Time*, is its best volume for some years. The ending, not surprisingly, is sombre, but my feeling when I laid the book down came partly from another source. It was like the sadness that descends when the last chord of a great symphony fades into silence.

Observer, 7 September 1975

Mr Maugham's Notions

Somerset Maugham: a Biographical and Critical Study, by Richard Cordell, Heinemann

I have a notion that the artist is a man much like other men. He shares to the full their vain, egotistical dreams, their pettiness and cruelty, their lust and greed, he is capable equally of the self-sacrifice and the nobility of spirit which form the other half of the contradiction that is human nature and raise it fleetingly above the brute creation. And yet, such are the paradoxes at the heart of things that he will not be a good artist unless there are moments when he is indescribably moved at the contemplation of some ideal beauty, when his heart beats strangely and on a sudden his whole being seems borne aloft towards he knows not what . . .

If you feel at home with that sort of notion, then you will notoriously have so felt with many of the works of Somerset Maugham, and, now that the supply of these seems to be running thin, the publication of Mr Richard Cordell's volume offers the chance of similarly comfortable sampling of similar notions. From Boswell onward, what a biographer does to his subject has been approached in interest by what subject does to biographer. I have no idea how Mr Cordell writes when he isn't writing about Mr Maugham, but in these pages, or in such of them as he is not actually quoting or paraphrasing his way, he puts on a remarkable impersonation act. He assures us, for instance, of Mr Maugham's acquaintance with the notion 'that human nature is complex, that divided loyalties often make man's motives obscure to himself as well as to others'. Quite a few of us, you see, might have managed to work out the bit about *to others* unassisted, but it takes Cordell-Maugham to spot that prizewinning *to himself as well.*

Some of Mr Maugham's admirers may simply not recognise that this book is about him instead of by him: I think of those who wrote to ask for a picture or an autograph of Larry Darrell (the hero of *The Razor's Edge*), a phenomenon recorded by Mr Cordell as a pretty impressive tribute to something or other. Others may welcome the assiduity with which, like a border-line candidate in some pass school, he retells the stories of Mr Maugham's stories or, moving up now to the beta-query-plus level, restitches material from Mr Maugham's autobiographical works and prefaces; there is a place for the literary equivalent of an 'Operatic Gems' pot-pourri slung together over the weekend by an arranger's devil. But others again—surely there must be others again—will tire eventually of collecting specimens of blurb-writer's criticism ('a simple but powerful study of antipathy that grows into intense hate'), and will cease to marvel at the long and variegated roll-calls of Maugham fans which, together with information on sales and translations, are about as much as Mr Cordell can do in the way of establishing his subject's credentials.

There is an obvious appropriateness about all this, as obvious as what we learn about Johnson from noticing that it was Boswell who wrote his life. The totality of Mr Cordell's achievement here reflects a sizeable part, at any rate, of Mr Maugham's, the part that seems to depend on the meagreness of most of his notions about life and art, whether these are expressed as such or are deducible from his practice.

His insistence on the primacy of narrative interest, for example, would be all very well if it were not so often accompanied by a too easily satisfied curiosity about his alleged speciality, the complexities of human behaviour. He writes of the people he met on a trip to the South Seas: 'I found it possible without conscious effort to pigeon-hole each one in my awareness', the sort of remark which would come better from a dendrologist on a stroll round a friend's estate. Similarly: 'I learnt very quickly when a place promised me something and then I waited till I had got it', as if 'it' were a set of native pottery or an unusually potent local liqueur.

The connection between deficiencies of approach and poverty of language is clear enough. We have all in our time recoiled from the strangely tender smile that hovers endemically on the lips of Maugham characters and the mischievous twinkle that may at any moment dance in their eyes. The gimcrack antitheses, whereby most folk accept their lot, if not with serenity, at all events with resignation, of a man who is presented as one you could not approve of, but could not help liking, are as hard to bear. Worst of all are the sudden wild forays into imagery, perhaps recalling the fact that their author grew up in the 1890s: Mr Cordell makes one of his few mis-statements—they are as few as his statements—when he speaks of Mr Maugham's 'deliberate avoidance of fine writing'. Anyhow, to narrate in all apparent serious-ness that 'slumber fell upon their tired eyelids like the light rain of spring upon the fresh-turned earth', and to leave it uncancelled, is no mere local blemish. It charts the limits of Mr Maugham's celebrated sense of irony with uncomfortable precision.

Other limitations are easily recalled. Passion, as a word, turns up all over the stories and novels; the thing itself is usually absent. When George Peregrine cannot believe that his wife's poems refer to a tem-pestuous love-affair she has had, it is hard not to share his incredulity. When Red and Sally, years after their love-idyll, meet by chance and fail to recognise each other, this strikes one as less a symptom of moral coarsening than a highly civilised tacit agreement to keep buried the memory of an intolerable silliness. The author's predilection for odd or exotic attitudes to sex—hidalgo-ism in 'The Point of Honour', Gallic practicality in 'Appearance and Reality'—may be part of his function as chronicler of the curious, but it also represents a flight from the subject itself. Even Rosie Gann never comes to life as the recipient of Willie Ashenden's or anyone else's 'passion'.

But Rosie is completely real when she steps outside her overtly sexual role and becomes the befriender of the schoolboy Willie, or rounds off the novel in her old age with a burst of triumphant vul-garity. *Cakes and Ale*, indeed, carries the effect of a great deal of Mr Maugham's fiction: that of a picture dull or out of drawing at the centre, sharp and lively elsewhere. The account of Alroy Kear, the pushing, Walpole-like man of letters, with its inextricable compound of malice, fairness and pretended fairness, has not lost an iota of its bite. Most of all, the brilliant construction of the book, the exact sense of timing, the unobtrusive logic of the transitions, the accumulation of dramatic irony, are the index of an achievement that makes *Eyeless in Gaza* and all its analogues look vaguely arid. That this is not an isolated success is proved by such minor masterpieces as 'Flotsam and Jetsam'. Here again the 'passion' stuff is botched: 'they fell madly in love with one another', as Maugham couples so often do, a mere *donnée* that arouses no more interest or conviction than, say, the faster-than-light drive in a science-fiction story. But the figure of Norman Grange, the beefy, surly rubber-planter who murders his wife's lover, is solid enough not only to keep the melodrama anchored down, but to render the isolated bungalow a haunt of nightmarish boredom and hatred, from which Skelton, the unexpected visitor who has learnt half of the story, is delivered at just the right point, a point that Mrs Grange's memories daily drive her beyond. It is skill of this order that makes Mr Maugham, like Mr P. G. Wodehouse on a quite different level, a writer's writer.

His finest performance, however, remains *Of Human Bondage*. Although the construction is not this time remarkable—theme and coherence have departed by three-quarters of the way through, at the latest—the treatment is everywhere invigoratingly direct and literal. We are certainly to take Philip Carey's club-foot as a 'symbol' of bondage, but it is a fully actual club-foot too, with a series of plausible consequences in both inner and outer life. The novel shows how one barrier, in the shape of lameness, loneliness, puritanism or stupidity, will set up others: suspicion, over-exclusive affection, vindictiveness, exhibitionism, obstinacy, intolerance, self-torture—the state of what a later generation has learnt to call the injustice collector. It is this which leads Philip into the central episode, his agonising involvement with the cold, trivial and vulgar Mildred Rogers. Mildred's eventual ruin brings a baneful whiff of Maupassant, Mr Maugham's evil genius, and Philip's escape from bondage, taps the author's special vein of the lyrical-banal, but until then the situation is totally believable, repellent without ceasing to be pathetic. It is adroitly counterweighted by Philip's early brush with Miss Wilkinson, the randy-respectable governess. Egged on by ideas about manliness and romance, mentally halving her evident age before the fact and almost doubling it after, he cuts a funnier figure here than most serious heroes are allowed to become.

Like all writers with energy and a degree of professional pride, Mr Maugham has managed on occasion to transcend his limitations. His notions of the writer's function and nature—teller of tales, arranger of patterns, not at the mercy of any obsession thanks to his ability to 'put it down in black and white', and thus 'the only free man'—is patently inadequate as a commentary on his own best work. When the mean, timid, pompous vicar of Blackstable, Philip Carey's guardian, reappears in *Cakes and Ale*, we recognise only the most obvious of the agents of bondage who haunt Mr Maugham's world. That that world is more than the narrow corner it so often seems to be emerges unmistakably in two novels and parts of several more, perhaps a dozen stories, and *The Summing-Up*, that further honest self-portrait in which Mr Maugham is characteristically disavowing any hope for literary immortality, says 'it is pleasant to think that he may find a place in the history of his country's literature'. He has found that place.

Spectator, 7 July 1961

The Demon of Progress

Kipling: The Glass, the Shadow and the Fire by Philip Mason, Cape

Philip Mason is promisingly equipped to write about Kipling. He has behind him twenty years in the Indian Civil Service and he has studied both the administrative and the military masters of British India, and so he can tell us, for instance, that Findlayson in 'The Bridge-Builders' should not have been taken unawares by the rising of the Ganges, because the month in which the story takes place must be June, there being three months to go until the Viceroy is to declare the bridge open, which he could never in fact do until October. More usefully, perhaps, Mr Mason knows and likes his subject and is neither an academic nor an American. Notwithstanding the honourable exceptions of C. S. Lewis and Steven Marcus, Kipling is peculiarly vulnerable to these two breeds, who see in him very little that is there. In particular, Edmund Wilson's essay of 1941, 'The Kipling that Nobody Read', is far and away its author's worst performance, made expert short work of by Mr Mason, although he is not at all polemical: another of his virtues. The last and not the least of these is that, despite his subtitle, he is a good writer, always lucid, never pretentious.

Near the start of his book, he sets himself three questions, which I will summarise as why Kipling is so much hated as well as admired, why his earlier work is preferred to his later, and why that later work includes so much that is 'immature' or unsatisfactory. My own short answers to these questions will at least show why I found myself constantly disagreeing with Mr Mason's closely-argued analysis. On Nos 2 and 3 I can venture to be very short indeed: because the earlier work is better, and because, like many vigorous and original talents, he had in him an enduring streak of vulgarity. The first question will take a little longer.

People have disliked Kipling—they were doing so by 1900—because they thought of him as an imperialist, which of course he was, and the fact cannot be removed by any amount of contention that his imperialism was defensive, practical, unmercenary and up to a point conscientious, which equally it was. What has removed that fact from most kinds of discussion is the removal of the Empire. Other causes of dislike have not been so amenable to history. I wish Mr Mason had been readier to make concessions about Kipling's silliness (the choruses of 'The Song of the Banjo', elsewhere a fine poem), his unfunniness (*Stalky & Co.* passim), his excessive laughter ('My Sunday at Home'), his over-certainty of his values, his cruelty, his obscurity—but more of that one later. His readers will have their own reasons for admiring him. If I must suggest my own, they have to do with his tragic power, his understanding of pain, waste, loss and horror and the unargued stoicism that outlasts them, this and a grasp of scene and setting excelled by no other English writer. At his best he unites the two to a degree that recalls somebody not often thought of in connection with him: if anyone else could have written Tennyson's 'Mariana', it is Kipling.

Enough. Mr Mason pursues a biographical theme, one that seeks to illuminate the work by means of the life and vice versa. This is reasonable: one would expect a link of some sort between late stories like 'The House Surgeon' and the author's loneliness and depression in those years, and it would be hard to argue against the surmise that elements of ' "They" ' reflect Kipling's feelings at the loss of his daughter Josephine. Though Mr Mason does not do so, the method could be extended negatively, Kipling's boredom with life in Vermont suggested by its failure to give him local material, the flagging of his enthusiasm for the British cause in South Africa seen in his having spent some part of his 1901–2 visit there at work on his *Just So Stories*.

So much is safe, at least, but an approach of this kind must not be allowed to sway critical judgment. It seems to do so here more than once. *The Naulahka*, the novel Kipling wrote in collaboration with Wolcott Balestier (the young American publisher whose sister he married), is not really very good, but it is much better than Mr Mason will allow. To him, Balestier was a charmer, a thruster, determined to haul himself up in the world by getting his name on to a title-page under Kipling's, so the result *must* be bad. It is odd that Mr Mason's interest in biography does not propel him into clearing up at this stage one of the couple of small mysteries in Kipling's life, the suddenness and closeness of his attachment to Balestier. One place to look for clues is *The Naulahka*, the first four chapters of which are Balestier's work. They show a pleasant light wit, rising occasionally to genuinely inventive and funny turns of phrase, which was beyond Kipling, who loved good talk above most things; so, assuming Balestier talked as he wrote, we now have the fabric of an explanation.

I think Mr Mason goes astray too in some of his comments on *Plain Tales from the Hills*. He cannot be quarrelled with when, as others have done, he finds a knowingness in them; indeed, he defines that quality, which Kipling never quite shook off, as the trick of suggesting, in the manner of a clever examinee, that the knowledge shown is merely the tip of a vast iceberg. Excellent, but he forgets that a man can be wise and knowing by turns, and takes too much account of the circumstances of the composition of the *Tales*. They were written for an Indian paper, to meet a series of deadlines, to a prescribed length, so they *cannot* be as good as more considered work. He ignores the possibility that these circumstances were, on the contrary, accidentally helpful restrictions on an author much given to self-indulgence.

Mr Mason has a matching critical theme. For him, writers, instead of just changing a bit as they grow older, must advance, progress, develop, so the later stories *must* be the best. Or to put it crudely, any fool can admire, say, 'On Greenhow Hill'; you have to work at, say, 'Dayspring Mishandled'. Complication *must* be more interesting than directness, obscurity than clarity, and 'Mrs Bathurst' (from 1904, but 'technically a late story') defeats all attempts to explain it in the sort of way that life does. The true artist declares himself by leaving out a lot, even when what is left out is necessary information. No doubt unwittingly, Kipling himself encouraged this view in a passage near the end of the autobiographical volume, *Something of Myself*, written in his last months. He describes how he would keep a story by him for years, cutting and recutting: 'a tale from which pieces have been raked out is like a fire that has been poked'. But poked fires often go out, too.

New Statesman, 20 June 1975

Fit to Kill

Decline and Fall, by Evelyn Waugh, Chapman & Hall

Half a century ago this month there appeared the first—what? Modern novel? Post-Great-War novel? Novel written for me, and not for some porcelain-collecting multilingual gourmet?—thereby degrading Aldous Huxley, who had been doing well in my esteem on other but related grounds. Whatever it was, it changed things. No writer could go on in the old innocent, docile way after that.

I read *Decline and Fall* first in 1937, when it appeared as one of the new Penguins, and have reread it a dozen times since, though not recently till just now. Doing so showed it to be one of those books that change in the memory, like Jules Verne's works and some of Dickens's (while George Eliot, for instance, is as steady as a rock). If challenged, till just now, to say what it was, I should have mentioned among other things satire, smart set, adventures of young Candide type among said set. The blurb of my present Penguin (1962) goes on very much like that.

I ought first to have allowed for the fact that any comic or would-be comic novel having to do with a profession, institution, social group, etc, is apt to be taken as a satire on it. But the word seems more usefully reserved for pieces purposefully deriding vice or folly. Looked at thus, *Decline and Fall* has no more than some incidental touches of satire, a couple of which, amounting to less than ten pages, refer to the smart set. Others dig in passing at trendy photographers and modern churchmen, ie surpliced atheists (yes, first published 1928), and more thoroughly and just as undatedly at avant-garde architecture and interior decoration. The Sports Room at King's Thursday (before its rebuilding the most beautiful Tudor house in England, naturally), with lights in glass footballs, furniture made of bats and polo-sticks, telephone held by a boxing-glove, is hardly funny at all.

The chief satirical strike is at Sir Wilfred Lucas-Dockery and his liberal ideas. This monster is introduced as Governor of Blackstone Gaol, where the hero, Paul Pennyfeather, is confined—after committing no crime, naturally. Formerly a professor of sociology (yes, 1928), Sir Wilfred institutes far-reaching reforms that are flatteringly written up in a periodical with the mysterious title of the *New Nation*. In the belief that crime, as well as being a form of insanity, is due to repressed desire for aesthetic expression, the Governor allows one of the prisoners, a carpenter turned religious homicidal maniac, access to a mallet, a saw and other tools of his trade. The madman uses these to decapitate the chaplain, Mr Prendergast, an old friend of Paul's and the most harmless person in the whole story, naturally.

Few who know the book at all will have forgotten the hilarious and terrible passage, one of the most extraordinary in all our literature, where Paul hears of the murder from the words a fellow prisoner in the congregation sings to the tune of 'O God, our help in ages past' at the chapel service the next day:

> *A pal of mine what lives next door,*
> *'E 'eard it 'appening;*
> *The warder must 'ave 'eard it too,*

> 'E didn't interfere.
> Time, like an ever-rolling stream,
> Bears all its sons away.
> Poor Prendy 'ollered fit to kill
> For nearly 'alf an hour.

And the whole affair is soon quite forgotten.

These events are offered as no sort of warning about what could happen when you turn a progressive loose; that might indeed belong to a satire. As it is, Sir Wilfred and his antics are no more than gleefully elaborated instruments of the cruelty and arbitrariness at the heart of the universe. *Decline and Fall* is a pessimistic romance presented as a farce. What has caused Paul to land up in gaol is his love for Margot Beste-Chetwynde, the rich, beautiful, veronal-addicted white-slaver and probable murderess who is the mother of one of his charges at Llanabba Castle, a rather unnaturalistically described school in North Wales. (The locals are all indeed-to-goodness-whatever and poncing for their sisters-in-law in a kind of parody of satire.) Paul's love is deliberately presented as quite unreal; his revelation of it to his colleague at Llanabba, Captain Grimes, sounds—again on purpose?—just like Bingo Little having the news wormed out of him by Bertie Wooster. The whole point of Paul-and-Margot, apart from bringing in King's Thursday etc, is to show him dropped in the shit and her, the real criminal, not only getting away with it and feeling fine about that but marrying into the peerage and in general flourishing like the green bay-tree.

Yes, Captain Grimes: short, bald, queer, with a false leg popularly supposed to be the result of a Great-War injury but in fact that of being run over by a tram in Stoke-on-Trent when he was one-over-the-eight, always in the soup and always climbing out again—Grimes is seen by Paul as one of the immortals, by which he means little more than that Grimes would always survive. That too, but to the extent that the phrase means anything he is an immortal character in fiction. *He* gets away with it because the gods would obviously not think him worth bothering to destroy. (Sir?) Solomon Philbrick, sometime butler at Llanabba and possibly but almost certainly not shipowner, novelist or retired burglar, is a diverting creation, but I see him and his function less clearly; I also see him, very much unlike Grimes, without great clarity as a physical presence. Mr Prendergast, another Llanabba alumnus, plays a large part in the action; little Lord Tangent, superficially wounded in the heel at the school sports and later dead of what must be gangrene, reminds us that having only a walk-on part doesn't guarantee your safety.

No novel is a statement, and we should try to fight against making inferences about the author's state of mind. Nevertheless I will succumb to temptation by suggesting that the twenty-five-year-old Waugh, rather than go mad or commit suicide, was in real need of something that offered an explanation of or an excuse for the horrors of existence. We all know what Evelyn Waugh found—to his artistic detriment: what had been an enlivening bitterness sank to defiance and jeering, a struggle against the unalterable and inevitable on the secular and social plane. *Vile Bodies*, that admittedly brilliant and very funny successor, most likely written during the process of his religious conversion, is in some ways a merely chronological successor. Mrs Ape (the name in itself) and her angels were a new, facetious departure.

Waugh's one great book is the outcome not, as Edmund Wilson put it, of regarding cruel things as funny because he didn't understand them. ('*Interviewer*: Have you found any professional criticism of your work illuminating or helpful? Edmund Wilson, for example? *Waugh*: Is he an American? *Interviewer*: Yes. *Waugh*: I don't think what they have to say is of much interest, do you?') One way or the other, what *Decline and Fall* is the outcome of is trying to make cruel things as funny as possible, because that is one of the very few ways of making them a little less intolerable.

New Statesman, 22 September 1978

There's Something about a Soldier

Officers and Gentlemen, by Evelyn Waugh, Chapman & Hall

Mr Evelyn Waugh is continuing to check that farcical vein which founded his reputation, and upon which, even now, his status as a novelist may well seem to depend. It is true that his other, more serious, vein produced his best novel, *A Handful of Dust*, and was going to produce an even better one, as can be seen from the fragments published as *Work Suspended*; it also produced his worst, *Brideshead Revisited*. Here there were symptoms of radical decline so numerous and appalling that prognosis almost broke down: could the author of *Decline and Fall* really be going to turn into a kind of storm-trooper from the Sixth at Downside with nothing to offer his audience but a universal grudge and invocations of a fanciful past? The story *Love Among the Ruins* upheld this reading with a fidelity which, in such small space, put a strain on belief. With the publication of *Officers and Gentlemen*, in spite of the ominous overtones of the title, it is clear that

that danger has passed. The angry bitterness, at any rate, has cooled; the tones of denunciation, though still to be heard, are sad rather than hectoring; a great deal of the baronial wrought-iron, on which one was always barking one's shins at Brideshead, has been torn down. Even farce, in the shape of a ludicrous commando raid which succeeds for every possible wrong reason, is given a mild outing.

The main ingredients of the story are soon described. Guy Crouchback, the hero of *Men at Arms*, arrives home from West Africa with a small military black mark which, as with all Mr Waugh's characters, is undeserved. His subsequent adventures chiefly concern service with the Halberdiers, his regiment, and with the Commandos, either on the Isle of Mugg (near Rum), in the Middle East or in Crete. There are subsidiary matters involving the disposal of a quantity of 'gear' belonging to Apthorpe, a deceased brother officer, an encounter with a crazed Scottish Nationalist and a demolition maniac, going to confession, and so on. Much of the book centres on other characters: the shady Trimmer of *Men at Arms* reappears as a lieutenant of 'the Jocks,' has a brief affair with Guy's ex-wife, and is the leader, in a devious sense, of the commando raid referred to; a brigade major called Fido Hound cracks up in Crete; there is an old colonel named Jumbo, a lunatic dietitian named Glendening-Rees, an intellectual corporal major whose name doesn't matter. At the end of it all Guy is back with the Halberdiers under training.

If the above elements seem discursive and episodic, then they have been truly rendered. The continuation of this saga promised us by Mr Waugh may perhaps pull them together, but it seems more likely that his plan, like most large-scale plans, countenances a good deal of irrelevance, of including matters which are to justify themselves. I hardly think that this is decisively achieved here. A great deal of what is obviously offered as comedy is not quite funny enough to be that, however promising it may sound in summary. Even during life, Apthorpe was a bit of a bore with his silly field latrine and his aunts, and his shade hangs heavily over the early stages of this volume: the mystery of his 'gear' is not worth solving. The other eccentrics we meet are like him in being models of dull conformity, or alternatively models of cardboard and paste, compared with someone like Colonel Blount of *Vile Bodies*. And the war scenes in Crete, though rendered vividly and sympathetically enough, are no better, and in places a good deal less passionately realised, than the war scenes of quite a few younger novelists who have not yet hit the headlines of the Sunday book pages: Mr Alexander Baron is the obvious example. At one point—the beginning of Fido Hound's crack-up—it does look as if we are in for a dose of that disconcerting blend of the funny, the horrific and the pitiful which is Mr Waugh's distinctive contribution to the repertory of literary effects. But this episode is typical of the rest of this book, and its predecessor, in that the humour is purely decorative, a stray effect, not something which embodies the author's whole intention.

A ruder way of putting this would be to say that Mr Waugh is unwilling—I cannot believe that he is unable—to chance his arm and have a go and lay us in the aisles. The reason is not far to seek. If one is really going to satirise army life, in all its confusion and arbitrariness, then sooner or later one has got to start satirising the army itself, which contains in its nature confusion and arbitrariness just as much as order and custom. Mr Waugh's attitude to the army is much too serious to permit that. Although it is often risky to assume that a novelist shares his hero's feelings, Mr Waugh participates in Guy Crouchback's cause with an intensity which recalls the effect of complete fusion in *Brideshead Revisited*. If Guy's standards are too high for the modern world, they share this feature, it is implied, with every other kind of traditional (ie real) standard, and these days a lack of worldly wisdom, even a degree of naivety, can only be admirable. The two volumes are certainly packed with inferential approval for every kind of regimental usage, ceremonial and idiosyncrasy: the almost fanatically exclusive Corps of Halberdiers seem to spend most of their working day showing how differently they do things from other units. Some of all this will draw an embarrassed grin, as when we hear of new subalterns being sconced for mismanagement of the snuff-engine after dinner in the Mess; others will arouse mild incredulity, such as the discovery that the frightful Brigadier Ritchie-Hook, with his taste for decapitating enemy sentries, is not to be taken as a caricature of the 'mad major' type he seemed at first, but is a figure we are expected to admire. Admirable as a soldier he may perhaps be, though he conspicuously lacks that consideration for subordinates which, so I was taught, is an indispensable mark of the good officer; admirable as a person he certainly is not.

Reverence for the army is to be expected from a Waugh hero who derives from Tony Last and Captain Ryder rather than from Basil Seal. At odds with the modern world, longing for the certainties of a past age which are preserved chiefly in the public school, bitterly romantic or, in Mr Donat O'Donnell's expressive phrase, neo-Jacobite, the Crouchbacks and Ryders find in the army not only the stability they crave but a macrocosm of the world of school and a church-militant as well. Both by image and by direct parallel the traditional ritualistic and hierarchical aspects of army life and organisation get rubbed in. It is again no more than natural that actual combat, which disturbs this stasis, should be the field in which Guy's disillusionment is worked out, and that his crusading zeal, his feeling of having taken up arms against the Modern Age—all this is urged with complete literalness—should wither before the harsh and inconvenient realities of wartime diplomacy. A man to whom Italian fascism was merely 'a rough improvisation', for whom it was Nazi participation that 'dishonoured the cause of Spain', who was much more angry at the Russian invasion of Poland than the German, is going to take some knocks when 22 June 1941 comes along and England is 'led blundering into dishonour'. He is also a man with whom few, I hope, will want to identify themselves.

Crouchback is really a terrible fellow. He has none of the unpleasant vigour of Ryder, and compared with Tony Last his dream is a pipe-dream, his sufferings would be deserved if they were not so unreal. I suppose he may pull round a bit in later volumes, but he will have to pull round a lot to efface the memory of that scene in *Men at Arms*, as remarkable in its way as anything in recent fiction, where he tries to seduce his ex-wife in the flush of the discovery that theologically he would be committing no sin. If Mr Waugh had set out with the intention of discrediting him for good and all, he could not have done it more skilfully. The wife says, on discovering the set-up: 'I thought you'd chosen me specially, and by God you had. Because I was the only woman in the whole world your priests would let you go to bed with', and she adds with truth and finality: 'You wet, smug, obscene, pompous, sexless lunatic pig'. The next day Guy looks to Apthorpe to 'bear him away to the far gardens of fantasy', as well he might. They are the only place where he can live.

I implied earlier that an important difference between these two books and what preceded them lies in a toning-down or cutting-out of elements previously present. The trouble is that the new elements are, in comparison, thin, neutral and private. The next novel in the series will show whether Mr Waugh's invention is really impaired. When I think of *Decline and Fall*, *Vile Bodies*, *A Handful of Dust* and *Work Suspended* I cannot believe that it is.

Spectator, 8 July 1955

Crouchback's Regress

Unconditional Surrender, by Evelyn Waugh, Chapman & Hall

The major theme of all Mr Evelyn Waugh's novels has been disintegration, social and moral, and he has often made good use of structural devices to reflect this theme. Thus in the earlier books long stretches of narrative, heavily translated with variegated characters, would give place to tiny fragmentary snapshots of the same people singly or in pairs, held for the instant that enabled us to infer their destiny. The result is a looser but more widely ranging kind of unity than that which most narratives afford, and it is here, in this apparently quite casual attitude to matters of coherence and direction, that Mr Waugh's celebrated airiness of manner is largely to be traced. His style, an elegant instrument based on scrupulous attention to syntax and word order, is perhaps secondary.

With all its virtues of economy, mobility and breadth of coverage, the dangers of the open-ranch method of character-farming, as opposed to the enclosed-pasture technique of more cautious practitioners, are obvious enough: parts of the herd will wander off and set up on their own. Mr Waugh can be relied on to see to it that they are brought back in time for slaughtering—being a Waugh minor character is still almost as hazardous as being a Graham Greene hero—but their cavortings meanwhile, however spectacular, may bear little relation to even the freest overall plan. Tony Last's dash up the Amazon had better have been left in its original short-story form instead of furnishing an out-of-key, and unnecessary, coda to *A Handful of Dust*. And there are few parallels to the headlong vigour with which the author of *Work Suspended* rides off in two contrary directions.

Now that its third and final volume has appeared, a similar centrifugal tendency can be seen in the *Men at Arms* sequence. The figure of Apthorpe, brother officer of the hero, Guy Crouchback, in the Royal Corps of Halberdiers, seemed at the time to bulk unduly large in the first volume, not only in that he suffered his predictable demise at the end of that volume and was forgotten altogether soon after the start of the next, but also by reason of his lowly status in Mr Waugh's grotesques' gallery. When the Apthorpe portable latrine came up for the eleventh time, one had the unexpected feeling that comic material was being spread out thin. It is curious that, after giving his name to all three main sections of *Men at Arms*, he gets only the passing mention in the four-page authorial synopsis prefixed to *Unconditional Surrender*, and that as merely 'another officer'.

The second instalment, *Officers and Gentlemen*, promised more in the way of emergent unity among apparent diversity. It seemed to offer a firm but unstated contrast between types doing well out of the war and the social changes accompanying it (Trimmer, the ex-hairdresser turned fake-national-hero; Ludovic, the mysterious corporal-major) and types meeting or evidently heading for various levels of disaster (Ivor Claire, the dandy who abandoned his men in Crete; Crouchback himself, condemned to military ineffectiveness and emotional dehydration; Fido Hound, whom battle brought from regimental punctiliousness to appallingly comic degradation). If additional room had been found for Fido earlier, among the transients who thronged the pages devoted to training and preparation, his reappearance might have lent continuity, but one readily conceded that discontinuity and randomness better befit an account of the Cretan debacle.

Unconditional Surrender disappoints most of these hopes of final coherence. Trimmer vanishes, even though the fact that before doing so he has rendered pregnant Virginia Troy, Crouchback's ex-wife, does something to keep his memory green. Claire, whose dereliction of duty before innumerable witnesses might have preluded an interesting conflict of values, is let off by everybody, including Crouchback, the army, Bellamy's Club and Mr Waugh, who extends to him that indulgence for the ruthless egoist which he normally reserves for women of this type, from Margot Metroland to, in the present volume, Julia Stitch (described in the synopsis simply as 'a beauty'—that's enough, you see. She's a beauty all right, mate). And to take a small but significant example of the defeat of expectation, Grace-Groundling-Marchpole's counter-espionage department, whose mounting but baseless suspicion of Crouchback looked like issuing in a frenzy of injustice, fades quietly from the scene half-way through—I will suggest why in a moment.

What does tie the book to its two predecessors, and what abundantly justifies it in itself, is the continued history of Ludovic, now a major in Intelligence. While holding the post of commandant of a parachute training school he is terrorised by the arrival of Crouchback, whom he supposes to know about certain events in Crete. Unaware that shock and privation have removed these from Crouchback's memory, visualising imminent exposure as the murderer of Hound and another officer, Ludovic retreats into a sort of somnambulism, from which he emerges only to play with his poodle (which he names 'Fido', of course), plunge the Mess into leaden gloom and tinker with the volume of *pensées* he is compiling. Equally in this last role—that of a rather more sensitive and adult Palinurus—in his final appearance as a successful trashy novelist, and in his earlier career as valet-cum-secretary-cum-what-may to a diplomat of specialised tastes, Ludovic is a creature of the airiest fantasy.

This means that he and his doings score heavily over much else in the book, especially Crouchback and his. Even the latter's decent actions have a way of arousing suspicion, as when he tries hard to save a party of Jewish refugees from miserable internment in the Balkans: Greeks or Turks, presumably, would not give him such a signal opportunity of showing how he can put duty above prejudice. But the real trouble with Crouchback is his failure to act, his great and varied inabilities. He feels this himself, and his creator claims sympathy for him as a man trying in vain to find a place for himself in a great battle of our time. This would be acceptable if he seemed to be really trying, but he never looks back from that stage, early in *Men at Arms*, when he appears in England in the first weeks of the war 'looking for a job' by buttonholing powerful friends at Bellamy's and writing to Cabinet

Ministers' wives. What about all those jobs in the ranks of, say, Signals or the RASC? Unthinkable, naturally.

This, again, would be acceptable if Crouchback were another kind of Waugh hero, the sort to whom cruel and unjust things are always happening. But to be a Paul Pennyfeather of 1939–45 is inconceivable for the heir of a landed recusant family, a member of Bellamy's, an officer of the Halberdiers who *enjoys guest nights*. And so Grace-Groundling-Marchpole's bomb fizzes away into harmlessness, Apthorpe and Ludovic draw the laughs Crouchback cannot be allowed to draw, Hound and Trimmer meet the serio-comic humiliations reserved for persons who have no dignity to start with. The lopsided construction of the sequence faithfully reflects the predicament of a hero—and the difficulty of using a hero—who is surrounded by activity he cannot share, who can barely remain on his feet, propping himself up on Catholicism and peacetime regimental tradition. No wonder he is always hurting his knee. It is tempting to believe that Mr Waugh, *à la* Pinfold, sees this more clearly than anybody else. Certainly there is a strong hint of self-consciousness about some of those top-people-isms with which his later work is encrusted: things like:

When Guy rose to leave, all his little household, twenty strong, assembled to see him go,

and (the time is September, 1939):

Everywhere houses were being closed, furniture stored, children transported, servants dismissed, lawns ploughed, dower-houses and shooting-lodges crammed to capacity; mothers-in-law and nannies were everywhere gaining control.

You know, everywhere from South Shields to Llanelly. These are almost certainly put in specially to annoy the Labour Party, etc. But it would be too fanciful to say the same of the souped-up traditionalism with which, for instance, the funeral of Crouchback senior is recounted. That 'baronial wrought-iron on which one was always barking one's shins at Brideshead', and which one reviewer saw as having been largely 'torn down' in *Officers and Gentlemen*, is back in full profusion.

We might note here the small detail that we are invited to think it is all right for the Crouchbacks to call the local church 'the chapel' although it is not a chapel, but not all right for Box-Bender, Crouchback's brother-in-law, to call his den 'the business-room' because it is not a business-room. The Crouchback motto is 'It's all right when my family have always done it', or more shortly, 'It's all right when I do it', whether 'it' is studiously maintained uncharitableness for six years of war service or dining at a black-market restaurant. And conversely, of course, it's not all right when they do it, and this 'it' and 'they' have now multiplied exceedingly. Crouchback's original enemy, 'the Modern Age in Arms', has come to have less to do with Germany and

Russia than with jazz-lovers, diners on expenses, hirers of evening dress, Americans, pilferers on the railways, Trimmers of all sorts, holders of temporary commissions. (Crouchback had one of those, too, but it was all right when he did it.)

These would be valid targets if clearly seen. But Trimmer cannot be made the key figure he might have become, because the task of finding out about him would be too distasteful; his liaison with Virginia can only be alluded to and he must be dropped from the story. Ludovic must remain insulated from probability. An American officer can be introduced, but is not worth the effort of close observation: the result is the dullest and least differentiated character Mr Waugh has ever created. As for American enlisted men—well, Coca-Cola and peanuts and gum and whores will do for them, won't it? No, it won't, not even on TV. Guy Crouchback has maintained his integrity at the cost of keeping his eyes shut and his fingers in his ears.

Spectator, 27 October 1961

Waugh's Warts

Evelyn Waugh: a Biography, by Christopher Sykes, Collins

This book reinforces my thankfulness that I never met Evelyn Waugh. If I had, my lifelong admiration for most of his work might have taken a sad buffet from what I would surely have received: a courteous invitation to take off my collar if I would really feel more comfortable without it, perhaps, or an interested query about when I hoped to return to Wigan. Or something much, much worse.

It was his nature to go too far, most of all in the direction of outrageousness. He started early by being a bully at school—a refreshing change, true, from the legions of novelists and their characters on the receiving end. Throughout life, his rudeness in public was famous. Nobody was immune: old friend and new acquaintance, enemy and admirer, passer-by and servant. Even an old friend could not look after himself when Waugh cast him, as he loved to do, in the role of helpless spectator of a barbarism meted out to a third party. Hostesses were favourite victims. At a safe distance, one can rather half-heartedly deplore all this, but without this compulsion to say the unsayable he would never have come to be the writer he was.

There was the drink too. Readers of the published diaries will know that there was a lot of that. Mr Christopher Sykes takes a disapproving tone on it, understandable in one who for so many years had to help to pick up the broken glass. Nevertheless, I could have done with more detail about the actual tipples. There is not much of it here, beyond Waugh's discovery, when aged not quite seventeen, of the virtues of ginger-beer-and-burgundy in washing down dressed crab. We are not told whether, in later life, he really did as has been rumoured, kick off the day with a mixture of gin, Guinness and, again, ginger beer.

The drink led towards Roman Catholicism. Other things did that too: a Christian training, and a more personal agony of spirit to be seen in the first novels. *Decline and Fall* is in all senses a screamingly funny book, a wild farce pervaded by despair at the unjust order of things; the subject is not, *pace* Mr Sykes, the triumph of the wicked but the destruction of the innocent. Its author might have had to go mad or commit suicide or take to drink as a mode of existence (or non-existence) if he was not to seek the embrace of the Church. Waugh had remarkable insight into himself, as parts of *The Ordeal of Gilbert Pinfold* show, and he well knew that he was staving off destruction by becoming a Catholic.

One who shares that faith, Mr Sykes, is at pains to argue that Waugh's attitude to his religion was 'altogether unconnected with, uncontaminated by, any reverence for our "old" or "good" Catholic families'. I should like to think so but, speaking no doubt as the child of a non-old and non-good Protestant family, I have a special dislike for baronial Popery, which I find *passim* in *Brideshead Revisited*, that novelettish novel, lush and arid at the same time, in which Waugh's snobbery rages unchecked for once by the habitual austerities of his style.

Something like snobbery kept him for three months out of a British Army which, late in 1939, would have been quite prepared to welcome into its ranks a patriotic and physically fit man in his middle thirties. But the ranks would not do; he had to have a 'job', ie a commission. Eventually he got one, pursuing thereafter a rather mysterious military career that included, among several other interruptions, a leave of some months granted for the writing of *Brideshead*. His brothers-in-arms bore the separation with fortitude. The man who had wangled things, Brendan Bracken, then the Minister of Information, was rewarded by being offensively caricatured in the book. Later, there was an episode in Yugoslavia with Randolph Churchill that reads like an up-to-snuff part of a Waugh novel.

Back in peacetime England, he felt less and less at home, convinced that his country had taken a wrong turning. Acrimony and defiance soured his later work. His health broke down before he reached old age. To the end, he kept up several close friendships and, as he had always done, showed generosity and lasting kindness to the unfortunate. He was a man of honour. So much and more to his credit emerges from Mr Sykes's admirable portrait which does not spare the warts but is fair to the attractions too.

The book is full of excellent, skilfully recounted anecdotes, but others were omitted 'for the sake of literary economy'. A pity, I should have liked to have all the details confirmed in my version of the one about Donald Baverstock, Feliks Topolski and the strawberries, and should have welcomed some filling-in of the one about Randolph Churchill and Alan Brien in the bar at White's. Both these are too well known to be likely to perish unrecorded, but the one about the *Queen Mary* does perhaps stand in that danger, so I give it here.

A certain journalist—name unknown to me, but character clearly of the utmost foolhardiness—on an Atlantic crossing found the great name in the passenger-list and sent a note: would Mr Waugh do him the honour of being his guest in the cabin- (ie, second-) class bar? No, no, my dear fellow, be my guest in the first-class bar. Later: could Mr Waugh face being taken to dinner in the cabin-class restaurant? Delighted, my dear chap. Now that restaurant was not Claridge's, but it was not a Wimpy bar either. As the two entered (remember that they were going to spend the next couple of hours immovably fixed at their table), Waugh sniffed the air and bawled as loudly as he could, 'You can just *smell* the poverty, can't you?'

Observer, 28 September 1975

Dead Ringers

Waugh on Women, by Jacqueline McDonnell, Duckworth

What is meant by saying that a novelist has 'based' or 'founded' or 'modelled' a fictitious character on a real person is not obvious or straightforward, and may have as many answers as there are novelists, or even characters. Nevertheless people go on saying things like that with complete simplicity and confidence.

Jacqueline McDonnell is one of the latest of them. For her, when Evelyn Waugh gave a female character blue eyes it was not because, in some way difficult to fathom, he thought blue eyes were right for that character, it was because some woman he knew, or more 'significantly' two such women, had blue eyes. What went on in Waugh's head is a matter of opinion; Lady Whatsit's eyes are a matter of fact. And of course there are lots of other facts about her, some of them possibly amusing, which might as well go in for good measure.

A scrap-book about the women Waugh knew, put together from memoirs and his own diaries and letters and with some references to his works, could have made a pleasantly gossipy and non-educational read. Unfortunately Miss McDonnell will keep trying to draw 'critical conclusions' from the parallels she notes. She starts from the assumption that a novelist who is not constantly putting real people into his books is nothing but 'a pure fantasist'. A little later she quotes approvingly Christopher Sykes's view that the characterisation of Julia in *Brideshead* is weakened by not being 'drawn from life'. After that it comes as no surprise to find her critically concluding that the more demonstrably a character is based-founded-modelled, the better-drawn and more memorable that character will be.

In the course of trying to clinch this proposition by discursively identifying Julia Stitch of *Scoop* and *Officers and Gentlemen* with Lady Diana Cooper ('they are one'), the author succeeds in demolishing it. Mrs Stitch, seen across forty-eight and thirty-one years respectively, has dated to a calamitous degree, emerging now as silly and conceited when not repellently ruthless, trivial, dreary, above all unbelievable, making me feel quite sorry for Waugh in an embarrassed way. (Actually I thought she was all those things at the time, but it may have taken some of you a little while to come round.) Never were the dangers of trying to put a real person into a book—if that was indeed the attempt— more painfully demonstrated. I suspect on internal evidence that Waugh had something of that intention with the figures of Sebastian Flyte and Brigadier Ritchie-Hook, and took tumbles there too. Real people are paradoxically too static to be made part of a story.

One could leave it there, if not earlier, were it not that any enterprise of this sort tends to lead readers of fiction astray and to do some damage to fiction itself. To fancy that a novelist was 'really' writing about a living individual is too close for comfort to concluding he was 'only' doing so, and all talk of 'models' tends to trivialise and de-universalise what he has created. The integrity of fiction must be defended, by insisting among other things that to draw parallels between bits of it and bits of the writer's life is at best to leave out everything of importance.

But it's just the thing for a thesis, which is what this book reads like most of the time, and an American or Canadian thesis at that. Miss McDonnell is evidently unfamiliar with a number of details of everyday English life. She seems to think that *Animal Farm* is a card game like 'Happy Families', she is unaware that 'Oh for the Wings of a Dove' is part of the very well-known Anglican anthem by Mendelssohn, and she even finds it worth saying that lower-class English persons drop their Hs ('note how he captures the dialogue of the housemaids') and old-fashioned aristocrats their final Gs, an observation she launches with 'interestingly', her favourite adverb by far. The matter is settled by her descent into a distinctive North American illiteracy by writing 'As many admirers as Lady Diana had' to make a concessive clause.

More than any of this, Miss McDonnell is an American to the core — or more charitably an American graduate student — in her notions of what constitutes a pertinent or useful or bearable remark. Julia's green hat in *Brideshead* is a reminder of *The Green Hat* by Michael Arlen. 'Through Chokey [in *Decline and Fall*], Waugh was able to portray what he saw as the determined culture-hunting and defensiveness of the American negro in London.' Shockin' bad form, eh, what?

But this volume is thoroughly British in its physical form, in cramming perhaps 120,000 words into not much over 200 pages, something no American publisher known to me would have tried to get away with. The result is that the lines are crowded together and made too long for the size of type, so that the reader would follow them with pain even if he found the text worth reading. There are no illustrations.

Observer, 9 February 1986

How I Lived in a Very Big House and Found God

'Brideshead Revisited', Granada TV

Evelyn Waugh was a marvellous writer, but one of a sort peculiarly likely to write a bad book at any moment. The worst of his, worse even than *The Loved One*, must be *Brideshead Revisited*. But long before the Granada TV serial came along it was his most enduringly popular novel; the current Penguin reprint is the nineteenth in its line. The chief reason for this success is obviously and simply that here we have a whacking, heavily romantic book about nobs. (Indeed, almost any old book about nobs seems sure to do at least reasonably well in the English-speaking world, as is suggested by the prosperous career of Nancy Mitford, for instance.)

Nobs, of course, are in themselves not at all bad people to write or read about and, to take the small and inevitable step from nobs to snobs, they too are perfectly harmless as such and, with their eye for social nuance, actually well suited for writing novels. We may infer that a given novelist is a snob and still wish him well, though we will perhaps feel a little different if he brandishes the fact in our faces. The trouble comes when, as with *Brideshead*, snobbery corrupts judgement.

It is as if Evelyn Waugh came to believe that since about all he looked for in his companions was wealth, rank, Roman Catholicism (where possible) and beauty (where appropriate), those same attributes and no more would be sufficient for the central characters in a long novel, enough or getting on for enough, granted a bit of style thrown in, to establish them as both glamorous and morally significant. That last blurring produced a book I would rather expect a conscientious Catholic to find repulsive, but such matters are none of my concern. Certainly the author treats those characters with an almost cringing respect, implying throughout that they are important and interesting in some way over and above what we are shown of them.

The Flyte family, or the Marquis of Marchmain's family, or the family whose house Brideshead is, or what you will, are a band of bores. They hang about, idle rich in an extra sense, given too little to do by the author. Ironically, the one he himself regards as rather a bore, Lord Brideshead or Bridey, the elder son, emerges as the least boring of them because, on his smallish scale, he is the most fully shaped as a character. As a result he transfers successfully to the screen, with the admirable Simon Jones giving the most sympathetic and enjoyable performance of the six. Elsewhere, the cast have their work cut out.

In the original, there is nothing much to Lady Marchmain, mother of Bridey, Sebastian, Julia and Cordelia, also not fully acknowledged as a pal's-mum figure, long-serving hostess to Charles Ryder, the narrator. Is she just trying and predictably failing to keep Sebastian away from the drink or is she the agent of something more repressive, even destructive, something the self-exiled Lord Marchmain ran away from long ago? We never learn; the conversation shifts to her dead brothers, but nothing emerges about them either. All this, or what there is of this, is no more than reproduced in the serial. As repeatedly happens, the vacancy of the novel cannot help being thrown into prominence by the mere process of screening, the removal of the filter of literary presentation, but here the authority of the actress, Claire Bloom, makes it seem to matter less at the time.

Under-employment grips the figure of Lord Marchmain even more severely. All he is really needed for is dying a doctrinally edifying death near the end, and Waugh earlier allows him no more than a walk-on, a glimpse of him being in his house in Venice and comparing

Italian with Austrian pastry-cooks. But no television company is going to get its accountant's permission to send a unit to Venice and end up with a couple of minutes of screen-time. As it is we are treated to nearly half an hour of event-less sightsee blown up from a mere nine pages, a straggling Martini commercial rounded off with some corny Latin wisdom (all out of the novel) from the old fellow's girlfriend, or 'mistress' as she is quaintly called. This bit, coming where it did (second half of the second episode), must have done a good deal to depress the ratings. The lead-up to Marchmain's death is most affecting, but not particularly more so than any other character's would have been with Laurence Olivier to play him, and neither book nor adaptation has told us enough about him for his last-minute return to the bosom of the Church to seem very momentous.

Let me pause briefly and admonish those critics who, after laying about the acting, direction, etc with a will, join in a drowsy chorus of, 'But it must be admitted that the whole thing looks ravishing.' Well yes, but so it bloody *should*. From the way some of them go on you would think the camera-team had had a hand in building Christ Church or St Mark's instead of just pointing their instrument in approximately the right direction and remembering to take the cap off the snout. Any producer will tell you that keeping the public out of view is the real task.

Back, with a faint groan, to those Flytes. Cordelia is no less boring and officious on the screen than in the novel, and Phoebe Nicholls could do little to redeem her occasional lurches into poeticality. Such lurches are far more thoroughgoing and harder to bear in the case of Julia. There is nothing in this bad book worse, more embarrassing, more saddening, than her long pseudo-hysterical tirade after Bridey's 'bombshell'. Her character as illustrated by her behaviour is simply subject to mood and whim in a way that suggests insufficient opposition in early life, about as charming as that of Brenda Last, whom she powerfully evokes in her treatment of Rex Mottram. The most plausible explanation of her final dismissal of Charles Ryder is nothing more religious than a desire to be bitchy to him with God to back her up—after all, he (Ryder) did try to cross her over getting a priest for her father. But Diana Quick contrives to make this scene quite touching, no worse than something out of Graham Greene.

There remains Sebastian. Every time I read the book I ask myself if there is anything to him at all, and the answer is always no. The related question of what it is that drives an indolent, affected, greedy, queerish young nob to the bottle perhaps lacks urgency, but it is the sole matter of the least dramatic interest raised in the first 200 pages. No answer is given, though hints from Anthony Blanche and Cara could be worked up into a surmise that poor old Sebastian has realized he is too stupid to keep up in the adult world. Anthony Andrews does wonders with the part, arousing pity and concern for a helpless victim, something the book fails to do, but we are still not told what he is a victim of. 'He was sick at heart somewhere, I did not know how . . .'

The most disagreeable of the central trio, however, is undoubtedly Ryder, priggish, prickish, on the make, John Beaver to Julia's Brenda. Though cautiously taciturn in company, he is loquacious enough in his asides and comments. Something of these, not much in total but too much, John Mortimer's script preserves in voice-over. The producers evidently mistook for vivid writing the sickening floweriness of a great deal of Ryder's commentary, headlining on the front of their publicity brochure one of his most novelettish bits of attitudinising: 'My theme is memory, that winged host that soared about me one grey morning of wartime.' But as far as I remember we are spared that shaming Langour-of-Youth stuff, also the noble wine stuff and most of the sniffy stuff about the awful people who are taking over the world, so that, for instance, the famous dinner with Mottram (Charles Keating— excellent), in the book an orgy of vulgar disdain, becomes simply funny. But even trimmed down like this, Ryder's character is suf- ficiently offensive, or would have been without intelligent direction and the fine acting of Jeremy Irons, which between them transform him into a human being. An adaptation which so much of the time follows the original with calamitous fidelity here triumphantly departs from it.

One grave defect common to the portrayals of Cordelia, Sebastian and Julia is that they are not nearly posh enough. Those four are nothing if not upper-class in a closer sense of the construction than usual. But the actors all put glottal stops in front of initial vowels, pronounce the H's in unstressed words ('*he has* lost *his* way') and use a German or King's Road short A ('the cuht suht on the muht') and a short E that is half-way to an orthodox short A (half-way to 'jat sat'). Diana Quick calls her papa 'poppa', Andrews stresses the second syllable in 'café', Irons sounds the T in 'often'. Fault-finding? Well, producers who proudly describe how, unable to use plovers' eggs, they had a lot of pullets' eggs painted were not short of time. Perhaps it was decided that to have those four talking in the way young nobs between the wars actually talked would blow away any rags of sympathy and esteem they might have managed to acquire.

The TV version is very good whenever it comes to the good parts of the novel, all of them significantly irrelevant to the main issue: the army scenes, the interesting short story about Julia's marriage to Mottram, the lively sketch of the General Strike, Ryder's father, Ryder's wife, Anthony Blanche, Mr Samgrass—John Gielgud, Jane Asher, Nickolas Grace, John Grillo, all first-rate. But there was not much to be done about the boredom at the centre. The mistake was in the time allotted, or in picking the book in the first place. I hope no one will draw the false conclusion that faithful adaptations of serious novels can never be successful.

The production is very thorough and professional and might even have been called stylish if it had not tried a little hard to be. It could have done without the irritating convention whereby, for instance, two people at the far end of a restaurant are audible to us but not to those at the next table. The period stuff is fun to look at and the storm at sea is fascinating. I think the music is just right, grand, sad and rather brassy.

Times Literary Supplement, 20 November 1981

How to Behave

Mrs Palfrey at the Claremont, by Elizabeth Taylor, Chatto & Windus

Mrs Taylor is one of those novelists who look homogeneous, as if working within a single mood, and turn out to be varied and wide-ranging. There is a deceptive smoothness in her tone, or tone of voice, as in that of Evelyn Waugh; not a far-fetched comparison, for in the work of both writers the funny and the appalling lie side by side in close amity. After the fashion of *Angel*, her best book to date, though without any hint of self-repetition, Mrs Taylor presents to us here somebody both ridiculous and dignified—not just laughable and dignified, like, say, Fielding's Parson Adams.

> She was a tall woman with big bones and a noble face, dark eyebrows and a neatly folded jowl. She would have made a distinguished-looking man and, sometimes, wearing evening dress, looked like some famous general in drag.*

Adams would hardly have survived being introduced in such terms.

The one so introduced is, naturally, Mrs Palfrey, and the Claremont is a hotel in the Cromwell Road where old widowed people like herself come to spend their penultimate days; not their last ones, because, as she explains at one point, you aren't allowed to die at the Claremont. And the principal subject of the novel is loneliness, old age and approaching death, and I must warn those who dislike this triad of

---

* So the British edition. The author told me that she originally wrote 'like Lord Louis Mountbatten in drag' but the British publisher would not have it. The American one didn't mind.

prospects that they will not like it any better on finishing *Mrs Palfrey at the Claremont*.

Among her and other residents—Mrs Post who knits and thinks she means well; Mrs Arbuthnot who is in constant pain and knows she means ill because of it—there is perpetual competition. You must show you are not, in spite of all appearance, alone; you have relatives and friends who come and see you and take you on jaunts. There are some at the Claremont who can opt out of the contest: Mrs Burton who drinks and has blue hair and an easily amused brother-in-law; Mr Osmond who gets by on writing mainly unpublished letters to the *Telegraph* and telling the reluctant waiter dirty jokes—and who, after one of the most embarrassing marriage proposal scenes in all fiction, is the unwitting instrument of Mrs Palfrey's death.

Mrs Arbuthnot gets out of the relative-competition by becoming incontinent, being told 'in the nicest possible way, which in the circumstances could not be very nice', to leave, and going off to die in a nursing-home. Mrs Palfrey has no such recourse. She has a grandson who goes on conspicuously failing to materialize. After falling over in the street and being helped by a young man called Ludo, she manages to turn him into her grandson, and the dangers inherent in prolonging this deception under various beady eyes furnish a great deal of the comedy and awfulness.

Ludo, a decent, scruffy, rather solitary chap, plays up to the deception for a mixed and (on the author's part) scrupulously balanced set of motives. He enjoys it; he is a writer who actually writes, and finds Mrs Palfrey, with her grape-coloured varicose veins and such, marvellous material, also unintentionally funny; he likes her and feels sorry for her; he does come to look on her as a sort of grandmother. He is also quite often bored by her, as he is by his splendidly tatty mother and as an unhealthy-looking bird called Rosie is by him. The other part of the subject of the novel, closely linked with the main part, is the dreadful and irresistible sincerity of the boredom we feel with those we do not need. Mrs Palfrey, looking back at her life, tells Ludo that the only way of being free is to be not needed, and understands the implications.

She is not heroic; she is not called on to face the intolerable, merely the very hard to tolerate, and her death is easy. She is just 'sure how to behave', trained to 'be independent; never give way to melancholy; never touch capital', and so is able to avoid being a coward, to accept not life nor death but a dismal today and no prospect of tomorrow's being any different. The account of her fortitude is one of the celebrations of the wondrousness of the ordinary in which Mrs Taylor excels.

This is a continuously fascinating novel, always pushing the reader one way and another. He will be moved; he will wince at such unobtrusive but well-aimed jolts as Mrs Palfrey's calm observation:

that as she got older, she looked at her watch more often, and that it was always earlier than she had thought it would be. When she was young, it had always been later.

And he will every so often be provoked into yells—and I mean yells—of laughter.

New Statesman, 27 August 1971

Left-over Life to Kill

Blaming, by Elizabeth Taylor, Chatto & Windus

This is Elizabeth Taylor's twelfth novel, completed shortly before she died last year. Outside her family and friends, her death was not much noticed except among the smallish band who care for literature. Her genuine distaste for any kind of publicity—that rarest of qualities in a writer—and her deeply unsensational style and subject-matter saw to it that, in life, she never received her due as one of the best English novelists born in this century. I hope she will in the future. Meanwhile, those who are new to her work will find in this book all the qualities that gave that work its distinction.

Despite its title, of which more later, the subject of *Blaming* is in the first place widowhood, which is seen from time to time rather as a special form of loneliness. Amy Henderson's husband, Nick, dies suddenly while the couple are on a package tour abroad. Their recent acquaintance, Martha Larkin, a youngish anglophile American who writes novels (and very terrible they are made to sound), kindly accompanies her back to London. In the house she had for so long shared with Nick, somewhere on the river, Amy gets through the days and weeks.

What makes this hard for her is not grief as such but boredom, impatience and the inevitable, manifest inadequacy of others' efforts to help her. Ernie Pounce, ex-sailor, ex-barman, and now rather more of a housekeeper than anything else, does his best for madam with smoked salmon sandwiches and gossip, but he will go on about his false teeth, which click. Gareth Lloyd, the local doctor, is an old friend, but it was his dead wife to whom Amy was really close, and doctoring is to her a distasteful occupation. As for staying with her son James, his wife, Maggie, and their two little girls, she wonders how the hell she can get out and go home. And the vicar sets off instant rudeness.

The most serious threat to Amy's sovereignty over her diminished life, which is what all attempts to do anything for her soon become, is posed by Martha. She is unconventional, or bizarre, enough to beat aside the Englishwoman's instinctive defences, and for a time wins her reluctant tolerance, 'rather taken for granted than welcomed'. It is Martha who provides most of the movement of the novel, having an affair with a fellow American called Simon, marrying him, departing for the US with him, leaving him, returning to England and, to some unknowable degree through Amy's neglect, taking an overdose in a Paddington hotel. Most of this, however, happens off-stage: Amy remains at the centre of the story.

We are shown that she is not cut out for bereavement without its ever being suggested that anyone else is or could be. She becomes grudging and resentful, giving nobody credit or charity. James keeps sticking his nose in to find out how she's getting on. How dare a girl of Maggie's age have to go into hospital to have her womb fixed and so oblige her, Amy, to look after the kids for a couple of days! Martha's concern and trouble-taking win precious little in the way of benevolence — 'Is she a counter-irritant?' asks Gareth. 'No, just an irritant; sometimes like a dead albatross. Talking of irritants, that awful Vicar came again the other day. . . ' When, near the end, Simon flies to London for Martha's funeral, Amy's first thought is, 'God, don't let him come here.' And, for one crushing moment, she remembers how her marriage bored her and knows that, if Nick could come back, she would be bored again.

That moment, of course, like others, takes Amy beyond any sort of ingratitude or selfishness and into accepting something dreadful about her own life. Painful insights visited on people with no tendency to introspection, no gift of detachment, have always tended to come the way of Elizabeth Taylor's characters, and it is in the nature of things that Amy's should give her no help at all in facing her future. She is helpless to change because she is helpless to be different, and totally reconciles herself with the reader by her final question, put to nobody, 'What else could I have done?'

This is not in the least a gloomy book. There are dozens of those Taylorian digs, tiny bolts of a malice that almost rises to a kind of gleeful affection, some launched by Amy, just as many at her. At Christmas dinner, her wonderfully sly, fake-pious granddaughter (aged eight) asks her to pull the other end of her cracker, because she always thinks 'old wrinkled hands get a better grip'. But naturally Martha takes more punishment than anybody else, a lot of it from the author. She is a thoroughly good person who is at the same time a monster of crappy sensitivity, walking about while eating, studying her reflection all possible ways in a spoon, burning an entire box of matches one by one as she stares broodingly at Gareth—'what a terrible man', she characteristically says later. I started by laughing at her, but was soon screaming with incredulous horror.

Hypochondriacal, house-proud Ernie is a small classic in another favourite vein, the genteel-shabby ('I merely said, you know, sarcastic. "You'd have thought," I said, "the telephone had never been invented".'). And Amy's other granddaughter is as good—as bad—in a quite different way. But other characters are not filled in. Gareth, James and Simon are almost featureless; you have to search back to find what the last two do for a living. Maggie is given nothing to get her teeth into. Smaller parts—the vicar, Martha's landlady— that would formerly have been made lovingly finished cameos are reduced to walk-ons. There is an air of underpopulation and, despite some splendidly, almost chillingly, spare descriptive sketches, underfurnishing.

The novel is not incomplete but is not quite fulfilled, not completely shaped. I connect this with the unsuitability of the Henry Greenish title. The author herself insisted that no other one would do. I could not see it applying much until near the end, and then only in the person of James. Well, she was writing, let us say, against time. And even so, how much was achieved, how much mind and feeling did reach the page. After Martha had visited her:

> Amy could notch up a little score of hours passed—not in pleasure but passed—of a long day broken into. She discovered that something she had missed and needed were day-to-day shared trivialities; sudden thoughts, not important enough for saving, and an untidy trail of events.

That is wisdom.

Observer, 12 September 1976

Dodos Less Darling

Anglo-Saxon Attitudes, by Angus Wilson, Secker & Warburg

The spectacle of a writer of fiction deliberately taking steps to increase his range is one that must arouse sympathy and encouragement. When Mr Nigel Balchin tried to break out of the small back room into symbolic fantasy or the Italy of the Borgias, it was the action of a churl, however sensible a churl, to tell him to about-turn and report to Professor Mair's research team the next day. And only the hyper-sensitive could greet without warm emotion an attempt by Mr Evelyn Waugh to chronicle the struggle for power in the supporters club of a Lancashire soccer team, say, or an imagined invasion of Earth by Vegan vegetables from the pen of Miss Ivy Compton-Burnett. The work of that undervalued writer Mrs Elizabeth Taylor makes one long to ask her to take up one of the few weapons she has so far never tried: adventurousness. Yes, there is a lot too much re-tilling of the private allotment going on, too many hermits contented with their cells. Two cheers at least, then, for the man who has a shot at a new line.

The trouble with saying all that is that it renders a little disagreeable the necessary task of pointing out that such an attempt has slipped up when in fact it has slipped up. But all the sympathy and respect in the world could not have made my reading of Mr Angus Wilson's new novel less of a task. From his brilliant short stories, and in a different way from his earlier novel, *Hemlock and After*, it was plain that his most congenial method was that of presenting rather than developing a situation. His large long scenes existed so that relationships should emerge rather than alter, and character, not incident, seemed his main interest. An initial approach via technique, however arid or niggling it may appear, may be justified in discussing so self-conscious and painstaking a writer as this, and would at least be some sort of corrective to the prevailing mode of criticising a novel on the score of its attitudes. Even when these are Anglo-Saxon ones, the way they are presented makes a lot of difference, perhaps all the difference.

Half the length of this book has gone by before all the characters have been brought on to the stage. There are a great many of them. One group consists of academic historians, who are much concerned about the editorship of a new medieval series. One of the historians has a grown-up family who, with their various wives, husbands, mistresses and boyfriends, compose the second group. The third group is the expected little posse of pansies, one of whom has a Dickensian grandmother and another a reciprocated interest in the chief historian's younger son. Other figures are scattered round the fringes: a bitchy novelist, a frightful French biographer, a put-upon market gardener. By the time everybody has been assembled, a number of lines of interest have suggested themselves. Some of these prove to be dead ends, one or two fall easily apart into marginal decorations, and it would be truthful, though uncharitable, to describe large areas of the book as short stories about darling dodos suspended piecemeal from a tenuous central thread. This thread is spun, rather over-luxuriantly, around the figure of the chief historian.

Gerald Middleton, the man who did the standard thing on Cnut, is a dodo all right, and if not a very darling one he is a good deal nicer than that fearful old humbug, Bernard Sands. Gerald is sixty (p. 5), or sixty-two (p. 28), or sixty-four (p. 6), but anyway he still has a heavy handsome dark face, or a handsome sensual face, or a dark flushed face. There is something vaguely women's-magazine about him, a streak of the man of distinction both in what is said of him and in how it is said—a very unlikely defect in a character that Mr Wilson wishes us to side with, and an intimation that extension of range can include extension downwards. The dark flush on Gerald's face also derives in part, perhaps, from his anxieties. He has published nothing for years, he is worried about a noteworthy archaeological find which he suspects of being a bit phoney, he is estranged from his wife and his children elude him, his ex-mistress drinks and he feels he is to blame. By the end of the novel, although the wife and children situations are back to a virtual as-you-were, the others are clearing up. He is ready to give Edward the Confessor the treatment, he has denounced the archaeological Piltdown, and the mistress has stopped drinking.

These, to be sure, are modest enough victories, and the sad thing about them is that they just happen. A grinding penury of invention saps the narrative, which in spite of its many discussions and explanations and long speeches (Mr Wilson's dialogue unit is the paragraph) still fails to explain why Gerald stopped working and why, apart from having a rest-period for cogitation and mulling over the past, he feels he can start again. The gaff-blowing about the find, too, is preceded only by further cogitation and a long series of scenes in which evidence is collected from minor characters. And anyway, he knew all the time there had been dirty work. The find business is clearly supposed to be the powder-train which leads to the final explosion, but it is such a long powder-train and it splutters so much, that the explosion is muffled and mainly smoke-producing. Why did Gerald sit on his knowledge for forty years, and why did he get off it? No such questions plague the matter of the mistress's reform. She switched to bubblegum after being got at by Alcoholics Anonymous—aagh!

It is at this point that technical defects merge with, and affect adversely, attitudes presented. Since drama and even dramatisation are so lacking, since nothing of importance is found for Gerald to do, he is left hanging about brooding for 400 pages, too inert for sympathy. Since nothing is made to happen whereby Gerald can affect the destinies of the other characters, nor they his, he is reduced to the mere passing of judgements, portentously upon himself, priggishly upon them. Priggishness, righteous discomfort, goat-voiced didacticism are explicably the Anglo-Saxon attitudes which finally emerge. In some cases (though not, unfortunately, in the more important ones) these are skilfully deflated, with all that wealth of legitimate malice that distinguished the author of *The Wrong Set*. There is nothing here that quite touches 'Crazy Crowd' or 'Mother's Sense of Fun', but the bitchy novelist is magnificent and there are some well-assorted comic foreigners. It is part of the adventurous writer's fate that it is the familiar elements in innovatory work which are likely to draw the cheers. There are, however, parts of this novel which are both new and successful.

Two important female characters stand out from the rest. Inge, Gerald's huge Danish wife, is a creature given to agonising whimsy, to little frenzies of sentiment which arouse all his censoriousness, but which evoke only amusement and compassion, mixed about equally, in the reader. Elvira Portway, granddaughter of an aged—and superfluous—actress and mistress of Gerald's heterosexual son, sees herself as a kind of hammer of cocktail-party young men ('*Every single* English intellectual is *provincial* and bloody') and is regarded by Gerald with an intolerable snooty lust. Mr Wilson seems not to realise how deftly, and how sympathetically, he has portrayed these two, who almost alone in his enormous gloomy cast have real grounds for gloom and try to do something about it. He writes them down or writes them off, passes superficial judgements about them *in propria persona*, tells us lies about them in a curiously off-hand and bored, almost angry way. It is almost as if he was conscious that they were stealing the show from old heavy, dark and handsome.

Anglo-Saxon Attitudes is clearly a failure, but it is the sort of failure which makes one impatient to read its successor. In it I hope Mr Wilson will have done with complexity (equals having lots of characters) and breadth (equals length). I hope too that that fug of judicial self-righteousness, asphyxiating in *Hemlock and After*, yawn-engendering in the present book, will have finally blown away. May he take his place, not as our Galsworthy or our George Eliot, between whom he seems at present to be uncertainly hovering, but as our Thackeray.

Spectator, 1 June 1956

Dodos on the Wing

A Bit off the Map and Other Stories, by Angus Wilson, Secker & Warburg

In this latest volume Mr Angus Wilson has switched his faintly alarming attentions from Chelsea and North Oxford to the coffee bars and new housing estates that are widely held to typify the post-war era. As before, his subject is most often the explosions and embarrassments touched off when people of differing class, training or culture are made to confront one another. *A Bit off the Map* shows us a pampered young Jewish sensitive uneasily involved with a grubby but twee floosie, a 'county' vicar's daughter married to a village shop-keeper, a mandarin-level critic trying to be urbane to a lacquered Teddy boy. This last encounter is a high point in the title story (one of the three longer pieces in the book), which is a brilliantly funny satire on Soho geniuses. The stars of the group are the philosophaster Huggett ('he says real genius means Will Power') and the novelist-to-end-all-novelists Reg ('we'll light such a blaze that all their nice little civilized fire-engines won't be able to put it out'). The climax, whereby it is the bewildered Teddy boy who proves himself the genuine Out-sider by slugging a helpless dotard, comes not as an arbitrary resolution but as a stroke of ironical justice.

In this story, as in most of the others, Mr Wilson wields his precision instruments with all the skill that distinguishes his earlier collections; in fact one detects occasionally a ruthless farcicality which gives them an added cutting edge. The most conspicuous novelty, however, is to be found in another of the longer pieces, 'More Friend than Lodger'. Here the author's absorption in social collisions operates at reduced volume, and this is perhaps connected with the fact that this time the reader is never led to wonder, as he has to rather too often even with Mr Wilson at his liveliest, whether people like this do actually exist and whether, if they do, they talk as they are shown to. On the contrary, the charmingly catty, animated and devious heroine-narrator of this story is real in every phrase, especially when one of her little verbal squibs fails to go off or her sophistication is momentarily holed, and her accounts of her pedestrian husband and snobbish-fake lover throw as plausible and clear a light upon her as upon them. And she differs sharply from the protagonists of Mr Wilson's existing novels in never taking herself seriously. The outlook is bright.

Spectator, 18 October 1957

The Road to Airstrip One

A Study of George Orwell, by Christopher Hollis, Hollis & Carter

Orwell is one of those writers you can never quite get away from. I do not just mean that the stream of books and articles about him shows no signs of abating. Nor is it merely that his influence seems inescapable, so that any intellectuals who may submit to having a list of their heroes wrung from them are likely to put him in the first two or three whatever their age (within reason), whatever their other preferences and—more oddly at first sight—whatever their political affiliations, if any. And if they have none, incidentally, this is as much Orwell's doing as anyone else's. However: Orwell is hard to get away from because no view of him can ever be final. No sooner have you established him in your mind as a fearless honest critic of society than you come up against little bits of journalistic fudging in his reportage and big bits of subjective fantasy where, whatever is being criticized, it is something far larger and more dimly apprehended than society. When you think you have him taped as a fanatic, his similarities to Lawrence spotted and his writing tied down as the record of personal obsessions, you find yourself rereading *Homage to Catalonia*. So unsatisfactory as a novelist. So unsatisfactory as a propagandist too. And yet so good. And so on.

Mr Christopher Hollis's critical biography is the best contribution to the Orwell problem that I have read. Certain eccentricities of style—in particular an infatuation with the word 'but' that sets the reader oscillating from one side of the question to the other like a spectator at Wimbledon—made me want to invite his presence at my desk at the end of the hour, but these are small prices to pay for a most admirable informality and unpretentiousness. The biographical material is valuable. We now have the full story about Orwell at Eton: that he was neither ugly nor unpopular nor, compared with many of his contemporaries, particularly rebellious, and that if he kept himself apart it was because he was, like the central figures of most of his books, a natural solitary. Mr Hollis takes us through the Burma period, giving a first-hand account of the oddly jingoistic Orwell of 1925, and on to the semi-mystical, and perfectly voluntary, retreat into the world of the down-and-out. We are shown the part played here by Orwell's sense of class-guilt and by his compulsive desire (shared by Gordon Comstock of *Keep the Aspidistra Flying*) to reach 'the mud', although I doubt whether the full story of his motives in this regard, as in much else, will ever be known. As it is, the general portrait of Orwell which emerges is a very sympathetic one, full of amiable qualities: humour, good nature, love of England, fondness for animals, belief in decency, conscientious readiness to admit inconvenient facts.

Mr Hollis's account of Orwell's work and ideas is always vigorous and in the main balanced and just. Where he fails it is because he cannot resist drawing Orwell in his own image. If *Animal Farm* stops annoyingly short of saying that a moderate conservative regime would be the best of a bad lot, then Mr Hollis is on hand to let us know that this can be deduced from it, or anyway that it is the conclusion its author 'ought to have drawn'. There is no doubt that Orwell's constant denunciations of the Left (founded on fact as most of them were) have done a great deal to drive the post-war intelligentsia to the Right—or, as I said earlier, into political quietism—but this is propaganda by negation only. It is again reasonable, if one is of the Left, to be irritated with Orwell for his 'betrayal' of it, but the most diligent search would not, I think, find in him any trace of positive right-wing sentiment. And I cannot believe he would have countenanced for an instant the idea, urged on him by Mr Hollis, that an aristocracy is necessary for the preservation of liberty—or for anything else.

Be that as it may, the field where Orwell dances unmistakably to his biographer's tune is that of religion. Unlike many of his fellow-Catholics, Mr Hollis shows himself free of the bigoted or the uncritical, and so it is possible to forgive him for interjecting an occasional bull on the virtues of the Spanish Church or on the firmness of Swift's faith, even, perhaps, for taking Chesterton seriously. And since Orwell, like many other people, clearly did have vague, intermittent and inert hankerings after belief, there is a sort of reason in ticking him off for not seeing that some of the questions he raised could have (not 'must have') a religious answer. But where Mr Hollis shows himself badly limited in dealing with a man like Orwell is in his continual insistence that ethical beliefs have got to be propped up with religious beliefs. He must know that it is logical to pursue goodness and so on for its own sake. To reject this is to come dangerously near to the evangelical-canvasser view that all moral activity is 'really' religious activity. Orwell was no more in search or in need of God than the next man.

He was, however—and not merely towards the end of his writing life—tortured, embittered and hysterical. Mr Hollis is too observant to miss these traits, but he does not allot them the emphasis they demand. Although they are absent from the best of Orwell—*Burmese Days, Animal Farm, Homage to Catalonia* and the first half of *Coming up for Air*—they must be set against the equally real qualities of honesty and objectivity with which they were so often at war in him. He was, as Mr Hollis expresses it, 'concerned to analyse reality', but one would be hard put to it to find any reality at all in a book like *Keep the Aspidistra Flying*, let alone the slightest concern to analyse it. Elsewhere there is a pessimism that out-does Swift—one of Orwell's heroes—in its insistence that man is not only bad but getting worse, that he is moving at an increasing rate towards being as bad as possible: 'the autonomous individual is going to be stamped out of existence', or more colourfully, 'if there's anything you care a curse about, better say good-bye to it now, because everything you've ever known is going down, down, into the muck, with the machine guns rattling all the time'.

This was not an eccentric view in 1939. What distinguishes it is the obvious relish with which these maledictions—they are not warnings—are uttered. A kind of ecstatic glee pervades the bombing episode in *Coming up for Air* and the prophecies of sadistic totalitarianism, imminent and universal, which accompany it. The war came and went, however, without bringing the smash-up any nearer. Prophetic generalities could no longer satisfy: the nightmare of endless brutality must be rehearsed at length and in detail, shown as actually taking place. There is some sort of incoherent political message in *Nineteen Eighty-Four*, but the real emotional weight of the book falls not upon that nor upon the various techniques for defeating love and individuality, but upon the succession of extravaganzas about violence and torture which pervade it, and its real hero is not the sapless Winston Smith but the inhuman O'Brien. 'If you want a picture of the future, imagine a boot stamping on a human face—for ever.' It was Orwell's own picture, and being divorced from probability it was offered for its own sake. Why? In a brilliant article, published in the *New Yorker* of 28 January 1956, Mr Anthony West argues that Airstrip One, the setting of *Nineteen Eighty-Four*, is actually a paranoiac version of Orwell's preparatory school. A string of parallels, culminating in the bracketing of the headmaster's study with Room 101 in the Ministry of Love, is adduced to suggest that Orwell's unconscious purpose was 'to send everybody in England to an enormous Crossgates to be as miserable as he had been'. This is the kind of perception about Orwell that needs investigating. Not until his fantasies have been exposed and discarded can we properly value the truths he told.

Spectator, 31 August 1956

Orwell and Beyond

1985, by Anthony Burgess, Hutchinson

The energetic and unclassifiable Mr Burgess has once more broken new ground, which in the case of so protean a performer is saying something. He has clearly done it again. What exactly it is that he has done is not altogether clear. To be sure, the volume consists of two parts; '1984', a number of dialogues and essays partly devoted to *Nineteen Eighty-Four*, George Orwell's novel and '1985', a short exercise in the genre of that novel with comparisons invited. A couple of postscripts conclude.

Mr Burgess opens sensibly enough by reminding us of Orwell's Oceania, Eurasia and Eastasia, the proles, the Outer Party, the Inner Party and of course Big Brother, though without throwing light on the vexed question of whether, in that perpetual and much-advertised world war anybody was actually fighting. The trouble starts in the short section that follows. There are three 'tasks' ahead, of which the first is 'to understand the waking origins of Orwell's bad dream', ie what went on in him and his surroundings, what made him write the book, and the second 'to see where he went wrong and where he seems to have been right'. (The third task is the making of '1985'.)

There are indeed parallels between *Nineteen Eighty-Four* and the reality of 1948, from cigarette shortages to the presence of television — a bad example, with that presence ranging from omni in the novel to mini or little more in fact. But to notice these, along with such resemblances as that between the Ministry of Truth and Broadcasting House, gets nowhere near justifying the view that '*Nineteen Eighty-Four* is no more than [*sic*] a comic [*sic*] transcription of the London of the end of the Second World War'. If Orwell put in some of that London it wasn't because he could see nothing else or thought it must stay like that for ever; he merely seized on an 'accidentally available embodiment of the drabness and penury generated by totalitarianism'.

It seems strange to find a novelist as imaginative, as genuine as Mr Burgess finding Orwell wrong here and right there, ending the perorations of '1984' with the statement that '1984 is not going to be like that at all'. (He says once that Orwell wasn't really forecasting the future but takes it back several times.) Must I observe that a novel can no more be right than a symphony be true? Orwell was not prophesying; if he had been, the best — the only good — parts of the book would have been those few references to metrication, by which he meant not to predict, but to illustrate the homogenising and de-flavouring of life under Big Brother. In general he was saying not 'This is how 1984 will probably be', but 'If some of you go on as you are doing in 1948 something like this, not of course this itself but something as awful and irremediable as this, may happen'. *Nineteen Eighty-Four* is as unaffected by its discordance with any possible 1984 as is *The First Men in the Moon* (1901) by improved lunar observation.

Quite soon Mr Burgess moves beyond Orwell and, scattering etymologies as he goes, takes us through freedom, good and evil, right and wrong, the State, freedom again, Bakunin and anarchism and youth (excellent), free will and freedom again, brain-washing, the inefficiency of Russian restaurants and love. None of this is less than entertaining. The best part argues that there are no free societies, only free individuals. I think that that view fiddles with what 'free' means, but it is well argued here.

'1984' is at any rate more successful than '1985'. In seven years' time we shall still have soccer, supermarkets (and shoplifting), the Health Service, television (not like Big Brother's, just horrifyingly more and worse than what we have in 1978) and inflation. We shall also have rampaging union power (what is now the London Hilton will have become New Transport House), the firemen on strike, the army on strike, everybody on strike and an Arab-backed private army called the Free Britons brought in to hold the country together. The prospect of civil war will advance, recede and finally be sent packing by the intervention of King Charles III.

The predictions here vary in plausibility. It seems quite probable that even under full nationalisation, with the union membership supposedly having come to power, management would go on behaving like management and workers treating it as such. What is most improbable is that within seven (or seventeen) years there will be groups of youngsters learning Greek and Latin on the quiet from the State system's learned throw-outs and supporting themselves by theft and violence. The other difference between these two ideas is that the second is much more interesting, incomparably more interesting, than the first, that is to say it belongs to the sphere of fiction, not that of likelihood.

But Mr Burgess has set out to combine the two, to tell a story that shall be tied to fact and free of it at the same time. In one of his postscripts he takes himself to task, rather half-heartedly in my view, for having been 'foolish' enough to write a fictional prophecy that his readers will soon be able to check. Foolhardy rather than foolish, perhaps, though not because of the impending check, which can only leave him as unscathed as Orwell will be. Fast in a self-cleft stick, Mr Burgess has had to try to reconcile the claims of what 1985 can reasonably be expected to be like (very little different from 1978) with what a novelist can do with it (up to him).

Luckily for us he keeps taking the novelist's option, which even so can't save him from being damaged by the Orwell comparison, not or not necessarily on grounds of merit but to the extent that ordered societies, like that of *Nineteen Eighty-Four*, differ widely, while states of chaos, as in '1985', resemble one another. This is not new ground any more.

Observer, 18 March 1979

A Man on Rockall

Pincher Martin, by William Golding, Faber

Pincher Martin is a naval officer who, after the torpedoing of his ship, drifts aimlessly about in the Atlantic for some hours before being cast up on a small, barren, isolated rock. Here he survives for several days, living off mussels and sea-anemones and doing what little he can to increase his chances of rescue, until madness, delirium and (presumably) death overcome him. Except for the last chapter dealing with the recovery of his body, the novel is a record of his thoughts, his memories, his few positive actions, what he sees and what he thinks he sees.

All these things are described with the utmost inventiveness, assurance and power. One wave is much like another, one view of the sea from a fixed point is much like another, the sensations of a man in mortal danger and a great deal of the time in moral terror cannot but be appallingly restricted and repetitive, but Martin's nightmare is self-perpetuating: it spirals, never circles. As it progresses it reveals Martin's life as that of a ruthless despoiler (pincher?) of the cherished possessions of others, a helpless victim of his own greed and selfishness, and yet we are left in no doubt that what we are being shown is the pathetic shabbiness of humanity in general. At the end, in the teeth of his own childish protests, something divine seems to take charge of Martin and show him the paradox of 'a compassion that was . . . without mercy'. The last sentence of the book shows the mysterious extent of that compassion.

To discuss *Pincher Martin* in such terms is at least to indicate the force of its impact, the seriousness with which it requires to be taken. No reader will soon forget the world it reveals. But it is the narrowness and remoteness of that world, whatever its status, which rob the novel of the universality it appears to claim. Although Martin is in some sense doing duty for man, the context of this performance is too remote from the world of men to excite that continuous recognition and self-recognition upon which depends the novelist's power to persuade. The brilliance of the many nightmare passages is too akin to that brilliance which we attribute, implying a reservation about the significance of what is being done, to the triumphant solution of technical difficulty. One admires, one is impressed; but it is only when Martin is shown as actively human—working out his chances, erecting a pillar of rocks to draw the notice of any passing ships, treating himself for fever—that one in the fullest sense sympathises. To put it another way, Martin is most interesting when he nearly approaches the condition of those other Crusoes, the schoolboys of Mr Golding's terrifying and haunting *Lord of the Flies*.

Every review not just done for the guineas is among other things an impertinence, for it is bound to imply that the reviewer knows better than his author what he ought to be doing. I hope Mr Golding will forgive me if I ask him to turn his gifts of originality, of intransigence, and above all of passion, to the world where we have to live.

Spectator, 9 November 1956

What Marriage Did for Our Joe

Scenes from Provincial Life, by William Cooper, Penguin
Scenes from Married Life, by William Cooper, Macmillan

Outside the classics, very few books have appealed to me as strongly as did Mr William Cooper's *Scenes from Provincial Life* when it appeared in 1950. This appeal, which a rereading has in no way diminished, was a broad and diverse one extending over almost the whole range of the novel's qualities, so that it is hard to decide where to begin an appraisal.

The most obvious point is the provincial setting, the deftly rendered ambience of market stalls, teashops, grammar school, clock tower, trams. But to some of us at any rate, especially those who have never lived in any major city, this was hearteningly recognisable rather than inspirational; we had already worked out, in our fumbling way, the possibility of subjecting the provinces to literary treatment, as other, larger writers had done a good deal earlier.

What impressed me most about Mr Cooper's book was that Joe Lunn, its hero, was just like me (and just like, I imagine, tens of thousands of other young men all over these islands). To begin with, he had a job, and not as a publisher or a rich-man's secretary either, but in the middle reaches of schoolteaching. His friends, instead of being masochistic expatriates or well-connected Roman Catholics or suicidal chiefs of police in West Africa, were chartered accountants, minor commercial artists. And his relations with his young woman, the meek, innocent, smirking, evasive Myrtle, were casual and tender, selfish and sympathetic, non-cosmic and non-operatic: entirely believable.

There were other, similar, attractions, all traceable to a central core of unsensational common sense. It was refreshment, for instance, to read a novel set in 1939 that was totally free both of antedated prophecy and of souped-up laments for the snuffing of all the lights in Europe, civilisation crashing about our ears (oh, my dearest) etc. Without any hint of the 'brilliant' or the 'witty', there were plenty of what I thought, and still think, were penetratingly funny remarks: Joe doesn't like cafés with cruets on the table at tea-time; his friend tells him, 'You wouldn't notice the cruet if you were interested in the human heart'; another friend complains of his girl's taste in films. Joe says, 'If girls aren't ignorant, they're cultured. You can't avoid suffering.' Above all, perhaps, *Provincial Life*, did not (*pace* the Penguin blurb) 'poke fun at' our taboos of sex and class. It did something much more acceptably offensive: it ignored them.

Queries and reservations were few, but they were there. Although I enjoyed the absence of 'style' in the pansy travel-book sense, I felt that the laconic informality came near at times to a nudging chumminess with the reader. I was slightly bothered, too, by the function of Robert, a great wise friend of everybody's kept waiting in the wings throughout; by the thinness of the link between the main Joe-Myrtle plot and Joe's dealings with his pupils and colleagues; and by the fact that Joe was a novelist when all that was necessary was that he should be something for Myrtle not to take him seriously as: since his creator was demonstrably also a novelist, anything else—amateur architect, educational theorist, baritone saxophonist—would have been preferable.

It would be cracking up my powers of discernment too far to claim that I saw at the time where these dissatisfactions were tending; conceivably Joe's status as a writer of three novels, while, for all I then knew, Mr Cooper was a new writer, blinded me to the dismaying possibility that I was reading not fiction but half-heartedly-tidied-up fact.

I call this dismaying because once per lifetime is probably more than the average frequency with which direct experience sets us up with all the materials for a novel. For one reason or another, either the one I have suggested or some radical failure of invention and constructive power, the new Joe Lunn novel, *Scenes from Married Life*, has no more shape or direction than an average diary. Joe is a Civil Servant in London in 1949 and thereafter. He still writes books, the most recent of which, a friend foresees, may be 'the progenitor of a whole series of similar books', that's a neat one, I must say. Some nasty senior Civil Servants try to get Joe sacked. In the end they fail. The Home Office authorities may object to parts of his next book, the one after the progenital one. In the end they don't. At the beginning Joe has a mistress, but he chucks her, so heartily that she never reappears, and gets married to a schoolteacher called Elspeth, who blushes a lot. They are very happy and have a baby girl.

There are other characters: Robert, now a senior Civil Servant, comes on stage and stays there; he is shown, but not seen by Joe, as cold and self-important. A man called Harry wanders in and out; he is shown, but not seen by Joe, as a spiteful meddler. Elspeth is, without qualification, a bore. Mr Cooper evidently sat down to describe an unrelievedly happy marriage, a project as foredoomed as that of turning out a Western in which all the Apaches shall be beneficent, the bad men fresh from psychological reconstruction, the United States cavalry commanders models of competence, enlightenment and amiability.

What he has produced is the least dramatic, least significant, least interesting book I have ever read by a writer I regard with respect and gratitude. The appealing wryness has become mechanical; nothing is left of that invigorating blend of high spirits and sadness; Joe's dragons are all laid to rest, which no doubt makes him easier to live with, but has been the death of him as a literary figure. Do you realise that he actually puts a notice of his marriage in *The Times* and the *Telegraph*? I know what the original Joe Lunn—my Joe Lunn—would have had to say about that.

Observer, 29 January 1961

Second Time of Asking

Scenes from Metropolitan Life, by William Cooper, Macmillan

I have never looked forward more eagerly to a new book than to William Cooper's *Scenes from Metropolitan Life* (ML). All my crowd have enjoyed and admired its predecessor, *Scenes from Provincial Life* (PL), when it came out in 1950, drawn to it in the first place by the title, probably—the author was then quite unknown. Thanks to his descriptive gifts, that provincial setting made a strong and fresh appeal. The story of Joe Lunn and his girl Myrtle, and secondarily of Tom and his boy Steve, was straightforwardly and also cunningly told, with admirable writing about sex. And there was nothing modern anywhere.

When, in 1957, ML was announced, the title was again informative— the PL people were to turn up in London. The new effort got as far as the Selected Books feature of the *New Statesman* and then disappeared. Word went round that somebody had threatened to sue Cooper down to his socks.

This was a double disappointment to me. I was deprived of ML, and my view of PL would have to be revised. Put it like this: all things considered, it appeared most unlikely that two such books could have been written in two totally discordant ways, PL comparatively pure fiction, ML libellously exact chronicle. No, my venerated PL had turned out to be about the doings of a bunch of real people—now I came to think of it, there were those few boring removable bits about Joe being a novelist.

Joe reappears, naturally, also Myrtle, obviously. In PL they had an affair, she wanted them to get married, he didn't, and they didn't. In ML they have another affair, he wants her to leave her husband and marry him, she hesitates, and finally doesn't. This second time round, nothing much like love drives him on, merely the calculation that the years are rolling by and she suits him well enough. Myrtle just drifts.

Tom and Steve from PL have gone. In their place we find Robert, a shadowy great friend figure in PL now shifted into the middle, and Julia. Will Robert be able to detach Julia from Wladislaw, her Polish husband or perhaps just boyfriend, and marry her himself? No. I never for a moment thought he would—marry her, that is. She drinks and sleeps around a bit; he is far too cold, cautious and selfish to take her on, and also to sustain the reader's sympathy over anything like the required distance. Here the author is surely the prisoner of his commitment to fact. He could neither make Robert nicer nor purposefully portray him as cold, etc. Robert is shackled to 'Robert', the great friend of 'Joe'.

The best parts of the book concern Julia and Wladislaw, both vividly depicted characters, and his attempts to remove her from Robert and to subdue her egotism with his own. An exploration of conflict between 'romantic hope and the reality' is promised but never embarked on, presumably because life failed to deliver. That, in Joe's phrase, would be a different novel. Perhaps a more interesting one.

I have said that an important attraction to PL was not just the provincial scene but its handling. There are plenty of bits of London on which one might have thought that keen but affectionate eye could profitably have fastened, but no. In what must be a connected way a civil service sub-plot, unlike the school episodes of PL, is unrewarding—inescapable, though, because 'Robert' and 'Joe' were in the Civil Service. By a crippling stroke of literal-mindedness, we are not even allowed to know the nature of the piece of machinery or item of equipment, from nuclear reactor to pencil sharpener, on which the intrigue turns. The A16 it was and the A16 it stays. There is much talk of novels too.

There was a lot going on at the time that may have hindered a steady view of PL. Now all that is over it seems to me an even finer book than it did, a triumph against the odds, a classic.

Observer, 10 October 1982

Onwards and Upwards

Billion Year Spree: the History of Science Fiction, by Brian W. Aldiss, Weidenfeld and Nicolson

A s his nervously jocose title suggests, Brian Aldiss has had to face a plaguey problem over the potential readership of this giant compilation. Any book about science fiction, any published matter with the least bearing on the subject, will be gobbled up by thousands of people who read virtually nothing else. There are plenty of others for whom it is one interest among many, who perhaps know something of it and would like to know more—a few may even read the *Observer*. The two audiences are not incompatible, but their co-presence calls for delicate steering: the fans must be told who Aristophanes or Baudelaire or Ruskin were in a way that will not bore or offend the more learned.

This recurring difficulty is one that Mr Aldiss solves adroitly almost every time. Defoe, Hawthorne and others are allotted routine mini-biographies; Voltaire is conscientiously identified as 'a French philosopher who wrote over ten million words'; but only the ultra-snooty will object. A second problem confronting the author must have been just as rough: what and whom to leave out. Dante, though claimed for science fiction (it says here) by a Croatian authority, can pretty safely stay where he was. But what about William Morris, *The Castle*, *Animal Farm?* This is got round by the simple and admirable expedient of claiming to leave a lot out and actually putting everything in. Or nearly everything. In the search for 'surprising omissions' which every reviewer of this kind of book seems to feel bound to conduct. I could come up with only a single major one. Bram Stoker's *Dracula*, which just appears on a list. I suppose Mr Aldiss might argue that the book falls outside his terms of reference, or else he simply doesn't care for it.

To take the second plea first: nobody who cares for pulp-purveyors like E. E. Smith and Jack Williamson enough to write two or three pages on each ought to be allowed to get away with snubbing Stoker. The answer to the other notion would be similar: if *The Dynasts* and *Alice in Wonderland* qualify here, as they do, *Dracula* does, with honours. It is surpassed only by *Frankenstein* as a source of popular myth, and the two are linked in other ways—the remote setting, the strong sense of the uncanny and of the dreadful violation of divine laws.

Frankenstein comes in appositely here, for it constitutes Mr Aldiss's starting-point. It is 'the first science fiction novel', largely in that we find there 'science replacing supernatural machinery'. This is vital: the place of science in science fiction has never been finally settled, but some version of it must be really in the story if we are not, at last, to start wondering whether we might after all have to admit Dante, Homer, the Book of Genesis, etc. Everything in the tale, and much that was yet to be written, would have been different if Frankenstein had called up his monster from the dead by incantation instead of assembling it from actual bodies by surgery.

After his illuminating essay on Mary Shelley, Mr Aldiss moves on to Poe, whom he characterises very aptly as 'the first poet of the Great Indoors'. It soon turns out that Poe gets at best a lower second as a science-fiction writer, but never mind. Mr Aldiss wants to write an essay about him too, and does so with success. The same engagingly omnivorous attitude brings up a brief discussion of John Milton's *Paradise Lost* (as distinct from Joe Milton's poem of the same title) and a longish one about another work that 'does not count as science fiction', *Gulliver's Travels*. Here, as elsewhere, Mr Aldiss shows himself to be an excellent literary critic, correcting the Orwellian fallacy that sees the Houyhnhnm society as the object of Swift's, not just Gulliver's, admiration. By way of Bulwer-Lytton, Samuel Butler, Edward Bellamy (*Looking Backward*), Verne in a rather sketchy account, Col Chesney (*The Battle of Dorking*), and other writers sometimes more written about than read, we arrive at H. G. Wells. In dealing with him, Mr Aldiss here and there dredges a little deep for my taste. He will see as a message what I would take as an implication, a possible added view; thus Wells's Martians are 'in effect' European colonists of primitive lands, Dr Moreau 'is intended to stand for God'. The final judgement, however, that Wells is the Shakespeare of science fiction, is entirely acceptable, deflationary as it is, on reflection, to some of the more reckless apologists of the genre.

Not long afterwards, Mr Aldiss starts running out of space, a common hardship when the present topic is under discussion. He progressively finds himself committed to summaries of careers and plots, with some thoughtful remarks thrown in: '[Jack] London has no real vision of a future; his future is just the present and the past, only more so.' True; but isn't it always true of what can properly be called science fiction? Wasn't it precisely when Wells developed and wrote about some 'real visions of a future' that he began to go off as an imaginative writer?

So to yesterday and today. By this stage, the author is reduced much of the time to listing names and titles. He doesn't really face the task of saying what the writers of the so-called New Wave in science fiction—or, loathsome phrase, 'speculative fiction'—are up to. Perhaps, as one professionally interested in the standing of the genre, he finds reticence advisable. But he does unerringly pin down the predicament of J. G. Ballard, that great self-destroyed talent: Ballard has never resolved 'the central problem of writing a novel without having the characters pursue any purposeful course of action.'

This book gives constant pleasure and continual insight, provokes murmurs of agreement and mutters of disagreement. I recommend it equally to those who want to know and those who think they know what it's all about.

Observer, 4 November 1979

Intense Inane

Aniara, by Harry Martinson, adapted by Hugh MacDiarmid and Elspeth Harley Schubert, Hutchinson

After being for some years a serious interest of a small and fragmented minority, science fiction is showing signs of becoming a highbrow fad. William Burroughs has introduced some of what he takes to be jargon of the mode into his recent work. The result is, perhaps predictably, an oafish illiteracy never descended to by his namesake of *Princess of Mars* fame. Now comes Harry Martinson's space epic, with a reported sale in Sweden alone of 36,000 copies, a substantially higher figure, I should guess, than the circulation there of any science-fiction magazine.

It is not that Mr Martinson is merely cashing in on a trend. Parts of the present work were written at least ten years ago. But he betrays a disastrous unfamiliarity with both science fiction and science fact. Jupiter, for instance, is a planet, not a star (I don't think this is a translator's error). The chances that 'snow' from outer space will ever fall on Earth are negligible. There is no such thing as roentgen—ie X-ray—light. A device that, in full working order, can show 'television' pictures of distant parts of the cosmos, but does not 'know' the location of these, seems improbable.

Now an ordinary science-fiction writer is dealing with such improbabilities all the time, but if he is any good he makes them sufficiently important in the story to need an explanation, and does his best to furnish one. He doesn't just throw them off casually as Mr Martinson does: that looks much too much like not knowing your stuff. And this is not quibbling. *Paradise Lost* would have been fatally damaged by Milton's not knowing his stuff. Nor will it do to take the line, popular with Poundians, that illiteracy somehow doesn't count if your intentions seem serious enough. The same goes for the line that 'it's a symbol, you see', that in the 'television' example quoted all that really matters is that something or other is being said about the limitations of the intellect or something. A decent symbol makes sense in actuality too.

Aniara ('a combination of letters, rich in vowels', by the way, 'which represents the space in which atoms move') fairly totters under its symbolic load. The story concerns a space-ship, bound for Mars with 8,000 emigrants on board, which is thrown off course in a meteoric storm and heads irreversibly into the intense inane. It doesn't get anywhere, and neither does the story. At an early stage the 'television' thing blows up through some unstated cause; at a late one destruction in another storm seems inevitable, only it isn't really. That's about the lot. Our ordinary science-fiction writer would have felt impelled to give his readers much more to bite on, as well as—while I remember it—avoiding silly made-up terms like gopta calculus, loxodrome, jender curves (no, nothing so interesting: 'a graph in higher mathematics', the glossary says), a habit now practised in only the very worst magazine stories.

A writer can be forgiven this kind of laziness, and others too, if he offers a narrative. Jules Verne was years behind the science of his time, but those followers in the Nautilus were always up to something. All Mr Martinson can provide is some resolutely unspecified sexual activity, a song or two from a space mariner or so, and a great deal of wondering about where they will all end up. Aniara's voyage is a symbol, you see, of the human journey towards death, an interpretation hard to avoid after the first few times the author has slammed it home. In actual fact, however, that journey is diversified by a lot of activity; Mr Martinson's characters use up all their time personifying this and that, so much so that I got to the end without learning for certain whether some of them were people, spirits or machines. We find out no more about any of them than we do about, say, Virgil's stout Gyas and stout Cloanthus, while *Beowulf* appears in comparison a jostle of intolerably vivid personal portraits. Give me the dynamic non-people of the average story in *New Worlds Science Fiction*, any issue of which shows more genuine imaginative power than is shown here.

But perhaps the verse itself has something? (The Mima in what follows is the 'television' nonsense.)

> *In their unguarded moments sometimes,*
> *able to read their expressions. I can see*
> *despair shines like the glow of phosphor*
> *in their still ceaselessly questing eyes.*
> *This shows most clearly in the case*
> *of the woman pilot. She often sits*
> *gazing at the Mima: and then*
> *a change came in her lovely eyes.*

A change came in my lovely eyes, all right. The lids kept drooping.

Spectator, 1 March 1963

Inner Space

Inner Space: The Drowned World, by J. G. Ballard, Gollancz

In J. G. Ballard's new book we have something without precedent in this country, a novel by a science-fiction author that can be judged by the highest standards. To my knowledge, this level has as yet been attained by only two American writers, Algis Budrys and Walter M. Miller. Mr Ballard may turn out to be the most imaginative of Wells's successors, though he has expressly repudiated Wells as an influence.

The setting is among the super-tropical swamps, lagoons and jungles that, as a result of an increase in the sun's heat, now cover most of Earth's surface. Plant and animal life is reverting to the giant bamboos and reptiles of the Triassic age. Among the members of a survey team, sent south from Greenland to determine whether parts of Europe may some day be reclaimable, a parallel but far more complex and disturbing regression can be glimpsed.

Those so affected share a recurrent dream in which they appear to be reversing the process of their birth, losing their identity in a warm sea that is at once the uterine fluid and the primeval ocean from which life emerged. In their waking hours they withdraw more and more irrevocably into the consciousness of their remote biological past, and the book ends with the hero's departure on a lone trek southward towards some kind of paradisal graveyard of the species.

There is plenty of drama, notably after the arrival of a diabolical freebooter, bone-white in a world of darkened skins, whose ship is crammed with salvaged altar-pieces and equestrian statues and whose entourage consists of a band of half-civilised Negroes and a pack of quarter-tamed alligators. By his agency the main lagoon is drained and a paranoid *Walpurgisnacht* enacted among the slime-coated buildings of what proves to be Leicester Square. But the main action is in the deeper reaches of the mind, the main merit the extraordinary power with which whatever inhabits these reaches is externalised in concrete form. The book blazes with images, striking in themselves and yet continuously meaningful.

There are perhaps faults of luxuriance, not very reprehensible anyway in a young writer. The similes, though often marvellously appropriate, sometimes crowd too thickly, and the author sees fit here and there to tell us that such-and-such is strange while amply demonstrating its strangeness. But he triumphantly achieves his object, set out in a fascinating article of his in a recent *New Worlds Science Fiction*, of exploring 'inner space'. His emblem is the metaphorical diving-suit, as against the literal space-suit of most of his contemporaries.

Observer, 27 January 1963

The Lesson of the Master

Rendezvous with Rama by Arthur C. Clarke, Gollancz

At fifty-six Arthur C. Clarke is still the leading science-fiction writer of his generation. (By 'generation', that slippery term, I mean in the present case those who started their careers between 1940 and that time in the mid-Sixties when the genre began to be afflicted by modernism.) Clarke's first story was published in 1946; since then he has brought out nearly fifty books, some of them general works on the future of space-flight and other technologies. The range of his fiction is wide indeed, from severely probable, day-after-tomorrow tales of action (*A Fall of Moondust*) to far-off visions of a humanity on the verge of becoming something else (*Childhood's End*). Even at is boldest, his writing is sharp, lucid and logical, embodying imagination in the true sense of the word: common sense with wings. While his contemporaries repeat themselves at declining levels of energy, and blunder through the arid wastes of experimentation Clarke continues to invent as he has always done.

Rendezvous with Rama might have been expressly designed to show, against a lot of evidence, that the old vein is not worked out. With almost cynical aplomb, the author takes some of the hoariest themes in the whole science-fiction repertory and blends them into a fresh and genuinely exciting whole. The year is 2131, and the habitable worlds of the solar system have been colonised. A body new to astronomers is found to be approaching the sun at a tremendous velocity. On inspection by space-probe, it turns out to be an artificial object, the first product of an alien civilisation to be encountered by man. Accordingly, the interplanetary craft *Endeavour*, under supervision by an ad hoc committee of the United Planets' Science Organisation, is dispatched to investigate and report.

Rama—the classical pantheon having long been used up, celestial novelties are given Hindu names—Rama is a vast cylinder, fifty kilometres long and twenty across. Its outside is practically featureless, but its inside, soon reached, is a sort of world that stretches round the skin of the cylinder. Thus there is no sky; to an observer standing at any given point (enabled to stand by the lateral spin that imparts pseudo-gravity) the 'land' curves away and up on either side until it arches above his head. There is sea as well as land, a continuous ring-shaped body of water held in place by centrifugal force. And light is given by six regularly-spaced suns.

The exploratory team from *Endeavour* consists of just the right kind of people, efficient, tough, loyal, and otherwise differentiated only by their technical specialities: they would not do for a novel of character, but this is science fiction. They find structures that might be buildings without entrances, or machines with no ascertainable function; they encounter beings that are part robotic, part organic, engaged in mysterious tasks; they endure hurricanes caused by temperature changes as our sun starts to heat the outside of Rama; they sail the sea and meet a tidal wave; they find a single flower. Only after they have had to leave does Rama declare its purpose.

All this is visualised by a keen, expert eye and set down by a master hand, one that allows the various wonders to speak for themselves without stylistic fuss. Nothing is fudged and there are no loose ends, though a purist might complain that the attempt to sabotage the project, lively as its results are, is detachable, and that the superchimps in *Endeavour* (IQ 60, worth 2.75 men apiece for rough jobs) never leave the ship. On the other hand there are some splendid throwaways, careless references to a tenth solar planet, Persephone, no doubt beyond Pluto, to the popular Church of Christ, Cosmonaut. And with similar lightness, great cosmic absolutes are tossed in to give a far from light effect:

He was looking at the largest enclosed space ever seen by man . . .
. . . in this one direction, parallel to the axis of Rama, the Sea was indeed completely flat. It might well be the only body of water in the universe of which this was true . . .
Faster and faster Rama swept around the sun, moving now more swiftly than any object that had ever travelled through the solar system.

These and other uniquenesses are brilliantly twisted aside in the final sentence.

Rendezvous with Rama is not Clarke's best novel, but it is consistently, continuously good. I hope there is no truth in the horrifying report that the author intends to write no more science fiction. In these days of the New Vague (or New Far-Too-Explicit), we need him more than ever. After all, with due allowance made for one-off triumphs like Walter M. Miller's *Canticle for Leibowitz* or Algis Budrys's *Rogue Moon*, the body of his work will stand comparison with any since that of

Wells. If he behaves himself and goes on producing, we may yet be forced to call Arthur Clarke the greatest since the greatest.

Spectator, 4 August 1973

Here Comes a Chopper

Bloody Murder: From the Detective Story to the Crime Novel: a History by Julian Symons, Faber

They're all on about it—about the detective story, or crime fiction, or the *roman policier*. At least five leading American journals have published long reviews or articles on the subject in the last few months; as recently, the work of two learned Danes, *The Murder Book*, took a a swift dash from end to end of the field with a lot of rare and interesting illustrations and probably far fewer inaccuracies: only four mistakes about me in well over 100 words. Again in the US the venerable Jacques Barzun and another professorial savant have brought out *A Catalogue of Crime* that runs to 831 pages and sets you back the equivalent of eight quid—I have not yet seen this volume; and, here and now, Julian Symons, by most standards the best-qualified candidate possible, presents a remarkably comprehensive and yet concise history of the genre.

Before I get down to it, however, I will just parenthetically wonder whether this upsurge of critical interest heralds, even accompanies, the start of a new golden age or points to the demise of the whole thing. Books about genres, however glad one may be to have and read and refer to them, are questionable symptoms. Wilder Hobson's *American Jazz Music*, the first in its field, appeared in 1939, just when a (perhaps supernaturally) keen ear might have detected the first faint sour notes in that once wonderful noise. After—I hope no more than after—my own *New Maps of Hell*, a survey of science fiction, had appeared in 1960, that whole form of writing promptly set out on a brisk and confident march downhill. And not only the genres: has poetry got better or worse since people started writing discursive books, as opposed to polemical pamphlets, about it? Even if we don't murder to dissect, what we dissect tends to show some cadaverous signs.

Still: begone, dull care—any medium that can inspire the vigour and enjoyment with which Mr Symons writes here must have more than a few kicks left in it. His book can be heartily recommended to anyone who has ever enjoyed a detective story or a crime novel. This is the sort of thing reviewers usually say (if they say it at all) to round off their notice, rather than near its outset. I say it now to get it out of the way, before settling down to the congenial task of registering my numerous disagreements with the author, who wrote, I am sure, partly with the object of provoking disagreement.

I can find no fault with his opening. He remarks irrefutably, if unpalatably, that very few actual tales conform to the classical rules of deduction: early mention of the criminal, all clues shared with the reader, no poisons unknown to science, etc. 'The truth is that the detective story, along with the police story, the spy story and the thriller, makes up part of the hybrid creature we call sensational litera-ture.' The last expression there sets disagreements stirring. I would not call a science-fiction masterpiece like James Blish's *Case of Conscience*, or M. R. James's *Ghost Stories*, sensational in any but a very stretched sense. Genre fiction is a phrase harder to get one's tongue round, but I find it more accurate.

Disagreement rampages in me when Mr Symons offer to explain why we read stories about crime. He finds first a psychological basis, invoking a psychoanalyst called Geraldine Pederson-Krag, whose potted views, as well as whose name, might have come out of Peter Simple. 'The murder represents parental intercourse, the victim is the parent, and the clues are symbolic representations of mysterious nocturnal sounds, stains, incomprehensible adult jokes.' Whew! That reminds me of the Freudian critic who 'explained' Lear's rejection by Goneril and Regan as the rejections suffered by the infant Shakespeare when his mother successively produced two further offspring, and—I can't resist adding—Lear's insistence on keeping his hundred knights round the place as the infant Shakespeare's anti-maternal retaliation by dirtying his nappies.

Next, and more horribly, Mr Symons puts forward a sociological basis, suggesting that, 'What crime literature offered to its [earlier] readers . . . was a reassuring world in which those who tried to disturb the established order were always discovered and punished . . . [making] its chief appeal to those who had a way of life and a position in society to preserve.' Ow! *That* reminds me of the Marxist critic who wrote of *The Tempest* that 'Caliban is [*sic*] the bestial serf and Ariel the free wage-labourer.' Anyway, Mr Symons throws some doubt on his own views when he confesses to having become addicted to crime literature at the age of eleven. If he had a way of life and a position in society to preserve then, he must have got on in the world a good deal earlier and faster than most of us.

For the remainder of his book, Mr Symons drops his psychological basis, but that old sociological basis keeps cropping up, and the soci-ology is, in the way of sociology, situated left of centre. Here (some might say, predictably) is the heart of my disagreements. The trouble with a sociological basis is that it is non-literary and can be anti-literary, in the sense that it judges one kind of thing by the standards of another kind of thing. Indeed, that literary basis that I was expecting Mr Symons to outline, having furnished his other two bases, never gets outlined, and is less often appealed to throughout the book than I should like.

His overt theme is that the detective story has been virtually replaced by the crime novel—agreed—and that 'the detective story is an inferior thing to the crime novel'—disagreed. One would think he had never read, let alone written, a detective story himself from the way he goes on about its artificiality, its narrowness, its necessarily shallow characterisation, its failure to offer anything but a puzzle followed by a solution. I cannot answer all his charges here, but I might just suggest that, in this kind of writing, as in science fiction, characterisation of any depth is likely to impede plot and action, and that the best examples offer not only an ingenious puzzle, but atmosphere, suspense, and a fast-moving story as well. That very narrowness imposes a discipline, a something to push against which the crime novel so often suffers from the lack of. To the latter, any old bit of violence or sex, or, far worse, 'psychological interest' is all too readily available. Mr Symons does praise rather highly the work of John Dickson Carr (among others), but books like *The Burning Court* and *The Crooked Hinge* in their highly-wrought, perfectly finished complexity, offer far more than the exploiting of a formula he finds in them.

Well: the explanation proffered for the replacement of detection by crime pure and simple is that society has changed, so that we can no longer trust or like or identify with the forces of law and can, under certain conditions, regard the criminal as a heroic figure. Disagreed again, on two counts; not all, probably not even much, of our society has changed in that way, and secondly, there is a better, literary reason for the decline of the detective story, in that, once more like science fiction, it has run out of the specialist ideas on which it depends. The number of possible methods of murder, to take the obvious instance, is very large, but it is not inexhaustible, and has been pretty well exhausted. As regards the alleged superiority of the crime novel, this seems to rest largely on the sociological, or political, notion that detective stories are reactionary and crime novels progressive, the one reprehensibly glorifying the police, the other laudably depicting them as no better, perhaps worse, than their prey.

What I, from my position of Olympian detachment, would call Mr Symons's political prejudices betray him, here and there, into unconscious humour, as when he tells us that Conan Doyle condemned the Russian Revolution in the strongest terms and *yet* was *also* a man of generous impulses. (He adds the curious remark, in disparagement of Doyle, that 'his mind was on the level of Macaulay, not of Carlyle'—I know which mind I'd pick, given the choice.) Then, it puzzles him that Baroness Orczy, in her Old Man in the Corner stories, never used them to make 'social comments' as she could so easily have done. And how could the Coles, in their detective novels, have 'ignored the very existence of the social realities with which in life they were so much concerned'?

It is no laughing matter when Mr Symons awards his palm—'the peak of the crime writer's art in the Twentieth Century'—to *The Glass Key*, by Dashiell Hammett. I remembered, thirty years or so ago, reading the first couple of chapters of it before finding something better to do, but, in my conscientious way, went back to check. I found it quite as boring as before, but had forgotten, or not noticed how relentlessly mannered it was, in a way that, this time, recalled some other writer of the period, vividly but at first untraceably. Where else had I come across such an obsessive concern with tiny, unrevelatory physical or facial movements preceding, accompanying, following altogether insignificant remarks, such that everything grew charged with a weight of portentousness hard to sustain by a character the size of Beethoven or St Paul, let alone a faceless churl like Ned Beaumont, the hero? Then I had it—Virginia Woolf, whose novel *The Waves* was published in the same year, 1931. It is true that people get murdered a bit in *The Glass Key*. Not enough, though.

Mr Symons clearly does not see any of that in Hammett's book. What he does see, among other things, is the author's cynicism, his portrayal of the violence and corruption in American life—'the police, of course, are crooked almost to a man.' Of course. He was, as Mr Symons says, probably a communist; could that be an attraction for some readers? Anyhow, there are three and a half pages on Hammett here and not much more than a half on John Franklin Bardin, whose *Devil Take the Blue Tail Fly* is, to my taste, streets ahead of anything in Hammett, the only crime story, in fact, that has ever really frightened me. Mr Symons, too, praises it highly, in ten lines. The trouble with it, from his point of view, must be that it is not up to much when judged on a sociological basis. Nor, it transpires, are Fleming or William Haggard, but John Le Carré and Len Deighton—'a kind of poet of the spy novel'—are. They are realistic (disagreed) where the first two purvey pipe-dreams.

I wish I had room to go on and quarrel with Mr Symons about Raymond Chandler, Patricia Highsmith, Sapper (who gets eight lines), but I must restore the balance a little. The chapters on the early stuff, before Sherlock Holmes, are excellent; and the account of Poe's contribution, in particular, is the best I have seen, critical in the true sense, informative and completely fair. I also join hands with the author over the later work of Dorothy Sayers ('pompous and boring') and S. S. Van Dine's intolerable Philo Vance. The table of differences between the detective story and the crime novel is a model of clarity and succinctness. There are some good odd facts, too; I never knew that the composer George Antheil wrote a couple of crime stories, that

Dylan Thomas wrote a thriller (unpublished) in collaboration with John Davenport, that Konrad Adenauer was a fan of Edgar Wallace and Jean Cocteau of John Creasey. By the way, everyone knows that John F. Kennedy was a James Bond fan, but had you realised that 'the attack on the Bay of Pigs may well have begun in some private Bondian fantasy'? Such, at any rate, is the view of a man at a College of Education (where else?) in a recent letter to the *Guardian* (where else?)

I notice a few surprising omissions. (That funny swishing noise you can hear is me rubbing my hands.) Nothing on Helen MacInnes, nothing on comparative newcomers like Philip Atlee or James Munro. Nothing on Guy Boothby, whose Dr Nikola was still a household name in the 1920s. And nothing on Dornford Yates, who would surely have been just the chap for Mr Symons to get the boot into from his sociological basis. On the very first page of *Blind Corner* (1927), the narrator is sent down from Oxford for 'using some avowed communists as many thought they deserved' and the author shows a typically fascistic affection for dogs. Perhaps, as they say, in the second edition . . .

There seems to be only one error, and it cannot be laid at Mr Symons's door. Until the other week, Melville Davisson Post's Uncle Abner stories were indeed unavailable in Britain, but this has now been rectified. Dating from the 1910s and set in Virginia before the Civil War, the stories offer only intermittent deductive interest, but their feeling for atmosphere, place and period is very marked. Connoisseurs and addicts had better grab a copy.

Spectator, 8 April 1972

Holmlock Shears

Sherlock Holmes and his Creator, by Trevor H. Hall, *Duckworth*
The Last Sherlock Holmes Story, by Michael Dibdin, *Cape*

The Baker Street Higher Criticism (not my phrase, nor my cup of tea), pretends that Holmes and Watson were real people and that for some reason and somehow or other Watson got Conan Doyle to publish the 'records' of Holmes's cases. Since Doyle quite properly didn't bother with immaterial detail, not checking what the weather had been like on a given date and so forth, the Higher Critics have plenty of inconsistencies and other spurious problems to get their teeth into, and they are still clashing away.

Not my cup of tea, as I said, and very likely not a lot of other people's either, but it would be a pity to be put off Trevor H. Hall's book because he sometimes operates like that. Thus he opens his collection with a 'biography' of Dr James Moriarty—not 'Professor' even though Holmes so calls him—and goes on to disparage *The Seven-Per-Cent Solution* (1975) for its incompatibilities with the canon. This bestselling (so they say) novel by Nicholas Meyer, supposedly based on a typescript found in a Hampshire attic and denounced by Mr Hall as a 'forgery', relates how Holmes goes to Vienna so that Freud may cure him of his cocaine addiction, dispel his delusions about harmless old Moriarty, etc.

But at about this point one's interest begins to pick up. Incompatibilities with fiction are one, rather trivial, thing; to be at odds with fact is another. Watson is made to describe Hugo von Hofmannstahl, Richard Strauss's librettist, as a 'grave, middle-aged man' whereas he was actually seventeen at the time (1891); when Holmes's Stradivarius is sent on from London the parcel is opened by an unborn daughter of Freud's; the chronology demands that Holmes and Watson spend at least eight months on the train between Paris and Vienna. To a Higher Critic such gaffes are the penalties of impiety, while others will see them as results of the laziness that goes with pursuing a dull idea.

'Thomas Stearns Eliot and Sherlock Holmes' is an essay title to make the heart quail, but the text is fine. We had noticed that there was a good deal of Moriarty in Macavity but not, I think, how close some of the parallels were, and I for one had no idea that the word 'grimpen' in 'East Coker' derived, plainly, unmistakably, from the Grimpen Mire in *The Hound of the Baskervilles*, nor that a part of the Musgrave ritual reappeared almost unaltered in *Murder in the Cathedral*. After that, things take a turn for the worse again with an account, unwanted by me, of how 'Holmlock Shears' gets on in the adventures of Arsène Lupin by Maurice Leblanc, and with a demonstration that the character of Holmes was based, founded, modelled (whatever those words mean in this context), not on one Wendel Scherer, a German private inquiry agent operating in London in the 1880s, but on Dr Joseph Bell, under whom Doyle had studied at Edinburgh, as we had always known and as he said at length more than once and slightly what of it?

The best and much the longest piece in this short book is about Doyle and spiritualism. It emerges that if some spiritualists are more easily and willingly fooled than others, then Doyle was one of the some; the attribution to him of 'versatile and eager credulity' is extensively borne out. How, Mr Hall asks in effect, could a clever chap like the creator of Holmes fall for such a load of mumbo-jumbo? Well, he fell for it in 1916, a year when plenty of people less compassionate and warm-hearted than he needed to believe that the grave was not the end; he had broken with the Roman Catholicism he had been brought up in; he was too decent a man to suspect others of charlatanry in a matter so serious; he had always been fascinated by the bizarre and obscure, which sounds the likeliest reason of all.

Whatever did it, it got done all right. For the last twelve years of his life (1918–30) almost everything Doyle did was in order to advance the cause of spiritualism. He wrote thirteen books on it, lectured incessantly—for expenses only—and doled out a quarter of a million pounds of his own money. Oh, and from 1921 to 1927 he published in the *Strand Magazine* the stories collected in *The Case-Book of Sherlock Holmes* (1927). These have always seemed to me, and seem to Mr Hall, much below the average of the other four volumes. What with the dates mentioned or implied in the stories. (1896–1907) and other evidence, he convinces me that they were written, or at least drafted, and rejected by their author long before their eventual resurrection and publication—to raise cash for the cause. So the Higher Criticism can have its critical uses.

This is a sensible, well-written and fascinating essay, enough in itself to make the volume necessary to all Holmesians, even mild ones like me who think the tales are merely works of genius; I was going to call it overpriced, but that 'necessary' brings such a judgement into question.

I wish—rather inertly, though—I could say the same for Michael Dibdin's novel. Meyerlike, he has found his manuscript in a box on deposit at Watson's bank. He modifies the Higher Critical assumption so as to make Doyle the author of the canon working from information supplied by Watson. This allows Mr Dibdin to get in a good crack from Holmes about a flagrant implausibility in *A Study in Scarlet*— foisted in by the bungling ACD. It also lets him off the uncomfortable hook of having to write in Doyle's style. Fair enough, or nearly, but a work supposedly written in 1922 by a man supposedly born in the 1850s must not contain modernisms like—I pick three out of a couple of dozen—'minimally' in a non-technical sense, 'massive' meaning only 'extensive' (massive injuries) and, God save the mark, 'hopefully' meaning 'with luck'—this in a letter *from Holmes himself*.

The plot is wrong too: Holmes called in by Lestrade to catch Jack the Ripper. The horror of those real crimes, not at all stinted here, won't blend with the undistressing fictions of the Holmes-Watson-Doyle world. Mr Dibdin is vivid and convincing about the people and places of late-Victorian Whitechapel, but that doesn't help much. Taking one thing with another, I rather hope this is indeed the last Sherlock Holmes story.

New Statesman, 30 June 1978

The Natural Death of Crime

The Best of Winter's Crimes, edited by George Hardinge, Macmillan

The forty-one stories in these two volumes are selected from seventeen anthologies, *Winter's Crimes*, published yearly since 1969. Every story in the original series was specially commissioned, most of them by Lord Hardinge, editor of the present compilation. So this is the result of an impressive double handpicking process. The names, as the jacket says, speak for themselves: Eric Ambler, Agatha Christie, Edmund Crispin, Dick Francis, Patricia Highsmith, P. D. James, Ruth Rendell, Julian Symons and a dozen others no less eminent.

I have enjoyed crime stories for many years, though admittedly I have not been able to find many good new ones of late, and the feelings of eager anticipation with which I opened the first volume may be easily imagined. What I had not imagined at this stage was the speed and irreversibility with which my eyes would glaze over as I read. Frankly, if it had been left to me I should not have cared much to have to throw together an issue of a run-of-the-mill monthly magazine from the material on show here.

As some heavy hand must already have written, no mystery offered in Dame Agatha's work is half as knotty as the high repute of that work. It is a measure of the low general level in these volumes that her story looks almost rather good. It is shoddily written, true, and over-complicated for its length, and flat, and pestered by the presence of Mr Harley Quin, one of those semi-supernatural beings who pass by from time to time and lend slow-witted mortals a helping hand. But at least it has an *idea* in it, about red and blue teacups and colour-blindness and poison, something, however flimsy, for readers to get their teeth into.

Anything like that is thin on the ground elsewhere. Simon Brett has a nice variation on the method of art-theft that involves substituting a fake, and he tells his story engagingly, but not to the point of making me believe it. Michael Z. Lewin is engaging too with his reluctant detective, but the twist here is not ingenious or surprising enough to make up for studied lack of tension. Established masters come off worse. Edmund Crispin, once a fountain of ingenuity, ominously brandishes a ridiculous twenty-word title and seems to have no excuse for telling his tale—about a busy writer who wastes a couple of bothersome visitors in a fit of vexation—beyond being tickled by its opening and closing sentences. Dick Francis ambles round the course at a slow canter. Anthony Price . . .

To cut this lugubrious catalogue: those who do a bit better appeal by taking you back to a more propitious era, Anthony Lejeune with his conniving clubmen, Elizabeth Ferrars with dark deeds among upper-crust villagers. Or, more often, they produce stories whose main focus of interest is not any sort of crime but character or situation or setting, for instance 'inner-city' degradation (Patricia Highsmith), hospital life (James McClure), the growth of an obsession (Miles Tripp). But they still do only a bit better, I'm afraid.

The old-style crime story not only centred on a crime, it had something original or unexpected to go with the crime and justify the attention paid to it, some cunning clue, awful revelation, disastrous mistake, the biter bit, the fraud unmasked, the clever-dick outman-oeuvred—in other words an *idea*, and a new idea at that. The stock of such ideas is doubtless very large, but it is not infinite, and some time over the past twenty years or so there seems to have spread an unexpressed feeling that stock was running out. The same thing, after all, had happened twenty years or so earlier still to that much tighter and more demanding form, the detective story, in which most of the senior and departed writers in this gathering made their reputations.

What about science fiction?—or rather I will advise you that science fiction ran out of ideas about twenty-four years ago. Ghost stories? How long would you like to give spy stories? The prospects for genre fiction as a whole are far from bright. Already a science-fiction story is merely one that mentions space or telepathy in passing or is nothing more than the work of someone who used to write science fiction. Crime writers seem to be moving in a similar direction.

Independent, 18 December 1986

The Art of the Impossible

The Door to Doom, by John Dickson Carr, Hamish Hamilton

The detective novels and stories of John Dickson Carr (1906–77) have received the highest praise without ever becoming either a popular success or a highbrow fad. He is the acknowledged master of that classic rarity, the tale of detection in which detection is seen to take place, the clues really are shared with the reader, and crimes of majestic and multifarious impossibility are shown at last to have been possible after all, if not always very plausible. His villains sometimes get, and (less excusably) are revealed as having banked on, more than their fair share of luck, but he never assists them by coincidence, obscurity or any kind of cheating.

So much is evidently not enough for some. There are those like Julian Symons who give Carr full credit for inventiveness and professionalism but find in him an excessive reliance on formula and a lack of human warmth amounting to an absence of characterisation. Not a few would go further and charge him with disastrous facetiousness on occasion, instancing *The Blind Barber* as a fair idea exemplarily ruined by the notion that drink, anything to do with drink, is funny. Again, at every emotional turn he is likely to plunge into the style of the novelette.

Carr's admirers would not argue with these objections, which for them do not diminish the brilliance of the puzzles or the smouldering menace behind them. What some see as adherence to a prescription appears to others as the following of a ritual or a recurring dream: the approach and escape of the murderer by way of bolted doors and barred shutters, across an expanse of smooth sand or untrodden snow, most typically through a well-lighted place watched by several alert and truthful witnesses who saw nothing. And of course there are no secret passages, hidden trapdoors or concealed compartments any more than there are twin brothers or poisons unknown to science. Sooner or later the reader protests, 'But *nobody* could have done it!'

Impossible crimes were the stock-in-trade of Chesterton in the Father Brown stories. Bodies vanished and living men were snatched up into the air (to all appearance) by magic. Only Father Brown saw the truth, the overlooked possibility—but so often it could not have been seen, or would not have been overlooked, or was not a possibility. In that marvellous and much-echoed story 'The Invisible Man', for instance, one or more of the four sentinels would have been sure to mention the unmysterious intruder. It was Carr's great stroke to make good such perceptible gaps, to devise the contraption that created an apparently perfect illusion of miracle and still held one tiny, out-of-sight weak spot which enabled the detective finally to dismantle the whole elaborate concern. That detective was as likely as not to be the scholarly Dr Gideon Fell, a jovial caricature of G K C in the flesh, unworldly, shrewd and devoted to beer.

If Carr owes something to Chesterton he owes about as much to the kind of stories that began to be written in the 1920s by Agatha Christie among others, those set in the villages and country towns and grand houses of southern England. Coming from the USA to live here in 1933, he made his own characteristic contribution to this sub-genre, laying out his neo-Gothic enigmas among the summerhouses and tennis-courts. He soon developed a feeling for the nuances of local life sometimes denied grander visitors, and his ear for English turns of phrase, though not quite infallible, is unsurpassed by any other foreign-born writer known to me. In their minor way these novels supply some sympathetic insight into the social history of that vanished era.

Carr had already settled on his speciality—the locked-room prob-lem—but not much else; his earlier novels (1930–2) are melodramatic in style, have harrowing bits in them and feature a tiresomely flamboyant French detective, Henri Bencolin. As soon as Carr had produced Dr Fell (*Hag's Nook*, 1933) he was in full control. He wrote so fast there-after that in the following year, presumably to evade charges of over-production, he began publishing under a pseudonym, Carter Dickson, as well as his own name. The Dickson novels naturally display a different detective, the eccentric Sir Henry Merrivale, Bt, who seems to many readers as tiresome as Bencolin in his way, and also out of drawing. H M is a member of the English aristocracy, whom even English people find it hard to understand, and keeps saying things like 'Burn me!' and 'Lor' love a duck!' and referring to the Lord Chief Justice as 'Boko'.

In the dozen years of his heyday Carr/Dickson turned out over thirty novels and some twenty shorter tales of an ingenuity altogether his own. One thinks of *He Wouldn't Kill Patience* (Dickson), in which a perfectly ordinary room is sealed on the inside from the outside; *The Judas Window* (Dickson), with its calm announcement that there is such a homicide-facilitating aperture in most rooms (though my exper-iments indicate that the window, easy enough to open with a screw-driver and a knitting-needle, can only be closed after entering by the door); *The Black Spectacles* (Carr), the most accomplished fusing of the far-fetched and the domestic, unless *The Crooked Hinge* (Carr) is that in a different way. There for once the master's mind can be glimpsed at the moment of inspiration, the foundation-stone of the whole intricate structure identified in the quotation from the opening of the first Father Brown story, 'The Blue Cross', that Carr uses as the epigraph to his final section: 'There was one thing which Flambeau, with all his dex-terity of disguise, could not cover, and that was his singular height. . . .' Carr's murderer can lose six inches in a few minutes, and his method is quite simple, indeed obvious once you have thought of it, only you never would have thought of it—the mark of all the author's best inventions. (The trick of height variation, by the way, is not performable by more than a small minority of persons, and requires a certain apparatus, though this would be on open sale. It is not any form of stilts.)

The Burning Court (Carr, 1937) is many people's favourite and also extraordinary. Yes, but the detective, a non-recurring character, is commonplace; true, the structure demands that he should be common-place, but I still miss Dr Fell. That apart, the enterprise is of irreproach-able quality. As a series of crimes develops, it seems more and more inescapable that they have been done by witchcraft. In due course the investigating detective propounds a solution of the crimes whereby every known fact is naturalistically and convincingly explained. That brings matters to the last couple of pages, of which I will say nothing.

Words like 'gripping' and 'absorbing' should have been allowed to remain in the womb of language until the advent of Carr/Dickson. His reader feels more than the pressure of ordinary suspense or the desire to follow an exciting and puzzling story. There is an almost painful curiosity besides, a looking for deliverance from the incredible. The hero of *The Burning Court* comes across, in the most prosaic way possible, a photograph of a Frenchwoman who according to the caption was guillotined for murder in 1861. 'He was looking at a photograph of his own wife.' End of Chapter One. There must be those who, on reaching that point for the first time, would be able to lay the book aside and go out to a Mahler concert, say, without turning a hair. Not I; I had a hard enough time just now getting my copy back on to its shelf after checking that reference.

By 1948 Carr, never progressive in his outlook, had ceased to like it here and he and his English wife took off for the States. They were back in 1951 after the Tory victory at the election, but things were never to be the same for him again. There may or may not be a link between the traditional detective story and the pre-war world, but there can be no doubt that, after the final departure of that world, Carr showed a loss of energy and imagination in the Dr Fell and H M tales and others with contemporary settings. Nor can it have been a matter of whim that between 1950 and 1972, the year of his last novel, he spent half his time writing historical romances. These have crimes and clues and deductions and many clever moves, but not one is any substitute for, say, *Murder in the Submarine Zone*. To put matters more simply, Carr said about 1955 that he had devised eighty-three solutions to the locked-room problem. Well, the eighty-fourth and eighty-fifth were not going to be as easy to come by as the fourth and fifth. Like his colleagues, like the science-fiction writers of almost the same period, he was coming to the end of his material.

The Door to Doom, though legitimately called that after a—terrible—story included in the volume, should without doubt have been called something else. It consists of uncollected material, most of it from earlier years. There are four Bencolin stories, the first of which demonstrates most expertly and precociously how to get out of a locked room unseen by a dozen close-to witnesses. The last is a barefaced piece of licit misdirection about a murder on a train, rather thrown away in so few pages. Taken together, these four show in their style and presentation the formidable speed with which their twenty-one-year-old author was developing.

There can be few kinds of writing that look colder in print (apart from the text of a rock musical, possibly) than a radio play. A writer like Carr, heavily concerned with situation, setting, physical and other detail, clues and so on is at an added disadvantage, and his characters here do tend to lead off by standing toe to toe gabbling instant information at each other. Nevertheless, these half-dozen scripts from 1942–3 are full of cunning bits and what read very much like passages conceived for radio rather than translated from the page. The best is a brilliant variation on the familiar Paris Exposition story, about the old girl who develops bubonic plague there and is spirited away so thoroughly that, when her daughter returns to their hotel, there is no trace of her. An account of this is hauled into Carr's first scene, but with thirty minutes for everything, what would you do?

This volume also contains a couple of unsuccessful but readable attempts to combine deductive and macabre elements, an entertaining account of English highwaymen from Isaac Atkinson to Dick Turpin, an essay on detective stories that has dated a little over these last thirty-five years, and a splendid remark about Raymond Chandler to the effect that he *might* have been some good if he had ever bothered with 'the fatigue of construction and clues' — middle-aged trendies, take note. There is a useful but too-short biography and bibliography. All in all, as perhaps has already been guessed, general readers will not much concern themselves with the present offering.

What readers will? Those interested in the author and his works, those interested in detective stories and those interested in popular literature in its golden age, 1890–1950; but chiefly, of course, the first-mentioned group. The detective story at its best consists of Sherlock Holmes stories, especially the first three volumes, the Father Brown stories, especially the first two volumes, half a dozen or more novels by Carr/Dickson (*The Hollow Man, The Ten Teacups* and *The Reader is Warned* besides those already mentioned), and some individual volumes and scattered scenes by other hands.

Times Literary Supplement, 5 June 1981

Double-low-tar 7, Licence to Underkill

For Special Services, by John Gardner, Cape

Ian Fleming's last novel, *The Man with the Golden Gun*, appeared in 1965, the year after its author's death. I published *Colonel Sun: a James Bond Adventure* under the pseudonym of Robert Markham in

1968. The next Bond novel, *Licence Renewed*, by John Gardner, did not come along till 1981. Here now is *For Special Services*, by the same author.

Quite likely it ill becomes a man placed as I am to say that, whereas its predecessor was bad enough by any reasonable standard, the present offering is an unrelieved disaster all the way from its aptly forgettable title to the photograph of the author—surely an unflattering likeness—on the back of the jacket. If so that is just my bad luck. On the other hand, perhaps I can claim the privilege of at least a momentary venting of indignation at the disrepute into which this publication brings the name and works of Ian Fleming. Let me get something like that said before I have to start being funny and clever and risk letting the thing escape through underkill.

Over the last dozen years the Bond of the books must have been largely overlaid in the popular mind by the Bond of the films, a comic character with a lot of gadgets and witty remarks at his disposal. The temptation to let this Bond go the same way must have been considerable, but it has been resisted. Only once is he called upon to round off an action sequence with a yobbo-tickling throwaway of the sort that Sean Connery used to be so good at dropping out of the side of his mouth. No ridiculous feats are required of him. His personal armament seems plausible, his car seems capable of neither flight nor underwater locomotion, his cigarettes in the gunmetal case have the three gold rings as always and M calls him 007.

Nobody else does, though. The designation is a pure honorific like Warden of the Cinque Ports; some ruling from Brussels or The Hague has put paid to the pristine Double-0 Section and its licence to kill long ago. Even the cigarettes are low-tar. But these and similar changes would hardly show if he had been allowed to keep some other interests and bits of himself, or find new ones. Does he still drink champagne with scrambled eggs and sausages? Wear a lightweight black-and-white dog-tooth check suit in the country? Do twenty slow press-ups each morning? Read *Country Life*? Ski, play baccarat and golf for high stakes, dive in scuba gear? What happened to that elegant international scene with its grand hotels and yachts? No information.

One thing Bond still does is have girls. There are three in this book, not counting a glimpse of Miss Moneypenny outside M's door. The first is there just for local colour, around at the start, to be dropped as soon as the wheels start turning. She is called Q'ute because she comes from Q Branch. (Q himself is never mentioned, lives only in the films, belongs body and soul to Cubby Broccoli, the producer.) Q'ute is liberated and a champion of feminism. Luckily she only has two lines, but one of these contains a jovial mild obscenity, and a moment later there comes a terrifically subtle reference to the famous moment in the film of *Dr No* when Bond said, 'Something big's come up' in ambiguous circumstances and got the hoped-for laugh from the first audiences, thus, legend says, turning the subsequent films on to their giggly course. When you consider how much the original Bond would have hated these small manifestations of what the world has become since 1960 or so, you might be led to suspect a furtive taking of the piss, but nothing like it occurs again, as if Gardner, not the most self-assured of writers, had repented of his daring.

Bond's second girl has the cacophonous and uncertainly suggestive name of Cedar Leiter—yes, kin to that Felix Leiter of the CIA whom sharks deprived of an arm and half a leg in *Live and Let Die* (1954). Cedar is his daughter, a superfluous and unprofitable device that raises that thorniest of all questions, Bond's age in 1982. Bond keeps his hands off her throughout, perhaps out of scruple but more likely because only a satyromaniac would find her appealing. She is described as short—a deadly word. An attractive girl may be small, tiny, petite, pocket-sized and such, but never short. Poor Cedar has no style of presence, no skills or accessories, no colour, no shape. And it is this wan creature whom Bond instantly accepts as his partner for the whole enterprise. In a Fleming novel—I nearly wrote 'in real life'—Bond would have outrun sound getting away from her. To be accurate, of course, he would have done that even if she had been Pussy Galore or Domino Vitali all over again. *He* knew all about the way women 'hang on to your gun-arm' and 'fog things up with sex and hurt feelings'. But then that was 1953.

Bond scores all right with the third of the present trio, Nena Bismaquer, née Blofeld and the revengeful daughter of his old enemy, a detail meant to be a stunning revelation near the end but you guess it instantly. Nena—let me find the place—Nena looks fantastic and has incredible black eyes. Her voice is low and clear, with a tantalising trace of accent. She wears exceptionally well-cut jeans and has that special poise which combines all the attributes Bond most admires in a woman. When she sees him first she gives him a smile calculated to make even the most misogynistic male buckle at the knees. As she comes closer, he feels a charge, an unmistakable chemistry passing between them. From expressions like these you can estimate the amount of trouble Gardner has taken with the figure of Nena and indeed the general level of his performance. It remains to be said about her that she has a long, slender nose and—by nature, not surgery—only one breast, an arresting combination of defects. Nobody really cares when she gets thrown among the pythons on the bayou. Well, there are pythons on *this* bayou.

There are two other villains round the place about whose villainy no bones are made from the beginning, Nena's husband Markus and his boyfriend Walter Luxor. One is fat and cherubic, the other of corpse-like appearance, but neither exudes a particle of menace or looks for a moment as if he would be any trouble to kill, and Nena casually knocks them off one after the other on a late page. The three had schemed to steal the computer tapes governing America's military space-satellites, having fed drugged ice-cream to the personnel in charge of them. Bond, brainwashed by other drugs into believing himself to be a US general, is at the head of the party of infiltrators, but a third set of drugs, administered by a suddenly renegade Bismaquer, brings him to himself just in time. This sounds, I know, like a renewed and more radical bid to take the piss, but seen in the context of the whole book and its genesis the absurdity, however gross, is contingent, mere blundering.

I have suggested that *For Special Services* has little to do with the Bond films. In one sense this is its misfortune. Those films cover up any old implausibility or inconsistency by piling one outrage on another. You start to say to yourself. 'But he wouldn't—' or 'But they couldn't—' and before you can finish Bond is crossing the sunward side of the planet Mercury in a tropical suit or sinking a Soviet aircraft-carrier with his teeth. Hardly a page in the book would not have gone the smoother for a diversion of this sort. Why, for instance, does the New York gang boss set his hoods on Bond when all he has to do is ask him nicely? Echo answers why. The reader is offered no relief from his bafflement.

What makes Mr Gardner's book so hard to read is not so much its endlessly silly story as its desolateness, its lack of the slightest human interest or warmth. Ian Fleming himself would have conceded that he was not the greatest delineator of character; even so his people have genuine life and substance and many of them both experience and inspire feeling. So far from being 'the man who is only a silhouette' Bond is shown to be fully capable of indignation, compunction, remorse, tenderness and a protective instinct towards defenceless creatures. His girls have a liveliness, a tenacity and sometimes a claim on affection beyond the requirements of formula. Most of the Fleming books also have a more or less flamboyant figure assisting Bond and acting as a foil to him, such as Darko Kerim, the Turkish agent in *From Russia, with Love*, and Enrico Colombo, the virtuous black-marketeer and smuggler in 'Risico'. By a kind of tradition, however, perhaps started by Buchan with Dominick Medina in *The Three Hostages*, the main character-interest in this type of novel attaches to the villain. Mr Big, Hugo Drax, Dr No and their like are persons of some size and power. They are made to seem to exist in their own right, to have been operating since long before Bond crossed their paths, rather than to have been run up on the spot for him to practise on. But then to do anything like that the writer must be genuinely interested in his material.

Times Literary Supplement, 17 September 1982

Shaken, but Not Stirred

James Bond, the Spy Who Loved Me, by Christopher Wood, Cape

Ian Fleming's ninth novel, *The Spy Who Loved Me*, was published in 1962. Except perhaps for one short episode, it is not a spy story but a mildly touching thrillerish romance, recounted in the first person by the 'me' of the title, a nice French-Canadian girl with an unfortunate sexual history and a nasty current predicament in an Adirondacks motel. A kindly, capable English policeman called James Bond turns up just over half-way through and sorts everything out. Some male reviewers, though no female ones, assailed the book as 'unpleasant' and 'pornographic' (we've come a long way in fifteen years) while in fact disliking the naïvely patriotic and anti-Soviet attitudes of author and hero without quite caring to put it that way.

Always sensitive to criticism couched in moral terms, Fleming stipulated that this story of his should never be filmed; the title alone might be used. So it has been. A plot in which the baddies' grand design is burning down the motel for the insurance (admittedly with the heroine thrown in) would in any case hardly have done for a Bond film of the later 1970s: space stations, laser bombs and global takeovers are *de rigueur* here. There is plenty of that sort of thing in *James Bond, the Spy Who Loved Me*, which is the book of the film *The Spy Who Loved Me*, out soon.

Christopher Wood is part-author of the screenplay of this film. His Bond is largely unreconstructed, still drinking shaken dry martinis and still alive in spite of still being unable to draw and fire his Walther PPK in under three-fifths of a second (even FBI men are expected to manage in one-quarter). M has gone soft, allowing his desk-top to be specially prepared for a briefing demonstration and looking at Bond not without affection. The new 'me' is Major Anya Amasova of SMERSH, a sad come-down from her archetype, Corporal Tatiana Romanova in *From Russia, with Love*. And the chief heavy, one Sigmund Stromberg, an insane pelagiophilic ex-undertaker endearingly bent on sparking off the Third World War, lacks the presence of Goldfinger or Mr Big.

Enough of comparisons: Mr Wood has bravely tackled his formidable main task, that of turning a typical late Bond film, which is basically facetious, into a novel after Fleming, which must be basically serious. To this end he has, by my count, left out nine silly gadgets and sixteen silly cracks which were in the script. He has also left out, to my surprise, a marvellous fight on a train that challenges comparison with the one in *From Russia, with Love*. The heavy concerned, a seven-

and-a-half-footer with steel teeth, name of Jaws, is the best thing in both book and film. Mr Wood is not always exact: Bond, out skiing, muses that you 'can lay for a long time in the bottom of a crevasse'— I doubt if even Bond could manage more than a brief lay in such circumstances. But the descriptions are adequate and the action writing excellent.

What nobody could have cut out is the element of second-sight contingency planning (or negligence) that gets by in a film, indeed is very much part of the style of these films, but obtrudes in a book. Your enemy has an explosive motorbike sidecar ready to launch at your car in case he's forgotten to kill you for certain and in secret a few minutes before. In case that misses, he has already aloft a helicopter fitted with jets and canon. Your car is submersible in case you meet such a helicopter while driving on a coast road. In case you submerge your car he has a midget submarine waiting. In case he has you have underwater rocket-launchers.

Later, in his supertanker, which is really a giant submarine-trap, your enemy has a revolving gun-emplacement and four inch armoured shutters with machine-gun slits over his control-room in case the submarine crews he's taken prisoner and forgotten to kill break out of the 'brig' and start trying to take over with spare weapons they find in the magazine, where there's also enough stuff just lying around to build a bomb that'll blast through the armour-plate. Second-sight sportsmanship?

And earlier . . . but forget it. You safely can.

New Statesman, 1 July 1977

Buckets of Blood

The Dracula Scrapbook, edited by Peter Haining, New English Library

What makes some otherwise sensible people enjoy being mildly frightened by tales of witches, werewolves, ghouls and above all vampires, while others are left quite untouched, is still a mystery. Something to do with childhood, no doubt, but that says very little. It may be that the peculiar grip of the vampire legend comes from the fact that the horrid assault is generally made when the victim is alone, in bed and in the dark, the very time at which a child is apt to feel most vulnerable. But the grown-up version of that child ought presumably to stay at home clutching a crucifix when Dracula stalks the local Odeon. I don't; I turn up and love it; I can't think why.

I am certainly one of a large section of the public stretching back, in this country, well over a century, indeed to 1847, when 'Varney the Vampyre; or, The Feast of Blood', was published in penny weekly parts. It was not till 1897 that Bram Stoker's 'Dracula' appeared and, so to speak, swept the pool—nobody I know of has even tried to compete with it at any sort of serious literary level. Modern readers may not find it easy going: the narrative is awkward and the style pedestrian in parts, but there are passages of great impact and, if you like, mythic force. Perhaps it's enough to say that the book has never gone out of print in eighty years.

The latest of the long line of publications to follow on its trail of gore is a most entertaining and very full researched volume called *The Dracula Scrapbook*, edited by Peter Haining (New English Library). We are given the article on VAMPIRE in Chambers' Encyclopaedia which Stoker is known to have consulted, though he took from it not very much; an informative and satisfying detailed piece by Charles Dickens Jnr (son of the novelist) on Vampyres and Ghouls; a very jolly slice of Varney; press reports, including one about vampirism in Rhode Island found among Stoker's papers and significantly dated 1896; some early reviews—not too friendly; and among much else a recent travel brochure describing a 'Dracula Tour' you can go on in Transylvania, now part of Romania.

This tour is in one sense quite genuine, in that you visit places associated with a real man called Dracula, but the brochure makes no bones about his having anything to do with Stoker's character. Prince Vlad Dracula, or Dragkwlya—'son of the dragon' (from an armorial bearing) or 'son of the Devil' according to taste—flourished in the Fifteenth Century as a hammer of the invading Turks. His other nickname, 'the Impaler', referred to his favourite method of knocking off prisoners and those of his own subjects who displeased him. He did drink his victims' blood a bit, but this must have been a public-relations exercise designed to show his remorselessness; it was no sort of vampirism, and quite likely Stoker didn't even know about it. He just used the name and perhaps, to judge by the portraits reproduced in this book, something of the facial appearance.

The origins of the vampire superstition can only be guessed at. On the one side, the wasting effects of TB and (my own tip) anaemia helped on by bad diet might have suggested the workings of some external malignant force. On the other, there is the reported habit whereby criminals and vagrants would live rent-free and out of the public eye in crypts and mausoleums, emerging by night to get food— from burgled larders, not human veins—and returning towards dawn. The behaviour of a certain Countess Báthory in the 1600s would have given any such imaginings a powerful boost. A sadistic lesbian, she was finally convicted of murdering 650 girls whom she tortured with much ingenuity and whose blood she drank and bathed in, supposedly as an elixir of youth. This is the sort of thing that gets vampirism a bad name.

What is nowhere discussed in Mr Haining's otherwise comprehensive album is the origin of the vampire's various powers and limitations: ability to change into a bat (there is no European vampire bat), knack of calling up fog, storm and thunder, absence of shadow and mirror-image, allergy to garlic, inability to cross running water, etc. Nor is any explanation attempted of the attraction of a story that, as soon as you start thinking about it, reveals itself as either silly or revolting. But that's the biggest mystery of the lot.

October 1977

Horror! Absolute Horror!

The Edgar Allan Poe Scrapbook, edited by Peter Haining, New English Library

Some artists are honoured because of what they made possible rather than what they did, which is all right if what they made possible is large enough. We can put up with Monteverdi if he really was needed to produce Beethoven. Perhaps Poe is one of these. Certainly what he did looks rather thin today.

> *Helen, thy beauty is to me*
> *Like those Nicean barks of yore*

that took chaps home o'er a perfumed sea, etc. Nicea, or Nicaea, an inland city of Asia Minor, gave its name for a time in the Thirteenth Century to the remnants of the Eastern Empire. The passenger craft plying in the waters of that neighbourhood were never, as far as I know, renowned for either good looks or efficiency. But not quite any old barks of yore would have done here; wondering why they should be Nicean would have distracted Helen from the suspicion that her face reminded Poe of a lot of broken-down boats.

When the Raven, which also comes from of yore, hops into the poet's study and perches on the bust of Athene over the doorway, he

133

at once and very sensibly asks the bird its name, and we all know what the Raven quoth to that; but most of us forget what follows:

> Much I marvelled this ungainly fowl to
> > hear discourse so plainly,
> Though its answer little meaning — little
> > relevancy bore;
> For we cannot help agreeing that no
> > living human being
> Ever yet was blessed with seeing bird
> > above his chamber door —
> With such name as 'Nevermore',

whereas birds or beasts with such names as Darren or Keith sit on sculptured busts above half the chamber doors in the English-speaking world, and nobody turns a hair. *Could* he have been taking the piss?

> And it was then (oh, I beg you, I entreat you not to call me mad), *then* that — horror! horror! absolute horror! — I realised that I *had entered into the LIVING PRESENCE of . . . DEATH!!!*

Poe never quite wrote that, but it is what his art was often aspiring to the condition of. Before he turned up, there had been plenty of writers who were no good — Herrick, Cowley, Cowper; Poe's distinction is to have been the first who was positively bad.

But then he was also remarkably unamiable as a man. He was 'a very devil when drunk', which he often became; he was a chronic liar; he never had a good word to say of any other writer, living or dead; he treated his friends and benefactors badly; he screwed money out of people; in general he was a monstrous egotist. When we reflect that he was also a poetical prodigy who recited his works in public and died after a drinking-bout at the age of forty, his resemblance to a plumper poet born over a century later and much nearer home becomes striking. There are differences, however. Poe gambled and played the flute, was usually well turned out, could be polite and even charming. One would like to believe the story that in 1827 he set off to fight for Greek independence and got as near to the scene of conflict as St Petersburg (Russia, not Pa, or Fla), but on all grounds it seems unlikely.

Mr Haining's *Scrapbook* is a slight let-down after his companion volume about Dracula, which had more fresh material to offer. Poe's lies about his own career, and the tendency of commentators either to perpetuate them or to spend time refuting them, make some of the earlier pages unprofitable and repetitious: the length of his stay at West Point for instance, whether five months or two years, is not settled here. But there are some revealing essays, even if what is revealed isn't always quite what the writer intended.

Jules Verne admired Poe: he actually finds 'The Murders in the Rue Morgue' convincing. Then, passing quickly over 'The Balloon Hoax' (the source of his own *Eight Weeks in a Balloon*, just published), he chides him for being unscientific in 'Hans Pfaal'—this from the most unscientific science-fiction writer of them all! That term, of course, didn't exist then, nor for long after; Hugo Gernsback, the Luxemburger-American who founded *Amazing Stories* in 1926, is supposed to have coined it after a preliminary boss shot with 'scientifiction' (not, I think, 'scientification' as given in the text). Anyway, whichever it was, Gernsback hailed Poe as the father of it, and a fairish parody by the one of the other is included here. We also have Ellery Queen hailing from the detective-story corner and H. P. Lovecraft, Poe's closest disciple and very nearly as awful as a writer, doing the same for the horror story: 'before Poe,' he explains, 'the bulk of weird writers had worked largely in the dark.'

Fathers of things are in fact disallowed merit but seen as the cause of it in others. *The* cause—even in metaphor, multiple fatherhood ought not to be admitted. This collapses Poe's science-fiction claim at once: he is no more father of it than Bulwer-Lytton, Butler, Stevenson, Rider Haggard and the dozens of others cited in the days when the genre was not reputable. The detective stories are merely stories with a detective in them—they are wild fantasies strung together on pseudo-logic, but that detective admittedly started something, or someone: it was ungrateful, however accurate, of Sherlock Holmes to call Dupin 'a very inferior fellow'. Horror stories? All Poe did there was to mention a few genuinely nasty ideas—premature burial, living corpse, immurement, etc—which set going acres of meritless rubbish. So what he made possible isn't much. And yet he stays in print. Funny, that.

New Statesman, 5 August 1977

Macabre Legacy

The Collected Writings of Ambrose Bierce, with an Introduction by Clifton Fadiman, Picador

Ambrose Bierce (1842–?1914) must be the last writer in English to boast a query in his dates. The fact of his death was reported in 1916, but nobody knows how or why or just when it happened. The place, however, was undisputedly Mexico, where as usual in that era there was enough assorted violence under way to swallow up any number of unaccompanied gringos. Bierce was not forthcoming about what had taken him there, but apart from curiosity, which in his case would have had a morbid edge to it, he might well have gone to report the current disturbances. He had been a journalist most of his life in San Francisco, later in Washington and, in 1872–6, in London, where he was engaged to edit a periodical founded expressly to defend the exiled empress Eugénie against hypothetical newspaper attacks. The project folded, perhaps understandably, and his London years, like his spell as a miner in Deadwood, South Dakota, seem not to have left much mark on him.

Other experiences had. The ninth child of an Ohio farmer, Bierce underwent a log-cabin upbringing and almost no formal schooling, but his father, Marcus Aurelius Bierce, is known to have had a lot of books, which Ambrose presumably read. When he came to write the few dozen short stories he is remembered for, he showed the results of his lack of education, not in stylistic crudity but in its compensating opposite, a tendency to verboseness, elaborateness, almost at times pomposity. In this he recalls his younger contemporary Kipling, also short of schooling though not as grievously, also a journalist to begin with, and similarly determined to show he was no mere journeyman of letters—though in Kipling's case this betrayed itself in showy presentation and structure rather than style.

In 1861 the American Civil War broke out, and the nineteen-year-old Bierce volunteered for the Union forces, enlisting as a drummer-boy with the 9th Indiana Infantry. He served through to the end, was twice severely wounded and was breveted a major for bravery. What he witnessed in those four years most evidently left its mark on him. Although he seems not to have started writing about it till the 1880s, very nearly all his best work reflects his experience as a soldier in that war. (And oddly enough Kipling likewise wrote best about the India he left at the age of twenty-three.)

The very best of Bierce occupies not much more than the first sixty-five-odd out of the 810 pages of the collection under review, what was in fact the first third of his first volume, *In the Midst of Life* (1891), plus a single story with the splendidly Biercean title of 'A Tough Tussle' left over till later in his drawer or his mind. But this small sheaf includes some of the most horrifying and harrowing images of war ever recorded. There is always, I think, a feeling of the macabre somewhere present, witnessing not only to the presence of Poe over the author's shoulder, but also to the truth of the view that the American genius in fiction is for the Gothic. And here Bierce's decadent-patrician style is in effective tension with the awful and bizarre events he recounts.

One of these first stories is known in outline or by repute to thousands who would not recognise Bierce's name, partly because of the worthy though inadequate film made of it some years ago: 'An Occurrence at Owl Creek Bridge'. Its nine pages incorporate an idea that would serve for a whole novel, as William Golding discovered in his *Pincher Martin*. Anyway: the Confederate spy who is to be hanged on the bridge seems to escape at the last possible instant and somehow return home, or nearly. What he meets on the way—the two lines of trees that meet on the horizon, the unfamiliar, malign stars, the whispers in an unknown tongue—is as haunting as anything in this vein I have ever read.

At least two of the other tales deserve to be on the short list for any comprehensive anthology: 'Chickamauga', named after the battle in Georgia in 1863 that saw the fiercest slaughter of the whole war, and, rather outside the Gothic manner, 'Killed at Resaca', with its splendidly withering last line.

Bierce's only assured triumph off the battlefield is in lots of anthologies, but they are anthologies of science fiction, and *Moxon's Master*, while owing something to Poe, inaugurated a whole sub-genre of stories about games-playing automata. Characteristically, Bierce has the man beat the machine, to his cost.

Bierce is also dimly and differently remembered as the author of *The Devil's Dictionary*, to be found here out of chronological order between the two main sets of short stories. The entries in it presumably first saw the light as column-fillers in one or another American newspaper, or at any rate are fit to have done so. Served out in quantity they very soon feed the reader up with their cracker-barrel knowingness: 'diagnosis—a physician's forecast of disease by the patient's pulse and purse . . . vote—the instrument and symbol of a freeman's power to make a fool of himself and a wreck of his country'. The omnidirectional cynic is apparently an acceptable figure in American media punditry to this day, but over here he more or less has to stick to parliamentary notebook stuff.

This book rather lazily reprints an American publication of 1946. Although not complete it has all of Bierce that anyone not a bibliographer would want. Clifton Fadiman's introduction is better than nothing, even if it has too little biographical information and too much of the reach-me-down pessimism to which Bierce himself was prone. The running headlines unhelpfully refer not to the titles of individual stories but merely to the volume in which each supposedly first appeared. And surely there must be a better picture of the author somewhere.

Sunday Telegraph, 15 May 1988

PART THREE
Anthologies

Anthologies

A few years ago I compiled a pair of verse anthologies, *The New Oxford Book of Light Verse* and *The Faber Popular Reciter*. They weren't planned as a pair, of course; the commissions just turned up one after the other. In both cases the remuneration has been adequate, but it can't matter now if I admit I'd have done them for much less. They were irresistible, partly because of the interest of the material in each case, partly because they made a change from novelising, partly for a less obvious reason. Like a lot of writers, at any given moment I would rather be reading than writing—who wouldn't? But my temperament and/or my Nonconformist upbringing make reading illegal during the working day—except in furtherance of work. Nothing beats sitting around with a book on your lap at eleven o'clock in the morning and saying to your conscience, 'What do you mean, slacking? I'm doing a job and getting paid for it.' I'm sure this is the chief reason why people review books for, nearly always, less than they would earn by writing their novel or article for the same number of hours. And also why people agree to judge literary prizes for not very much money. I recently did that for the Arts Council. Who would spend a day reading novels too bad in many cases to deserve publication, let alone a prize, for any of the intrinsic or usual pleasures of reading?

The *Light Verse* was the first of the two I worked on. I began by looking at a great many anthologies—what else? One would naturally expect that a field of this sort would have been well worked over. I was only surprised at how well. The earliest collection of light literature known to me is *Wits' Recreations*, published in 1641. The steady trickle that followed had become a flood by the beginning of the Nineteenth Century. Finding each one seemed too difficult and too dull. I read the complete works of all the poets who in their different ways seemed to me to be light-verse poets, like Praed and Gilbert, poets who had written some light verse, like Chesterton and Auden, poets who might be considered to have written light verse if you looked at them in a certain way, like Betjeman and Larkin, and poets who might turn out to have written the odd bit of light verse if you read their complete works, like Hardy and Hopkins. All this was very productive, also frustrating at times; there was nothing to compare with coming across a single light poem by some monolith of sobriety, like Southey or Masefield, reading through his complete works in search of another, and finding just that one and no more, nothing except doing the same and not finding that one. That experience brought on the nightmare of every anthologist, that somewhere just round the corner but eternally out of reach lies a pile of stuff that would electrify his book, indeed change the world and make him a great man. In my case it would have been limericks by Wordsworth, scandalous lampoons by Shelley, an obscene epic by Coventry Patmore.

Nothing so wonderful revealed itself to me, though I did find a couple of Victorian recitations that had eluded previous inquirers, a marvellous light poet called Godfrey Turner who turned up in a comic paper of that period and nowhere else that I know of (further information welcome), and someone who had so to speak been around all the time without anybody noticing much. This was John Byrom (1692–1763), the mystic, shorthand pioneer and neglected versifier who is represented in a hundred anthologies by a good second-rate epigram, which I may say is higher than most verse epigrams get—you know the one:

> God bless the king, I mean the faith's defender;
> God bless—no harm in blessing—the pretender;
> But who pretender is, and who is king,
> God bless us all—that's quite another thing.

That sent me in search of Byrom's complete works, at any rate his complete poetical works. Some of these turned out to be comic narratives or comic fancies in an easy, jaunty, colloquial, technically-accomplished style that reminded me strongly of another poet I found difficulty in naming. That was because of the other poet's name: Byron, with an N. And it wasn't just Byron, it was the Byron of 'Beppo' and 'Don Juan', incidentally the greatest writer of light verse we have ever seen. I also noticed that Byrom with an M had experimented with verse forms in a way that brought him within a stone's throw of Byron's metre in those two poems, ottava rima. Then I noticed that Byrom's poetical works, having been first printed in 1773, received their second edition in 1814. Byron began work on 'Beppo' in 1818. There is the awkward fact that the second edition appeared in Leeds, not London; but I know what happened: on a visit to the north of England, where his family came from, Byron saw a copy of the Leeds reprint on somebody's shelf and was struck by the coincidence of the name—the two variants have a common origin, of course, meaning, rather piquantly, 'dweller by the cowsheds'. Anyway, that's how Byron came to write 'Beppo'.

I got to the end of my reading. In it, I don't know how consciously, I had been doing what any anthologist might have been expected to do, preparing a selection that should tread some middle path between the demands of the publication and the demands of my own taste, between doing what I thought was expected of me—doubly important in the case of an Oxford Book—and doing what I wanted to do. There was also the matter of what Auden had done in his *Oxford Book of Light Verse* of 1938. Reconciling those three pressures made the task of preparing a text quite good fun in its way.

Auden was not a big problem. His understanding of what light verse was and mine lay so far apart that the matter of overlapping, which obviously might have been serious, didn't arise. But I wasn't sure of that when I set out, and while I didn't want to steer towards his choice I didn't want to steer away from it either, so his book stayed on the shelf till I had finished. I felt vindicated in some way when, after the die was cast, I compared my selections from 'Don Juan' with his and found there wasn't a single stanza in common. Now and then, with other poems, I used his text, rather a different thing. For instance my version of 'She Was Poor but She Was Honest' was based on his, though I incorporated what I thought were some better readings from a nineteenth-century anthology and from my own memory. I also followed the tradition whereby those who transmit a piece of folk poetry are permitted, indeed half expected, to make a small personal contribution.

I settled my chronological limits early on. For me, English poetry in general starts with the Elizabethans: I can't bear all those heavy jollities about 'I cannot eat but little meat/My stomach is nat good.' I decided it would be forgivable and fitting to begin with Shakespeare, and I thought at first of putting in the Pyramus and Thisbe episode from *A Midsummer Night's Dream*, which of course is light verse and of the highest quality, but it proved impossible either to cut out or to leave in the asides and interruptions from Theseus and his party, so I settled for a little song from *The Tempest*, the only one that suited my purpose. Shakespeare's songs as a whole are well enough, but they are not light verse. Well, what is light verse? I didn't have to ask myself that question once while I was collecting material, only when I came to write my Introduction. There I gave several answers, but I wasn't really doing much more than naming the common characteristics of the poems I had already chosen by feel or instinct. Nothing I said was very original, though as far as I know it hadn't been suggested before that there was a connection between the rise of English light verse in the Restoration period and the imposition of French models and rules on English non-light verse by the king and his court, back home after ten years in Paris. In other words, light verse was an English counterblow against the Frenchified manner of Dryden and his mates. It's an interesting thought, though it doesn't tell us much about the reason why the great age of light verse, in both quantity and quality, didn't begin until the time of George IV and didn't end before about 1914.

This brings me back to my chronological limits, or rather allows me to say that since about 1914 light verse has declined in both quantity and quality. Of my thirty-four living contributors only six were under fifty and only one under forty. Can it be that there's a lot of good stuff written by youngsters that I just don't know about? I shouldn't think so, would you? Light verse has declined because non-light verse has collapsed. One way of describing that collapse would be to point out that it would be impossible to parody the work of any poet under — what? Forty? Fifty? Although parody is a favourite mode of the light versifier, the bulk of light verse is clearly not parody of a particular poem or a particular poet, but all light verse is to some degree parody of the whole of non-light verse; the one mocks the other, and when there's nothing to mock . . . After all, what seems so surprising about the decline or disappearance of light verse? That's what's happened to everything else: jazz, serious music, science fiction, the short story, education, cricket . . . But I could go on talking to you in that strain all night.

I had accumulated enough poems to fill a book of twice the pre-scribed bulk, on purpose of course; it's comforting to know you have much more stuff by you than you're going to need. It was in the reduction of this lump to size that I did my final balancing act between my duty and my preferences. I now discovered a second one, between merit and unfamiliarity. The best light poems have been anthologised many times before. Should that be a deterrent? Quiller-Couch had written in his robust way, 'The best remains the best even though a hundred judges have declared it so', adding that he wasn't going to search out the second-rate merely because it happened to be recondite. And yet an editor feels he must add something. That's it: something, not too much. You must grit your teeth and throw out all those pieces that invite the reader not to enjoy a splendid poem he's never seen before, but to say, 'This anthologist fellow has done a lot of work, hasn't he?' I've already mentioned a few poems that I hope were worthwhile discoveries; I was lucky too with some contemporary stuff, a privately-printed satire-parody by Anthony Powell, unpublished or uncollected limericks and pastiches by Robert Conquest, who appears under three pseudonyms.

The reviews were fine on the whole, but there was some niggling. Why no Ogden Nash? Why no Dorothy Parker? they said, sometimes implying that I'd never heard of Ogden Nash or Dorothy Parker, had read nothing that I hadn't included. But why? Because I don't like Ogden Nash or Dorothy Parker. Why so few Americans? Because the Americans, having failed to set up a non-light-verse tradition of their own, aren't often good at light verse. Why no Pope? Why no Burns? Not because they aren't great poets but because they didn't write light verse. Why so little Edward Lear? First, because nearly all the time *he* wasn't writing light verse either. Second, because except for most of one poem, 'How Pleasant to Know', he makes me want to get down on all fours and crawl out of the room. It was D. J. Enright, in the introduction to his recent anthology, *The Oxford Book of Contemporary*

Verse, who put the real answer to such niggling. 'It is common among reviewers of anthologies to complain, often with some justification, "If A and B are in, why are Y and Z out?" . . . Yet if Y and Z are in, neither they nor A or B will get much of a showing.' End of quotation. But I can't end this bit of my talk without mentioning Germaine Greer, who accused me of guess what: sexism. Why only one woman poet? Because I only found one. Ms Greer sadly failed to mention the names of the other sixty-two who would have supplied sexual parity and rescued me from what was presumably tokenism as well as sexism.

My other verse anthology was a much less anxious affair. *The Faber Popular Reciter* was an excellent title supplied by the publisher. The quickest way of describing what sort of book it is is to mention Gray's *Elegy*, 'Ye Mariners of England', 'Lead, Kindly Light', 'Horatius', 'Say Not the Struggle Naught Availeth', and Kipling. No problems of unfamiliarity and discovery here. No poem that wasn't, or hadn't once been, tremendously well-known to people who don't think of themselves as readers of poetry at all was going to get in. My research for the *Light Verse*, end to end, took a year. Ninety-five per cent of the contents of the *Reciter* was in my notebook after a couple of evenings with *The Oxford Dictionary of Quotations*. I discovered incidentally, and not surprisingly, that the kind of popular verse in question stopped being written soon after 1914. It wasn't just that the Great War made it difficult to go on being patriotic and devout in the old way; to write a poem like 'Horatius' you need confidence in your civilisation and its values, and the battle of the Somme put paid to that.

Lecture, given in 1980

Lines from Mr Baker

The Faber Book of English History in Verse, edited by Kenneth Baker, Faber

This anthology, compiled by the present Minister of Education, looks highly educational in one sense, presenting as it does a series of poems that speak of 'great events and great figures' and offer 'a true sense of the narrative flow of our history'. Almost anything that might do that is wanted today.

With commendable obviousness the book takes the reign of each successive monarch and groups poems written either at the time or after—sometimes long after—the events concerned (Kipling on James I, Robert Graves on Nelson's funeral). Surely a good idea. And yet, as soon as one starts on the detail, those initial misgivings about the value of studying history through poetry, one thing by means of another, begin to mount.

The opening section is of course the pre-Norman, before there were any reigns in the national sense, and the first poem is William Cowper's on Boadicea. Dating from the late Eighteenth Century, this is a good second-rate piece, historically interesting for the light it may throw, not on 'the British warrior queen' and her time but on its and Cowper's time, that of 'Rule Britannia!' as song and as idea. Cowper includes a famous and fascinating anachronistic prophecy of an empire encompassing 'regions Caesar never knew'.

So the great events spoken of in this case are not quite what they seem, though Mr Baker's note on the poem does not say so. What it does say is that 'Julius Caesar came, saw and conquered in 55 BC.' Not here he didn't, nor then. As every schoolboy once knew, Caesar uttered that rather flatulent boast eight years later after overcoming Pharnaces, son of Mithridates, and 2,000 miles away in what is now Iran. After that it is no surprise to come upon an epigram of sorts about King Alfred and the burnt cakes. Nothing on Gog and Magog, though.

The pre-Norman gathering also includes a couple of contemporary efforts, Caedmon's Hymn of *circa* AD 670 both in the original Old English and translated, supposedly the first poem in anything that could be called English—I can still remember the sinking of the heart with which I read it in 1941—and a translated extract from 'The Battle of Maldon' omitting the only two good lines. The section closes with Tennyson's pallid little effusion about Lady Godiva—'there are so many sources for this legend that we may assume something like it actually happened', says Mr Baker indulgently. Golly, sir, you are a sport!

I move now across a millennium or so to the penultimate reign, that of King George VI in 1936–52. Inevitably, alas, the choice includes John Pudney writing about Johnny-Head-in-Air in the Battle of Britain ('For Johnny'). This is surely forgotten now, but at the same time and for years afterwards it was the best-known poem of the Second World War, recited in a popular film on the subject. A comparison with Rupert Brooke's sonnet, 'The Soldier', taking it as the best known of the First World War, would have strikingly illustrated the enormous plunge in English literature and culture generally that took place in the intervening thirty-odd years, but Mr Baker's book would have been unrecognisably different if he had started to deal with that kind of historical event.

The only piece here that gets good marks for both history and poetry is an extract, far too short, from Louis MacNeice's *Autumn Journal*. This brings me for one a sharp reminder of what it was like to be around at the time of the Munich Agreement in 1938 while also, I should guess, transmitting something of the experience. Otherwise the poems with a possible score for documentary value are short on the literary kind. Something by A. S. J. Tessimond on England in 1938 gives the old place a fair knocking in familiar lefty terms: 'England of wagecut-sweat-shop-knight . . . half-hearted snob and shamefaced bully', etc. The reason for its inclusion must be to show that such vile creatures as this poet were indeed saying this sort of thing at this period, or perhaps to reassure Mr Baker's pals that he is not the type of Tory who can see only one side of the question.

Over the page we come to part of Auden's poem for 1 September 1939, the date of the German invasion of Poland, written in New York. One little bit of history that cannot be retold too often is that in January that year the poet, having been terrifically active in the struggle against fascism in Europe, had decided that he would be better able to conduct it from the perspective of the far side of the Atlantic. In the circumstances his line about feeling 'uncertain and afraid' must refer to the state of his bowels, since he had clearly forfeited his right to talk about the state of nations, at any rate for the time being.

It may be felt that I have taken too headmasterly a tone towards Mr Baker, and certainly to thumb through the book, being reminded for instance of the merits of Kipling's *Danegeld* (however little it really has to do with Ethelred the Unready), is agreeable enough. It might have been more, though, if his obviously conscientious and much enjoyed reading had unearthed a few worthwhile unknowns, but having finished the book I can remember none.

And he should not have been so happy to include extracts: any decent poems are injured by cutting. However handy the practice may be for the history-monger, it tends towards literary philistinism. I hope I am not being either too harsh or too fanciful if I connect anthologist-Baker, using poems as a means to an end, with education-minister-Baker, to whom knowledge is a tool.

Sunday Telegraph, 17 April 1988

Raising a Smile

The Faber Book of Comic Verse, edited by Michael Roberts with a supplement chosen by Janet Adam Smith, Faber

This book is designed to replace the original Michael Roberts selection of 1942, somewhat revised by his widow, Janet Adam Smith: enlarged too, the publishers claim, but an increase from 340 pages of text to 344 seems not a very large enlargement. The new material is everywhere in slightly paler print than the old, which is at least handy once you have caught on to it, though revision might have corrected a couple of printing errors and avoided introducing new ones. This otherwise well-produced volume, however, including as it does a good deal of copyright material, seems most reasonably priced, and is quite indispensable to anyone interested in the kind of writing it contains.

What kind of verse is comic verse? Any kind that produces a smile, or comes within measurable distance of doing so, though any given example is not required to keep up its smile-production throughout its length, and indeed may deliver a jab to the emotions that is the more poignant for being sprung on the recipient. (This is a characteristic of light art; a famous musical example comes something over two and a half minutes into Rossini's otherwise rather limply jolly 'Silken Ladder' overture.) Anyway, satire of the less malevolent sort is going to qualify, together with parody, pastiche, burlesque, epigram, technical set-pieces like 'An Austrian army awfully arrayed', poems that are simply funny poems, and some nonsense verse—a dodgy category. Well on the far side of dodginess, to me, are bits of awfulness from bad poets or from famous poets on an off-day; embarrassment works against the smile. There are only a few of such in this collection.

Sooner or later the reviewer of an anthology has to start niggling about the inclusions and exclusions, so one might as well get on with it. First, the nonsense-verse problem. After you have written, or read, 'Jabberwocky' where can you go? Not, please God, to 'The Walrus and the Carpenter', which is unmistakably what 'Jabberwocky' is unmistakably not, the product of a nice old bachelor who thinks he knows what clever little children will like. Children are good at noticing things like that, and the implied flattery must often override their natural boredom or distaste at what they are being given: compare Beatrix Potter. Another place not to go is Edward Lear, whose only successful avoidance of meandering whimsy, 'The Owl and the Pussycat', is omitted here. I quite see that the compiler of such a book has to include fat chunks of both Carroll and Lear, and he is to be congratulated on limiting to four his choice of the latter's terrible limericks.

The dozen or more of these by other hands unfortunately constitute an affront to that greatest of comic-verse forms.

The selection of parodies is rather on the short side: Chesterton's entertaining and clever variations on Old King Cole, after Tennyson, Yeats, Browning, Whitman and Swinburne, find no place; so too with Housman's 'Fragment of a Greek Tragedy', though this, perhaps, is *sui generis* not what we usually think of as parody. Calverley is in, with, among other pieces, 'The Cock and the Bull' (a title that has gained force since Victorian times), not only a marvellously funny and irreverent going-over of Browning but also the embodiment of a sharp critical insight. Charles Causley's 'Betjeman, 1984', newly gathered here, is a real discovery, an affectionate pastiche (rather than parody) which is an excellent poem in its own right.

Together with a number of readily forgettable efforts, E. V. Knox's 'Everlasting Percy', for instance, Janet Adam Smith has dropped Owen Seaman's beautifully casual demolition of Alfred Austin, doubtless on the reasoning that nobody remembers Austin any more. Her additions to the anthology are something of a mixed lot. They kick off with Ogden Nash, who has many admirers, I know, but to me is the purest example of that sadly numerous breed, famous American humorous writers who are not funny and not good in any other way either. And I could have done without . . . but enough! Here are Causley, Betjeman himself, Graves, Lawrence Durrell (yes), Anthony Burgess, Gavin Ewart, Peter Porter and, confounding my ignorance, Osbert Lancaster. A man so accomplished and entertaining with the pencil has no right to be just as much at home with the pen. Are there more than the three 'Afternoons with Baedeker' printed here? Where are they?

The great continuing merits of *The Faber Book of Comic Verse* are its inclusiveness, its tracing of an important thread in the rich, variegated tradition of English poetry, and, most practically, its rendering available a large number of pieces not of easy access elsewhere, the work of obscure or anonymous writers. Apart from acknowledged masterpieces like Browning's 'Soliloquy of the Spanish Cloister' or well-known squibs like Tennyson's 'Hendecasyllabics,' both of which acquire an added freshness when come across in an unfamiliar context, the best poem in the book is the anonymous 'Hye Nonny Nonny Noe' of the Seventeenth Century. This is a kind of artificially rusticised pastoral elegy on the death of a certain Mrs Overall, whose beauty was only matched by her fondness for adultery. I know of only one other poem in our language—Rochester's 'Song of a Young Lady to her Ancient Lover'—which so combines the obscene and the affecting.

I owe my information about Mrs Overall to George Orwell, who got it from John Aubrey. In his essay, 'A Good Word for the Vicar of Bray', Orwell makes a couple of comments which may serve to round off this review. One is that the poem in question 'never gets into the anthologies'—which says a little about Orwell, since he was writing four years after the Roberts book first came out. The other comment:

> The suffering which she presumably caused, and the misery and futility in which her own life must have ended, have been transformed [by the poet] into a sort of lingering fragrance like the smell of tobacco-plants on a summer evening.

Presumably? Must have? To my mind, this says quite a lot about Orwell; but it also perfectly describes the effect of a magnificent curiosity of our literature.

Observer, 21 July 1974

Beware the Jabberwock

More Comic and Curious Verse, selected by J. M. Cohen, Penguin

It is a pity in a way that (as can readily be guessed) the 'curious' in the title of this volume bears no relation to *curiosa*. There need be nothing facetious in the speculation whether some of the best light verse of our day might be found among the various unprintable though unpornographic efforts one hears from time to time, but speculation it will remain while no texts are available. However, one would not want, perhaps, to see brought to an end the last poetical genre entirely dependent on oral tradition, and anyway one is not likely to. All that can be said is that a few verses of you-name-it would have done wonders for the anthology under review. Only one poem in it, and that a short one, would so much as wring a snigger from a fourteen-year-old schoolgirl.

But that, of course, is perfectly legitimate: there is more than one kind of light verse. What is depressing is that there often seem to be very few more than one—about one more than one, in fact, if you go by Mr J. M. Cohen's compilation. This second kind can be indicated by devising the ideal occupant of the guest room in which, on an Australian walnut bed-cubby and next to a Swedish glass ashtray, *More Comic and Curious Verse* will find its ideal setting. Precisely what sort of sixtyish, unmarried, pipe-smoking, ex-Sidney-Sussex East-Anglian-benefice-holder will he be? 'Well now, it always seems to me that in the matter of light–verse–writing, or the writing of light verse—give those matches a fair wind, would you, Roger?—we should really hand the palm to that much-maligned gang, the Victorians. Not that I'm saying a word against the Chester-Belloc syndicate, or, er, one or two of the younger people. But, when all's said and done, where could you pick a team to stand up against Calverley, Praed, Leland (the Hans Breitmann merchant, you know), Barham (incidentally I was agreeably tickled to see that nice *Ingoldsby Legends* on your study shelves, Roger), and old Thackeray's stuff too, of course, and Hood, though I suppose he's a bit earlier, but above all there's Carroll and Lear, if they're not impossibly fuddy-duddy these days, eh?' Harriet nudges Roger: 'Oh no, we think Carroll and Lear are absolutely riveting, don't we, darling? That heavenly old Dong and the poor, sweet Yonghy-Bonghy-Bo . . .'

I doubt if it is just the thought of the people who like them which makes me heave very slightly when Carroll and Lear are mentioned. Has anyone for a long time read attentively to the end of 'The Hunting of the Snark' (here given in full)? Does 'The Akond of Swat' deserve to be known so much better than George Lanigan's 'Threnody' on the same theme? Perhaps pure fantasy can never be funny because laughter demands the realistic or at any rate the recognisable. This might explain the superiority of 'The Walrus and the Carpenter', which is a mock-ingenuous satire on hypocrisy as well as whatever else it is, and of 'Hiawatha's Photographing', which is anecdote topped up by some observant parody ('But he opened out the hinges,/Pushed and pulled the joints and hinges'). But a good deal of Victorian whimsy might have been spared from this book in favour of the great, savage, hurtful humour of earlier satire, from *Hudibras* to *The Dunciad*. Too well known? Or is it Sidney Sussex's objection that 'I always think that real humour in the best English tradition—this nut-brown's really alphasplus, Roger—has got something, well, essentially kindly about it'? Like Hood, I suppose, the merry, old sadist.

Altogether it seems that if funny verse is to be funny its writer must have his eyes fixed hard on something else. One might instance the aim of writing verse that is technically good, being careful to distinguish this from the kind of ingenuity that rhymes 'rhinoceros' with 'prepoceros' (name Ogden Nash for century's unwittiest bard). At any rate some extra-comic element is necessary: if not satire or parody, then the amiable vindictivness of a Belloc or the moralistic concern that gives vapidity a cutting edge in Barham's 'Hon. Mr Sucklethumbkin's Story'. Otherwise one gets left with a welter of roguish ballades, clerihews on Diodorus Siculus, translations from the Ish, old men of Darjeeling and two-line poems with titles like 'To a Covetous Woman who Rouged her Cheeks while recovering from the Yellow Jaundice'— as in this collection, which adds a final twist of horror by careless proof-reading. It is bad enough encountering the Yonghy-Bonghy-Bo in any form without being subjected to five different schemes of indention in the first five stanzas. 'I expect you're browned off with hearing this, Roger, but don't think I'm just playing *laudator temporis acti* when I say that some pretty shoddy jobs get done these days.'

Spectator, 5 October 1956

Pobbleboskle Abblesquabs

The Faber Book of Nonsense Verse, edited by Geoffrey Grigson, Faber

The trouble with nonsense is that any fool can write it and any one bit of it is as good or bad or indifferent as any other. In this and much else it resembles modernist 'art', there being no substantial distinction between two piles of bricks or two successions of random noise. Try to arrange the following in order of merit, wit, interest or anything else:

(1) Blake's song beginning 'Fa ra so bo ro/Fa ra bo ra'

(2) Lear's letter beginning 'Thrippsy pillivinx, Inky tinky pobbleboskle abblesquabs?'

(3) Chesterton's song beginning 'O Rowty-owty tiddly-owty/Tiddly-owty tiddly-owty.'

Actually I think I want to hit Lear most, but then he keeps making me feel like that (see below). The interesting thing is that the Chesterton, inexplicably omitted from Mr Grigson's anthology, was not offered by the author in and for itself: it comes from a short story, put into the mouth of a judge in open court very shortly indeed before his retirement. So the passage is the more intelligible because the song is not. But most nonsense has no context beyond the mere co-existence of sense, which is not enough to lend it the autonomy of art.

The above extracts are of course hard-core nonsense. I find such stuff slightly less intolerable than that in which the writer deviates into sense and out of it again fast, constantly offering the reader the cup of reason and then dashing it from his lips:

> There was an old person of Hove,
> Who frequented the depths of a grove;
>   Where he studied his books,

With the wrens and the rooks,
That tranquil old person of Hove.

Lear again: who else? The poem seems to be courting a response like that caressing noise made by soft-hearted old ladies who see a picture of a winsome child or a kitten playing with a ball of wool. The sheer doggedness of his whimsicality is disquieting. How uncomfortable to have been his doctor in the following exchange (there are a number of prose pieces given here):

Hassall irritates me by his damned Thermometers and Barometers. As if I couldn't tell when an East wind cuts me in half in spite of the thermometer by reason of sunshine being ever so high! I told him just now that I had ordered a baked Barometer for dinner, and 2 Thermometers stewed in treacle for supper.

Quick as a flash and witty too.

Lear shares a third of the book with Lewis Carroll, who comes very well out of the comparison. Although the author of the unfunniest poem in the language, 'The Hunting of the Snark' (reprinted in full, all twenty pages of it), he shows elsewhere that he knows how to introduce enough stiffening in the way of argument or purpose to prevent matters from imploding into fatuity.

Thus 'The White Knight's Song' is held together (a near thing though) by the Wordsworthian element, and 'Jabberwocky' is as marvellous as it is partly because it functions as a parody of the heroic ballad with unintelligible words in it. But looking at 'The Walrus and the Carpenter' yet once more suggests that only the well-known parts are much good, that the poem as a whole suffers from the lack of any close reference or analogue and, more generally still, that the nonsense poet is at the same time feather-bedded and severely weakened when it comes to rhyming, feather-bedded because almost any word with the right sound can be made to do, weakened because his best results, like his worst, will seem to come from chance, not art.

Plenty of the other selections seem to approach merit, or adequacy, precisely as they leave the realm of pure nonsense behind. Hood's 'Ode to the Cameleopard' is advisedly absurd, a skit, a burlesque of the 'Pindaric' ode ('Great Anti-climax, hail!'). Lewis Carroll's 'Poeta Fit, non Nascitur' is a good example of a familiar type, the unmalevolent satire on some contemporary poetic fashion, in this case the 'Spasmodic' school of the 1850s.

Mr Grigson, in his note on 'The Cock and the Bull' (Calverley), calls it 'nonsense in the mode of Browning'; well, it is indeed a very funny critical parody of Browning at his most verbose and rambling, but it would miss its mark if it were not toilsomely clear. The general and even the particular drift of Housman's 'Fragment of a Greek Tragedy' is again discoverable, but the extravagances of its style must appear as no more than random monstrosities to anyone unaware that they are literally translated from the weird lingo, strewn with rhetorical figures, in which the Attic dramatists wrote: in that sense all are genuine. The nonsense in Swinburne's take-off of Tennyson . . .

I could go on, but it is more important to make it clear that to wonder what a poem is doing in a particular anthology falls a long way short of questioning its right to appear anywhere. Mr Grigson's criteria, or his application of them, may seem thoroughly questionable, but his taste is not, or not often—I am thinking of that category of the intolerable. He perhaps forgets that the Horatian sentiment quoted in his Introduction, 'It is sweet to talk nonsense in season', says nothing about the sweetness of listening to nonsense. No matter: although the field is pretty well worked over by now, this selection is indispensable. I have to say that Lear buffs will find much unfamiliar material among the familiar. There are some poems written by Lewis Carroll in his early twenties and (I think) never anthologised before, including a splendid Shakespearean duologue; later pieces of his, too. Thomas Hood the Younger earns his place; but among the poets whose work will be new to almost everyone it is Anon who scores.

Mr Grigson has dug wide and deep, coming up no more frequently than is reasonable with a rarity that is nothing but rare. After 1914 the vein peters out rather. Of course it does.

Observer, 18 March 1979

Eighteenth-century Verse

The New Oxford Book of Eighteenth-century Verse, edited by Roger Lonsdale, Oxford University Press

Although it does not say so, this book is designed not merely to succeed but to supersede David Nichol Smith's compilation of 1926, *The Oxford Book of Eighteenth-century Verse*. The present editor sets out to display a more comprehensive and diversified view of the field and, at least as usefully, to rescue for contemporary readers a number of good poets and poems previously unknown to them. He seems to me to have succeeded very well in both these aims.

According to Nichol Smith and others in the Oxford of the 1940s and later, eighteenth-century poetry was by and large what it had been to the Victorians, a matter of Augustans, pre-Romantics (though this label was beginning to become eroded), and Blake and Burns, with some blurring at the edges when it came to 'Eloisa to Abelard' and such, and Swift treated chiefly as a prose-writer. The existence of another range of styles and subject-matter would have had to be inferred from outcroppings in anthologies and in the lesser works of the masters. Now for the first time—that is to say, through the agency of much material never reprinted since its own era—that other range can be fully explored.

A mere list, far from complete, may give some idea of the inclusiveness of the interests pursued there: the kitchen, prostitutes, a non-U wedding, golf, coalmines, street traders, builders, laudanum, homosexuality, a country fair, old soldiers, Whitbread's brewery, what it was like to be a woman, what it was like to be unemployed, what it was like to work on the land. A concern with the underside of things, then? Yes, but the others, from Pope to Crabbe, had gone into that in their own way. Wider social curiosity? Well, yes, but there again . . . More realistic? That dread word compels a pause.

It is not so much that the subjects reflect in some more largely truthful way the life of that time, as that—part of—the writing itself is more direct, more particularising than the established mode. The business of—many of—these poets runs counter to that urged by the philosopher Imlac in Johnson's *Rasselas*: it is that of examining not the species but the individual, of numbering the streaks of the tulip if not of some humbler growth, in such a way as to make an Augustan landscape or townscape and its figures seem remote, even prettified, 'unreal' like the robed and garlanded ones in a classical painting. The cattle in these fields are heifers, calves, oxen, not kine or even a lowing herd. To be sure, general pictures and generalisations are there all right, but they seem led to, arrived at, rather than started with.

All this may sound like an assertion of superiority, but it is not meant as such: for contrast's sake I am putting the best of the one up against the worst of the other. The newly-reprinted poets are no strangers to the faults of all mediocre verse, especially lack of verbal finish—there are hundreds of false rhymes—and uncertainty of tone, so that a pastoral scene can wander in and out of straight description, burlesque and bitter social polemic: not an Augustan vice. And it must be stressed that plenty of the new are merely unknown, often no more than unsuccessful apes of the high style, their chief use to illuminate the greatness of Pope or Gray.

Nevertheless there lingers a preference that may be nothing more than a prejudice. I omitted from the above list of subjects written about the one written about most often and most passionately: marriage. Of all natural magnets for anything that could be called realism or a realistic inclination, marriage is incomparably the most powerful. The order of things ensures that it will mostly be written about from an inside position or, if the writer is young enough, in interested contemplation of one. It cannot be a coincidence that, with some significant exceptions, marriage was a state the incumbent poets seem to have taken every opportunity to avoid. Like work, in the sense of having a job: they worked hard enough at their poems and other writings, of course they did, but how many of them ever worked *for* anyone? Is what we were used to thinking of as eighteenth-century poetry a characteristic product of the unattached self-employed?

That would doubtless be going too far. What we have here is certainly a most readable, most valuable, indeed indispensable collection. As I read it I jotted down the names of a dozen impressive newcomers, in other words, poets unknown to me. On inquiry they turned out to be more widely unknown, not to be found in Nichol Smith by definition, and just as naturally not mentioned (apart from a line and a half on the dramatist Thomas Holcroft) in George Saintsbury's classic, encyclopedic (797 pp) and lastingly influential *Short History of English Literature* of 1898, but less naturally missing (with two exceptions) from Geoffrey Grigson's highly regarded and supposedly revisionist anthology of 1946, *Before the Romantics*. So to most of us, 'newcomers' will seem the right word.

To one of Grigson's exceptions, Mary Leapor, I award the palm. The daughter of a Northamptonshire gardener, dead at twenty-four, she writes here with rare skill, reason and imagination on woman in society, knocking askew any easy line-up of 'new' with 'realist' by doing so in the general manner of Pope, with whom she has no need to fear comparison. George Farewell, with no proper dates, only a *floruit*, is of another persuasion with 'An Adieu to My Landlady' and 'Privy-Love for My Landlady' and, in blank verse, is wonderful and wonderfully detailed on animals. My salutes go to William Woty on tradeswomen, to Captain H—(just that) on marital sex, to John Wright on poverty, to the anonymous naval chaplain who wrote a heroical petition to be allowed to use the officers' bog, and many others.

They—my salutes—obviously go too to the known great and good, all of whom seem to get a fair look-in here: any temptation to foist on us an alternative Cowper or an underground Collins has been resisted. I could have done with some different John Byrom and some more Crabbe, but what of it? This book is a great catch.

The Listener, 6 December 1984

Poets in Mothballs

Everyman's Book of Victorian Verse, edited by J. R. Watson, Dent

According to Prof J. R. Watson, Victorian verse is in a bad way. Sixty years ago, T. S. Eliot formally expelled it from the main tradition of English poetry and put the Metaphysicals there instead. I. A. Richards and F. R. Leavis between them made sure that it never recovered. Now the time has come for someone to rescue the stuff from its present neglect, because it can actually be quite good, a bit patriotic, true, and privileged in outlook, and over-sensitive here and there, but often self-revelatory and, of course, responsive to social cross-currents.

Prof Watson is the kind of friend of Victorian verse from whom some of its other friends might well pray for it to be delivered. Even the task he sets himself is a dubious one. Where is all this neglect going on? As far as I can make out, just in the sort of collegiate bayou that still follows the Eliot line on the primacy of Donne and your old unified sensibility. Elsewhere, I suspect, the Metaphysicals' stocks are low, except for those of Marvell and George Herbert, as always, and the Victorians in the mass have never lost credit or popularity.

Let us agree, though, that there are people, especially among the young, who are indeed ignorant of Victorian verse and might well find it more 'accessible', as the jargon goes, than some of the other kinds of verse they are ignorant of. By its title, Prof Watson's compilation seems to be recommending itself to just such wayfarers. It will serve them ill. In fact I find it hard to imagine the sort of person who would benefit from a perusal of this volume, except possibly those in danger of forgetting that the Victorian period, like other periods but perhaps more than some, produced a great deal of dull verse.

It must have been his interest in social history and such that gave Prof Watson the bad idea of dividing his text into four sections to correspond with four imagined ages of poetry 'as it develops through the century'. The first of these—Early Victorian, 1837-51, get it down—opens with a short, unfamiliar, second-rate piece of Tennyson and then goes into some pious sententiousness by Richard Monckton Milnes, best remembered today for his great collection of pornography. Then, R. S. Hawker, though not the poem of his that everyone used to know, 'And Shall Trelawny Die?' Then, Anne Brontë, William Barnes, E. B. Browning, Hood's 'Miss Kilmansegg'—worthy enough, no doubt, but hardly right for Everyman.

What is right for Everyman now is probably what was right for him long ago, at the time when the general reading public was silently deciding which poems of that period were its favourites, were to form part of its stock of treasured cultural possessions: 'Break, Break, Break' and other short and shortish Tennyson pieces, 'Drake's Drum', a fair amount of Kipling, O'Shaughnessy's 'Ode', large parts of 'Horatius'. These are accessible all right, even today, perhaps too much so for Prof Watson's liking, too apt to distract from social questions. It is in any case a besetting temptation to anthologists to demonstrate their independence of mind by withholding the obvious, however essential. So here we have Henley but not 'Invictus', Francis Thompson but not 'The Kingdom of God', John Davidson but, surprisingly, not 'The Runnable Stag', Alice Meynell but not 'Renouncement' ('I run, I run . . .'), Housman but not '1887' — of course, it is rather patriotic.

Which reminds me: when I first came across that splendidly positive poem in about 1936 I suspected it of being ironical, so alien had anything and everything Victorian become at that stage. My education helped me only slowly to adjust my attitudes. Although I was not as badly taught as Prof Watson, it was years before I stopped being nervously on the alert for pomposities in 'In Memoriam' and complacency in the works of Browning, apologising for Arnold's literariness and keeping altogether clear of Kipling and Newbolt (and, incidentally, trying to admire Hopkins). But in the end it was done.

It was a special strength of Victorian poetry that, along with a measureless hospitality to new or strange verse-forms and an often under-regarded readiness to admit unauthorised, even dangerous subject-matter, there went a very firm set of assumptions about the pre-eminence of technique, the poet's duty to be as lucid as the occasion permitted and the perils of affectation and self-indulgence — and how mercilessly those who stepped out of line were ridiculed and parodied. This helped not only to make the great poets great but the second-rate ones good and the third-rate ones not too bad. Snatch up Coventry Patmore, James Thomson, Philip Bourke Marston, Jean Ingelow and put them down in the Twentieth Century, and where would they be?

Well, we know where they would probably be, sunk in formlessness and egotism like most of our contemporaries, unable to set about developing their talents, unable even to distinguish their accidental moments of relative success. One of the things that stops the Victorians being too accessible to us is their trick of making us look rather shabby.

Observer, 25 April 1982

For the Duration

Poems of the Second World War: The Oasis Selection, Editor-in-chief: Victor Selwyn, Dent

The Oasis Trust was set up in 1976 to collect and publish manuscripts mainly of poetry written by members of the Forces serving in 1939–45. Its beginnings were in wartime Cairo and nearly half the items here, which are grouped not very helpfully by the theatre they refer to, come from the Middle East, North Africa and the Italian and Balkan campaigns. This hardly counts as tendentiousness in view of the amount of fighting we did there and how long it went on.

The selection is unusual for its type in that three-quarters of the 200-odd contributors are represented by only one poem each, an arrangement more to be expected in a schools' anthology, which this resembles in several ways. An obvious one is that most of the poets are in a sense not poets at all, or duration-only poets who went on to do something quite different afterwards. This makes them more truly war poets than some of those normally thought of under this title.

The subject matter ranges widely over the discomforts and deprivations inseparable from service life: drills, assault courses, NCOs, padres, whores, rations, troopships, troop trains, lice, rice, often celebrated in appropriately caustic terms. There is some good straight travel writing, much of it again concerned with less than edifying experiences. Some poems lament the death of a comrade or paint scenes of bloodshed, but in a sombre, sorrowful way, rather than passionately. The note of outrage proclaimed or latent in so many written in 1914–18 is absent here.

This cannot in itself be any kind of weakness, and the contrast is no more than a reflection of manifold historical differences. Nevertheless comparison between the poetries of the two periods is unavoidable and enlightening. It is most recklessly instigated in the very blurb of this volume and followed up in the extensive introduction by Victor Selwyn. He affirms that all the poems here were written if not actually on the spot then while the writer was still on active service, and it is true that this distinction lends the anthology its special flavour and immediacy, but it is the immediacy of a good news dispatch, not in most cases that of a finished poem. To argue, as Selwyn goes on to do, that, because his poets wrote about what they had themselves done or were doing, 'their poetry often goes deeper than that of the First World War' is to distort and undervalue what poets do, poets of any era. When he says that 'we' find Owen and Sassoon condescending in their writing about the troops ('The Chances'? 'Conscripts'?) I at any rate lose sympathy.

But Selwyn has asked for it and he shall get it. If the most famous poem of the First World War is Rupert Brooke's 'Soldier' sonnet, now about as unfashionable as a poem can become but a proper poem all the same, the most famous one of the Second World War is almost certainly John Pudney's 'Johnny Head-In-Air', included here despite not being based on personal experiences or written in the field and—well, let us just say bad enough to go down most effectively in the 1945 film *The Way to the Stars*. The contrast between the two lots is not usually as stark as that but any attempt to turn it the other way round is doomed . . .

Against the First World War team of the three poets already mentioned and Graves, Edmund Blunden, Robert Nichols, Wilfrid Gibson and (some would add) Isaac Rosenberg, the Second World War can put up Roy Fuller, Alan Ross, Keith Douglas, Alun Lewis and Sidney Keyes. However high the merits of the first two, I doubt if either would claim he was writing war poetry in anything like the First World War sense. The other three are unfortunately not around to claim anything. When I look at them today I find them mediocre, thin: Douglas and Keyes egotistical and wilfully singular in not very different ways (though Keyes has a tin ear all his own), Lewis bumblingly decent but soft-centred and humourless. It is not their fault that lack of competition thrust their names forward.

If the poetry of the Second War actually is nowhere near as good as the poetry of the First, might there be a reason? Rather than psychologising about the national mood in the one case and the other I suggest that the falling-off was simply the military department of a falling-off in English poetry as a whole. To take a short cut: the poets of the First World War had reliable models to draw upon—Tennyson, Hardy, Kipling, Housman. The men of the Second World War had among others Hopkins (first published 1918 and all the rage in the Thirties), Eliot, Pound and, most insidious of all, Lawrence. No wonder so many of them, like their civilian contemporaries, took a toss.

But many did not. Forty years of further decline have seen to it that this book is bursting with poems one would be delighted and most surprised to come across in a magazine of today. If there are no first classes there are two or three dozen very good seconds, a great deal of fascinating versified journalism and some nice comic pieces. Room for a few more poems could have been found by dropping some of the eighty pages of editorial matter, which include an account by Spike Milligan, an Oasis trustee, of how or why he wrote his poem but no index of titles or first lines.

Anon does particularly well. He provides the poem that sticks in my head, 'The D-Day Dodgers', an eloquently sarcastic retort to a politician's stupid sneer at those troops who happened to be fighting in other places than Normandy. It evidently goes to the tune of 'Lilli

Marlene', essential information for working out how the lines run but not given here. I remember a similar effort, 'Don't Freeze Us In', sung to another popular tune of the day in Western Europe in the weeks after VE Day, and had hoped to find it in his book, but no, alas. Gone for ever, I dare say.

Observer, 19 May 1985

Poets in Uniform

Not Without Glory: Poets of the Second World War, by Vernon Scannell, Woburn Press

To go by his new book, Mr Vernon Scannell did not in the least enjoy his service as an infantryman in the Second World War. He offers no complaint about its dangers and not much about its physical discomforts, but mentally and morally he seems to have had an altogether frightful time of it. Over thirty years after the event, when most of his contemporaries look back with sentimental affection or at least with tolerance, he is still smarting at the humiliation of being reshaped by the military machine, the mindlessness of the soldier's life, the isolation, the anxiety, the enslavement, the boredom—especially that.

I would not keep on about this if Mr Scannell did not, but he does. Like billy-oh. When I stopped counting he had launched himself on his litany of vexation twenty-one separate times, with 'bored', 'boring', or 'boredom' featured in twelve. His dislike of officers, based on a kind of socialist-pantomime stereotype, is comically undiminished. Nor has he much more time for other ranks. The degree of his understanding of his brothers-in-arms can be gauged from his observation that the racial prejudice among them was 'perilously close' to that of the Nazis.

This singularity of outlook makes him a not always trustworthy witness to the general mood and morale among the uniformed masses from which the poets of the Second World War emerged. His critical sense is similarly imperfect. If a poet beavers away at the humiliation, mindlessness, boredom, etc, good; if not, not so good. So Keith Douglas's work is the poorer for saying nothing about wartime Britain;

Alun Lewis's the richer for being 'representative of the common soldier'; Bernard Gutteridge and F. T. Prince are culpable respectively for
not writing about fighting the Japanese and for being insulated from
hard facts. Alan Ross's 'Night Patrol' is a superficially attractive poem
weakened by its silence about the feelings of the men on the patrol,
but then he soon became an officer you see—'such was his natural
role', the amount of emotion in his verse always having been kept
down to what was 'commensurate with good form'. Can a man who
has written poetry as genuine as Mr Scannell's really think things are
ever as simple as that?

I am afraid I knew he and I were not going to get on as early as the
opening of his second paragraph:

> During the years immediately preceding the First World War
> popular preferences in poetry among the educated middle classes
> in Britain were more misguided than ever before or since. [A
> questionnaire showed] Kipling as the leader with William Watson,
> Robert Bridges and Alfred Noyes as runners-up.

Whereas if people had been properly guided they would have voted
for Hardy, Yeats ('fast approaching his maturity'), Pound and the
imagists. This begs questions of both date and taste, but never mind:
Mr Scannell's effort is to persuade us that the poets of the First World
War were landed with obsolete, inappropriate equipment for rendering
their experiences. Here one wants to suggest that the tension between
style and subject matter in those poets' work is just what gives it its
quality, but must move on again, this time to the author's further
design, which is to reduce the standing of the greatest poet of that
war, Wilfred Owen. So treated, he will tower less embarrassingly
above Douglas, Lewis, Sidney Keyes, *et al.*

'The notion', writes Mr Scannell, 'that from the First World War
came a wealth of fine poetry and from the Second little of any merit
is still extraordinarily widespread even among educated people.' Good!
Because it's true, isn't it? One can take one's choice of reasons: in 1939
there was none of that fruitful incongruity of style and material; in
1939 in place of such as Tennyson, Hardy, Housman and Kipling, the
chief tutelary figure available, as Mr Scannell observes, was Auden; in
1939 it was simply twenty-five years farther on than in 1914, and so
more difficult to write anything well. But to the truth itself there is
convincing testimony in the present book, when Rupert Brooke's
sonnet 'The Soldier' feelingly characterised by Mr Scannell as 'sentimental advertising copy for good English fertiliser', is compared with
a poem by Keith Douglas called 'Simplify Me When I'm Dead'. This
begins:

> *Remember me when I am dead*
> *and simplify me when I'm dead.*

As the processes of earth
strip off the colour and the skin:
take the brown hair and blue eye

and leave me simpler than at birth
when hairless I came howling in
as the moon entered the cold sky . . .

Wherefore should I do this? I have perhaps quoted enough to show off the bald, flavourless diction and short-winded rhythms in a hurry to get nowhere much: a full reading is needed to bring out the emptiness of the piece. It is an egotistical emptiness, with the poet there in person in every thought; Brooke's Soldier quits the stage at the end of the first line. All in all, clean contrary to Mr Scannell's intention, there could be no starker demonstration of what was lost in the quarter-century between these two poems.

I have no more space than inclination to go into Lewis's decent sententiousness, Keyes's accomplished bits of solemn drivelling, or anything by any of the assorted Americans who clutter up the last quarter of the book. I could not see what Mr Roy Fuller was doing in it: he was an established poet when he enlisted and was not specially given to warlike themes even at the time. And he does shame most of the other people rather painfully.

It must be said for Mr Scannell that he is informative, lucid and—on the verse itself—undogmatic, and that his quotations are copious and apt. Nor can he be blamed for the absence (from a book at this price) of photographs, apart from the two on the jacket: a modest amiable one of the author and, in front, a squaddie exuding as much mindlessness and boredom as anybody could desire.

Observer, 2 May 1976

Old Chestnuts

Poetry Please!, Foreword by Charles Causley, Dent

'Poetry Please!' (no comma) is the programme of listeners' requests that goes out every Monday morning on Radio 4 and has been doing so since 1979. Complete with introductory matter by one supposed practising poet or another, each show lasts twelve minutes, or just over a quarter of the weekly time allotted 'Jazz Record Requests' on Radio 3, which is quite good really.

Now, inside a jacket design unfairly evocative of the flooring in hotel cloakrooms, there is published a choice of these choices, a round hundred of the most popular among the more than 3,000 poems some of the public have troubled to write in and ask for.

Some limits are set: only one poem per poet, and the poem is far from necessarily the poet's most often requested. This I boldly deduce from the representation of Blake by 'The Little Black Boy' rather than 'Jerusalem' or 'The Tiger', Kipling by 'The Glory of the Garden' rather than 'If', 'Recessional' and a dozen more, Longfellow by something that is not 'The Slave's Dream', 'The Village Blacksmith', etc. Perhaps editorial feeling was that some poems are well enough known not to need reprinting, too well known not to be within arm's reach of anybody who reads poetry. This cannot be true today.

Blake, Kipling and Longfellow along with, say, Christina Rossetti, Keats and Henley ['Invictus'] unsurprisingly indicate the run of much of this selection, though not by any means all of it. Of course we get a bit of 'Omar', Turner's 'Romance' and Leigh Hunt's 'Abou Ben Adhem', the last a poem much more famous than its author and, the producer of the programme tells me, more often asked for than any other. Less inevitably there are a few poems more famous for their titles than their texts with their authors nowhere: 'The Green Eye of the [? Little] Yellow God' (J. Milton Hayes, 1884–1940)—irreparably and delightfully spoiled for some older folk by Leslie Henson and Fred Emney; 'An Arab's Farewell to his Steed' (Lady Caroline Norton, 1808–77)—historically interesting, as they say; and 'The Gate of the Year'.

This short piece by Minnie Louise Haskins (1875–1957) starts off in prose but breaks into verse towards the end. It owes its eminence entirely to its having been quoted by King George VI in his 1939 Christmas broadcast, which I heard, and very effective the Haskins words were on that occasion, and very terrible they look now. They quite fail to rise to the level of good bad poetry Orwell saw in Clough's 'Say Not the Struggle Naught Availeth' (also to be found here) quoted by Churchill in a broadcast of a year or two later. Together with an anonymous and allegedly traditional 'Indian Prayer', the Haskins is the worst thing in the collection. Yet I know there are people who will think it worth the full price by itself, and it seems hard to judge them sternly when very different people are buying whole books of poems by . . . I decline to continue on the ground that to do so might incriminate me.

As I implied earlier, plenty of this material lies off the beaten track in one direction or another, if not so far that an Edwardian or Georgian taste would strain at it. Nevertheless two leading themes tend to recur in some form or other throughout the book: affection for rural or village life and sights and sounds, often in a *rus in urbe* form, and admiration for unspectacular virtue, kindness in detail, benevolence rather than religious faith (Ben Adhem again) and the inoffensive self-sufficiency epitomised in the title, rather than the vaunting text, of Sir Edward Dyer's 'My Mind to me a Kingdom Is'. Yes, 'Grantchester' has a lot to answer for.

There is a temptation with a book of this provenance to hail (or revile) it as a phenomenon, a marker in the history of taste and then pass on. To do so would be a disservice to potential readers. My copy will go on the anthology shelf for the sake of Hayes and Norton, together with poems previously unknown to me by Jenny Joseph, Eleanor Farjeon and Edna St Vincent Millay, and a couple known but not in stock: Francis Thompson's 'Daisy' for purposes of ridicule ('She gave me tokens three:—A look, a word of her winsome mouth,/And a wild raspberry') and a rousing effort lost to me since my schooldays, 'The Highwayman' by Alfred Noyes.

The latter furnishes as apt a jumping-off point as any for a modest homily to those readers of this newspaper, sadly numerous as I take them to be, to whom the contents of this collection will sound like material for patronage, those at the furthest possible extreme from Haskins fans. I think it would do such persons good to see if they can claim to be quite unmoved by 'The Highwayman' and not stirred at any point by Charles Kingsley's 'Ode to the North-East Wind', whose 'jingoism' and fascist references to fox-hunting they are to do their best to overlook. The similar task of learning to put up with large bits of class and empire in Sir Henry Newbolt's 'He Fell Among Thieves' may be too much for some, leaving them shut out from one of the greatest poems of the last hundred years. These and other such exercises may be rendered easier and more congenial by first looking through the poetry selections in the *Times Literary Supplement* or the *Listener* in an average week.

This marvellous Treasury of Untrendy Verse should be bought by everybody who cares for poetry and will make an ideal present for any youngster who might be interested to learn what poetry is. It is a worthy memorial to the much-missed Brian Patten, the original producer of the radio programme.

Observer, 14 July 1985

A Rueful Shrug at Life

The Young British Poets, edited by Jeremy Robson, Chatto & Windus

Well, pretty young anyway—average age thirty-three or so, which admittedly is quite enviable when you get to my time of life. Their general situation is enviable, too: half of the couple of dozen of them have already collected a prize or an award or a book-club choice, one (I quote from the biographical entries) was the subject of a recent television documentary, another has appeared in relevant anthologies, a third has published translations of *Beowulf*. And then they all have their photographs in this book and again on the front of the jacket! Nothing much of that sort ever came *our* way, I don't mind telling you.

However: Mr Robson's Introduction is short, unpretentious and unpolemical, disavowing any notion of schools or movements, pointing only to his chosen poets' common language and domicile, showing a welcome aversion equally from two complementary heresies now current: the one that wants verse, or non-prose, to become a performing art, even an adjunct of the pop industry, and the one that wants to doodle wordlessly with typewriter or tape-recorder. He goes so far as to suggest, with due caution, that a poet might do well to aim at intelligent rather than stupid readers, and actually says that 'almost all' protest verse is cheap and ephemeral.

A look through the text bears out these heartening declarations; the volume is nowhere near as bad as some might have expected. No shock tactics, no word-salads, no obscenity, no trip-taking, very little mere showmanship or introspection. Instead, there is an overall concern to communicate, to render honestly scenes, events and people—individual people, too, and not only lovers but, to a perhaps surprising degree, fathers, uncles and aunts, children.

What emerges—to generalise—is a poetry of feeling rather than of thought, though not often of feeling that tries to dispense with thought; of suggestion rather than of statement, though, again, it is often coherent and controlled suggestion; and of the particular and personal as opposed to the generic and social. Not all of this is very new: no blame to it that it should not be. More distinctive is a prevailing attitude to experience definable as a non-self-indulgent melancholy, a resignation and regret for what has been lost or is passing, a (to me) sympathetic, if perhaps limited, rueful shrug at life, a feeling of 'Well, that's how it is.' That is indeed how it is, and I am probably being inconsistent or impatient in looking, mostly in vain, for a bit of anger, drive, spite, etc, to season all this acceptance.

The best of these writers, of course, tend to elude generalisation. Hugo Williams catches and fixes a mood with a sharpness that ought to be impossible in what seem at first sight so much like hasty, abbreviated scrawls. Looked at properly, the results drift into focus. Seamus Heaney has keen eyes and half an ear, or one ear, the faculty of rendering natural, external sound through his verse well developed at the expense of the written, internal sound of the verse; he can rumble and slam, but he can't yet make the cadences always fall right. John Fuller shifts with virtuosity between a clear, rather tinkling treble and a bass that sometimes becomes muddied to the point of obscurity. I should like to hear him in the middle register of the keyboard. He nearly gets there in—yes—a *sonnet*.

Nobody else stands out much. It is that sort of collection; indeed, if it is not as bad as I expected, it is also not as good as I feared— hoped, I mean. Its weaknesses are the ordinary endemic weaknesses of contemporary and recent, and less recent, verse. Mood can fall away into anecdote or whim, lumps of experience remain insufficiently moulded, reluctance to draw anything like a moral make a poem read like notes for a poem, if not for a short story or a couple of pages of novel: Mr Williams cannot altogether escape this last charge. And sometimes idiosyncrasy, or the simple withholding of information, is used to fuzz up what would otherwise, one suspects, reveal itself as a rather ordinary, underpopulated snapshot.

What is most widespread and disappointing here is lack of finish, lack of art—the oldest fault in the world. Punctuation becomes more than ever important when the syntax of the verse is jerky or compressed; it is not clever to skimp it. Unrhymed poems must be swept quite clean of accidental rhymes and near-rhymes, and all poems must be gone over with a careful eye on similar word-endings: -tion, -ing, -y. And it really is not, never has been, good enough to go peg-legging on from one row of type to the next with an occasional cock/jack sort of rhyme tossed in if it should happen to come to hand. He who forgoes metre as well as rhyme forgoes memorability too. That doesn't matter at a reading, or bawling; but these, so their editor says, are poets of the printed page.

Some such objections, among others, could be urged against this first stanza of an elegy for Fats Waller:

> *Lighting up, lest all our hearts should break,*
> *His fiftieth cigarette of the day,*
> *Happy with so many notes at his beck*
> *And call, he sits there taking it away,*
> *The maker of immaculate slapstick.*

To happen to know (no footnote is provided) that to 'take it away' is what jazz musicians used to be urged to do when embarking on a solo—equals roughly 'it's all yours'—will not much improve this passage with its compound-fractured third line topped up with the wild

bathos of 'And call' and the clatter of its fifth: not meant as onomato-
poeia, I hope on Waller's behalf. And what was it about that fiftieth
cigarette? And 'lest'? And 'slapstick', immaculate or not, for *his* piano-
playing?

Yes, it has an old look, oddly emphasised by the fact that Waller
died in 1943, when the poet was aged four.

Observer, 13 June 1971

The Red Muse

The Penguin Book of Socialist Verse, edited with an introduction by
Alan Bold, Penguin

I first read of this compilation a couple of years ago (when Mr Bold
was a candidate for the Oxford Poetry Chair) and dismissed the
project as a joke on his part, or else the foisting of a drunken interviewer: 'Alan Bold is now preparing an anthology of socialist verse
from Heine to the present day.' The Heine detail—perfectly accurate,
as it now proves—finished me: surely no one could be preparing a
thing like that with serious hope of publication, even in 1968.

But now we are all two years trendier, two years further from the
time when a mind and an ear were thought indispensable, or at least
valuable, to the poet and to the verse translator; and I had momentarily
forgotten the existence of Penguin Books. Now comes the reality: not
by any means the new number in the Shortest Books in the World
series some people might have expected, but a thumping great volume
of 550 pages, over 300 poems by 130–odd poets whose birthplaces
range from China (Chairman Mao and seven others) to Peru (Javier
Heraud and Cesar Vallejo).

Mr Bold has worked hard, contributing twenty-seven pages of introductory matter, twenty of biographical, two indexes, helpful explanatory footnotes, and several of his own poems and translations. The
book has been most carefully proofread. Its cover reproduces part of
Walter Crane's pictorial allegory, 'The Triumph of Socialism'—the
original, it seems, belongs in what must be indeed a fascinating reposi-
tory of non-bourgeois art, the James Klugman Collection.

In his Introduction, which is temperate in tone, but which excludes the faintest breath of humour or lightness, Mr Bold says that socialism is a word in daily use. It 'connotes progress, equality, protection from corruption, human mastery over initially hostile surroundings'. To some of those living outside the West, I imagine, it connotes, and denotes, other things, and anybody might wonder why, under connotation (4), no poems by colonists and empire-builders have been included here. But I pass over such points, suggesting only that the contention, 'a socialist poem which fulfils poetic criteria is likely to be more powerful, more lasting, than an entirely internal poem', rests on a false antithesis. There are two other such in these opening pages, one between political poetry and poetry deriving only from other poetry, the other between political poetry and experimental poetry. It is the body of the anthology, however, that presumably matters, the socialist poems which must fulfil the editor's poetic criteria.

> The impulse to extend knowledge, to find new ways,
> Penetrates the massive forest of being like a novice,
> And despite some feet struggling through the bushes,
> Man masters the limitations of his laws.

So runs part of Mr Bold's own translation of Emile Verhaereren's (1855–1916) poem, and in itself it goes far to explain the sadly low level of the run of pieces in this collection. Nobody passing it for publication (in particular, possibly, its second line) can be fit to pass any verse for publication. Now, my Chilean Spanish is weak, my Finnish, Korean, Urdu, etc, weaker still, and therefore I cannot pronounce on the merits of the originals of the 250-odd poems here translated. The versions of Yevtushenko look good, but then Milner-Gulland and Levi, and another team that includes Geoffrey Dutton, have been at work there; Vosnesensky seems fine, but his intermediary is W.H. Auden. These are exceptions: most of the translators show a shocking indifference to their authors, and contempt for their work, by turning out an oddly homogeneous series of chopped-up prosaisms that betray a corresponding disrespect for the English language and English verse.

The truth is, I am afraid, that those fine poetic criteria have been pushed clean out of the way by political ones. Any old poem that plays over one or other of the meagre selection of available themes—the West stinks, the poor have a rough time, war is bad, except against Western oppressors, fascists and so on—could and did go in. Any old poem, political in content or not, can go in if it has the right name on it: Mao, Ho, Ché—yes, really—or Auden. What has Auden's 'Musée des Beaux Arts' to do with socialism? Nothing, but he used to be a sort of socialist, and the poem is about suffering, which means it must be a sort of attack on capitalism, and (for those who know the text) you can say if challenged that the people who omitted to rescue Icarus from the sea could have been landlords and bankers. Bung it in—who cares? Few of those who do care, whether for socialism or poetry or both, will still be reading by page 300.

Only about fifty of these poems were first written in English, half of those by British poets, half again, a dozen or so, by Englishmen. To paraphrase Peter Cook, it's a feature of your English life. You get people remarking on it. They say, Hallo, not much socialist poetry getting written round here. Thank God is one of the things I say.

Observer, 4 October 1970

Poetry in the Mirror

Article written when Kingsley Amis stepped down as Editor of the Daily Mirror's *poetry column, which he had launched a year before.*

Who reads poetry nowadays? And what sort of poetry is most read and liked—modern, romantic, classical? Do readers enjoy Tennyson, or do they prefer T. S. Eliot? What do they look for?

I have known the answer to the first question since soon after starting my column: poetry is read by a great many people of all ages and levels of education. The other questions are more difficult. Nobody has ever tried to answer them; inquiries about taste in poetry have always been confined to specialist groups. Until, that is, questionnaire papers on the subject were sent out a few weeks ago to *Daily Mirror* readers who wrote in for them. These readers were asked to award marks out of ten in respect of twenty carefully selected poems printed in the column in January and February. Six hundred and thirty-one completed questionnaires were returned. The results are striking.

The poem scoring the most marks was 'In a Notebook', by James Fenton, who was born in 1949—convincing evidence that people enjoy modern poetry when they find they can respond to it. If not, then not: the four least popular poems were by Dylan Thomas, Sylvia Plath, Ted Hughes (the Poet Laureate) and John Ashbery. Other high scorers were rather more predictable: FitzGerald's 'Omar Khayyam', Shakespeare, Henry Newbolt, Kipling. But surely not all that predictable in 1985: the most recent of those poets was born 120 years ago. Public taste has been slow to change because nothing much has come along to change it. There were less predictable high ratings for Goldsmith and Cowper, lowish ones for Tennyson and Emily Brontë, suggesting again that unfamiliarity is less of a bar to enjoyment than is often supposed.

Since a lot of poems and poets had to be left out of the selected twenty, votes for overall favourites were requested. The clear leader was Thomas Gray's 'Elegy in a Country Churchyard' (completed in 1750). The clear runner-up was Kipling with '18' (1910). Also near the top: Christina Rossetti, John Betjeman, Fenton again (this time in competition with Keats, Tennyson and others), Leigh Hunt (for 'Abou Ben Adhem') Philip Larkin ('Coming').

I also asked for short comments on poetry in general. Some agreement emerged on four linked points:

A poem must first of all be understandable, perhaps with the aid of information about the poet, the period, etc.
Poems read in school were remembered and liked; the schools are important here and are no longer doing their job.
Poetry is for everyone.
'Modern' poetry is disliked in general.

All in all this is a clear enough message, an important one, too. I hope it gets a hearing.

Now I step down unwillingly, because this is the most rewarding job I have ever had. My warm thanks to all the thousands who have written in with information, questions and encouragement.

Daily Mirror, 18 March 1985

From Anon to Eliot

The New Golden Treasury of English Verse, chosen by Edward Leeson, Macmillan

Unlike all its other readers, reviewers of an anthology turn first to the introduction. They are likely to find there some account of what the editor has tried to do, or thinks he has tried to do, and so obtain grounds for a quarrel with him about whether he has actually done it or should have tried to do it or both. This pursued, and their intellectual and academic bona fides established, they can get on with the easier and more congenial exercise of disputing the editor's choice, demanding to know why A is in when B is out.

It does no good to sidestep matters by having no or virtually no introduction at all, Philip Larkin's procedure when compiling *The Oxford Book of Twentieth-Century English Verse*. This really annoys the reviewers, who are thrust into the position of having to work out for themselves whatever may have guided the editor in his choice. They retaliate by conducting the why-A-but-not-B exercise with live ammunition. And always, of course, they suggest that A is there merely to show off the breadth of the editor's reading and imply that the only possible reason for the omission of B is that he has never heard of him.

I hope to avoid some of this. But as you will see I did go first to the introduction, which has the merits of being short and readable. Mr Leeson opens with a respectful account of F. T. Palgrave's original *Golden Treasury*, first published in 1861 and often reprinted more recently with additional poems. It soon becomes clear, however, that this selection has nothing to do with Palgrave's, which was made on entirely different principles. Why, then, suggest that the two are connected, that one is the successor of the other in something more than the mere chronological sense? I think I can guess why.

The text starts with some early stuff (avoided by Palgrave): Anon, Gower, Langland, Chaucer, Lydgate, Henryson, Dunbar, Skelton and Gavin Douglas all in twenty-five pages, which is enough and to spare for me. My spirits sank at the sight of 'Sumer is icumen in', that dull little rigmarole, and stayed low at meeting for the hundredth time the Knight, the Prioress and the relentlessly rumbustious old Wife of Bath. Chaucer is without double the most repellent of our great poets. The difficulties of his text and the other ancients' are aggravated here by the lay-out, with the glosses adjoining the lines of verse instead of being segregated at the foot.

Once we have struggled through these first poems, which I suspect are there as much to justify a claim to comprehensiveness as to delight the reader, matters improve sharply. The brief but sound selection of Sir Thomas Wyatt and the Earl of Surrey reminds us what good poets they are, and being able to compare them readily with their predecessors does reinforce the conventional view that between them they managed to set English poetry on course for nearly four centuries. They were not always, incidentally, as inseparable as they have more lately become: Wyatt is represented in Palgrave but Surrey, whom some will see as the more varied and interesting poet, is absent.

Donne is another such omission, startling until we remember that not much was ever made of him before nearly the end of the Nineteenth Century. Mr Leeson does him proud and as expected gives the Metaphysicals in general much greater coverage than any nineteenth-century anthologist would have done. There are similarly lavish portions of verse in heroic couplets, a measure eschewed by Palgrave, who saw the Eighteenth Century as the age of Gray—in those words. That once prevailing view still carries enough momentum to make it natural for Mr Leeson to include 'The Bard', as well as the 'Elegy'.

If I may particularise for a moment, I think we should start planning to ditch 'The Bard'. 'In all Gray's odes there is a kind of cumbrous splendour which we wish away'—Johnson, who nevertheless thought the 'Elegy' was fine. I wonder how many people have, like me, had about enough of its condescending benevolence, its utter conviction that the mute inglorious Milton is better off in that condition, most of all its sonorous truisms: 'Can storied urn or animated bust Back to its mansion call the fleeting breath?'—no *way*, squire! But neither can we ever hope to ditch the 'Elegy'; as long as there are anthologies, it will be in them.

The Romantics are generously represented here, and on the whole by the right poems, though it is unfair to Byron and his potential readers to give them nothing of 'Don Juan' but 'The Isles of Greece'. The middle, and later Nineteenth Century comes off less well: not enough Tennyson, not enough Christina Rossetti, no FitzGerald at all, despite the prefatorial promise to include: 'important translations'. (And, while we are about it, no Tom Hood, no Sir Walter Scott, no Thomas Campbell, very little Burns.)

One could say that the Twentieth Century comes off better than it deserves, with about the same space devoted to it as to the corresponding period of its predecessor. Anyway, the choice seems mostly fair, and, if the allocation of twenty-five pages to Eliot (one more than Milton and two more than Coleridge) seems a bit extravagant, only people who like Campbell or William Drummond will mind much. When I noticed that there was no Ezra Pound my eyebrows had time to rise in astonished admiration before I realised that of course he was out for being American, not for being no good.

Mr Leeson has compiled a thoroughly serviceable anthology that is not afraid of obvious choices and has enough poems of immediate attractiveness to make it an excellent, initiatory volume. Its best feature is the large number of extracts it includes from long poems, a practice it mysteriously seems to reprehend in its introduction. At the same time, it is unlikely to replace any of the standard anthologies already in existence.

Observer, 18 October 1987

The Sound of Dying Laughter

*The Oxford Book of Humorous Prose: from William Caxton to P. G. Wodehouse —
a Conducted Tour* by Frank Muir, Oxford University Press

An Oxford Book, usually of verse of a particular period or kind,
used to carry its authenticity and authority in its title. But the
last dozen years — after the OUP published my own selection of light
verse, probably — greed or trendiness has changed all that. If they have
not yet brought out the Oxford Book of Bluebottles or of Handbags,
it can only be that they are biding their time.

The appearance on the horizon of the present work, its title and the
name of its compiler, seemed to promise a return to respectability.
But as soon as it arrived on my desk I began to have doubts. The
grinning parson on the cover made me think of the Rev. Sydney
Smith, represented inside and, to my taste, one of the unfunniest
fellows in the world before the advent of Philip Roth, also represented.
And instead of plainly announcing that the volume is 'edited by' someone, cover and title page excitingly promise 'a conducted tour' by that
person.

It is an extended tour, taking up just under 1,200 pages and altogether
weighing in at 1.5 kilograms. This means that the intending reader
would be ill advised to move the book off his or her desk. The thing
is too heavy and big to be held in the hands and falls off or through
the lap. The paperback promises to be unmanageable. Size is easily
obtained with a selection that starts with Caxton in 1477 and roams
slowly all over the English-speaking world before ending up chronol-
ogically with Sue Townsend and Adrian Mole in 1984. As well as
being unwieldy, this bulk is unjustified. The early pieces lend an air
of scholarly completeness, but all they really do is to assure us that the
sort of things we laugh at now — sex, love, dirt, malice — were also
found laughable by a lot of those old guys way back.

And I am afraid that the inclusion of innumerable Americans and
quite enough Canadians, Australians, *et al* testifies less to an editor's
desire to cover all the ground than to a modern publisher's desire to
increase the selling potential of the book in those places. The old OUP
was not daunted by the thought that *The Oxford Book of Medieval
Verse*, for instance, had no overseas contributors.

There are at least three difficulties facing the compiler of any book
of humorous prose of almost any length. All taste must be personal,
but here, more than in serious fiction, say, or drama, it differs sharply
between individuals and groups, so that no reader can fairly expect to
enjoy anything approaching the whole and will be left cold or actively

repelled by large parts. Secondly, humour in prose especially, doubtless because of its intimate dependence on shifting nuances of behaviour and language, fades more quickly and thoroughly than in other literary forms. (Thirdly comes later.)

So, for example, to this elderly Englishman, Somerville and Ross, Dorothy Parker, Sellar and Yeatman of *1066 and All That*, were never, in their notably varied ways, just never funny from the year dot, however hilarious they may seem to others of all ages. As for *The Diary of a Nobody*, still going strong after nearly a century, a benign Providence kept it and me apart till only a few years ago. It went straight to my guts as a rabidly laughter-free performance, all based on a single supposed joke, and that a snobbish one, promising the reader a sneer in every line. Those who are with me so far are invited to follow my example and use *Nobody* as a shibboleth. Get a chap to admit a liking for it and he reveals his 'sense of humour' as a sham, an empty and a vile thing.

I see the fading process at work on the erstwhile-funny writing of Dornford Yates, on Angela Thirkell, James Thurber, A. G. Macdonell (not Macdonnell, as here), whose famous cricket match in *England, Their England* I once thought a feast of laughs and high spirits, but see now as a tissue of blown-up facetiousness and whimsy. (*Can* this just be me?) Sadder still, Stephen Leacock, formerly a hero of mine and of many others, has long bitten the dust. Even his very best story, 'Soaked in Seaweed', not included here, is as dead as a doornail or the Marx Brothers films. Poor Leacock's Canadian upbringing laid him low in the end.

Now for that third difficulty I mentioned as besetting the editor of humour, of a volume of the stuff. Even with its contents sunnily viewed they become too concentrated when packed together, varied in style no doubt but directed to a single end, and mental indigestion soon supervenes. P. G. Wodehouse mentions this danger in introducing his Jeeves Omnibus, and recommends a maximum intake of three stories a day.

Very well, read *The Oxford Book of Humorous Prose* like that, then. But Frank Muir discourages that approach by offering mostly small portions not enough to get one's teeth into. Yes, he has all those pages, but he also has nearly 240 writers, which gives each one an average of five pages a head, including editorial information. Not enough—all right for the work of newspaper columnists, but tricky for fiction, whose effects are cumulative. Paragraphs and bits of scenes pasted together with commentary gives a fatally snippety, stop-go effect.

One of the most damaging cases is the attempt to give an idea of Sir Henry Bashford's unfading masterpiece, *Augustus Carp Esq.* by Himself, in five and a half pages, of which the first one and a bit is introduction. The rest is slivers of text, only two of them stretching to more than a dozen lines, separated by ten pieces of explanation. Apart from travestying and degrading a great comic novel, this meat-cleaver approach encourages the pernicious idea, already widespread enough, that funny writing is just a matter of stringing funny sentences together.

The book has been set out and copy-edited with a remissness the old OUP would never have fallen into. It may be all right to keep deviating from chronological order of contributors so as to put them in national groups, but in that case their dates should be given on the Contents page, not left to be ferreted out from under the end of each piece. And it is Humphry Berkeley not Humphrey, Nathanael West, not Nathaniel, Peter De Vries or DeVries, not de Vries (Dutch, not Latin descent), and the *South Wales Evening Post*, not Daily.

I had high but not unreasonable expectations of this book. On his day, Frank Muir is one of the funniest men around; at the Cheshire Cheese once, he gave the most entertaining after-the-meal speech I have ever heard. He is learned, too, of an inquiring mind and conscientious, and he has worked long and hard here. He could probably have done a successful personal anthology of a couple of dozen comic stories in a standard-sized volume. But this job would have been impossible for anyone.

Sunday Telegraph, 29 April 1990

PART FOUR
Poets

Anglo-Saxon Platitudes

Beowulf: A prose translation, by David Wright, Penguin

Deciding which is the most boring long poem in English is, even given the existence of *Piers Plowman*, by no means an easy task. If the matter is probed, a correlation emerges between a proneness to the more spacious or inflatable poetic forms and an indifference to what has often been considered the prime literary subject, relations between human beings. Thus *The Faerie Queene* and *Paradise Lost*, in their different ways the two most ambitious poems in our language, are also among the most remote and frigid. Despite several valiant and well-argued attempts, made over the last twenty-five years or so, to present these works as constructional or thematic masterpieces, they remain triumphs of dexterity, ultimately sterile demonstrations of magnificence conducted in the units of stanza or blank-verse paragraph. By this argument, Spenser's announcement of his moral purpose and Milton's claim to treat the most important of human events seem vast unconscious ironies when compared with their performance, which in making such themes the objects of mere versifying, however sumptuous, ends by adding frivolity to frigidity. The total of that sum is boredom.

The Old English poem *Beowulf*, though not on the same scale as the works I have mentioned, has the property of seeming to be. It occupies a unique position in both English literature and English studies. Its 3,200–odd lines account for something like one-tenth of the whole corpus of surviving Old English verse, an accident which has had some remarkable results. The poem, after more than a century of peaceful ransacking and discussion by antiquarians and philologists, has comparatively recently attracted some attention as a literary work. This development can be traced back to the foundation of the Oxford English School and the inclusion within it of Old and Middle English studies in the evident hope of causing the syllabus to be, or look, as hard as that of other Schools. *Beowulf* naturally became a star turn of this part of the subject, which undoubtedly has its value, not of course as an adjunct to literary study, but for its own sake. It seems, however, as if a growing nervousness about the propriety of offering purely linguistic teaching to literature students—and within earshot of literary dons—led the language men at Oxford to look for other justification than the perfectly respectable view that English philology is, considered in itself, a fit subject to be studied at a university.

The result was a stealthy upgrading of Old and Middle English texts into a position of alleged aesthetic importance. This manoeuvre had already been carried out on behalf of Chaucer, Langland and Gower, though here, too, the line was strengthened when *Troilus and Criseyde*, that footling rigmarole, emerged as 'a psychological novel'. Certificates of merit were drawn up for other Middle English poems of which it is tempting to say that nobody in full possession of his faculties could enjoy them: *Sir Gawain and the Green Knight, Havelock the Dane, The Owl and the Nightingale*, the last named of which, even in selection, is as powerfully moving as the whole of *The Revolt of Islam*. But it was the Old English stocks, helped on (perhaps in spite of much talk about 'sophisticated culture') by sentimentality about primitiveness, which really soared. *Beowulf*, again naturally, soared highest. After all, the thing was an epic, at least it had some narrative about it, and a hero, and one great single action—well, three actually, the last taking place fifty years after the other two, but that could be got over by discovering an 'essential unity'. *Beowulf* became a great poem—*nem. con.*, for the experts were all in the movement, and what inexpert dissenter could endure to gather ammunition by studying the text?

With this established, there was now a theoretical extrinsic reason for going into all that stuff about the scribes and the transcripts and the relative frequency of the weak form of the adjective used without the article: it was like, or fairly like, getting up the references in *Paradise Lost*. The new situation, however, aggravated instead of lightening the burden of the student, who was henceforth required to think up reasons for admiring the poem as well as remembering why the impossible MS reading *hrærgtrafum* in line 175 is significant. But let this flash of science deceive nobody; I am not, thank heaven, an expert, and the merit I think I can glimpse in two or three Old English poems, and even here and there in *Beowulf* itself, is to that extent faint and far off. If I were an expert, no doubt I should be throwing imputations of greatness around with the best of them. Most scholars are men of foggy aesthetic sense, the ideal audience for their own propaganda; even so, the confidence with which these claims are made is astounding and discreditable. The body of Old English poetry is so meagre, one might have thought, as to defeat inquiry on many points prerequiste to the forming of a literary judgement. A good poem is not just good, but good of its kind; when, as with *Beowulf*, there is only one of the kind in existence, the critic would do well to move cautiously.

Mr David Wright, introducing his prose version of the poem, is ready to affirm that *Beowulf* is great—a point, he adds quaintly, 'until recently often overlooked'. And why, or how, or in what is it great? The answer, for Mr Wright, lies in its theme: 'it is about how the human being ought to behave when he is without hope.' Is this true of any but the closing stages? Alternatively, the theme is 'the conflict of good and evil.' Is it? Granted that it is, this conflict remains one between a man and three assorted monsters, and whatever weight of symbolism we may attach to these it is hard to see the core of the poem as existing in any but non-human terms. *Beowulf*, in fact, exhibits to the full that endemic weakness of the longer poem referred to earlier: poverty of human interest. This is perhaps debatable, but Mr Wright's emphasis on theme has other aspects which connect with his emphasis on matters of construction and narrative—odd focuses of interest, incidentally, in a work so episodic, so slow-footed and so sparing of incident. His view of the poem has helped to incapacitate the translator.

Such virtues as *Beowulf* has lie in its style. This is not to say that they lie in the mere use of the compound words and periphrastic variations which are the common coin of Old English poetry, though something of the strong characteristic flavour of these ought to be aimed at in any version. My point is that the possible strength of the poem resides in what it means and not in just any old account of the events narrated. Mr Wright does not see this. His translation, on a student academic level, is accurate enough and does echo something of the poem. But the naïve concept of style as an ornament, lurking at the back of his mind, has led him to write far too often with the flat briskness, the explanatory paraphrasing and the all too neat syntactical subordination of a goodish sixth-former doing an unseen. One small example must suffice. The poet writes:

> *Oft Scyld Scefing . . .*
> *monegum mægthum meodosetla ofteah*

(literally, Often Scyld Scefing deprived many tribes of their mead-seats) which Mr Wright renders as 'Scyld Scefing . . . used often to bring nations into subjection,' thus missing altogether the note of concrete deprivation conveyed by the reference to the banqueting hall, the source and scene of the brighter side of warriors' lives. The darker side, the brooding sense occasionally caught by the poet that all the ways of our life can suddenly dissolve into a nightmare of destruction, Mr Wright misses too. He adds to his misconceptions a lack of poetic skill and poetic feeling.

Spectator, 5 April 1957

Dark Fears in Wimpole Street

Robert Browning: A Life within Life, by Donald Thomas, Weidenfeld & Nicolson

Edward Moulton Barrett, who tried so hard to keep his daughter Elizabeth from marrying Robert Browning, has not endeared himself to posterity. For many people he survives entirely through the genius of Charles Laughton, who played him in the 1934 film of the Broadway stage success, *The Barretts of Wimpole Street*. Laughton's Barrett was a fairly straightforward domestic tyrant, possessive and dog-in-the-mangerish, with a touch of submerged incestuous feeling thrown in. Something like that can be made into an entirely satisfactory reason for the old boy's perfervid opposition. A little lateral thinking, however, supplies another motive, one he could never divulge or allow to be inferred.

The Barretts were a family of West Indian slave-owners, so much so that Elizabeth was the first of them for some generations not to have been born there. Her colouring was dark. (More than that, her complexion was distinctly olive or sallow, causing Browning to give her the pet-name of 'his little Portuguese', which by a private joke was used to mislead the world in the title of her sequence of love poems to him, 'Sonnets from the Portuguese'.) Mr Barrett would very quickly have learnt that the Brownings also had connections with the West Indies, the poet's paternal grandmother having come from a family with extensive plantations in the island of St Kitts. And he, Robert Browning, was also of dark colouring, in his case to such a degree that there were rumours in London of Creole, ie, part-Negro, ancestry.

Pity Mr Barrett! Nobody could be absolutely sure about any Caribbean pedigree. Then, the laws of genetics were even more deeply wrapped in ignorance than now. Who, placed as he was, would not have been thoroughly dismayed at the thought of a 'throwback' and a black grandchild? You and I know that, whatever their descent, Browning and Elizabeth could not have produced offspring darker than whichever was the darker of them, but Mr Barrett had not been told so, nor might he have believed it if he had. One hardly dares imagine his feelings the day at the Wimpole Street house when he encountered the six-year-old Robert Wiedemann Barrett Browning and found him all blue eyes and golden curls.

Donald Thomas's new biography of Browning unfortunately omits any reference to my theory of what animated Edward Moulton Barrett. All the contributory facts cited above are present in it, however, except the passage in brackets about the Portuguese. For years I had taken this for an established and characteristic detail of Browning biography, and was quite dashed to find Mr Thomas talking about a real Portuguese, the sixteenth-century Luis de Camoëns, as the feigned source of Elizabeth's poems. The joke could be true as well and would suit the style of the relationship the two had, which was full of humour, not all of it honeyed.

One way or another, Browning was an exception in an era full of exceptions. Circumstance determined some of this. Like Robert Graves he came in for a certain amount of earnest Germanic Nonconformism from his mother's side of the family. He grew up in Camberwell, still in those pre-Victorian days a rural spot but with nature put in its place, London in full view across the fields and Dulwich art gallery down the road. In those days too (and until 1854) Oxford and Cambridge excluded all Dissenters, and Browning became almost the only known Englishman of his time not to go to either place.

The place he did notoriously go to was Italy. Byron and plenty of others had been before him, but Browning went there in a new way, in a spirit of eager, devout inquiry, like an American. This approach influenced both the strengths and the weaknesses, as examiners call them, of his splendidly readable Italian poems. He knew a lot, but was sometimes too much aware of the fact.

Browning loved Florence and Rome, and the climate suited Elizabeth's frail health, but he pined too for the dinner-tables and drawing-rooms of London, and lost no time in returning there after her death in 1861. Yet, though strenuously involved in the fashionable-cultural life of his time, he seemed to remain distanced from it, a spiritual American even at home; Mr Thomas is very good on what Browning made of his Victorian contemporaries and they of him. The famous remark of one of them, 'I like Browning, he isn't at all like a damned literary man', comes in appositely here. He was apt in youth to be mistaken for a racing man or a dandy, in maturity for a vulgarian, loud-voiced, often coarse in his language and sometimes an unstoppable talker. Throughout his life he was tough, energetic and self-contained.

More than any of his contemporaries Browning turned away from the narrow, remote interests and pure styles of the first English Romantics. As well as new subject matter he developed new interests for poetry, new things for it to talk about and ways of talking about them. These interests sometimes take him into territory that looks at first more like a novelist's than a poet's, not only as regards theme but as regards the handling of physical detail. It is this among other things that makes poems like 'The Englishman in Italy' and 'Garden Fancies' so fascinating, not to speak of 'Soliloquy of the Spanish Cloister'.

Browning's most memorable invention was none of this, but the poetic language that makes most of his work instantly recognisable, lively, compressed, colloquial and yet like no speech that was ever spoken. When I hear it in my head I find it not impossible to believe in that wild notion of an exotic strain in his make-up. One would like in any case to claim a place for him as the English member of a distinguished trio alongside Dumas (black grandmother) and Pushkin (black great-grandfather), contemporaries of his who surely have more in common with him than the mere matter of dates.

Despite its silly subtitle, this is a good straightforward biography, pleasingly informative about its subject's career and the society in which he moved. It could have done with a few photographs and a table of principal dates.

Observer, 29 August 1982

On Tennyson

It is not very much longer than ten years ago that Tennyson's poetry began to regain the kind of serious attention and acclaim it had begun to lose a century earlier, when the poet still had thirty years to live: surely a record length of time for any comparatively modern artist to spend in the wilderness. T. S. Eliot published in 1936 an eloquent defence that remains the best short account of Tennyson's genius; W. H. Auden brought out a selection of the verse, with some helpful and provocative introductory remarks, in 1946; but these, along with a few lesser names, made little lasting impression on what had become a massive prejudice.

There are perhaps three main reasons for this history of neglect—a neglect at or near the top, we should notice, rather than among the wider poetry-reading public, who have always seen to it that Tennyson's works remained very much in print. The first reason is that, from a distance, he can look just like an incarnation of Victorianism, pompous, unthinkingly patriotic, Poet Laureate (a crime by definition), the dutiful voice of the hierarchical system of that day, the bedside reading of Prince Albert and the Queen herself. None of Tennyson's best poems are vulnerable to this sort of charge, but it was the basis of a large and lasting reaction against him among people to whom the kind of society he seemed to stand for had produced the First World War and its aftermath.

Secondly, and more recently, his verse has turned out to be resistant to modern techniques of literary criticism. It holds no interesting ambiguities, intentional or unintentional; there are no puzzles, no 'levels of meaning' within it, it just is. All the critic can say about most of it comes down to, 'Look at this. Good (or bad), isn't it?' This is as much as a great deal of what passes for criticism is really saying, but with other poets—Donne, for instance, that notable purveyor of mere complication—it is easier to seem to be saying more. Tennyson eludes such attempts. His symbolism, moreover, is plain and transparent, and, as Auden remarked, 'no other poetry is easier, and less illuminating, to psycho-analyse'.

The third factor that has told against Tennyson's repute is more difficult to dismiss, if not impossible. A reading of his early verse, that written by the time he was twenty-one, say, shows him to have been possessed of stupendous inborn gifts, a child of the Muses who makes the Keats of that age look all fingers and thumbs. We should have to go back to Milton (whom Tennyson greatly admired) to find an English poet of comparable natural endowment, or, since Milton's early efforts smell of ink as well as inspiration, it might be more instructive to go outside literature altogether and invoke the youthful Mozart. Like the composer, Tennyson grew into and remained a quite uninteresting man, though, again like him, he was a very interesting phenomenon: a genius. But Mozart made only the most temporary compromises with the demands of his gift, whereas Tennyson deliberately threw his away, to become in time a figure uncomfortably close to that pensioner of the establishment taken by many in the past to be all he had ever been. So, at any rate, I would argue, as the latest of a thin but unbroken line of commentators beginning a good hundred years ago. The story really starts, however, earlier still, when Tennyson's first books appeared in the 1820s and early 1830s.

Their critical reception was largely hostile, and the nature of that hostility is significant. Some of it was directed at supposed technical flaws: Coleridge recommended a course in versification, a piece of advice that seems little short of absurd today. What was bothering him and others might have been the spectacle of so young a newcomer (two complete volumes and a large contribution to a third by the age of twenty-three) not only very much at home in any established poetic form, but able to invent fresh ones in which he moved with equal facility. This line of attack we can discount, though Tennyson did not, as we shall see. Far more telling were accusations of a lack of intellectual and moral content. Here, to all appearance, was another Romantic poet, and England had had, or should have had, enough of them.

It was clearly felt, if never openly stated, that a new and potentially great poet—even the sternest detractors saw that—must not be self-indulgent and perhaps sensual like Keats, nor an irresponsible atheist like Shelley, nor a republican and a debauchee like Byron. (All three, having died in the half-dozen years before Tennyson's first appearance, were fresh in the public mind.) No, such a man must be staid and pious like Southey or Wordsworth—respectively the current and succeeding Poets Laureate. Victorian in the grimmer sense before Victoria was on the throne, such critics condemned in Tennyson an 'unbounded indulgence in the mere luxuries of poetry', a failure to 'instruct', an ignorance of the vital fact that 'true poetry must benefit humanity'. John Stuart Mill, in an otherwise friendly article, told Tennyson that he must cultivate philosophy as well as poetry; a few years later, Monckton Milnes informed him that 'the function of the poet in this day of ours is to teach still more than he delights'—this from a man who was to become notorious as the owner of the largest collection of pornography in Victorian London.

Tennyson was sensitive to criticism. Nearly all artists are, major and minimal alike; Shakespeare surely was not, but we should run a mile rather than generalise from him. Milton never forgave a slight; Virgil, another hero of Tennyson's, would certainly have behaved in the same way, had the practice of reviewing flourished in classical Rome; it was impossible to converse with Beethoven except on the basis that he was the greatest composer who had ever lived. None of these three, however, would have swerved an inch from the course he had set himself if God had given him a hostile notice. Tennyson was made of less stern stuff. He minded adverse criticism in a double sense: he was stung by it, and he took notice of it. He introduced technical revisions, arguably for the better, in the directions suggested to him; he also, and disastrously, went against his nature by abandoning the luxuries of poetry, cultivating philosophy, and trying to teach more than he delighted. To give Pope's line a different bearing from that intended, he progressively 'stooped to truth, and moralised his song'.

One man really understood and appreciated the true nature of Tennyson's gift: Arthur H. Hallam, whom he met at Cambridge in 1829 and who soon became the closest friend of his life. In an article which would have been outstandingly acute whoever had written it, let alone somebody of twenty, Hallam drew a distinction between the poetry of reflection, exemplified in Wordsworth, and the poetry of sensation (or feeling), as seen in the work of Keats, Shelley and Tennyson. Hallam argued a preference for the second category on the grounds of its superior immediacy and beauty; we need not agree with him on that point in order to see at once that he had placed Tennyson where he belonged. Of the two friends, Hallam, though a year and a half the younger, was the dominating partner and certainly the more intelligent. Had he remained on the scene, he might well have lent Tennyson the support to continue along the path of lyrical expression for which nature had designed him.* But all too soon Hallam, away

---

* 'Whenever the mind of the artist suffers itself to be occupied, during its periods of creation, by any other predominant motive than the desire of beauty, the result is false in art'—not Oscar Wilde, not Walter Pater, not D. G. Rossetti, but Hallam in the article referred to. That he was able to forecast so early the direction English poetry was to take in the second half of the century is an impressive feat. He was also, however, making a terribly accurate unconscious prophecy about what was going to happen to the poetry of Tennyson.

on a trip to Vienna, was dead of a brain haemorrhage at the age of twenty-two.

The loss of Hallam was, obviously enough, the crucial event in Tennyson's emotional life, and its reverberations can be felt in his work until the end. It is equally plain that he had loved the dead man, often falling into the language of love in writing about him; but we had better be clear in our mind that, as certainly as can be in such matters, there was nothing physical in their relationship. The importance to us of that loss is that it made Tennyson into a great poet, in one sense despite himself and his attempts to alter the direction of his development, in another sense inevitably. For his whole poetic nature was made to express loss and the feelings that lie close to it: despondency, ennui, nostalgia, loneliness, despair and the desire for reconciliation and resignation.

So much is clear from poems of his that antedate Hallam's death, notably 'Mariana' and 'Œnone', while, in a less specific way, 'A spirit haunts' reads like a forecast of grief. 'Mariana' is a very easy poem to like, and, what is rarer, to like for the right reasons. It embodies to perfection that characteristically Tennysonian power which generations of critics have tried to define, but none more successfully than the unknown contributor to *Tait's Edinburgh Magazine* for August 1842, who praised Tennyson's 'power of making the picturesque delineation of external nature illustrate the mood of mind portrayed'. (At that time, 'picturesque' retained its original meaning of 'pictorial, in the style of a picture' and had not yet degenerated into a vague journalistic synonym for 'odd' or 'intriguing'. 'Sharply visual' would be a rough modern equivalent—but nobody could miss the tremendous aural effects of 'Mariana'.)

'Œnone' embodies the same theme in a totally different style. The tune, too, is different: blank verse that sounds as if nobody else had ever used the form, an achievement in itself for a young poet who had Milton looking over his shoulder and Wordsworth, so to speak, at the next writing-table. Here, twice at least, Tennyson brings the inner and outer worlds, mind and nature, to the point of coalescence. Œnone's memory of Paris's kisses can hardly be distinguished from the present reality, in her eyes and ears, of the whirling river, and, a little later, the loudness of the stream and the trembling of the stars are not only things experienced but also the prelude or accompaniment to a hysterical swoon.

'The Lotus Eaters' deals in similar ways with another aspect of melancholy, definable as languor, about which it manages to become energetic, ending indeed in a kind of rocket-burst of lassitude and capitulation. 'Ulysses', Tennyson's first important poem after the news of Hallam's death reached him, is a much less straightforward affair. It looks like a downright, almost artless call to action, a pre-Victorian exaltation of the heroic virtues and correspondingly an attack on loafing. Tennyson himself said, 'it was written under the sense of loss and that all had gone by, but that still life must be fought out to the end'. Well, he should know. Yet all sorts of critics have felt that the piece is not quite doing what it claims to be doing. As early as 1855, the historian Goldwin Smith wrote of 'the Homeric Ulysses, the man of purpose and action' shown by Tennyson as roaming aimlessly, 'merely to relieve his ennui, and dragging his companions with him. We should rather say, he intended to roam, but stands for ever a listless and melancholy figure on the shore.'

Smith connected Ulysses's deficiency of genuine vigour with what he saw as Tennyson's overall inability to paint 'the active life with real zest'—a sound observation, if not as damaging as Smith evidently thought. Another view, well argued by E. J. Chiasson, is that the poem is doing the exact opposite of what it seems to claim to be doing, and is actually an attack on irresponsibility,★ like 'The Lotus Eaters'. At least two points strongly support Chiasson's reading: the hypocrisy which leads Ulysses to praise Telemachus for qualities which, as the opening lines show, he himself has no time for; and the 'jovial agnosticism' with which he considers the expedition's eventual fate—it may be this, it may be that, and the verse at that stage does seem to carry a bored shrug of the shoulders. What weighs against this interpretation, apart from Tennyson's statement, is the squaring of the shoulders that at once follows the shrug and ends the poem on a note of conviction and nobility, a rather self-conscious nobility, perhaps, but noble all the same. Let the reader decide, or decide he need not decide.

There are no mysteries about 'Morte d'Arthur', to the subject of which Tennyson may have been immediately drawn by the coincidence of Hallam's Christian name, though he had long been interested in the Arthurian myths. The pictorial passages are splendid, and the musical ones too, notably the final journey to the lake and the violent change of key on arrival there. Nevertheless, all is not well. There are contrived austerities of diction and syntax, the earliest signs of the rift within the lute—Tennyson's own phrase in a different context. He was not yet cultivating philosophy very assiduously, but he was casting a colder eye on the luxuries of poetry. When we read 'Morte d'Arthur' as incorporated virtually unchanged in *The Idylls of the King* (published in instalments, 1859–85), it does not stand out from the arid wastes of that ersatz epic as boldly as we should like.

For a dozen years after the original poem was written, roughly 1834–45, Tennyson's development followed a winding course. He was already at work on what was to become *In Memoriam*, but with no clear intention of ever publishing it. Much of what he wrote he considered unworthy of inclusion in his final collected edition. He was casting

---

★ Auden, seeing the same things in the poem as Chiasson, but interpreting them differently, had asked, 'What is "Ulysses" but a covert—the weakness of the poem is its indirection—refusal to be a responsible and useful person, a glorification of the heroic dandy?'

about, trying lighter verse ('Will Waterproof's Lyrical Monologue'), trying, with untoward results, to ape Wordsworth, occasionally recalling his earlier lyrical simplicities ('Break, break, break'—Hallam again—or 'Come not, when I am dead'), once or twice successfully shaping something new ('Locksley Hall'—successful against all the odds). Then, at the end of this period, he did what a large section of opinion had been telling him to do and got down to a long poem that would teach moral lessons, show human sympathy, and concern itself with questions of the day.

The result was *The Princess*, and most, though not quite all, of it is a hard read. He had attempted to tell a story, and he could not tell a story; to create character, and he could not create character; to be dramatic, and he was no good at that either. All that is of value, and it is very valuable, is the lyrics he smuggled into the narrative. Some of these went under the camouflage of being in blank verse, like the main body of the poem, and at least two of them are among the finest things he ever wrote. 'Tears, idle tears' (Hallam again) is probably the most poignant cry of despair in the language, and refutes by itself any notion that Tennyson was nothing but a complacent Victorian. (Some recent critics have tried to implant difficulties in it; these shrink as soon as we see that 'idle' means not worthless or trifling, but useless, vain.) 'Come down, O maid' is a sustained flight of the purely lyrical, a vehicle of excitement and exultation unique in Tennyson, a sound-piece again unique in English. The rhymed songs he infiltrated in the 1850 edition of the poem are less fine, but still fine; indeed, yet again it is hard to think of anything in mere words that suggests actual music more strongly than 'Sweet and low'.

1850 was the pivotal year in Tennyson's life. Very nearly all his best, even his good, poetry was already written; it could be argued that most of that very nearly all had been written by 1843, and a lot of that most by 1834. More specifically, in May of 1850 he published his greatest work, *In Memoriam A. H. H.*, after sixteen years' preparation; in the June he got married, after twelve years' delay; in November he was appointed Poet Laureate, after seven months' interregnum since the death of Wordsworth. One event of that year, taking place on its first day, he most likely did not notice: the appearance of a new magazine, *The Germ*, the organ of the Pre-Raphaelite Brotherhood. This curious body, though mainly concerned with the visual arts, and though intermittently dogged by what we should now call social-realist convictions, had rediscovered Hallam's notion that the prime duty of art was to be beautiful, not moral, not useful, not acceptable. The PRB and their disciples could have formed Tennyson's ideal audience, could have encouraged him to remake himself as a lyric poet, had they cared to do so. But, even if they had, it would have been too late. He was set on his course, for the remaining forty-two years of his life, as the Christian, humanitarian, democratic poet of official Victorianism.

The greatness of *In Memoriam* starts from the fact that, in it, Tennyson had as if by chance come across the form that perfectly reconciled his gifts, his destined subject matter and his aspirations. It is a long poem that is not a long poem at all, but a series of lyrics loosely connected by continuity or change of mood, without narrative, characters or dramatization. Rather as the tension of *Paradise Lost* springs from Milton's quarrel with himself about the difficulty yet necessity of justifying the ways of God to men, so Tennyson is torn between despairing grief and the need and duty to resist it. He called *In Memoriam* 'rather the cry of the whole human race than mine'; it is both; for once, but what a once, he spoke for his fellow-man *without having set out to do so*. Eliot's splendid essay calls it 'a poem of despair, but of despair of a religious kind' (adding, no less truly, that its author was 'the most instinctive rebel against the society in which he was the most perfect conformist'). Ostensibly, the poem comes out for faith and optimism; really and poetically, despair carried the day. To feel this, we need look no further than the contrast in conviction between sections CVI and CVII (the first half of the latter), but it is at the heart of the whole, so that even the most unfelt assertions of eternal Providence carry the pathos of a whistling in the dark.

It remains to try to justify the assertion that Tennyson's gift had effectively perished by 1850, if not at some rather or considerably earlier date. The merits of *In Memoriam* might seem to refute the more extravagant versions of such a charge, but we know that at least half of the poem was already drafted by 1842, and we can fairly safely assume—at any rate I would strongly suspect—that a good deal more than that was there then. Other apparent exceptions to the suggested rule tend to disappear on investigation, or at least to become fuzzy. 'Tithonus' was first published in 1860, but 'Tithon', written in 1833 and not disinterred until 1949, provides a good four-fifths of the official version. It may show lack of taste to erect any kind of question mark alongside 'Crossing the Bar', undeniably written in 1889 and a genuine and touching poem; all the same, we may doubt whether Tennyson at his best would have let pass the minor but distracting enigmas in the first and last stanzas.

'Milton' (1863) is a more interesting, not to say fascinating, case in point. It is not only a magnificent piece, deeply romantic and Romantic, unashamedly lyrical and stuffed with the luxuries of poetry; it is also, in its conclusion, shamelessly personal, unedifying, unmoral, exotic and pagan—all qualities the Laureate was pledged to abjure. Or rather, it was not shamelessly, not openly, any of that; Tennyson smuggled it in, in the manner of the *Princess* lyrics, as an experiment in the use of Latin metres in English. The result is a technical feat unequalled in our language (one of the things that marks Tennyson as a great poet is the tally of his uniquenesses) in that 'Milton' makes metrical sense in English while adhering strictly to the utterly alien prescriptions of the Latin form—a feat appreciable only by those disap-

pearing few who know Latin. But, of course, the point of this performance is that it gave Tennyson sanction to say what he would not have
dared to say in his natural voice.

The 'Epigrams' were never printed in any form in his lifetime.
They reveal not only the sensitivity to criticism already described, but
something less predictable, a spiteful humour and vulgarity that was
very much part of the man, though its chief outlet was in remarks to
friends and others and recorded only in their memoirs. He wrote a
pompous, but as always competent, ode that was set to music by
Sterndale Bennett and sung by a choir of thousands at the opening of
the International Exhibition in 1862; on a visit there he is supposed to
have peevishly asked a companion, 'Is there anywhere in this damned
place where we can get a decent bottle of Bass?' The gap thus revealed
between two aspects of Tennyson is dismayingly as well as comically
wide. The Bass-seeking Tennyson could never have hoped to find a
hearing in Victorian England, unless under a pseudonym, and that
suppression weakens the Tennyson we have.

W. H. Auden has drawn attention to the difficulty facing any lyric
poet, that of finding work to do in the long and frequent intervals
between his necessarily brief bursts of activity. Such a poet finds no
difficulty today: he writes fiction, journalism, even advertising copy.
But in the Nineteenth Century, and above all for a Poet Laureate, this
kind of solution was not available; a poet was expected to be a poet
all the time. Just as many of us would give large parts of Keats ('The
Cap and Bells', for instance) for a few short stories by him, large parts
of Browning (*Sordello*, for instance) for a travel book, etc, so I at least
would give very large parts of Tennyson, from *The Princess* onwards,
for some of the down-to-earth comic poetry he had it in him to write.
In that medium he might have become the true commentator on those
old 'questions of the day' he grievously failed to be.

As I have said, the view that Tennyson in some sense yielded to
critical and social pressure, unmade his genius by an act of will, is far
from being a new one. The reaction against him did not begin in the
1920s. Lewis Carroll produced a cruel and very funny parody of one
of his styles in 1856, Swinburne another such in 1880. An acute French
observer, the critic Hippolyte Taine, wrote of Tennyson in 1864:

> He has chosen his ideas, chiselled his words, equalled by his
> artifices, felicities, and diversities of style, the pleasantness and
> perfection of social elegance in the midst of which we read
> him . . . [His poetry] seems made expressly for these wealthy,
> cultivated, leisured business men, heirs of the ancient nobility,
> new leaders of a new England. It is part of their luxury as of their
> morality; it is an eloquent confirmation of their principles, and a
> precious article of their drawing-room furniture.

And Alfred Austin, a third-rate poet who, by a sort of irony, became
Laureate in 1896, wrote in 1870 a curmudgeonly and envious article

which nevertheless contained the inescapable truth that Tennyson's 'fame has increased precisely as his genuine poetical power has steadily waned'.

If he has never been short of detractors, Tennyson has had his defenders too, not least on the matter in hand. A modern critic, W. W. Robson, has argued effectively against the view that Tennyson 'made himself express the attitudes of his age to large public subjects not because he really wanted to do this or was capable of it but because he felt he ought to'. But that is not quite the issue. No doubt he did feel he ought to, but what he felt more strongly was that he would have to if he was going to be what he had always set his mind on becoming, the poet of his age. Early in life he told one of his brothers, 'I mean to be famous.' And, although in most respects a very unworldly man, he was astute enough, or intuitive enough, to see how to be famous in the England of his day.

That England notoriously had its doubts as well as its certainties, its neuroses as well as its moral health, its fits of gloom and frustration and panic as well as its complacency. Tennyson is the voice of those doubts and their accompaniments, and his genius enabled him to communicate them in such a way that we can understand them and feel them as our own. In short, we know from experience just what he means. Eliot called him the saddest of all English poets, and I cannot improve on that judgement. Tennyson spoke for everybody in a sense he never consciously intended—not everybody all the time, in any mood, but everybody at some time or other, when the whole world seems to have gone wrong. He was the deeply unofficial, small-letter poet laureate of that feeling.

First published as Introduction to *Tennyson* ('Poet to Poet'), (ed.) Kingsley Amis, Penguin, 1973

Brandy to Brown Ale

Swinburne, by Philip Henderson, Routledge

After all these years and all those books, Swinburne remains one of the most engaging characters of mid-Victorian London: absurd in appearance and yet endowed with real dignity, an aristocratic republican who later became a virulent jingo, a flagellant who treated his vice in the style more of the *Magnet* than of de Sade. And all that drinking!—inordinate not so much in quantity as in the extravagance of its effects, the shouting, the breakages, the insults, all sincerely denied the next morning as behaviour impossible in one who knew himself to be a gentleman. An engaging character but, as so often, more fun to read about than to meet. He was artless, chivalrous and affectionate; he was also, clearly, a most tiresome little man, for ever reciting, reading aloud, launching into tirades against Napoleon III or for Mazzini in his squeaky voice and with ceaseless fluttering of his arms and shoulders. He stands out, in fact, as a bore, a tremendous achievement in a milieu that also boasted Burne-Jones, Morris, William Rossetti, William Bell Scott, Hall Caine and, notoriously, Theodore Watts. It must be this quality in Swinburne that caused the famous breach with Gabriel Rossetti in 1872.

Philip Henderson's portrait is very fair and very full. It quotes copiously and illuminatingly from the letters and other writings; it adds to our knowledge, not only of Swinburne himself but also of his age. In particular, Watts receives his total due. Far from having crushed the creative life out of the poet by keeping him virtually locked up in Putney, Watts gave him thirty years of physical life, and happy, healthy, active life at that: almost no good work came out of that period, agreed, but Swinburne's talent had effectively perished long before Watts came on the scene. One might even argue that Gosse's label, 'the old horror of Putney', fits Swinburne better than Watts, whose boringness emerges as a passive thing, no more than an almighty dullness, easier on the nerves than all that capering and chattering.

Quite rightly, Mr Henderson reprints Coulson Kernahan's sharply funny account of how Watts got Swinburne off brandy ('a drug, a medicine . . . beastly stuff'), on to port and off again ('apt to clog the liver'), through burgundy and claret and finally settled with beer ('Shakespeare's brown October'). Unfortunately, I find no confirmation of the anecdote—perhaps never committed to paper—in which some inquirer looked into the private room of the pub which Swinburne, on his daily walk from The Pines, was allowed to visit 'for a glass of beer', and found the place littered with empty brandy bottles. More serious omissions involve Swinburne's sexual life. Were those birchings ever more than a token or a game? Was he on homosexual terms with Richard Burton or was he not? Above all, what were his precise relations with his sadistic cousin, Mary Gordon, and how and why were they broken off?—'a climacteric experience' which, it transpires, 'we know very little about'. Quite likely: it would be unfair to chide Mr Henderson for not finding non-existent evidence.

His book contains critical as well as biographical matter. The general approach is the sensible one of stressing the virtues and scope of Swinburne's writings without turning a blind eye to their faults. I did not know before of his merits as an art critic, however 'melodramatic' in style, as Mr Henderson accurately puts it. The fiction reads well in extract, especially the passages of natural description, but I cannot really buy Swinburne as a novelist. And I am left cold by the 'immense scholarship' of *Bothwell*—the longest play in the language, I was once told, and surely longer (if performed) than the mere six hours and three-quarters of Patrick Funge's *O'Casey*. Similarly, I cannot much care if Swinburne influenced a lot of people, or if he was like Turner, or if Ruskin thought he was good. I am left, at the end, clutching almost the same handful of poems as the one I grabbed in youth.

Which poems? I still cannot quite swallow the real hundred-proof sado-masochistic stuff like 'Faustine' or 'Dolores'—just slightly too funny, especially if imagined read in a Swinburnean voice. For me, it comes down pretty well to 'The Triumph of Time' (real feeling for once), 'Ave atque Vale', the first couple of choruses of 'Atalanta in Calydon', and a few other pieces like 'In the Orchard'. They are charged with a kind of incantatory energy unequalled in English; even the iambic lines seem to fall over one another in their eagerness to be heard. Nobody could claim that the content of such poems was very striking, but they are not vapid, and the charge that they should be cut is answered by pointing to the extreme difficulty of settling which parts to cut.

Swinburne's worst fault is his defective ear, a rather serious short-coming in a poet so wedded to sound-effects. Mr Henderson quotes, with evident admiration, from 'Songs before Sunrise':

> *For the outer land is sad, and wears*
> *A raiment of a flaming fire;*
> *And the fierce fruitless mountain stairs*
> *Climb, yet seem wroth and loth to aspire,*
> *Climb, and break, and are broken down,*
> *And through their clefts and crests the town*
> *Looks west and sees the dead sun lie,*
> *In sanguine death that stains the sky*
> *With angry dye.*

Starting with '*land/sad*', I can count eight failures of euphony in those nine lines. As all observers agree, Swinburne habitually wrote at great speed; he could hardly otherwise have produced over 2,000 pages of verse, plus *Bothwell*, 'Lesbia Brandon', etc, etc. As in his reading, he was always being carried away, and, alas, it shows.

Observer, 24 May 1974

Nasticreechia Krorliuppia?

It may look churlish to heave a brick at such an apparently harmless figure, but to me, at least, harmless is the last thing Edward Lear was. Until Beatrix Potter came in on another flank, he did more than any other individual to foster the arch, twee, whimsical, etc tendency that so disfigures English literature, humour, even character. It was not Lear's invention (Shakespeare's fools are tainted with it), but he did much to found its favourite vehicle, nonsense verse, piffle verse, twaddle verse.

The lands where the Jumblies live may well have been far and few, but neither far nor few enough to suit me. Going to sea in a sieve can never, surely, have been more than a mildly funny or appealing idea, and well before the end of the sixth long, elaborate stanza it has dimmed a good deal further; four lines, the span allocated the wise men of Gotham, might not have been too much. I pass over the courtship of the Yonghy-Bonghy-Bo and the doings of the Dong with the luminous nose—the very titles ought to set any decent, trustworthy person wincing and grimacing—and come to one of the great nadirs of our national intellect and feeling, *The Pobble Who Has No Toes*. In the course of fishing for his Aunt Jobiska's runcible cat with crimson whiskers:

> *The Pobble swam fast and well,*
> *And when boats or ships came near him.*
> *He tinkledy-binkledy-winkled a bell . . .*

Just typing those lines has upset me, brought me to the verge of panic like the sight of Woody Allen or Spike Milligan, made me consider resigning from the human race. More rationally, perhaps, they conjure up a vision of innumerable wool-clad, amber-beaded aunts and cousins all squealing, 'Oh I *say* darling how perfectly *super* and *spiffing* and *side-splitting*!' It is against *that* that we are fighting.

Lear's limericks are more insidious. Their whimsy is less of the bull-in-a-china-shop variety and here and there may even raise a wan smile. But with their tamely repetitive last lines ('Oh but *darling* that's the whole *point*!') and paltry little narratives already beginning to drag after four, they are part of an only slightly less damaging blot on our culture: amateurishness, the notion that a gentleman, like Lear's quaint old pest from Thermopylae, never need do anything properly and that only drudges and artisans see the job through.

Louis MacNeice once wrote that Lear's Nonsense Songs were a fad of the 1920s. That fits like a glove. One gloomy deduction from it is that this centenary of his may have come along just in time to rescue

him and his works from richly deserved and much-to-be-desired
oblivion.

Sunday Telegraph, 31 January 1988

The Last Lyric Poet?

A. E. Housman: Collected Poems and Selected Prose, edited by Christopher
Ricks, Allen Lane

Housman's collected poems have been published before and so has
a selection of his prose. Now for the first time his 'double genius'
as poet and as Latin scholar is displayed in one volume. It is not really
so much of a double genius as all that, more a case of two abilities
present in the same man. Unlike Dryden or Coleridge, say, poetry-
Housman and prose-Housman do not interpenetrate very much. Each
merely wrote the sort of thing that might well have been expected of
the other, leaving the reader muttering unhelpful tags like classicism—
restraint—erudition—precision—tradition. But lovers of the poems
will, even so, be prepared to buy them over again in order to get at
some of the prose.

True, 'The Name and Nature of Poetry', a lecture Housman gave
at Cambridge in 1933, though famous at once and for perhaps twenty
years afterwards, reads rather disappointingly today. His assault on the
poetry of the English Eighteenth Century (with exceptions made for
the quartet of estimable madmen, Collins, Christopher Smart, Cowper
and Blake) has turned into little more than quite good fun. His indifference to meaning as a constituent of poetry, his 'affective' definition of
it as simply that which brings a shiver to the spine—well, the advent
in Cambridge of F. R. Leavis, whose first book dates from the same
year, 1933, must, however falsely, have promised an invigorating way
out of all this stuff.

But other pieces here have in effect improved over the years. Housman's assertion of the essential disinterestedness of scholarship, its
devotion to the discovery of truth and nothing else, was never more
needed than now, with knowledge increasingly regarded as nothing
more than means to an end and 'relevance' prized above truth. When
he remarks in discussing Wordsworth that 'the European view of a

poet is not of much importance unless the poet writes in Esperanto', he reminds us of something we are going to have to say louder and louder as the European 'community' takes over more and more of our life. And nobody, I think, has ever been as effectively crushing about the pretensions of literary critics.

For the production of all this and much more of value, nothing rarer was needed than a mind trained to discriminate with the utmost nicety and staggering powers of expressing itself. The poems written by the same man were and are more exceptional. Only the presence of Robert Graves doubtfully prevents Housman from being the last great lyric poet in the language.

Guided by a superlative ear and a craftsman's temperament, he remained utterly individual within the established verse forms, treating the old primary themes of loss, pain and deprivation as realised and reflected in the English landscape. His work has nothing to do with the great modernist development in poetry seen in that of Hopkins, Yeats, Pound and T. S. Eliot. It belongs instead to the other, older, home-grown tradition of Matthew Arnold, Hardy, Edward Thomas and, in poems like 'First Sight' and 'Cut Grass', Philip Larkin.

There, already, can be seen part of the reason why Housman has only fitfully had his due. No poet could have turned his back more comprehensively on the modern world or (what has come to be part of the same thing) written in a way less cut out for study in modern universities, where the standing of poets seems nowadays to be determined. From such places he looks a disagreeable figure, elitist, embittered, pessimistic and utterly unsuitable for appearing on television. This view of him was summed up in Auden's famous sonnet, a clever, shoddy, falsifying piece that enabled a whole generation to feel superior to one who had never bothered to hide his own, perhaps justified, feelings of superiority.

Owing to the physical length of the pages of this volume and the shortness of most of Housman's poems, a lot of paper in it remains blank. Some of it could usefully have been filled with informative notes. His verse in general is transparently clear, but today's average readers of 'The Oracles', for instance, will need to have the significance of Dodona mountain and the midland navel-stone explained to them, and likewise the position and significance of the sea-wet rock on which the Spartans sat down and combed their hair.

If he had thought about it, Housman might have said with Milton that he had in mind fit audience, though few, the few who among other things would appreciate his classical allusions. In the half-century or so after 1896, when he published his first volume at his own expense, he acquired an audience that was very far from few while remaining reasonably fit. Unfortunately all that has changed. What little can be done about it, for example by clarifying the poet's references, should be done.

This publication includes, as it says, Housman's collected, not complete, poems. It tells us that 'a full and exact edition of all the poems' is now in progress. Those who prefer to wait for it will presumably be getting all the light verse instead of just most of it, as here; a small gain. They will also get the considerable fragments from the notebooks, of which Christopher Ricks might have included a few. One of these ('Stand back, you men and horses') is thirteen strange, haunting lines of a poem in fifteen that he interestingly and perhaps necessarily failed to finish.

The back of the jacket of this volume shows a drawing said to be of Housman that does not look like him, as the photograph on the front makes clear. One is used to newspaper caricatures that hardly resemble their subjects in even the broadest way, but newspapers are gone tomorrow, unlike books, and this representation distorts its victim's face deliberately and for the worse. I wonder why.

Sunday Telegraph, 26 June 1988

The Pity of It

Wilfred Owen, by Jon Stallworthy, Oxford University Press and Chatto & Windus

Wilfred Owen is the greatest of our war poets, however that elusive term is defined. His war poems (to spell it out) excel both those of his fellow-victims and those of men who survived to write of other things. Certainly, he took as his subject 'War, and the pity of War', in the words of the famous fragmentary preface to what was to be a collection of his verse. He never saw it; only five of his poems had appeared in print by the time he met his death on the morning of 4 November 1918. He was twenty-five years old, the same age as Keats, on whose work he had consciously modelled his own. Other attributes in common were small stature (Owen was 5ft 5½ in.), chest weakness and Celtic descent, the last no more than a supposition in Keats's case, but surely a tempting one.

War in the sense of warfare, of active service and action, is an unpromisingly narrow theme for poetry, and one of Owen's distinctions is the range and variety he achieved within set limits. He handles with equal confidence and success the short angry outbursts ('Futility'), the tranquil elegy ('Anthem for Doomed Youth'), the dramatic mono-logue ('The Chances'), the detailed evocation of a trench landscape ('Exposure'), the elevated general statement ('Insensibility'). This diverseness is accompanied by an unusual skill in the devising of new forms to fit the matter in hand—'The Send-off' must be the outstand-ing example.

Mr Jon Stallworthy's fully detailed, irreplaceable biography is in part a record of the development of that unique poetic nature, a develop-ment that was late but was rapid. It may seem odd to speak of anything 'late' in so short a life, but history shows that most poets are in full possession of their powers by the age of twenty-one, if not several years before. From the many uncollected poems and fragments (some in autograph facsimile) included here, and from the datings of others already familiar, one can see clearly that Owen came of age poetically some time in August or September 1917, when he was already turned twenty-four.

The place was Craiglockhart War Hospital, Edinburgh, where mental and nervous cases were treated: Owen was in the middle of a four-month course of treatment after a breakdown at the Front earlier that year. The friendship and encouragement of Siegfried Sassoon, a fellow-patient; the discovery of Yeats's work; the delayed effect of the experience of warfare; whatever might have actuated or assisted the change, it happened. One moment, so to speak, Owen was writing 'From My Diary, July 1914', a callow, fulsomely Keatsian compote of nostalgia for the days of peace; the next, he had produced that fine, haunting little poem 'Six O'Clock in Princes Street', in which the feeling is genuine and the diction entirely natural. Not a war poem, by the way.

Mr Stallworthy's critical comments are both sensitive and sensible, but he has little to say about Owen's major technical innovation, the use of chime or pararhyme or consonantal rhyme or alliterative assonance, as in *killed/cold*. It appears that the origin of this practice is still a matter of debate; I myself can see no plausible alternative to the view that it comes straight out of Welsh verse. Nobody as conscious and proud of his Welsh ancestry as Owen was, or as interested in poetic technique, could have failed to make the necessary investigations (I am not suggesting that he read Welsh, only that he could have spared the ten minutes necessary to find out how chime works in that language.)

As before, the cause is less important than the effect. Overnight, English poetry came into possession of thousands of fresh rhymes: *love*, for instance, after centuries of struggling along with *dove* and *above*, acquired *live, alive, leave, believe, relieve, slave*, etc. And with the new end-ornament, so much less emphatic to an English ear than conventional rhyme, new tones of voice became possible and were heard: the early Auden, which is almost the only Auden, could not have happened but for Owen. Yet there is no gain without a loss: the day when *killed/cold* became possible brought nearer the advent of, say, *killed/bold*. When mere likeness of the final consonant(s) is thought to make a sort of rhyme, there is a modest liberation, and some saving of trouble, and a little decadence.

No fault of Owen's any of that, and it would be unfair to him to make any more of this discovery of his. He had the poetic discretion to master it as he used it, to be unmoved by the self-generated excitement of novelty. Like all true poets, he was more than truthful: his verse has its characteristic movement and its own sequences of sound. When we read:

> *Men remember alien ardours*
> *As the dusk unearths old mournful odours.*
> *In the garden unborn child souls wail*

we find something more than just *ardours/odours* to tell us we must be reading Wilfred Owen, and that something more can never be imitated. One subject Mr Stallworthy does not discuss is Owen's homosexuality, though he neither avoids the word nor passes over the evidence in the verse—also possibly in one or two suppressions in a letter to his much-beloved mother—that Owen's feelings ran in that direction. No doubt this is the wisest course, especially since I should guess Mr Stallworthy shares my own conviction that those feelings never ran as far as being translated into practice. Their presence in Owen, however, deserves recognition because, as with Housman, Beardsley or Tchaikovsky, they were an essential part of his artistic nature, causing him perhaps to experience a peculiar agony on the battlefield and to convey a peculiar tenderness in his work.

This is an outstanding book, a worthy memorial to its subject, valuable too in its additions to our knowledge of the period, above all, it struck me, of that terrible time in 1915 when what had started the previous summer became the Great War.

Observer, 10 November 1974

Against the Current

Robert Graves: His Life and Work, by Martin Seymour-Smith, Hutchinson
In Broken Images: Selected letters of Robert Graves 1914–1946, edited by Paul
O'Prey, Hutchinson

Of course there have got to be lives of the poets, big modern ones
full of extracts from diaries, letters, reviews, memoirs, even
poems—everything has to be there. But such books turn out to be
mixed blessings. The biographer has a story to tell, after all, and
naturally feels he must make the great man's poems an important part
of that story. So far so good: he does a valuable service in reminding
readers that, whatever a poem may be, it is not just a text on a page but
also a part of somebody's life. Unfortunately, whenever he connects a
given poem at all closely with an incident or limited period in the life
he cannot help damaging the poem.

So here the work of Robert Graves undergoes examination for the
biographical light thrown upon it and reflected from it. A chilling
nightmare monologue ('The Pier-Glass') is taken to show his state of
neurasthenia in 1921; a brisk and effective variation on the theme of
world weariness ('Callow Captain') is quoted as a summary of his
feelings at the beginning of 1930; a fine early poem ('Reproach'),
manifestly something to do with original sin, is diminished or even
distorted into something to do with a soldier's feelings in the Great
War. How much more edifying it would have been to learn that Graves
had had bacon and tomatoes for breakfast the day he sat down to write
it!

Martin Seymour-Smith is poet enough himself to see perfectly well
what is at stake. He is at fault over 'Reproach', but elsewhere I think
he never slips into actually substituting his biographical gloss for the
meaning of a poem as it stands, and the critical comments he offers
are in general quite fair. The trouble is that poems are peculiarly
vulnerable to the kind of reductive, de-universalising, anecdote-hatch-
ing process the biographer cannot help subjecting them to. Novels are
made of sterner stuff; they easily recover from that amazing treatment
in which literary journalists and other unliterary people speculate about
which real person this or that fictitious character is 'based on'.

It seems a pity in a way that Mr Seymour-Smith could not have
followed the example of Johnson, who by the custom then prevailing
kept his observations on a poet's work quite separate from those
on his life. He likewise followed practice in offering few extracts or
quotations in his text, and I suppose it might be said that respectable
literary criticism ceased at about the time they began to be generally

admitted. But they—extracts—are all the rage now, as I said, and anything like that makes a book look more diverting. This is useful in the present case because Graves's life has been for most of its length as boring to be told about, however satisfying to lead, as that of most professional writers.

He started off admittedly with a bang, in France in 1915 with the BEF at the age of nineteen. His letters of these years are perhaps surprising: nothing about the awfulness of the war, but then soldiers' letters as a whole rarely touched on that, and he reserved his account of it for his devastating autobiographical book, *Goodbye to All That* (1929). What he wrote home about was poetry, as an art, as a passion, but also as a career for R. Graves when the war was over. I find this reasonable and normal, a wholesome corrective to any image of a lonely, bardic unworldliness which his later self-exile may have fostered.

He married early for those days and it was not a great success, though productive of children. When he was thirty he ran into someone who instantly set up a *ménage à trois* with him—though quite soon he and she were away in a *deux* together while Mrs Graves looked after the children—and who went off with him in 1929 to Majorca, where, apart from an involuntary absence from 1936 to 1946, he has lived ever since. (I still cannot understand this removal, at the time a most unusual step for a heterosexual not wanted for fraud.)

The interloper was called Laura Riding, a name somehow inappropriate to that small dark beaky-nosed apparition from New York, *née* Reichenthal, the poetry-scribbling daughter of a left-wing Jewish tailor. For over ten years she and Graves continued in close association. The physical side of this, which lasted only a short time, may well have relieved his sexual difficulties, of whatever mild sort these were. Intellectually, her effect on him might have been disastrous if it had been less superficial. They collaborated on two influential books about poetry which would seemingly have been much the same without any contribution from her. He cannot really have had any time for her unmetrical verses. She did bring drama into his life, which he liked.

That comprised the first of the two intriguing or faintly sensational parts of Graves's life. The second was briefer and more decisive. On a visit to America in 1939 he and Laura Riding broke up. At about the same time she renounced poetry, an action which she regarded as 'the outer manifestation of an inner experience of discovery' of something or other. Not long afterwards Graves settled down in what became a tranquil and lasting second marriage. The rest is writing.

Though he perhaps devotes too much space to some trivial and venial follies of his subject's old age, Mr Seymour-Smith's portrait is a full and fair one. Robert Graves emerges as a man not greatly at ease with his time. In particular, his poetic contemporaries displease him: Pound, Eliot, Yeats, D. H. Lawrence, Auden, Dylan Thomas, Edward Thomas (surprisingly). Only Norman Cameron, James Reeves and others of lesser note pass muster. It is hard not to see a dislike of competing eminence there, and certainly in his personal relationships Graves has seemed to want to dictate, to dominate, a great one for quarrels and shifts of allegiance.

A difficult man, then, also vain, humorous, warm, brave, not very happy, inquisitive, self-willed and capable of the most passionate absorption in others. Some of these qualities can be seen in Roberta Booth's marvellous jacket photograph, very recent, with the master unshaven of course, in non-glamorous clobber but wearing a special Spanish or Mallorquin hat. Has he overdone the part of poet a little? Maybe, and his personal cult of the Muse and the White Goddess has rightly or wrongly hindered his being accepted where he belongs, in the front rank. But when the events of his life have receded to a blur, his poems will be as clear, as hard-edged and as sound as when they were first written.

Observer, 16 June 1982

Digging up Graves

Robert Graves: The Assault Heroic 1895–1926, by Richard Perceval Graves, Weidenfeld & Nicolson

The author of this book is a son of John Ranke Graves, younger brother of Robert (I use the plain Christian name for brevity). The blurb describes him as 'a full-time biographer' whose previous subjects include T. E. Lawrence, Housman and the Powys brothers. He was helped in his present task by privileged access to unpublished memoirs by respectively Robert's mother Amelie, brother John and half-brother Perceval, together with various family diaries and letters. This is the first volume of what is intended as the definitive, very long biography.

Robert was the third child of middle-aged parents; his father, Alfred Perceval, Irish Protestant, his mother German with some Norwegian blood. He grew up in a well-off, respectable, indeed dry household, strong in morality but rich in affection too, populous in the sense that it was constantly full of relatives: there were five children of a previous marriage of Alfred's and innumerable aunts and uncles. Their comings and goings make difficult reading. Alfred was an Inspector of Schools, also like other senior Graveses a literary man, a poet whose song 'Father O'Flynn' must be better known than any one of his son's poems. (He sold it outright in a batch, eighty pounds the lot, being no better at money than the rest of the family.) Perhaps Robert was inspired by his father's creative example; this biographer more than most tries to clarify complicated and never really explicable events, like becoming a poet, by ascertained and easily grasped facts. Perhaps, then, and perhaps not. In rather the same way, Robert began as a poet very early, in other words he made verse-type scribbles from time to time, like many little boys who develop into writers and very many more who don't.

With the schooldays we are on firmer ground. Robert went to a lot of schools, six in all by the time he was fourteen, and hated every one of them. Charterhouse, where he ended up, took a turn for the better when he began to do well at cricket and boxing and later poetry, but in his last month there he wrote to his brother John that it was 'one of the vilest places on God's Earth'. In this respect Robert showed himself to be significantly like other writers and artists in general.

The reason for the prevalent unpopularity of school with creative persons is perhaps straightforward, even syllogistic. All schools, at least in the day when they were still schools, provided the entrant with inexhaustible reservoirs of opposition and competition. These are the two things most hated and most bitterly resisted by egotists. All artist are egotists. There. Not all egotists are artists, of course, and it does seem that other types, like those who eventually become industrialists or trade unionists, say, or critics, have no discernibly worse a time at school than anyone else, so perhaps we should insert some intensifier like 'screaming' before egotists in my conclusion just above.

Hereabouts somebody often pleads that the egotism is needed to get the art into being and is therefore worthwhile, though the relevant wives and husbands are not always consulted on the point. But this is a large subject. Before leaving it I might remark that artist-egotists can be cowards and dissemblers too, which is why some of them miss the conventional bad time at school.

Robert was manifestly not one of them. He left school in July 1914 and by May the following year was serving with the Royal Welsh [later Welch] Fusiliers in France. He shirked none of the dangerous and harrowing tasks that fell to an infantry subaltern, in due course a captain, at that appalling time. He was lucky not to have died of a wound from shell-fragments and his nerves were severely affected for years afterwards. After demobilisation in 1919 he went to Oxford, got married, lived on Boar's Hill and entered the literary life. The story ends with Robert's departure for an academic post in Egypt in the company of his wife Nancy and of the American poetess Laura Riding Gottschalk, who had crossed the Atlantic on purpose to become his helpmeet and collaborator.

As told here it is not a very interesting story. All those family sources seem to have yielded precious little of much consequence. On and around Boar's Hill, for instance, Robert got to know or ran into all manner of literary figures—Bridges, Gilbert Murray, Edmund Blunden, Robert Nichols, Masefield, Yeats, T. E. Lawrence, Walter Raleigh, Siegfried Sassoon, who had been a brother-officer in France, even Vachel Lindsay—but on this showing they never did or said anything worth remembering. Here, as elsewhere, a mass of undifferentiated detail is piled up after the manner of a bad examinee, with the reader left to spot the connections and applications, if any. Even this is preferable to the author's attempts to impart relevance to his facts.

When he exerts himself to focus on his subject's actual writing it is to comment that his early religious conflicts 'fuelled his creativity', or that the 'cornerstone' of Robert's and Nancy's relationship was 'a shared commitment to the arts', though worse than this was surely to be feared after an introduction that begins: 'A true poem is like a spring of water in a desert land.' Golly, and here I am walking past springs of water in desert lands every day for years without ever tumbling to it that what they're like is true poems.

Something that might have alleviated matters is any show of penetration, liveliness or wit, any flicker of enjoyment in the writing or personal response to the material, were it no more than malice or boredom. But no: it is very much as if the full-time biographer of the family felt or was told that here was something he was uniquely equipped to do and had better get on with willy-nilly. The book does possess one great novelty, however: it presents Laura Riding in a favourable light.

Observer, 21 September 1986

Rimbaud of Cwmdonkin

Dylan Thomas, by Paul Ferris, Hodder & Stoughton

A biography that calls its subject 'a chronic liar' on its second page and describes him as having 'made begging into a cottage industry' on its third is unlikely to end up as a work of piety. If Paul Ferris has left anything out of his tale as too damaging, I should not much care to be told of it. According to him, Dylan Thomas could be the most engaging and entertaining of men at a safe distance, but this turned out to be pretty far. His cadging letters, with their vast range of tones from the ostensibly timid or inadvertent claims on pity to the straightforward demand to be given cash, were small masterpieces, but they could after all be resisted—yielding to them, by the way, was no kind of guarantee against being badmouthed behind one's back. What might be called invisible income was supplied by a smallish army of unpaid tradesmen and landlords. Unreturned advances for undelivered work were always useful. It was in sorning, however, that Thomas made his greatest contribution to the art of living off others.

To sorn—a Scottish word, oddly enough—is 'to take up free quarters or exact maintenance unjustifiably'. The unjustifiably detail needs slight qualification here. Thomas's favourite victims were those afflicted with a family tie to him or his wife Caitlin, herself no warden of the stuffier bourgeois virtues. The two would descend in the middle of the night (good thinking) on Nicolette Devas, Caitlin's sister, and get their 'sorning' off to a brisk start by demanding money for the taxi they always turned up in. Thomas would repay such exactions by urinating against the living-room wall, defecating on the floor, stealing shirts, the silver, the gramophone.

Anyone who still thinks that 'Dylan' was 'really' rather 'marvellous' after all this should study Mr Ferris's account of the care and devotion with which Thomas evaded first military service and then direction into war-work in 1939–45; he finally got to writing film-script propaganda for the cause he had sneered at. There is neither extenuation nor malice in such passages: Mr Ferris's whole tone and approach are scrupulously just. His object is to sort out fact from legend, no sitting target, in a case so confused by rumour, falsehood, fantasy, calumny and drink.

In the first place, Dylan Thomas was not the country boy or the son of the people or the Welsh-speaking or strongly Welsh Welshman he has often been taken for. Swansea, his home until he was twenty, is for better or worse a sort of English town, by language to start with, and the street where he was born and brought up, Cwmdonkin Drive, is in a very decent middle-class suburb there; I lived within a stone's throw of it myself for ten years, which ought to give you some idea. He loved Wales, but as the place he came from, not as the land of his fathers. He knew no Welsh and I (for one) can find nothing specifically Welsh in his work—plenty of stage-Welshmanship in *Under Milk Wood* etc, but I don't count that.

Thomas stressed his Welshness in public because it came in handy for the larger, self-created legend—Thomas the bard in stained pullover and baggy trousers, the roaring boyo, the young dog, always breaking things, talking bawdy, womanising and of course boozing. Although some of this was quite real enough, a lot of the womanising came down to histrionic lunges at parties, meant to fail, and the boozing was exaggerated: he often feigned drunkenness and lied about how much he had drunk. Mr Ferris's most valuable piece of demythologising lies in his inference that what killed Thomas was an overdose, not of alcohol, but of morphine administered as a sedative by an incompetent New York doctor who died in 1974.

Thomas needed his raffish persona for two reasons that correspond to his two main emotional drives. The first lay in his conception of himself as a poet. Mr Ferris makes the uncomfortable but necessary point that being regarded as such was more immediate to Thomas than the actual writing of poems, and he was set on being accepted by people who would not know one poem from another. To pose as a dandy, a rustic or a bank manager *à la* Eliot would not have done; the young-dog spot was vacant. Hence part of the reason for the cadging. No *poet* could take a job, which, he said somewhere, was 'death without the dignity'. Thomas was all too aware of what had happened to his father, failed poet and embittered schoolmaster.

Thomas's other compulsion was fear. The only time I met him I put his awkward behaviour down to shyness; Mr Ferris quotes a dozen other witnesses to the same thing. Hence not only the protective persona but very likely part of the reason for the obscurity of the verse: to be readily understood was and is to stick one's neck out. But the main fear was more terrible, and it was justified. In a letter of 1941, Thomas described himself as 'the Rimbaud of Cwmdonkin Drive'— too agonisingly accurate to be funny. Like many self-centred people, he knew where he stood, and the relevant point about Rimbaud was not that he had been wild or a boy genius but that he had given up writing poetry at nineteen. Most of Thomas's own poetry had been written or drafted by the same age. He recovered his powers to some degree for a short period at the end of the war, but for the last eight years of his life he knew he was finished.

All in all, a hilarious, shocking, sad story. Mr Ferris has sifted through a great mass of material, written and oral, and assembled his findings with outstanding care and skill. This is a brilliant book, necessary to that large number who continue to care for Thomas and his work—I am told that *Under Milk Wood* alone sold 38,000 copies last year—but also to be recommended to those with a general interest in human beings and what they can get up to.

Observer, 24 April 1977

On the Scrounge

The Collected Letters of Dylan Thomas, edited by Paul Ferris, Dent

Paul Ferris is the author of a superb Life of Dylan Thomas (1977), pre-eminent among modern biographies in conveying what its subject was actually like to meet and know and have to do with, a dismal tale for the most part, told without either censure or apology. Now Ferris has brought us the Letters too, over a thousand of them in a book the size of a Companion to something. With such exposure, even a correspondent as self-projecting and as manipulative as Thomas cannot escape being seen more closely yet.

He was always notorious for having consciously run his life as that of a poet, and not in any high-falutin Shelleyan sense either. Being a poet meant for Thomas being his own man, being above convention, especially the tiresome sort like keeping to agreements, refraining from theft and leaving places as most people would have wished to find them. But above all it meant not having a job, any other job than writing poems or stories, though in practice this meant in turn not taking paid employment: he was perfectly happy writing articles and scripts and giving readings as a freelance.

What is, I think, newly revealed here is the full extent to which that determined independence, admirable perhaps on a quick view, distorted the supposedly all-poetic life. In fact of course it was not independence at all, merely a form of dependence more clinging and corroding than any clerkly or educational grind. That sort of thing gives you some free time; getting hold of unearned money seems never to stop. Seven days a week it soils with its sickening poison, to misquote a different sort of poet.

Writing a simple begging letter perhaps calls for nothing more ruinous than putting your pride in your pocket, though if you make a habit of it you may find your self-respect and your reluctance to lie (if any) going the same way. But soon you come to the begging letter indirect, asking A to get money out of B or to ask B to suggest C, D, E, etc, who might send money or suggest someone else who might. The begging letter anticipatory, as here to Edith Sitwell or the American anthologist Oscar Williams, proffers engagingness, perhaps of a vaguely and rather fraudulently Cymric sort, or an affecting determination to battle through adversity—what you will, to soften up the mark. Anything as important as that needs taking through several drafts, like a poem.

A distinguished late-period effort, to Princess Caetani, proprietress of the affluent periodical *Botteghe Oscure*, perhaps falls into a begging letter topping-up category, but no such label could do justice to the lyric flights of imitation pathos and real cadging it sustains for much of its couple of thousand words:

> The whole fishy bay is soaked in guilt like the bad bits of poems-not-to-be oozing to the marrow on the matchsticked floor, and the half-letters curling and whining in the warped drawers . . . This weather gets me like poverty: it blurs and then blinds, creeps chalky and crippling into the bones, shrouds me in wet self, rains away the world.

Real love of the job went into that. By now (1952) Thomas was working on such stuff (and worse was to come) not just as if it were poetry but pretty much instead of poetry, though the drying-up of his gift was in progress by 1945 or even earlier.

It is tempting to see that decline as inevitable, given that when he had used up his childhood he had nothing more to write about because he had noticed nothing since. Taken together, these letters testify to a staggering indifference to what was around him. They show no curiosity about other people or their lives—I counted one remark that showed he had had a proper look at an acquaintance, though admittedly there are quite a few ventings of spite. No incident or circumstance outside his personal concerns seems to have impressed him. He evidently took little interest in literature, read nothing since his schooldays, saw nothing much in any contemporary. Poets are usually passionate about some irrelevance: cooking, racing, painting, budgerigars; not this one. Even the trees and the seas exist only to be plastered in style and tone of voice.

But then Thomas's poetry had aspired from the start to be all surface, all context, as near to the purely verbal as poetry can get. And that is self-defeating: a poem cannot just be and not mean, exist entirely within itself, while it goes on using words at all. But, again, why not be meaningless, why not be satisfied with conveying nothing in particular if you have nothing to convey and no one to convey it to? There is an odd appropriateness in the fact that at the time of his death he was preparing to collaborate on an opera with Stravinsky, that supreme exemplar of musical emptiness.

Not all of Thomas's work, even his later work, was like that, just most of it, and not all these letters demonstrate his almost solipsistic self-centredness. Those to his wife are not easy reading for third parties, not that they should be. Those to his parents show some affection and concern, as do his frequent references to his children. One comes to such letters with relief: for the moment at least nobody is going to be asked to send him money, find him a free house, help him to get out of joining the army, save him from having to pay income tax or being summonsed for non-payment of NHS contributions, publish his poem, *type* his poem, fix up his lecture, arrange his trip.

Whatever it was that made so many people put up with all that for so long can hardly be expected to emerge now: this volume looks like being the last we shall hear of him. Nobody interested in Dylan Thomas or his work can afford to miss it.

Observer, 3 November 1985

Life with Dylan Thomas

Caitlin—Life with Dylan Thomas, by Caitlin Thomas with George Tremlett, Secker & Warburg

Dylan Thomas is still so much a present-day figure and popular writer that it comes almost as a shock to realise he died in 1953 at the age of thirty-nine. Now to add to the story comes *Caitlin—Life with Dylan Thomas*, a substantial and entertaining book, based on many hours of interviews with his widow tape-recorded at her house in Catania, Sicily, starting just a year ago. George Tremlett, hitherto known to the world of letters chiefly as a biographer of David Bowie, The Who and other rock performers, has done a first-rate editing job. By careful cutting and revision he has produced a readable narrative while retaining as much as possible of Mrs Thomas's lively conversational style. It is a valuable supplement to Paul Ferris's *Life* of 1977 and other records.

Caitlin opens with her first meeting with Thomas, in London, inevitably in a pub, the Wheatsheaf, in what was then called Fitzrovia. He was too busy talking to notice her properly at first, but after a few minutes he put his head in her lap and told her she was beautiful, he loved her and he was going to marry her. Later that evening they booked into the Eiffel Tower Hotel and stayed there for five or six nights at the unwitting expense of Augustus John, with whom Caitlin was involved at the time. Thomas and she spent all day and every day round the pubs, drinking non-stop and apparently not eating a crumb.

This very much set the pattern for what followed. The romance took an early dip when the lady got tired of being ignored while Thomas was holding forth in the pub one evening and walked out, ending up on a trip to Ireland where her parents came from. She left no address and he evidently made no attempt to find her. But soon they were back together, in London, in Cornwall, where in 1937 they got married (someone else paid for the ceremony), in Swansea with Thomas's parents, in Laugharne in what was then Pembrokeshire, where after various sojourns, rent-free as far as possible, they finally settled in 1949. The end comes with a vivid, harrowing description of Thomas's death in a New York hospital from drink and faulty medication.

The two of them had done a great deal of pubbing—of course, but it could surely be said of very few other married men that they never spent a single evening at home. In one place or another they quarrelled a lot too, over Thomas's infidelities, more over his wife's unquenchable resentment of the hard fact that he attracted more attention than she, though never over the kind of life they should lead.

In the circumstances it may seem wonderful that they produced and reared three children but, like many couples whose marriages look awful from outside, they seem to have got along not too badly. There is an appealing and very believable picture of her scrubbing his back in the bath while he gorged the boiled sweets, humbugs, pickled onions and fizzy lemonade she had put out for him across the soap tray.

On this account, what held them together was devotion not only to booze but also to petty criminality, minor fraud, stealing from friends and messing up their houses, cheating, cadging, above all a shared conviction that rich, complacent people, ie those living on their own earnings, deserved to have anything movable taken off them by footloose creative souls like Mr and Mrs Dylan Thomas. I suppose that seems more or less right if you admire his work enough. I don't myself.

Mail on Sunday, 26 October 1986

A Poet for Our Time

High Windows, by Philip Larkin, Faber

How many poets qualify under the night-owl test? When everyone else has gone to bed, how many poets compete successfully with a new recording of the Tchaikovsky B flat minor as accompaniment to the final Scotch? In my case, the answer to this question (a more searching and serious one than anything involving hierarchies of merit) is—remarkably few: Housman, parts of Graves, Betjeman, the early Tennyson, the Macaulay of 'Horatius', the early R. S. Thomas, and Philip Larkin. The quality they share is immediacy, density, strength in a sense analogous to that in which the Scotch is strong. Greater poets need some distancing for their greatness to be apparent.

Taking this view, I find it disgracefully characteristic of our time that Larkin is not universally and unquestioningly accepted as one of the best three or four poets now writing in our language. What weighs against this acceptance is a loose combination of attitudes, some of them mutually incompatible. In outlining them, I must use some guesswork, I hope of a reasoned kind.

He cannot be a great or even an important poet (so the feeling runs) because he writes so little. Indeed he does write little—the new volume has thirty-four pages of verse, many of them partly vacant, and twenty-four poems, the fruit of ten years' work—and is always trying to have written even less: he has refrained from putting between hard covers a good deal of earlier work we could well do with, and now omits to mention, on the back of the half-title, his two excellent novels. He stands or falls, then, by a collection of jazz-record reviews, on the face of it a frivolous publication, and four books of verse, none of the earlier three much fatter than this.

Such a cavil is the product of Victorian literary values, usually the best of guides, but not here. The requirement of bulk as a witness of poetical status helped to pad Browning out insufferably; it ruined Tennyson; and does anybody really want every line of Hardy, the last of the tribe? Or, to start at the other end and finish somewhere not far from the same spot, perhaps our age does not deserve great poets and cannot generate them, in which case it had better make the most of its good ones.

Larkin (to continue the story according to a very different sort of person) is old hat: he rhymes and scans, he makes sense, he writes about other things than what he happened to be doing last night, he never turns up to shout his poems at a throng of the educationally underprivileged (and he shaves daily). Again, indeed he does rhyme, not always, for one of his merits is the variety of his forms and with that, the control of verse-movement in unrhymed poems that comes the way only of one who has mastered rhyme. And that he has done: how seldom it is that the reader can tell which of two or three rhyme-words suggested itself first to the poet—more seldom than in Dryden or Pope. Yes, of course, they wrote much more.

Objections to the evidence of craftsmanship are not simply the product of envy, or of the fear of being shown up as a mountebank by comparison. The demon of progress has made off with several intelligent and once reputable poets of Larkin's generation who—it takes no reading between the lines to see it—could not bear the thought of being left 'behind' in that old Fifties movement, even though it had never existed, and committed the lethal folly of setting about 'forging a personal style' by an effort of will. The more praise to the man who goes where his gifts lead him.

Larkin is gloomy, not life-enhancing, etc. There are at least two answers to that. One is that a poet of our time who means to write about it at all had better be gloomy, and that life is not enhanced by not facing it. Another answer is that Larkin is not gloomy in any glum, hang-dog sense, he never writes the oh-isn't-everything-hell kind of poem once so rightly thwacked by Robert Graves, and he never sinks to self-pity (he has learnt to rise to triumphantly comic self-pity in poems like 'Annus Mirabilis').

No, Larkin is serious, which also means non-trivial, though he is fond of starting with the trivial: in the past a jazz record, a holiday train, a photograph album, in the present book a seaside crowd, a gin and tonic, a provincial hotel. But then—what a dizzying, appalling, electrifying swoop into the midst of most things that matter: death, solitude, loss, change, the past, our relations with others, religion (what there is left of it), nature (what there is left of it; at least we still have seasons, and there is one fine poem here in praise of spring, another of summer). There are no love poems, nor, thank heaven, any gobbets of over-private, under-personalised chatter about the poet's wife or girl such as pass for love poems these days. I doubt if there can be love poems these days.

High Windows is the product of, among other things, a keen eye and an exact ear. They combine wonderfully in, for instance, 'Dublinesque', a street scene of tiny compass and enormous meaning. Poems like 'To the Sea' and 'Show Saturday' accumulate details chosen with the minutest care and given an appearance of haphazardness while, under the surface for the most part, a mood, a memory, a way of life is being simultaneously evoked and defined. With it, inseparable from it, goes the weight and memorability of verse. This is what Larkin the novelist has attended to. In his day, that novelist had his savage, bitter streak, translated here into some short pieces that jolt as hard as a Restoration lampoon.

Larkin's admirers need only be told that he is as good as ever here, if not slightly better. According to the night-owl, who turns over at once if he comes to a poem that doesn't entirely please him, the last volume scored eleven out of thirty-two, this one ten out of twenty-four. It seems overpriced for its length, and my copy—admittedly after several readings—has started to come apart and had two leaves creased in production. But you expect that sort of thing these days.

Observer, 2 June 1974

Collected Larkin

Philip Larkin: Collected Poems, edited by Anthony Thwaite, Marvell Press/Faber

'I certainly haven't got a great mass of unpublished poems,' Philip Larkin told Roy Plomley, his host on 'Desert Island Discs', in 1976. Well, with the publication of these *Collected Poems* we know at last that he certainly had, unless sixty-odd poems in a total output of about 200, not counting juvenilia, is no sort of great mass. Of course a man giving a broadcast is not on oath, and on this one Larkin also stated that he had never played any musical instrument but the drums, thus showing disrespect for his own delicately bluesy piano-playing as well as for history.

The volume also contains more than a dozen poems previously published but not collected, the contents of the four published books and those of the privately printed *XX Poems* of 1951. Nevertheless it is not a complete collection and does not set out to be. It excludes, 'a little regretfully', says the editor, Anthony Thwaite, an unknown number of light poems and genre pieces Larkin included in letters to friends. 'Many' of these will appear in his forthcoming *Letters;* by no means all, if the ones I have are typical of what I will call their candour.

Reading the first poems in their chronological order, from a sonnet written in 1938 at the age of sixteen up to about the year 1950, shows an always great and distinctive talent working out the way it should go. That talent took what some judged as a wrong turning, even a cul-de-sac, in the contents of the first volume, *The North Ship* (1945), classified here as 'early poems' and firmly relegated to the back of the book. Too much like Yeats, or not really Philip, it was thought; nothing much to do with his life, he said himself. There followed a switch to a less lyrical, more difficult and abstract style that by 1947 had thrown up enough for a new book, to be called *In the Grip of Light*.

This never found a publisher and I for one had never heard of it till a year ago. Those who turned it down might well have started kicking themselves shortly afterwards, but they need not have done so too hard. The poems in it, though beautifully crafted as always, seem thin-blooded and uninvitingly obscure, and Larkin himself rescued only three of them when he got going in 1955—began to attract public attention, that is. As the poet we now know, he had emerged at the end of the 1940s with the writing of 'At Grass'. It seems almost suddenly that he learnt to take his images from the world of reality and show us, in the vividly drawn picture of a pair of old racehorses, the evanescence of glory, of active life and of life itself. At almost the same time he discovered another, vernacular style, breezy and rueful by turns, to be seen later in the famous 'Toads' and its palinode.

Larkin eventually published the earliest of these colloquial pieces, 'Fiction and the Reading Public', but never put it into hard covers. Too trivial, perhaps? A different kind of poem of this period stayed in his drawer for easily presumed 'personal' reasons, though the latter might well not have deterred other poets one knows.

In this category, at the head of it, in fact, comes the marvellous and eagerly awaited 'Letter to a Friend about Girls'. The amorous friend, needles to say a composite figure, conducts 'staggering skirmishes/ In train, tutorial and telephone booth' while the poor old poet lives in a grey world where 'none give in:/ Some of them go quite rigid with disgust/ At anything but marriage.' By the end we have been given an insight into sexual frustration too penetrating to be funny, with an added poignancy imparted by the amazingly conscientious verbal finish of the whole thing.

'The Dance', also in print for the first time, begins in the same key with 'drink, sex and jazz—all sweet things, brother', but develops into a substantial narrative set at one of those provincial-academic beanos with a live band and a buffet supper, all sharply and bitterly described. The Larkin-figure in ridiculous, resented black tie wanders in hopeless pursuit of the 'innocent-guilty-innocent' beloved until, after several pages and a year of persistent work, the poem breaks off in mid-sentence. If taken significantly further, which I suppose it never could have been, this fragment might have become a remote successor of 'Don Juan'. It is all we have—as yet—of that third novel Larkin spent so long vainly trying to write.

He might have considered 'The Dance' in any form too plain-spoken to be publishable. Other poems, even from his later years, perhaps seemed too opaque, personal in another sense. He liked to think of his work as perspicuous—'it's all quite obvious what it means'—and at its best, in 'Dockery and Son', 'Mr Bleaney' or 'Reference Back', it triumphantly is.

But some of Larkin's finest performances are clouded here and there by little fleeting puzzles, especially towards their close. Nobody seems to know quite what those high windows are doing in the poem of that title. And I for one, more sadly, can make almost nothing of the sense of falling and the arrow-shower at the end of 'The Whitsun Weddings', which he grudgingly conceded to Plomley he thought as good as anything he had done. It is as if clarity was something he had to be perpetually battling towards.

That remarkable broadcast also contained the castaway's ready avowal that he would want very much to be rescued from his island because, as a gregarious sort of chap, he would soon start missing people and society in general. To many of us this will sound rather like Yeats confiding to somebody that he only felt really comfortable in dear old London. Larkin was not above teasing, and he was far from being one for obstinately telling the whole story when a harmless evasion would save trouble. His friends would agree that he kept his life in uncommonly rigid compartments.

In his poetry all is truth. There he says nothing he does not believe, whatever the easier distracting temptations. How any poet can convince us of this on the evidence of his poetry alone is a mystery, or a multitude of small mysteries, but it constantly happens, sometimes against the grain. Even at his most assured and eloquent, Swinburne never seems to mean what he says: Wordsworth can take us where we cannot or will not follow, but he is incapable of dishonesty. It is towards the latter rather than the former end of the scale to which Larkin can now be seen to belong.

Not every reader of this book will be happy with its division into Poems 1946–83 followed by Early Poems. In all other respects it seems to me to be provably well-judged, clear and attractive. The jacket photograph shows the man as a trifle more self-confident and brachycephalic than perhaps he looked in life, librarian rather than poet, but it is pleasant enough.

Sunday Telegraph, 9 October 1988

The Coventry Chaucer

Philip Larkin 1922–1985: a Tribute, edited by George Hartley, Marvell Press

George Hartley founded the excellent little poetry magazine *Listen* in 1954 and edited it till it ceased in 1962. In it he printed some of Philip Larkin's poems and in 1955, as proprietor of the Marvell Press, he published the first of Larkin's three principal books of verse, *The Less Deceived*. The two of them were close companions up to Larkin's death in 1985. Now Hartley has put together a miscellany in tribute, as he says and no doubt intends, to the poet and the man.

It is a mixed bag. We open with a score of poems in supposed commemoration. Except for the offerings from Elizabeth Jennings and John Fuller, their chief effect is to bring home to the reader how far Larkin surpassed his contemporaries, how thin, formless and unorganised he makes them look in comparison. This is unfortunately rubbed in by the immediately neighbouring presence here of seven hitherto uncollected or unpublished Larkin poems. Just one of these, 'Tops', in its twenty-four short lines, reduces the eulogists to the status of a Richard Rolle or a Thomas Hoccleve (on a poorish day) beside Larkin's Chaucerian eminence.

We continue with a short but characteristic 1960s interview ('Another thing I rather dislike is my voice—I come from Coventry, between the sloppiness of Leicester and the whine of Birmingham, you know'), and a couple of substantial reviews Larkin contributed to *Listen*. Both of these, on John Betjeman's *Collected Poems* (1958) and Auden's volume *The Shield of Achilles* (1955), were later reworked in pieces available elsewhere, but there is not so much of Larkin's criticism anywhere that we can afford to miss a paragraph of it. This part ends with a judgement of his on Robert Lowell (not very fervent, and quite right too) embarrassingly put next to one of Lowell's on him (just as rightly effusive).

There follow some morsels of memoir, of which those by Nick Russel (on Larkin at Oxford), Arthur Terry (Belfast) and R. L. Brett (Hull) are informative and agreeably written. Russel is good on the jazz. Terry describes some of Larkin's puzzling enthusiasms, for Emily Dickinson, D. H. Lawrence, Katherine Mansfield, the novels of Conrad Aiken. Brett gives an endearing and very Larkinian glimpse of the poet reading the Bible through in instalments each morning as he shaved, surely a good subject for a competition poem.

The trouble comes with the literary or critical or academic articles that occupy the second and longer half of the book. Like that of his admired Betjeman, Larkin's verse responds poorly to close verbal analysis. As he put it himself, 'Theres not much to say about my work. When you've read a poem, that's it, it's all quite clear what it means', and he was hostile to the study of literature as a 'discipline'.

But lecturers and thesis-writers are not to be put off so easily. Where there are no mysteries or hidden cross-references in a writer's work they must be invented. The favoured technique is that of trivial/accidental association, whereby anything in the text that reminds the critic of anything else, however uselessly, is fair game, as with the Burmese or Ghanaian or Californian student who is supposed to have remarked that the first two words of the phrase 'to be brutally frank' are reminiscent of Hamlet's soliloquy.

He, or she, would be eaten up with envy for someone called Steve Clark, who writes here that the rhyme 'decisions/imprecisions' in a Larkin poem 'suggests a Prufrockian lineage for the persona'. Actually the rhyme in the Eliot poem turns out to be 'indecisions/revisions'; but never say die, nobody can prove that bit of Eliot was not lurking somewhere in Larkin's mind at some time in his life. And if you still feel undecided about the method, consider the following ray of light on a Larkin line about 'fools in old-style hats and coats', obviously meaning one's grandparents' generation. Maybe, but wait a minute:

There's a passing intimation of fully-clothed marital relations, and one should not forget that in *The Interpretation of Dreams*, Freud equates hat with the male genitals, and putting on a coat with wearing a contraceptive.

Oh yes one bloody should, and go round seeing to it that everybody else who happens to be listening forgets it too! Anyone who knew Larkin will have no difficulty in imagining the yell of horror and loathing with which he would have hailed that revelation. And such people will hope, without much confidence, that he somehow failed to foresee the cloudburst of fatuity that would descend on his work once he was in no position to object.

I have singled out this Clark but there are other offenders enough. One fellow announces ominously that he proposes to discuss 'the importance of difference' in a Larkin volume and hastens to explain that by 'difference' he does not mean '*différance*—the Derridean term is too quickly interested in the general processes by which meaning is generated and "deferred" for it to help with the specific meanings of Larkin's texts'. Well, I should just about think so too, what? Another fellow says he reckons the rhythm of a specific Larkin line 'could be related' to that of what he inaccurately describes as Zutty Singleton's introduction to the Jelly Roll Morton recording of 'Oh, Didn't He Ramble'. Could it really? Or is he joking? Yes, he mentions the muffled drums in Purcell's 'Funeral Music for Queen Mary' as another possible analogue. 'Colonel Bogey' he passes over.

Whatever went into the assembly of this collection as a whole, the editorial attention it received was minimal. Nothing is said of the provenance of more than a handful of the pieces or of their dates or of who any of the contributors are, except the editor himself. There is no index. A college contemporary of Larkin's cannot be bothered to find out whether a close friend, Bruce Montgomery (*ob.* 1978), is alive or dead, and the editor cannot be bothered to give him a hand or to correct his false suggestion that Larkin and Montgomery had little in common and lost touch with each other. The photograph illustrations are interesting and valuable. The front cover is mildly disfigured with a colour portrait by the editor and the back bears his coloured sketch of Philip Larkin lying in his coffin, evidently from a photograph. The latter is unlikely to appeal much to anyone and will probably offend most of those who knew him.

Sunday Telegraph, 29 May 1988

Larkin Misrepresented

Philip Larkin and English Poetry, by Terry Whalen, Macmillan

The jacket design of this book reproduces what the flap calls a cartoon of Philip Larkin. Such a thing is no longer expected actually to resemble its subject or victim: that bastion fell years ago. But positive misrepresentation, amounting to a kind of graphic libel, is another matter. This travesty gives the image of Larkin a sidelong vindictive look and a mean thin-lipped mouth, not to speak of an outsize ear, that he never had in life. More seriously, potential buyers might be put off by its sheer ugliness.

Any who are will have been well served. Terry Whalen, who I see teaches English in Canada, shows the level of his understanding and literary style with stuff like 'Larkin's surface cleverness only thinly veils the decidedly more serious dimension of his personality' and 'There is a more serious underself to the speaker which moves past the confines of established personality'. His unsatirical reference to Dr Samuel Johnson (a poet said to throw light on 'the further dimension of [Larkin's] unillusioned aspects') will make readers of Larkin wonder if the fellow has ever got as far as the second chapter of the novel *A Girl in Winter*.

We are entitled to expect a scholar to quote accurately the text he is supposed to be studying (or anything else). Some of Dr Whalen's dozen garblings are perhaps no worse than slovenly: 'the high-builded cloud' for 'that high-builded cloud', 'my life, my perfect order' for 'my life in perfect order'. But when we come to:

And that much can never be obsolete

instead of

And that much never can be obsolete

we are dealing not with mere misquotation but with clear evidence that the misquoter does not know how a line of English poetry goes. There are four other equally clear instances, three of them from the same short poem. Again, this is not just a matter of crass insensitivity to one of our finest metrists since Tennyson. It indicates to me that Professor Whalen is not fit to write a book on any subject of this sort.

If that were all that emerged, there would have been no need to go on at this length. What also emerges is how low a reputable publisher is prepared to sink—and incidentally how cheeky he can get, charging twenty-five quid for these 139 greyly-printed pages of text. Take note too that this Whalen book is no random barbarity. It is the seventeenth in a series of Studies in Twentieth-Century Literature, where the works of Orwell, Patrick White, Iris Murdoch, John Fowles and others are no doubt given similar treatment by similarly semi-literate dons. Before another poet gets on to the list, would Macmillan consider hiring somebody who can tell that the line 'They serve also who stand and wait' must be wrong?

Independent, 13 December 1986

PART FIVE
Social Questions

Definitions of Culture

Socialism and Culture (pamphlet), by Richard Wollheim, Faber

The prefatory matter gives us no information about Mr Wollheim's age, but it is no doubt significant that he leads off with a quotation from William Morris: one can imagine the excitement with which the young Wollheim must have awaited each new issue of *The Commonweal* and its instalment of *News from Nowhere*. I see him now as a hale and vigorous octogenarian, more actively interested in the contemporary scene than many people half his age, keeping abreast of social and cultural change by unremitting study of *The Times*, listening with real attention to what his cook has to say about the television programmes she watches below stairs, not at all disconcerted to learn that his granddaughter has taken to travelling to and from her office by motor-scooter.

Some such hypothesis is needed to explain the astounding fact that in his discussion of mass culture, by far the longest section of his pamphlet, Mr Wollheim mentions not one single concrete, individual example, falling back instead on a few lazy categorical plurals: 'jazz sessions . . . magazines, records, cars, films . . . pop-songs'. He tries to defend himself in advance for this evasion by asserting that 'we should consider the phenomenon . . . as a whole'; we shouldn't judge it by the forms that correspond most nearly to what we, on our lofty pinnacle, find interesting in real culture, for instance what Raymond Williams calls (with characteristic pomposity) 'reading artifacts'. A strong temptation to judge on just these terms, Mr Wollheim tells us, besets 'highly educated people and intellectuals in particular, *confronted by* mass culture'.

My italics. As this significant phrase, and the whole tone of his essay, makes clear, Mr Wollheim approaches mass culture from the outside. If he has ever watched *77 Sunset Strip*, seen *Oklahoma!*, listened to a Connie Francis record, looked through a selection of keen neckties at the local outfitter's—and I mean as a *participant*, not as one confronted by anything, in search of material about cultural trends in anything, diagnosing anything—he evidently feels this to be irrelevant to his task, perhaps even a bit shameful. This is silly of him. For, unless he really is an octogenarian, it is almost beyond belief that he should have avoided experiencing mass culture to much the same degree, and in much the same way, as (schooling apart) he has experienced high culture. And if he acknowledged this he would see, among other things, that the partial fusion of these two, the 'plural culture' to which he looks, or peers, forward in his peroration, is already well on the way to becoming an accomplished fact—under welfare capitalism. (Where does that leave socialist cultural theory and effort, by the way?)

Real acquaintance with the field under discussion, or a readiness to avow such acquaintance, might have rescued Mr Wollheim from a second, related, error. It is just about possible to go on talking about the 'general level' of mass culture, the fact that 'it' is of 'low quality' and so forth, as long as you remain firmly aloft in generalisation, the favoured sphere of all writers I have read on this subject except Colin MacInnes. The moment you descend to particulars, you see unmistakably that there is no monolithic 'it'; that all these 'artifacts' vary enormously in merit, at least as widely as those of high culture; that the proportion of the really unreadable and unviewable and unhearable, though huge, is probably no greater than in the *whole* of high culture; and that the best of mass culture is very much better than the worst of high culture. Duke Ellington is not as good a composer as Mozart, but he is almost certainly more varied and adventurous than Leopold Mozart was, and I should bet on an up-to-standard Frank Wess flute solo using the qualities of the instrument more imaginatively than any but the best dozen, say, of Quantz's concertos.

The mention of jazz raises an interesting dilemma, one that has never been tackled, as far as I know, by any cultural clinician. If, as American observers like Dwight Macdonald are very ready to grant, jazz as a whole is worth taking seriously, where do we fit it in? It clearly isn't all high culture, nor, while men like Miles Davis and Thelonious Monk are still active and yet so far from making the Top Twenty, can it be all undifferentiated mass culture. Then perhaps the good bits of it have graduated to being a sort of rough and warty high culture, while the bad bits are still hopelessly limed in mass culture. But then we notice that the good bits and the bad bits are all muddled up together on individual records, that the finest modern jazz is riddled with *kitsch* and empty virtuosity, the finest traditional jazz with cliché and rabble-rousing. So we can have three and a half bars of mass culture, followed by seven of high culture, followed by five and a half of mass culture, can we? (The same sort of difficulty, obviously, goes for the cinema and TV.) It does almost look as if we shall have to judge all this stuff on its merits—just like literature and painting and that type of thing.

A third defect in the Wollheim approach is more serious. This pamphlet, one gladly admits, is on the whole clear-headed, admirably moderate in tone, cogent and forceful in its demolitions of sentimental or sinister Leftist fallacies—the notion that one could, or should, revive the old working-class culture, that the competitive element could, or should, be taken out of education, that the socialist state should extend patronage to individual artists, that a specifically socialist culture could be brought into being by any means short of imposing it upon the people. But unfortunately the externality of Mr Wollheim's view of mass culture means that he too, for all his caution and humanitarianism, is in danger of setting himself up in a welfare-officer relationship with his fellow citizens, of prescribing what We can do for Them. To acknowledge that nearly all of us are implicated in mass culture, rather than confronted by it, is an essential step towards doing something for ourselves.

New Statesman, 2 June 1961

Godforsaken

My grandparents were Baptists of the Denmark Hill community in south-east London. My parents, who first met in chapel there, moved eventually away from the chapel and towards the church, like not a few English Nonconformists of that era, but by the time I started taking notice of such concerns they no longer visibly practised any religion. When I was a boy they took me to a few services, at Easter and at Christmas and on Armistice Day, but they never gave me religious instruction, told me to say my prayers or anything like that. This was policy much more than laziness; my father, laughably as I once thought, considered himself a rebel in these matters, an emancipator.

What I missed at home I was given at school, in the measure then prevailing: morning prayers, weekly Scripture (I got a credit in the subject in School Certificate) and, when the war transformed us from daily grammar school into boarding school, Sunday chapel. I had less in the way of religion than some of my contemporaries—no parish and no Sunday school—but more than others—Greek Testament in the Classical Sixth and, a less superficial experience, the chapel choir. This I joined entirely for musical reasons, or so I would have said then. But I must also have been drawn to what was on offer besides the music, and come to be familiar with it. Choir practice is in itself an unregarded form of religious training.

Except in detail, I have described the common experience of many thousands of my age-group and those younger. It would hardly have been worth recounting if large parts of my subsequent experience, beliefs and attitudes were not also common, as they surely are, and connected with it in all sorts of ways, as they must be. Something, at any rate, has made me an unwilling unbeliever, one with a sense of deep and continuous attachment to the Christian religion, a fascination with its doctrines and its history and their history, and an inquisitive interest in the Church of my country and its doings and sayings.

My belief is not uniform. Notions of God's omnipresence, of his knowing everything I think, of my ability to reach him through prayer, even of my being a part of him, I feel I could accept if I could accept other things, anterior things. But I have no belief in the existence of God, not the first beginning of one, not a shred, and never have had as far back as I can remember—not no belief in him as all-wise, all-loving, all-powerful, difficult as these might be to acquire, just no belief in him as an eternal supreme being. How could the idea of such an entity be believable? Logic will not help and the rest is poetry at best: 'I believe in order that I may understand'—'It is believable because it is absurd'—'I believe because it is impossible' (Augustine? Tertullian?)—a lamentably discouraging and frivolous remark, the more so for its quibble between it-as-belief and it-as-thing-to-be-believed.

But there the belief under discussion was of course not God as a general concept but the Christian God and all the immense structure of Christianity. Once more I feel I could take the second step as soon as I had taken the first, and accept a God who became man. But how can all the rest be accepted, every piece of it, and if just one piece, even the smallest, can be dropped, then why not others, why not all? I will never understand how and why not, until I believe, and I know well enough by this time that belief does not come by looking for the answers to questions. Faith is evidently not an explanation or a discovery but a gift.

One principle I can accede to is that human beings without faith are the poorer for it in every part of their lives. But many of those in that condition are far from being entirely pauperised, indeed are decidedly rich compared to the truly godless, those who know and care nothing about God at all. To us who were brought up or partly brought up as Christians but who cannot believe, a world without religion in it would nevertheless be as sad and dreadful a place as a world in which art as we have known it might become impossible to create, and great tracts of existing art would for certain become fatally impoverished.

English poetry is such a tract. Specifically religious poetry in English is on any reckoning one of its great beauties. To read such poetry from the outside, with only a swotted-up knowledge of the religion in it, is to experience a bloodless simulacrum of it. Something ominous can be learnt from imagining what it would be like to have to read a poem of George Herbert's, as it might be 'Redemption' ('Having been tenant long to a rich lord'), with no more than footnotes for illumination.

This is doubtless an extreme case, but from beginning to end English poetry as a whole has been shaped by religion, constantly reflects it, looks back to it often when it seems furthest away. I imagine it would not be hard to make out similar cases where other arts are concerned.

We in this country, not uniquely, may be entering a world without religion, by which I mean a world without Christian belief. Any attempt to hatch such a thing by direct means, as we now know, will go wrong. This would have been the worst cruelty of the communists, because irreparable, but the attempt has been their most ludicrous failure.

What will bring it off, in this country, is the Church of England itself, out of no malice to anybody, in a general honest thought and common good to all, assisted by a number of less attractive qualities like stupidity, cowardice and—is there a polite word for it?—flattery, sycophancy, desire to appease *bien-pensant* sentiment at almost any cost.

I pass over for now the atrocities the Church has inflicted on the Bible and Prayer Book, though it is very much part of my argument to suggest that the total effect, or at any rate the strongest effect, of these is to help to render unbelievable the doctrine in and behind the original texts. 'The Lord be with you, And with thy spirit': that clearly means something, even if we cannot at once paraphrase it. 'The Lord be with you, And also with you' means nothing, can be forgotten. The motive for the assault is possibly less sinister: by destroying its special language, to damage the status of Christianity as something special in itself, something partly detached from the things of this world.

From the progressive point of view, the trouble with Christianity is that like other religions, but unlike modern systems of belief, it is pervasively elitist, indeed it has given us the word 'hierarchical'. Although open to all, it imposes rules, difficult rules, and introduces a struggle in which some succeed while others fail. (Think of that!) Most people in it stay ordinary sinners, a very few become saints, who are regarded as much more exalted than anybody else. Parsons or priests, once called 'men of God', know more and know better than the laity, and have or had a special dress to show their difference, accentuated on those (increasingly rare) ostentatious special occasions. Above priests come archbishops and popes. And above them. . . .

What makes the Archbishop of Canterbury most uncomfortable is his sense of being above other people and knowing more and better than they do. To tell them what he knows, especially what he knows about God, and how in the light of that knowledge they ought to lead their lives, would be authoritarian of him, or at best paternalistic. Better to keep quiet about all that. As he put it in his gloom-spreading interview with Bernard Levin in *The Times* recently:

If we are to have a free society, which is essential if love not power is going to rule the world, then we can't have some people—people who believe in God—in a position to order other people what they should believe and how they should behave.

His Grace's embarrassment is fascinatingly highlighted in a point of grammar. To talk of some people telling other people what they should believe sounds too harmless and commonplace. To talk of some people ordering other people to believe this, that or the other sounds daft, not what anyone ever does. So he coins a totally unEnglish construction and talks of some people—people who believe in God—being 'in a position to order other people what they should believe'. But of course 'we can't have' the first lot of people *in a position* to order or tell another lot of people anything at all. What, then, according to the Archbishop, should the Archbishop's position be?

Faced with all the difficulties of being a clergyman in a free society, most of them understandably shy away from the elitist propounding of doctrine (never the easiest of options) and settle down to discussing 'values'. Here at least Jack's view is as good as his master's, and all can agree that compassion and peace, for instance, are what to believe in. More popular than the Trinity, and much more fun, what with speaking out against Mrs Thatcher and demonstrating against the Bomb.

In a free society, in a liberal society, in a secular age, in sceptical times—however the clergy characterise the times, their nervous consensus is that the Church must move with them. Any Christian in the old-fashioned sense, and anybody in my own position, is likely to feel that this must be wrong. Let the times move as far as they like, the Church should stand still as it has done in the past. Or rather, things having gone as they have, it should move back to where it was before and preach the Christian religion, at whatever price in incomprehension, indifference and hostility, and wait for the times to return to it if they will.

It may be asked—I ask myself—by what right I lay down the law to a Church I have never embraced. Well, as an Englishman, I still call it and think of it as my Church. More important, it is my grandchildren's Church. I have said that faith is a gift, and so it is, but it requires a living religion to prepare its recipient and to invest it with meaning. A living religion is in turn inseparable from a living, believing, practising Church. Since I want my grandchildren to live in a society in which the Christian faith is still possible, I am surely within my rights in demanding the continued existence of the kind of Church that safeguards that possibility. Unlike many other human institutions and practices, but like a language and like a literature, its most intimate associates, a religious belief, once no longer current, is dead and gone for ever. (Some years ago I wrote a novel on that theme.)

The early Christians foresaw the Parousia or Second Coming as the return of Christ in glory, either to judge the living and the dead and to terminate this world, or to rule it in person for a thousand years.

Just as likely it will be much as before, and with everything to do over again. If so, the chances are not bad that there will still be the Jewish religion to build on, as before. But I gather that 'the prevailing Christian tradition' has opposed speculation on the time and manner of the Second Coming. I am sure that this is one part of that tradition that the contemporary Church has unswervingly followed. It has enough trouble with the First.

Spectator, 18 April 1987

TO THE EDITOR OF THE *SPECTATOR*

25 APRIL 1987

Help thou my unbelief

SIR: Anyone who had been following the argument of my piece about the Church (18 April) would have been thrown off on reaching the statement, 'My belief is not uniform.' What I wrote and intended to write was, 'My unbelief is not uniform.' Part of my argument was that Anglican believers and unbelievers had interests in common, but it would take a bishop of our Church to say that belief and unbelief are interchangeable expressions.

Yours faithfully . . .

Sod the Public: A Consumer's Guide

About this A-Z: 'Sod the public' is the working slogan not only of government, the service industry and the retail trade, but also, as 'sod the customer', 'sod the audience' and other variants, that of interior designers, providers of culture, playwrights, composers and many more. For further explanation *see* CAUSES.

ACTORS: Actors and actresses are so stupid, ignorant and eaten up with themselves that one can easily forget how lazy they are. Many cannot face the effort of articulating clearly enough to be understood. Of those who can, none bother to speak their lines properly, so as to make sense. In order to do so they would have had to read them through with some care and work out what they meant, asking for help if necessary. They would also have had to discover the general drift of the action and listen to what the other characters might be saying. Anything like that is too much trouble, beside the point, in fact, if all you care about is receiving attention and looking good. So, playing Isabella in *Measure for Measure*, feel absolutely free to say:

> O, it is excellent
> To have a giant's strength, but it is tyrannous
> To use it like a giant.

Why not, if that was how you first happened to think of it? And, when another character in another play tells you the bad men are out to kill some third party, nothing of the least importance is to discourage you from saying 'That's not what *they* want; he's no use to them dead'—certainly not the reflection that it would make better sense to stress almost any other of the first five words. And, on being told that a situation or event 'was like *that*', go right ahead and say 'It wasn't *like* that!' instead of 'it *wasn't* like that' because you think you look very strong saying it your way and nobody you care about is actually listening to the words—the fucking *words?*—least of all the director, who himself only wants it to look right, and is an artist too.

The public has nowhere else to go, except away, and is steadily being reduced to a state in which it listens only in a vague, general and inattentive spirit to the plays, films etc it pays to see. Well, who does it think it is?

ADVERTISING ON TV. As many had long thought and a recent survey confirmed, the 'good' commercials made by the 'good' directors are hopeless at selling the product. The public is presumably content with the arrangement, though now and again it might prefer to keep the extra couple of coppers off the price and do without the commercial. The customer, in the shape of the vendor or client, has a *prima facie* case for objection, but these days perhaps the honour and glory (among one's fellows) of having a 'good' commercial attached to one's name outweigh the failure to sell any more actual toffees or insurance. Such must have been the feeling of those who credited the Labour Party with the 'best' TV campaign in the 1987 election, and never mind the tiresome and irrelevant fact that the main competing product was favoured instead. The people who counted, those in that sort of journalism and communications trade, admired it. This time, however, the client might have felt a bit dissatisfied with the deal.

I got a *frisson* when I happened to come across a piece I wrote for the *New York Times* in 1972 about the Nixon-McGovern election campaign. According to the British media, I wrote, the Democratic convention was a spontaneous festival of sweetness and light, the Republican a carefully staged performance rehearsed down to the last hand-clap. In particular, the McGovern campaign film was called 'brilliant', 'beautifully made', and said to project him as 'a man of honesty, integrity, physical courage and prescience' [!!!]

'After rolling around in this warm bath of impending utopian fulfilment,' I continued, 'the fellow who has taken it all seriously gets a sudden dousing of ice-cold water in the form of a tiny paragraph saying that Nixon's lead is up to 29%, down to as little as 24%. What does it mean, such wild divergence between radical opinion and conservative fact? British experience suggests an answer: most people like facts and are conservative, the radical few have the opinions, and the two interests are irreconcilably opposed.' But perhaps that perception leads us to other pastures than this Guide.

ARCHITECTURE: Most artists, or people who think of themselves as such, have to get the public to watch or listen before they can sod it. The famous pile of bricks at the Tate Gallery was powerless against those who never went to see it, and while still on the shelf *Finnegans Wake* is impotent. Architects are different. They have the unique power of sodding the consumer at a distance, not just if he lives or works in the building concerned, or just when he passes it a couple of times a day, but also when he happens to catch sight of it miles away on the skyline.

ARTS COUNCIL: Grants and bursaries from this detestable and destructive body in effect pay producers, painters, writers and such *in advance*. This is a straight invitation to them to sod the public, whose ticket money they are no longer obliged to attract, and to seek the more immediate approval of their colleagues and friends instead (see CLUB). The system encourages a habit of thought whereby 'creative' people can be divided into *artists*, who deliver serious, important, innovative, difficult stuff and so of course have to have financial help, and *entertainers*, whose work is easy to understand, enjoyable and therefore popular—you know, like rock music and John Betjeman's poetry, and whose very title to the label 'creative' is shaky. Thus an organisation created to foster art and bring it to the public turns out to be damaging to art and cutting it off from the public. Only those in the trade profit. Compare NATIONALISED INDUSTRIES and MODERNISM. The Council's days are perhaps numbered. Its new chairman, Peter Palumbo, allegedly collects the work of Andy Warhol and is known to have campaigned long, but thank heaven without success, to have an office block in the city built by the wrecker Mies van der Rohe. More to our purpose, he is reported to favour experimental art, which for one in his position comes down to injecting public money into what would otherwise be dead of rightful neglect. Well, one more like him and something may snap somewhere.

BOOKSHOPS: Following a technique pioneered by Foyle's a good twenty years ago, the more 'popular', ie lazy and shoddy, bookshops have taken to grouping their (paperback) wares by the publisher, so that unless you happen to know in advance that the works of Anthea

Scheissenschreiber are published by Cockroach Books you may have to look round the whole shop before you find them, if indeed they are in stock. Foyle's had wall-lists showing author against publisher, but no doubt it was discovered that the only people benefiting from this arrangement were the public, and it has not been imitated elsewhere. A good example of the workings of EFTA (*which see*).

BUFFET CARS: These used to stay open until the train had finished its journey; now they shut in time for the staff to tidy up in slow tempo (and block the corridor with their rubbish) and hit the platform at Paddington or Penzance a couple of strides ahead of you and me. So for instance the 15.53 out of Cardiff the other day shut its buffet at 16.05 before terminating at Swansea at 16.46. Having lunched well at Gibson's in Cardiff I was all right, but any poor dabs who got on down the line at Bridgend, Port Talbot Parkway [where?] or Neath had had it. Not a huge atrocity but worth a mention as showing how little bits of sodding the public will burgeon of their own accord in the rich soil of organisations like BR that sod it on the grand scale. Compare the inventive, resourceful skiving of individual postmen, gas or electricity officials and other public employees.

CAMRA: The Campaign for Real Ale is an inspiring but lonely example of rolling back a powerful sod-the-customer tendency. Likely to remain lonely because not all such causes have this one's appeal. Movement for Cleaner Trains? Alliance for Sensible Poetry? It seems unlikely.

CAUSES: The cause, that is, of the phenomena listed. Among them must be centralisation and the tendency to monopoly, the growing power of bureaucracy and experts, and that affluence which has transformed the old relationship between shopkeeper and customer. The shopkeeper need no longer study the customer because if he loses one there will be another along in a minute, and the customer needn't study the shopkeeper because if one purchase goes wrong there is money left to try again elsewhere. The question of causes may well be worth following up and a single, primal one may perhaps be discoverable. What has interested me more here has been the diversity and yet the similarity of the effects.

CLUB, how will it go down at the: Whereas, a hundred years ago, a composer or a playwright or a poet was influenced to some degree by what the general public might think of his new work, today such a person is more likely to wonder instead how it will go down at the club, ie in the circle of his colleagues, his friends in the profession, certain critics and a more or less specialised expert section of the public. The effect of this is to drive him towards the technically stimulating, the obscure and the 'sophisticated' and away from the older goals and values of whatever can be called pleasing, straightforward, entertaining, popular; sod the audience, in fact. Over-concern with club opinion is often obvious in modern ARCHITECTURE, in interior design (*see* PUBS), and in several features of film and television style (thrillers made baffling rather than legitimately puzzling, distracting use of camera, 'clever' cutting and the whole flood of mischievous send-ups, delightful romps, tongue-in-cheek spoofs and hilarious take-offs, particularly to be found in espionage and gangster stories). Nobody outside the industry likes send-ups, as far as I know, though individual examples may be tolerated for their moments of straight action. But a few flip jokes will protect you from being asked by someone at the club, 'Going for the teenage market now, Cy?' It may be significant that the outrageous-romp school of spy-crime story has never caught on in printed fiction. *See also* FILM DIRECTORS and SPECTACLE FRAMES.

Note: The club in the present sense may well be typified by an actual association or place and its members or *habitués*, like the Green Room, the BBC Club in Portland Place, the bar at Pinewood Studios and innumerable places of arty resort.

COINAGE, decimalisation of: Never accepted by the public, in that nobody talks of tuppence or fivepence or tenpence, as whoever wished it on us might have thought we would one day, if he thought about it at all—always two p and five p and ten p.

CONCORDE: The turned-down nose of this aircraft is rather ugly. The original straight version looked much nicer, very pretty in fact, but it was discovered that the pilot couldn't see downwards properly from it. Sodding the public does sometimes stop short of actually killing it.

COUNTIES: Changing the names and boundaries of half the counties in Great Britain and abolishing others is an effective way of sodding the citizenry not only on a large scale but for a long time, until all those who remember the old ones are dead, in fact. Except for those who are part of the new system, none of them has ever accepted the change.

DENTISTRY: Once you sat in a chair, now you lie down on a sort of couch. Nastier for you, producing feelings of helplessness among the old and nervous, but nicer for him because he can sit down. A good textbook example of sod the patient.

EFTA: Easier-For-Them Association. This must have its cadres in every country in the world, even Japan, but is nowhere as powerful as here, where the ruling passion is not for money or power but for less work. (Not so much, by the way, for shorter hours, because more time at home could mean being expected to help in the house.) Other bodies are obviously at work, like NBC (Nasty But Cheaper) and NKVD (Nanny Knows Very Definitely). A growing affiliate is CBI (Costlier But Inferior), active in production as well as service.

FILM DIRECTORS: For some reason these have become peculiarly devoted to sodding the customer. Successful ones seem to become so powerful, through their ability to attract star actors and so on, that they can be as self-indulgent, whimsical, mannered and digressive as they please. If a new film comes along and you recognise its director's name, think twice about going. It may just be worth suggesting that the much-acknowledged decline in cinema audiences may have been largely caused by the increase in the power and standing of the director, who wants to show he is an artist and be damned to the rest of us, and the decrease in those of the producer, who used to try to please the public. The chronology certainly fits.

GPO: So called here to suit my convenience for once in my dealings with it. No need to go over Sunday collection, directories, telephone boxes, telegrams. One possibly new point: have you ever tried to find out the telephone number of your neighbourhood—or any other—post office? If you knew it, you see, you could ring up and ask about second-class postage to Zaire instead of having to go and queue up to ask.

HOTELS (British): No other institutions quite touch these in their single-minded devotion to the interests of those who work in them and indifference to those who use them. Illustrations unnecessary. Motto: 'Can I help you, sir/madam?' ie 'What the hell do you want?' Founder member of EFTA.

JAZZ: The first performers of 'modern' jazz in 1941 showed a remarkably clear sense of what they were doing by *literally* turning their backs on the audience. The first jazz musicians to be given an Arts Council grant were the North-Eastern Jazz Band in 1968.

LAVATORY BOWLS: The old design with a steep inside enabled a reasonably careful gentleman to urinate without spilling a drop. The new (newish) one makes it almost impossible not to bounce a couple on to the floor. But it is *new*.

LIGHT SWITCHES: When carrying a tray etc you used to be able to put the light on with your wrist or elbow (and also sometimes open the door catch in the same sort of way), but now you have to put the tray etc on the ground or somewhere. Compare TAPS.

MAGAZINES: The growing practice of not numbering advertisement pages, and so forcing the reader to turn through them while looking for what he wants, supposedly makes him more likely to buy and demonstrably sods him at the same time.

MEDICINE: Signs here of a turn of the tide. In America a revolutionary new technique is being developed of asking the patient how he feels on the new treatment, etc and paying attention to what he says.

MODERNISM: This is an immense subject. For now, consider only that the movement in its very beginnings of eighty or more years ago *set out* to liberate the 'artist' (the inverted commas are a bit cheap but are also time-saving) from the need to please or be comprehensible to or otherwise concern himself with the public. 'I believe that a real composer writes for no other purpose than to please himself. Those who compose because they want to please others and have audiences in mind are not real artists'—Arnold Schoenberg, who does not go on to say whether or not he considers Mozart, Beethoven and others to be real artists. The undoubted fact that Picasso (and not he alone) was immensely successful says a great deal about the art trade and not much about public taste, except its suggestibility. No modernist composer, film-maker, playwright, poet or novelist has ever appealed to more than a small, specialist group, nor ever will. In this country the movement would probably have expired altogether by now without the life-support machine provided by the ARTS COUNCIL.

MUSIC IN PUBS, ETC: Nearly all pubs now have a sort of music in them, here and there some variety of real music, much more usually what merely shares certain qualities of real music such as pitch, duration etc. Those who like it or benefit from it are the staff of the place, not the public. The staff of course don't *listen* to it, they just want to have it on, in the way that smokers don't so much like smoking as feel not quite comfortable when not smoking. As regards the public, no doubt some of them would as soon have it on as not, some can ignore it when it isn't loud and put up with it more or less willingly when it is, some hate it so much that they leave and don't come back: those are the ones who like music, a smallish minority, I suppose, in this country at least. We all know this, but what do we do about it? Does anybody know the relative sizes of the three sections of the public I have tried to distinguish? Do the brewers really do better out of customers who drink against a background (or foreground) of yelling and drumming? Do they, the brewers, think that people over (say) forty spend or would spend less money in pubs than those under? Is it actually impossible to get staff unless they can 'have it on' all the time? Why is there no campaign on the lines of the brilliantly successful CAMRA? A pronounceable acronym is needed. POTIPHAR (Project Outlawing Tintinnabulation in Pubs, Hotels and Restaurants) has its points, except for being overlong, fanciful, and forgettable too now nobody has heard of Potiphar. (Well, he comes in Genesis XXXIX. In the Bible, you know.) SIP (Silence in Pubs) is better. Promise to think about it.

Note: This is only partly an age thing and not really a taste thing at all. Restaurants have taken to giving you Mozart with your *moules marinières* and Bach with your beef: better than drumming and yelling, sure, but not that much. Trying not to be distracted by what you like wastes nearly as much energy as trying to shut out what you abhor.

MUSIC ON RADIO: There are several musical publics, including a large occasional one (A) that owns and plays some classical records, goes to a concert or the opera a couple of times a year and often listens to music on the BBC when it fancies the selection; and a much smaller one (B) that reads scores, goes to concerts and recitals at least once a week and keeps up with musical developments. What (A) likes best is the period roughly 1770–1920, especially its orchestral and operatic music. Although (B) cannot be described as caring exclusively for twentieth-century music, not many in (A) like it much, except for a few special works, chiefly operas. A quick survey shows that the music broadcast on Radio 3 divides about equally between (A) and (B), which considering the respective size of each is sodding most of the public most of the time. (By a terrific concession, about a fifth of the (A) stuff goes out at 7–9 am, when the car radios are on.) The point is that (B) is much more influential than (A)—it writes in all the time, it throngs the CLUB—and the programme planners and their staffs inevitably belong to (B). Why should they bother about (A)?

NATIONALISED INDUSTRIES: A recipe for sodding the public by providing an employer who can be struck against indefinitely with no risk of bankrupting him. What was conceived of as the means to general prosperity has notoriously become its chief obstacle. Remember that stuff about production for use and not for profit?

NEW BIBLE AND PRAYERBOOK: A big one, sodding congregation, Church and people at a single stroke. Nobody except those in the trade wanted it.

NEWSREADERS: Another lazy breed like ACTORS. These are likewise too lazy to read through their material before delivering it and constantly misemphasise it, pause in the wrong place, etc. Thus one of them will say forthrightly:

> This morning a Dutch tanker was shot up in the Gulf and this afternoon an *American* destroyer was attacked,

making the viewer wonder foggily whether it was not a Dutch destroyer that was first mentioned. Or just as likely:

> This morning a Dutch tanker was shot up in the Gulf and this afternoon an American *tanker* was attacked'

this time producing foggy wonderment whether it was not an American something-else that was first mentioned. Such readers might plead lack of time for rehearsal, but they are just as bad at 9 or 10 pm with stuff that was in that morning's papers. This excuse cannot cover reporters known as 'correspondents', who are presumably uttering their own words. They recite their pieces, whatever the subject, in a ghastly wheedling singsong, stressing the last word of every sentence no matter how inappropriately, that seems designed to rob them of overall meaning. The public will be able to glean little more than that there has been a bit of fuss about the air disaster, shake-up health report, cabinet crisis they read about earlier. Jolly good, because they consequently miss the little Leftist distortions the reporter has smuggled in.

PACKETS, POSTAL AND PACKAGED GOODS: Once, you could open these with your bare hands. Who would think of tackling one today with anything less than a power-saw? But *putting on* the packaging is lovely and quick. Note how on the book packs they have done away with that little tab-and-tear arrangement down the side, a tiny saving for them and much more trouble for you.

POLITICS: All politicians are, though in varying degrees, sodders of the citizenry, giving them not what they want but what it is felt they ought to have. A British society in which the majority were given what they want would not be attractive to anyone opposed to hanging and flogging, for a start. It should be remembered, however, that if years ago the majority had been given what they wanted about coloured immigration, or not given what they didn't want, a large existing problem would never have arisen.

PUBS: Any pub redesigned internally in the last ten years or so is likely to be uninhabitable. The designer will usually have concerned himself very little with what the customers might have liked. With what, then? With trend, I suppose, with the ultimate aim of winning a prize awarded by other designers (*see* CLUB), or having a photograph of the result published in a Swedish magazine. The customers have no way of getting back at the designer and if they go elsewhere they are unlikely to do better. Sodding the public works best either when you are a monopoly (*see* GPO) or when all or enough of your competitors are sodding it too, a general point perhaps worthy of a heading to itself.

RADIO TIMES: Nobody is going to stop taking this publication because of disgust at its non-programmatic content, and it exploits this strength by sodding the reader in depth. The main departments of this are:

1) Its fairly recently revised and disimproved layout, which makes it even harder than before to find the day and time and service (TV or radio) and channel or frequency (BBC1 or 2, Radio 1, 2, 3 or 4) you are after. In case you are lucky to start with, page numbers are left out where possible (*see* MAGAZINES).

2) Filling the programme pages with unwanted and often seriously repulsive drawings and interspersing equally unwanted articles in space partly won from

3) Short-changing you on programme details, especially in casts of films and plays. Even when all the wanted names are there, that of one or another character may not be given in full, so that Bill Jones will be just Bill or Jones on the page, not much good when he mostly gets called Jones or Bill on the screen. Radio 3 entries are often minimal, with individual works left untimed in gramophone concerts of two hours or more. (This item, and others on the list, may come rather near grumbling. Perhaps they *are* grumbling, but I would not much care to be the kind of boss who has to go round telling the folks that there are worse troubles at sea.)

All in all the *Radio Times* demonstrates most plainly and usefully that those in a position to sod the reader, customer and the rest will do so to the limit of their power. (*See* this list *passim*.)

RESTAURANTS: It took a spell as a restaurant reviewer to bring home to me that modernism, now in retreat in the arts, has spread to the kitchen and is advancing there by leaps and bounds. The modernist chef sets out not to please the palate but to 'challenge' it. If a helping of roast beef and Yorkshire pudding can be compared to a Constable landscape and a plain grilled sole to a Handel *concerto grosso*, he will serve you the equivalent of a Picasso figure with both eyes on the same side of its nose or an atonal chamber work for wind instruments by Schoenberg. The bible-cum-Pseuds' Corner of modernist cooking is the *Good Food Guide* as it has lately become. Here one can read of three-dimensional seasoning and self-congratulatory mousses and note the *praise* for boldly inventive, innovative, imaginative menus, sauces, combinations of flavours. Jaded by eating out five or ten times a week, food writers have come to seek novelty above everything else and so to encourage chefs to be 'adventurous', to go in for self-expression, to think of themselves as artists and give the writers the excuse to call *them*selves critics. And the trendies go along, though it beats me how anybody can actually prefer to eat, rather than write or read aloud, a dose of puff pastry 'wrapped around a noisette of lamb and accompanied by a pungent madeira sauce and a garnish of courgettes stuffed with mange-tout' to roast leg of lamb with runner beans and baked potatoes. The public just want a decent meal nicely served in a comfortable restaurant, not an exciting bloody gastronomic experience, and are duly sodded. One might have thought that avant-garde cooking, like avant-garde music, drama, etc would soon start needing the support of the Arts Council, but the British will fork out sums in a restaurant that they would never dream of paying for a seat at the opera. I suppose one should be grateful for any lingering sparks of philistinism.

SPECTACLE FRAMES: All the pairs of glasses I have had for the last twenty years have slipped down my nose within a minute of my putting them on. There is nothing to hold them up, since I lack a convenient trench between my eyes and the side-pieces would not hook round any human ear. The frames are supposed to stay up by gripping the side of my head just above the ears. This doesn't help them to stay up but it certainly hurts my head in those two places. But I bet they looked good photographed in *The Optician*, or whatever that is in Swedish.

SPELLING REFORM: No, not here yet, but probably nearer than you think because it has everything required of a quarry for bureaucratic interference, *viz*:

1) The present system is long established and works perfectly well.

2) No rational person who has given five minutes' thought to the matter wants a change.

3) It would be very expensive. (Transliterating all previous writings for a start.)

4) Any new system would be much worse than the present one. (In this case anything more than tinkering with words like *centre* and *favour* would be unworkable. An alphabet equally intelligible to an Aberdonian, a Chicagoan and a Hararean cannot be devised until we all speak English in exactly the same way. That is probably a little further off.)

5) The most irresistible attraction of the lot to the bureaucrat

with a roving eye: the present system is full of illogicalities, inconsistencies, exceptions and things you just have to know, all crying
out to be straightened and made uniform.

STAPLES: As paper-fasteners these are more trouble for the recipient
than paper-clips but easier for the sender. As ticket-fasteners on dry-
cleaned garments they are much more trouble than safety-pins at the
receiving end and not that much easier for the people at the shop, but
enough to make them worth while.

SUPERMARKETS: A stunning example of a sod-the-customer institution
passed off as a public benefit.

TAPS, kitchen and bathroom: If you had oily etc hands you used to be
able to turn on the water with your wrist or elbow; now you have
to get the oil etc all over the tap before you start. Compare LIGHT
SWITCHES.

THIS YEAR'S MODEL: I think I understand that manufacturers (in the
broad as well as the narrow sense) want customers to buy anew and
that this year's model must look a bit different from last year's to
encourage them, and also that customers like to have the latest. I
plead only that this year's model should be no more lethal/revolting/
inconvenient/uncomfortable/time-wasting/fast-eroding/unnecessarily
expensive than last year's.

TRADE UNIONISM: By definition a sod-the-public enterprise, today and
for many years. This is now so much taken for granted on all sides
that it was scarcely mentioned during the miners' strike.

TV CRITICS: Unlike other classes of critic, these concern themselves
with what has already and irrevocably happened, though without ever
showing themselves to be the least bit daunted by that thought. In
general TV critics avoid those programmes that the public actually
watch, though they may occasionally stress snooker or soccer coverage
to show how quirky or demotic they are, with England's cricketing
performances always good for a passing sneer. They prefer to mention
Thursday documentaries or Wednesday plays with a political message
acceptable to them or, if not, with some peg on which a political
message of their own can be hung.

Although a step further down in esteem, writers who preview TV
programmes have more actual power. They do their best to put the
public off stuff that might be bad for it, using phrases like 'routine [ie
non-anti-American] spy thriller' or 'uncritical [ie non-hostile] account
of police work in Liverpool'. Their use of words like 'enjoyable' and
of course 'stimulating' or 'irreverent' should be treated with reserve,
but they can be useful in alerting one to the threat of private-eye
spoofs, tongue-in-cheek Westerns, black comedies and other shopworn
novelties dear to retarded directors. (*See* CLUB.)

TYPOGRAPHY: If the newspaper is full of literals, transposed lines, etc,
what of it? The reader can sort it out, and if he can't, sod him. Similarly
with splitting the line halfway through syllables or in the middle of

digraphs. Why not print *chang/ed* or *chan/ged* or *cha/nged*, or *ende/avour* or *que/ue*, or *penk/nife* or *hig/hlight*? Such choppings used to be thought of as discourtesies to the reader, that's to say they're perfectly all right now. Telling the computer it mustn't do things like that takes time.

WEIGHTS AND MEASURES, decimalisation of: Nobody ever wanted this, except bureaucrats and—exporters? importers? Outside such contexts, adoption of it is a serviceable pointer to trendy pissers, as when a broadcaster says a mountain is so many metres high, or someone gives a distance in kilometres (pronounced, of course, kilómetres). Even children taught only the metric system know what feet and miles are.

stop press: I have just had the new (October 1985) A-D London telephone directory dropped on my doorstep. The outside is newly designed, so that, for instance, the letters A-D on the spine, visible across the room in the 1984 edition, are smaller, pale, some sort of italic, because their purpose is not to be legible but to look pretty, of course.

Spectator, 19 October 1985

Martians Bearing Bursaries

Britain in the Sixties: Communications, by Raymond Williams, Penguin
Britain in the Sixties: Education for Tomorrow, by John Vaizey, Penguin

There is an innocence, an unworldliness about most sociological writing which can be its greatest charm. With the possible exception of public relations, I can think of no field of cultural activity in which the expert seems to start off with so much less information than the ordinary citizen. This island is now full of voices announcing with an air of discovery that people do football pools and watch television and go dancing. What is at work here is not so much real ignorance (though there is that) as an error of approach. Encouraged, perhaps by deluding dreams of his subject one day becoming an exact science, this sort of sociological writer is determined to take nothing for granted and sets about rephrasing common knowledge with the assistance of figures, charts and tables. The result of these gestures towards objectivity is often that he begins to sound like a Martian—dazed by so much novelty, moving on from one topic to the next just when he seems about to say something that might interest a human being.

Raymond Williams's new book suffers here and there from the Martian fallacy. A long and elaborate survey of the press introduces such observations as that richer people read papers with richer things advertised in them, that there is nothing about current affairs in women's magazines, that the dailies angle their news. Twice at least Mr Williams offers to do more than document assertions of this kind. Rightly noting that 'it has become commonplace to complain that there is too much "sex" in certain Sunday newspapers'. he suggests that 'it is necessary to analyse this content further'. Perhaps this doesn't mean he's going to do the analysing here and now, just that somebody ought to some time; anyway, after pointing out that 'there is a fairly regular association of sex with crime', he goes on to distinguish three categories: court cases (in which the *News of the World* 'seems to special-ise'—no jumping to conclusions here), confessions and investigations and fiction. The *Pictorial*'s serial *Lady Chatterley's Daughter* is the only example quoted of the third category, as well it might be: there's really very little of this sort of thing about, nowhere near enough for a proper category. However, the samples of this work we are given establish hardly anything about it except that it's probably not as good as *Lady Chatterley's Lover*, and virtually nothing about what Mr Williams wants us to think of it. Is it especially dangerous? Lascivious? Illiterate? Glossy? Funny? No idea. And the same applies to the stuff in the other 'categories'. Honestly, to list a couple of dozen heads and sub-heads from stories featuring sex and leave it at that is no help to anybody. Where does Mr Williams think we've been all these years?

The same question could be asked about his account of the stories in women's magazines: he informs us that 'the whole ordinary range of industrial and shop work is only very occasionally touched . . . marrying "the boss" is quite regular . . . [there are] crises due to misunderstandings and secrets . . . the reader is evidently invited to identify with her . . .' It's escapist, you see. And so on. But it isn't difficult to see what these careful expositions of the totally accepted are doing here, any more than there is any final mystery about the fantastically detailed historical account of the growth of modes of communication—'Stamp Duty was reduced in 1836 and abolished in 1855', etc. All this acts as reassurance to the reader that the author knows his stuff and as preparation for the launching of a programme designed to cure the evils, mentioned at length and with pretension to exhaustively damaging detail, of our existing culture. The technologi-cal patter in a science-fiction story, offered as routine and probably unintelligible preliminary to some plot-device that outrages the laws of nature, has a very similar function.

When he comes to his programme, Mr Williams stops telling us that two and one are three and talks in his other voice, direct and construc-tive and moderately lucid. For a change, he sees that there is something good, and much that is potentially good, in what the mass media give us; he writes well on the damage our high culture has suffered by having been made the preserve of a social class or the expression of a class attitude. His solution for our troubles, put forward with a great deal of self-questioning, is that the various arts and entertainment media should be removed from commercial control and made to govern themselves through publicly accountable committees. These bodies would include 'representatives of the professions concerned' and would dispense public money to individuals or, in the case of television and other modes that need apparatus, facilities would be granted to groups. All decisions would be made openly and with constant right of appeal.

I myself can only attempt to imagine what this would mean in terms of the publication of books. The cultural bureaucrat as he now exists—editing, granting awards, chairing committees, organising festivals and conferences—is, I should have thought, quite powerful enough even while he remains balanced by the weight of the profit motive. Mr Williams's system would put him in control: the active author wouldn't have time to help run a State publishing house, and would not often be thought 'safe' or 'balanced' enough for the job. Any *Spectator* reader should be able to fill in the names of those he could expect to find on a National Publications Council alongside the men from the Treasury, the Society of Authors man, the man-in-the-street man, the Associated Writers' and Artists' Hostels woman . . .

The danger is not from any governmental interference, but of the entrenchment of a rigid self-perpetuating oligarchy impervious to what is new. I can think of nobody in this country, myself not excepted, whom I would trust to behave with complete integrity and sense when it came to exercising power of the magnitude envisaged, to 'guaranteeing . . . certain facilities . . . of living and working' to hopeful young writers who, evidently, would have been reduced to doing without publishers in our present sense. And I am not reassured by contemplating Mr Williams's notions of correction of injustice via appeal. Any really hopeful young writer would simply refuse to have any truck with the kind of body intended, one combining the worst features of an examination board and an appointments committee, with a touch of labour exchange thrown in. Better, I submit, to stick with publishers as they are, however wicked—and their wickedness does, after all, allow of some slight and intermittent attention to the merit of the books they publish.

It is to Mr Williams's credit that he is aware of these and other dangers, though not, according to me, acutely enough aware. He is deeply concerned to give people in this country the kind of culture he thinks they ought to have; there would undoubtedly be much to commend it; he is not remotely interested in any personal power that might accrue to him if that culture were imposed. But imposed, in any foreseeable future, it would, I am afraid, have to be. I visualise no obvious form of tyranny, merely some unusually benign form of the paternalism he rightly identifies as a danger to cultural freedom, one to which his system would be particularly vulnerable. I think myself that paternalism would soon be running riot in Mr Williams's world of administrators and grants, and I suspect sadly that he would not mind quite enough. He should consider the force of Henry Fairlie's observation that 'the mass of a people must find its culture, if it is to be real to them at all, by following their own tastes and their own pleasures'.

John Vaizey's lively contribution to the debate on British education is almost unique in at least one way: so far from being brought up as a scientific civil servant or some other professional administrator, its author knows about teaching at first hand. (He has more recently, however, become an educationalist.) He starts from a keen sense of the intellectual and moral shoddiness of so many parts of the national scene and from the central fact that 'the whole idea of social equality rests upon a substantial increase in educational provision'. He argues eloquently, and with abundant and well-selected evidence, that our present system is compounded of inefficiency and injustice. All his many concrete proposals are worth considering, from the abolition of the public schools as we now have them down to the provision of computers to work out school timetables.

An understandable impatience with fluffy and obstructive notions of class superiority, of the heaven-sent fitness of the old governing class to govern, and so on, leads Mr Vaizey into insisting several times that intelligence is an acquired characteristic. Here I am not qualified to argue with him, but I connect this view of his with another which he urges as strongly, that we ought to devote more thought and energy and resources to the education of stupid children than of the gifted. Again, one sympathises, or nearly; and yet it is not hard to see this, with suspicion, as a more embattled version of the currently dominant obsession with quantity as overridingly more important than quality. Sweeping university expansion might, Mr Vaizey concedes, lower standards a lot to start with, 'but they would almost certainly improve all round in the long run'. I wish I shared that almost-certainty.

The universities—Mr Vaizey will forgive me if I use up the rest of my space on this—need reform all right. But I think we should be chary of bringing this about in order to satisfy the desires of exterior groups, whether these are ambitious parents, personnel-hungry industrialists or schoolteachers who find admission requirements arbitrarily and confusingly varied. Anyway: I should certainly resist Mr Vaizey's proposal for bringing all higher education under the executive control of the Ministry of Education (not least because this would, he alleges, 'lead to a substantial improvement in the status of the Ministry'—that body has status enough and to spare). My resistance would spring, I hope, not from any deep yearning to be allowed to go on sipping my port in peace, but from some inkling of just how precarious the barriers have become between the free pursuit of knowledge and the direction of talent for ends that are, however well-meaningly or subtly, utilitarian.

There is always a temptation to pull two bits of a review together at the end, and I am probably being merely over-neat, or over-fanciful, if I detect a faint resemblance between Mr Williams's cultural bureaucrat off to his bursary-granting session and the Ministry of Education man on his way to tell a history faculty how to improve its teaching techniques. It'll all come right in the end, I'm almost certain.

Spectator, 27 April 1962

An Arts Policy?

From a lecture given under the auspices of the Centre for Policy Studies at the Winter Gardens, Blackpool, during the Conservative Party Conference in October 1979.

As you'll see soon enough, what I have to say carries no special authority. I've been selling my work for nearly thirty years and living off it for over fifteen. I have some experience of other arts as what's now called a consumer. I'm a member of the Writers' Guild, but not a very active one, I'm afraid, and I've never sat on any panel or board or committee concerned with administering the arts. So at any rate I have no vested interest in the matter. I've a vested interest in surviving, like everybody else, and also like everybody else another one in not being told what to do. More of that in a minute.

You may not think so, but I chose my title with some care. *An* arts policy? Only one single policy for all those different arts? An *arts* policy? What a horrible bureaucrat's phrase, with 'arts' used as an adjective. An arts *policy*? As Mr St John-Stevas asked, 'Why should a political party have an arts policy at all?'* and I think any Conservative approaches the subject not with the eagerness of the planner but with the feelings of someone reluctantly settling down to a not-very-exciting duty. I hope so, anyway. The question-mark in my title is meant to show that reluctance. It also shows my indecision: I'm not sure what

* In *The Arts: the way forward*, Conservative Political Centre, September 1978.

244

policy is best. And that's rare; my friends will tell you that for Amis not to be absolutely certain what he thinks on any topic from Aberystwyth to Zoroastrianism is almost unknown. The question-mark stands for another kind of uncertainty too: I had to give the organisers the title before I wrote the talk, and as usual didn't know a lot about what I was going to say until I was down to the job.

One thing I'm absolutely sure about is that any kind of socialist policy for the arts must be sternly resisted at every point. When the State takes a really passionate interest in the work and other activities of its artists, creative and executive alike, the artists had better start running. Many a writer in the Soviet Union, for example, must feel he could well have done without the kind of official recognition he's attained. It would be foolish to pretend that there are not plenty of people in the Labour Party and elsewhere who would like to see a British government concern itself with culture to the same sort of degree. Any kind of totalitarian hates all artists, not only writers, because he can never own, or direct, their talent, what makes them artists.

What is the official arts policy of the Labour Party? I strongly recommend *The Arts and the People;** notice it's not *The Artists* or *Artists and the People*; it's *The Arts*, the commodity, *and the People*, the consumers. I thought I was going to be bored, but I wasn't; I was fascinated, and horrified. If I spend a few minutes on it, that's not only because it pays to know your enemy, though it does. Preliminary thanks are offered to the people who made their experience and expertise available to Labour's NEC: government ministers, MPs, trade unionists and individual Party members—I suppose some of them might have been artists. First sentence of text: 'The arts are politically important.' Footnote: 'In this statement we use the term *arts* to include all cultural activities—including those activities often termed as entertainment.' Next page: 'Politics are inextricably sewn into the fabric of the arts'; quite a vivid image. There, of course, the authors are telling us something about their brand of politics, not about the arts. You won't find much political content in a given string quartet. I suppose they might tell you that that content is in string quartets as a whole, something to do with a leisured, affluent class, perhaps. That would be a pity, because what is interesting about any string quartet is how it differs from all the others written up to that time. After studying Shakespeare politically, which I did once, you can be pretty sure he wasn't a republican and he wasn't anti-English, and that's about it. Enough; we know where we are there.

What the authors call in so many words a socialist policy for the arts has six classes. (A) goes: 'To make the arts available and relevant to all people in this country'. To call something 'relevant' like that, as a synonym for 'meaningful' or 'interesting', is a very unpopular use

* *The Arts and the People*, The Labour Party, October 1977.

in some quarters. I'm all for it; it's a useful or even infallible sign that the writer is a victim of appalling herd-instinct, getting his ideas from some fashionable source and passing them on without taking them in or thinking for himself. Also, you can't do that, make the arts relevant to all people in this or any other country, nor even to most people, who are not interested in them. Before sitting down to frame an arts policy, it's essential to understand that. It's a traditional Lefty view, the belief that anybody can enjoy art, real art, in the same way that everybody is creative. In the words of that old idiot and very bad artist Eric Gill, 'The artist is not a special kind of man; every man is a special kind of artist.'* That's only possible if making mud pies counts as art, which admittedly is beginning to happen. Can you imagine a novel, say, that was relevant to everybody in the United Kingdom, including the ones with an IQ of eighty? But I think that's what these chaps are getting at. You notice they say 'available' as well as 'relevant'. Obviously a novel is physically *available* if it's in print; they must mean 'accessible', another fashionable use, 'understandable' by an eighty IQ. So the novelist is to write down to his readers and thereby cease to produce art. The trouble with bringing art to the people is that it tends to get fatally damaged in transit.

I may have come a bit too far too fast. Anyway, clause (B) of the socialist arts policy goes: 'To increase the quality and diversity of the arts with greater emphasis on those based in communities'. So my duty is clear. I must write better, which had never occurred to me before, and I must write more sorts of things, epic poems and introductions to catalogues of exhibitions of experimental paintings and gags for TV shows—remember they're art too, even though they are often termed as entertainment. Actually, more than this is required. 'A socialist policy', they say further on, 'requires more books, and a wider range and higher quality of books to be published, written by authors of every sort of social background.' Naturally. But why aren't people writing these high-quality books already? Our friends seem to think quality is a sort of optional ingredient or extra like HP sauce on sausages: 'Don't forget the quality, mum!' Years ago, when the universities were beginning to expand their intake, I wrote of university students, 'You cannot *decide* to have more good ones. All you can decide to have is more. And more will mean worse.'† So with books, so with paintings, so with everything. An artist is a special kind of man, or woman, there are never many around at one time and there's no way of making new ones, even by spending money. Authors are certainly going to have some money spent on them, though, because literature is 'an underfinanced artistic area'. Would you let someone

---

* Somewhere in the works of Eric Gill. I'm not going to read them through to find out where.

† p. 163, *What Became of Jane Austen? and other questions*, Cape, 1970.

who talked about 'underfinanced literature areas' recommend you a book?

What about those arts based in communities? What are they? There's community singing, of course, but I'm sure they don't mean that: much too spontaneous and uninstructive. It's hard to make out what they do mean. Community arts are a 'process of art activity' rather than a product. They include drama, but it's community drama; music and dance, also community; silk-screen painting, video, murals and neighbourhood newspapers—'all aimed at involving the community', they tell us, and—they don't tell us, but I know—all left-wing. Community theatre would be very, very poor man's Brecht, Arnold Wesker, etc. There's a good give-away passage about encouraging 'fringe experimental and community theatre which most regional and national theatres have neglected from lack of finance and lack of interest'. In other words, we'll supply the finance and you'd better supply the interest, a very clear example of the Socialists' habit of giving   the public not what it wants but what they think it ought to want. And it's the Tories who get called paternalistic! Happily, the public won't take what it doesn't want. It goes somewhere else. It changes the channel.

The last point I want to make about this vile document, which manages to disgrace the Labour Party, concerns its answer to the question, 'Who will run the arts?' Well, 'a policy-making National Conference for the Arts and Entertainment will be set up, comprising of'—this is really elegant stuff—'elected representatives from local authorities, Regional Arts Associations, arts and entertainment trade unions, individual artists, subsidised management, and other relevant bodies'—got it right for once—'such as those directly representing the consumers of the arts'. So this lot decides what the public ought to want and a reformed Arts Council doles out the cash. It, the reformed Arts Council, will comprise of, one-third, Ministerial appointees suggested by what they call 'interest groups in the arts', hold on a minute, and two-thirds, 'representatives of most of those interest groups represented at the National Conference', and a list follows. Since it's only 'most of', who's missing? Local authorities? No, they'll be there. Trade unionists? No. It's individual artists. We're not having any of *them* on our new Arts Council; who do they think they are?

So under a Labour government we'd have the TUC controlling the arts in this country. And it's well enough known that he who pays the piper calls the tune, except that these days it wouldn't be a tune but a succession of meaningless noises that nobody asked for. The principle doesn't change when a Conservative government comes to power, though I obviously wouldn't be here if I didn't think that such a government would exert its influence more wisely and far more gently than the contenders on the other side. And yet . . . The whole question of paying for the arts is a very difficult one, not only at the doling-out end but also at the receiving end, the end which isn't so often considered from this point of view. The truth is that the way an artist is paid profoundly affects his product, whether he's an opera producer, what used to be called a lyric poet or anything in between. Most artists are subject to two quite different pressures, one to do with their material, the other to do with their public. In the twentieth century a lot of artists have got heavily involved with their material at the expense of their public. In other words, they tend to produce something very technical, complex, unfamiliar, in some way unexpected, and the public doesn't understand it, is bored, baffled or outraged. And the public—I belong to it myself most of the time—is usually right. This was happening long before there was any government support for the arts, but that support encourages the tendency. In explaining his resignation from the Arts Council in 1977, the distinguished poet and novelist Roy Fuller wrote: 'The bestowal of money for the arts inevitably attracts the idle, the dotty, the minimally talented, the self-promoters.'* He might have added that their typical product is plays without plots, a canvas entirely covered with black paint offered as a picture, poems that are meaningless patterns of letters—I needn't go on. If you're paid in advance or have your losses underwritten, the temptation to self-indulgence is extreme. If you have to please to live, you'll do your best to please.

The standard answer to that, of course, is that I'm suggesting that artists should pander to the public's whim and that new work, innovatory work, should not be encouraged. The public's whim is better than the critics' whim or the experts' whim or the bureaucrats' whim and what we should encourage is good work, not new work. Actually the public's whim can be pretty constant, a whim of iron. Take one field, music. A new work, called say 'Distortions', is commissioned. It's to be played at a concert. You have to put in other works as well, by Beethoven, Schubert, Brahms, and other composers who pandered to the public's whim. When you work out the order of performance, 'Distortions' has to be played second. If you put it first, nobody comes in until it's over, except the composer's party and the critics. If you put it third, before the interval, everybody goes out before it starts. If it's after the interval, they all have a drink and go home. And it's been like that for fifty years—some whim. A cynical friend of mine, a very able keyboard player and conductor, said that the really rare event in musical life is the *second* performance of a modern work; no subsidy for that. Well, I could go on about this for hours, as you may well imagine, so I'll round off this bit just by stating flatly that if you really are interested in quality, one way of allowing it to improve would be to withdraw public money from the arts.

As well as being tempted to be self-indulgent, the state-supported artist is likely to be wasteful. We all spend other people's money more freely than our own, with less regard for value. It doesn't really matter

* In *Encounter*, October 1977.

if a chap overspends an individual grant, which is likely to be pretty small anyway. It matters rather more if he's in charge of a new production of *Carmen*. Let's call him Entwistle. He'll be very lavish on the production itself, because that's what gets talked and written about. It's Entwistle's *Carmen* you go to see, and when you've finished discussing that you go on to the singers' *Carmen* and after that you might get on to the conductor's *Carmen*, and possibly you might have a word or two to say about Bizet's *Carmen* if there's time, or room. I was told on excellent authority a terrifying story about a recent production of *Rosenkavalier*. There's a drunken-brawl scene in which, at every performance, half a dozen glasses were smashed on the stage. One of the singers noticed that they seemed posh affairs, and asked how much they'd cost. Seven or eight pounds, he was told. 'What!' he said. 'Why aren't you using tooth-glasses?' 'Oh, the audience would see, and it would seem wrong to have rich characters drinking out of cheap glasses.' I'm glad I'm not playing the Bleeding Sergeant in that fellow's *Macbeth*; presumably he'd stab me every evening before I made my entrance so the audience wouldn't be put off by seeing artificial blood. I don't think he'd be spending fifty quid a week on glasses if the money came out of the takings, do you? As a footnote, I similarly doubt whether you'd give £2,865 you'd earned and paid tax on to something called Harry's Big Balloonz, with a Z. Well, the Arts Council gave that sum to a body so named in 1975–6. Actually it's a performance art group, whatever that is, but I wouldn't give a cent of *your* money to anything called that, even if it were a charitable home for distressed old ladies. That strikes me as quite a good wheeze for go-ahead charitable homes. I offer it free.

So taxpayers' money paid to the arts encourages waste and irresponsibility in those who do the spending as well as self-indulgence in the artist. On the second point, I might have said further about 'Distortions' that as well as not writing for the public the composer *is* writing for the critics, which means he'll inevitably strive after originality. It's annoying, but originality will come of its own accord or not at all, and striving for it must have a harmful effect. Anyway, am I arguing for the abolition of subsidies? For the moment I am. A third argument on this side concerns the supposed experts who sit on the central panels, the awful Regional Arts Associations and so on. A full study of the rise of the expert in this century, especially its second half, would make enthralling and very depressing reading. It's all part of the great loss of confidence that has shaken our society, beginning at the time of the First World War. In the past, you didn't know anything about art, but you knew what you liked. Of course you did, and what was even more important, you weren't afraid to say what you liked, and didn't like. You were a Victorian businessman and you came down to London to Birmingham and you bought a Pre-Raphaelite picture because you liked it, not because some interfering git called Ruskin said you should. Now you ask an expert because you don't trust your own judgement. It's comically appropriate that one of the most totally committed expert-worshippers of our time should be Sir Roy Shaw, the amiable head of the Arts Council, or its Secretary-General as he's forbiddingly known. Roy Fuller, in his why-I-resigned article in *Encounter* magazine,* gave as one minor reason what he called 'the hideous contemporary paintings' bought by the Council and hung in its Piccadilly offices. In his reply the following month, Sir Roy Shaw said that Roy Fuller was an excellent poet, but 'he is not an authority on contemporary paintings and neither am I; the paintings were bought on the advice of people who are'.† We learn from that that Sir Roy must himself be an authority (up-market term for an expert) on contemporary poetry, or he'd have had to ask one to find out whether Roy Fuller was an excellent poet or not. Imagine telling Lorenzo the Magnificent that that painting he thought he liked had been pronounced bad by an expert.‡ Imagine telling our Victorian businessman. Their descendants are afraid of being thought unprogressive.

The present system exalts the expert and institutionalises him. The panels and study groups and regional boards he sits on officialise and bureaucratise and politicise art. They might have been designed for the needs of the Left and probably were: new and expanding bodies with ill-defined powers and fields of operation and endless public money, money the public won't pay. For the moment I'm objecting not to Leftist politics as such but to the consequences of those politics on the various bits of art that get publicly promoted and financed. It's strange that some of the members or supporters of what rather sadly still likes to think of itself as a mass party should have such elitist tastes, that left-wing views should go with an apparent liking for avant-garde, experimental, nonsensical and certainly minority art. The explanation must be that the Lefty's settled hostility to tradition, to things as they are, overrides his feelings of class solidarity, perhaps not very strong in the first place.

So do we phase out the Arts Council and all the other bodies, withdraw in the end every shilling of public support? It's tempting. Think of a Minister for the Arts with no functions at all, his title a pure honorific like Warden of the Cinque Ports, a symbolic figure to be seen only at first nights or private views. Certainly some parts of the system could be closed down: grants to individual writers and other artists whose materials aren't expensive could well go, and there seems an unanswerable case for closing down the National Film Fin-

---

* In *Encounter*, October 1977.
† In *Encounter*, November 1977.
‡ I have no quarrel with the expert as such, who can be very useful in his proper role of supplying me with specialist information and helping me to form my taste. If, instead of making up my own mind, I let him tell me what's good and what's bad, I'm abdicating my responsibility, encouraging in him an inflated view of his own importance and increasing his already-excessive power. Art is for the public, not for experts.

ance Corporation and the other bodies it has spawned, what with their classic demonstration that investment in failure ends in failure. But things like that wouldn't save very much, any more than closing down arts centres, however desirable that would be on every ground you can think of. The really big spenders are the national opera and theatre companies. What the question boils down to is whether we seriously think the day will come when Covent Garden or the National Theatre can get along without any taxpayers' money and also without lowering the quality of their productions, though putting a 50p ceiling on any glasses they may break. If we do think that, then the argument is over.*

Where's the money to come from? David Alexander, of the Selsdon Group,† thinks it could come from where it most certainly should come from: the individual as consumer, not as taxpayer. Enough private money would be set free by radical cuts in taxes on capital and on incomes to cover the gap left by the withdrawal of subsidies. Dismissing as a red herring the idea of business patronage, David Alexander sees what he calls mass patronage as the answer. Colin Brough, of the Bow Group,‡ sees things differently. He doesn't think the arts can ever be free of state support, but a large injection from business could be gained by changes in the laws affecting capital gains, covenants and such matters. I don't know what I think. I am very conscious of the idea that any transition involving a large increase in the price at the box office would have to be managed with almost superhuman care, and I hate the thought of any of these important institutions being endangered. If they had to shut for a month or two, they'd probably shut for ever. But what I do think is both important and practicable is the lifting of VAT on the arts, if not on all of them then on theatre, opera and concert seats. Even the authors of the Labour Party pamphlet agree with me here. To take this action would be to give a huge invisible subsidy of the best kind, one that doesn't benefit individuals or individual groups. I urge the government to consider this seriously and soon.

I've said nothing so far about the Conservative document about arts policy,§ because it's very disappointing, to put it as mildly as possible. The subtitle, *The Way Forward*, bodes ill. The first sentence goes, 'Any government, whatever its political hue, should take some active steps to encourage the arts.' No. The arts aren't like housing or public health; they have their own momentum and rate of development, and must be allowed to pursue it unmolested by encouragement as much

* Some part in that argument would be taken by the example of the Glyndebourne opera, which is privately supported. It is, however, a comparatively small-scale venture, and was founded at a time when conditions were more propitious.
† In *A Policy for the Arts: Just Cut Taxes*, The Selsdon Group, July 1978.
‡ In *As You Like It: Private Support for the Arts*, Bow Publications Ltd, nd.
§ In *The Arts: the way forward*, Conservative Political Centre, September 1978.

as by censorship. The extra reason why I said so much earlier about the Labour pamphlet is that long stretches of the Tory one read just like it, though they're rather better written. *The arts are menaced by public indifference.* No: public interference. *The bureaucrats who dole out the money lean towards the conventional and established.* No: they lean towards experimentalism and non-art, because they're afraid of being thought unprogressive. *Fringe activities should be encouraged.* No, no, no. I won't go on. Apart from suggestions that VAT should be reduced, state subsidies limited to fifty per cent of revenue and business support actively encouraged, the authors have nothing useful to say and a good deal that's pernicious. Their statement is a sad example of Tory me-tooism.

I'd like to say thank you to the government for establishing the principle of the Public Lending Right for authors, and to explain to the doubtful that payments under PLR would not be grants to individuals but returns for services already rendered to borrowers of library books, the money coming not out of those borrowers' pockets but out of taxation. Perhaps I might also point out that so far no money has even started to come. Action, please.

You'll understand if my final point is also about books. One of the simplest ways, not of bringing art to the people, but of letting the people get at art, is by way of bookshops. In this country there are about 500 chartered bookshops, that is, shops where you can't buy toilet requisites or pop records, just books. In West Germany there are 6,000. There are large provincial towns in Great Britain with no decent bookshop at all. Somebody willing to start one could be supported in one or more of several ways: with a grant or loan for fitting out the premises, buying the initial stock, meeting some of the overheads, etc. To bring such a shop into being would be a real community service, and those many who live out of reach of one will probably agree with me that it's as important as establishing any sort of theatre, and much cheaper. The arrangement would also benefit authors, which is no bad thing. Some of the expense could be offset by stopping the subsidies to little magazines that mainly or largely publish poetry. The provision of unearned cash, cash that comes in whatever and whoever you print, almost inevitably results in a magazine of that kind becoming the preserve of a clique, a disability to which poetry is peculiarly liable, and that is a bad thing, and not a trivial one either. As so often, public funds turn out to be harmful to the very people they were intended to help. It's odd that Conservatives of all people should seem not to have noticed that after thirty years.

TO THE EDITOR OF *THE TIMES*

3 AUGUST 1981

SIR: The argument about cutting public expenditure on 'the arts' is in danger of becoming over-simplified. Mr Arnold Wesker (letters, 27 July) and others treat it as if there were only two sets of people involved, good chaps who are in favour of art and therefore want as much public money spent on it as possible, and bad chaps who want to reduce or abolish that kind of financing and are therefore presumably indifferent or hostile to art. Let me try to sharpen the picture. I could start by questioning the motives of some of the 'good' chaps, and there is plenty there that is questionable. But it might be more useful to advertise the fact that part of the case for cutting expenditure is founded on that very concern for art professed by the 'good' chaps.

The way an artist is paid profoundly affects his product. To subsidise him, to give him other people's money on request and unconditionally, disrupts the all-important relationship between him and his audience, a relationship already in serious disarray for historical reasons. A composer under no pressure to attract ordinary concertgoers, in other words non-specialists, is inevitably under a kind of pressure to attract specialists, critics, experts, even trendies, perhaps to be self-indulgent. Subsidy maintains or erects barriers between the composer and those who could be his public, with the result that most new works played at concerts have to be sandwiched between familiar works, otherwise nearly everyone either arrives late or leaves early.

The situation is different, and worse, with the most private of all arts, poetry. Here the entrepreneur, a particularly dangerous intruder in this field, is helping to reduce it to one more fun thing or now thing like Space Invaders machines. The poet traditionally wants to reach the reader direct, the reader wants to find the poet for himself. That intimacy vanishes in a world of poetry readings (which these days are sometimes not so easy to distinguish from rock concerts), arts centre evenings, clique magazines, cassettes, visual aids and, any moment now, poems stencilled on to tee-shirts, the whole lot subsidised by the Arts Council. I think English poetry is in mortal danger, largely because of money meant to help it.

I have come some way from Mr Wesker and his worries about 'threatened' university departments of drama. There is a case against them too, based to some extent on considering whether English literature as a whole has improved or declined since it began to be studied in our universities, but that is a large and separable subject.

Yours faithfully . . .

16 FEBRUARY 1985

SIR: According to David Hewson (14 February), 'the sense of anger, disillusionment and even betrayal now being expressed over the direction of the government's arts policy is virtually universal'. But not quite. Surely I am not alone in welcoming anything approaching a cutback in public spending on 'the arts' as a step towards the distant but desirable goal of ceasing it altogether.

Subsidy damages art by tending to foster irresponsibility, showiness, cliquism and self-indulgence in the artist. At the same time the public's power to choose what art it wants, by financial pressure on the artist, is dangerously weakened. And, whatever might be said about public taste, it is better than the taste of the people the subsidised artist is likely to set out to please or impress: critics, colleagues, friends, experts, bureaucrats.

Yours faithfully . . .

TO THE EDITOR OF THE *MAIL ON SUNDAY*

28 MAY 1985

SIR: Congratulations to Paul Daniels for his timely attack on the spending of taxpayers' money to support the arts. Of course the customers should pay the full cost at the door. This is not only morally and politically right, it also gives them some say in what is produced and put on.

The moment artists are paid in advance (which is what a subsidy means) they are tempted to become wasteful and self-indulgent, showing off to their cronies instead of having to appeal to the public. What the public wants may not be the perfect guide but it's better than what administrators and bureaucrats decide we should have.

Yours faithfully . . .

Television and the Intellectuals

I got got my first TV set early on, in the mid-Fifties, long before the things were to be found in every or almost every home. Already, the attitude of intellectuals and others towards the medium, as it was not yet called, was wary, snooty, even hostile. *They* were not going to have television; some instinct had told them in advance that it was plebeian and mind-destroying, and there were frightful stories—from America, needless to say—about children who went into psychopathic rages or panics when separated from it. (The 'violence' business came later.) These attitudes tended to become more lenient when a notable sporting or royal event came along, or an adaptation of Shakespeare was shown, but of course that was not *television*, it was something decent and defensible *on* television.

I am not concerned here to argue the toss on what inveterate TV-watching may or may not do to the watcher. Demonstrably it goes with not reading, but from what I see of young inveterates I doubt whether in a television-free world they would be reading anyway, always assuming they could, and the notion that they might become passive and withdrawn only makes me wish some of them would start to get there a little faster. Admittedly I was rather disconcerted to read recently that more than half the patients in a general hospital some-where said they would rather not have visitors because it interfered with television, but there again even a programme like 'Terry and June', say, perhaps has an edge on a lot of the people who come visiting.

If this sounds flippant it may be because I doubt whether more than a fraction of those who profess 'concern' over the effects of television are particularly serious or sincere either. I leave out professional psychologists, who may be both. I sympathise with genuine Luddites, haters of the Twentieth Century, of whom the most eloquent is Peter Simple of the *Daily Telegraph*, who would like to see the total disappearance of television along with motorways, contraception, frozen food, youth leaders, plastics and certainly psychology, though not I think modern drugs or dentistry—peace to all such. The fellows I want to get at are the intellectuals and others who on various grounds take exception to television as what it has grown up to be: a vehicle of mass entertainment in an affluent, democratic society.

Some of them are not much more than survivors from those early days when it was smart or posh not to have television at all. Now that one's friends and enemies are to be seen on it from time to time this has become a hard position to maintain. The solution seems to be to have it but not watch it, or watch it as little as possible, preferably using one of those postcard screens for minimum involvement. A friend belonging to this school asked me the other day what the Benny Hill show was, a question that would have aroused genuine alarm in my family. I explained that it was the most vulgar programme on British television. 'The things we miss, darling!' she said to her husband with charming smugness. In New York it is only okay to watch the public-service (ie non-popular) channel.

This sort of thing is obviously harmless and may even serve as a healthy corrective to rubbish on the other side about the cultural potentialities of television. Not so when we consider a particular type among those who fuss about their 'concern' at the state of the medium. The real direction of his interest is soon clear. Whatever he may say his objection to 'Crossroads' would not be that it is 'mindless' nor even—more to the point—rather dull, but that it is about employed people in a motel and not people on benefit in a squat, to him a worthier subject in every way. As it stands, too, the show is fiction and so in all likelihood 'trivial' and distracting from harsh reality. A similar approach goes for any given episode of 'Starsky and Hutch'—'violent' this time, naturally, but more to the point it shows policemen in a not unattractive light and is also not an episode of a twenty-six-part 'investigation' into trade unionism. And just to round it off, 'Tom and Jerry' picks up one black mark for being 'sadistic' and ten for not being incomprehensible and made in Prague.

A great deal, perhaps too much, has been written on political bias in television and I will shut up in a minute. Most of that bias is probably inevitable and inevitably of the Left. If you are going to make a programme about our hospitals or sewage systems or pensioners or education arrangements you are not going to come out at the end with the message that everything is in a wonderfully good state. A programme about missile-launching sites in Great Britain is not going to take as its recurring theme the necessity of such things to our national security. And you cannot have an on-the-spot programme about dissidents in Russia because you will simply not be let in, so you make one about dissidents in South Africa instead, or even possibly by preference.

My interest for now is not with the message of such programmes, nor their fraudulent air of objectivity, but with the plain fact that they are all programmes *about* something, in other words they are documentaries or current-affairs 'reports'. The documentary cinema film started life fifty years ago as an ego-trip for arty cameramen-turned-directors who could not face the discipline of telling a story, and to this day the television documentary retains the fatal habit of self-indulgence. The Leftiness too was there from the beginning (see Lenin's views on the cinema). Well anyway, the documentary in one shape or another is all over our screens today and I should very much like it removed, not just for being biassed or boring but because it takes up good snooker and soap-opera time.

To say as much is not just to make an anti-highbrow gesture but to point out the great fundamental conflict in television between the mass of the audience, who want to be entertained but are not averse to a spot of news now and again, and the makers and planners and authority-members, who grudgingly accept the need to keep the punters' noses turned to the screen but much prefer trying to improve their minds, often by pushing them Leftwards, though by no means always. In practice this means an emphasis on documentary current-affairs, on certain kinds of drama and on 'the arts', of which more in a minute.

This is the type of thing that gets and keeps franchises for independent companies. The requirement generates a good deal of cynicism: there was jubilation at Granada when their 'prestige' news-discussion show, 'Weekend World', was slotted at midday Sunday, when everybody would be in the pub, rather than using up valuable peak viewing-time later. But the pressure is there.

In television, as in other departments of national life, the consumer, the customer, the purchaser, is faced with a semi-benign semi-conspiracy to foist on him what is thought to be good for him, what other people consider he ought to have, instead of what he naturally prefers. In short, the public is brought education when it wants entertainment. This may sound an impossibly crude antithesis—surely the two can and often do go hand in hand, always have done. What about Shakespeare and other serious drama? What about art-gallery, museum, stately-home, church-architecture programmes? What about all the wildlife series? What about the concerts and operas? Yes, yes, of course there are exceptions—my case is that as things are, *on television*, education and entertainment pull in different directions.

Even some of those exceptions tend to go to pieces on a second look. Directors of heavyweight drama by and large are still far too conscious of themselves and 'the medium'; they cannot forget for a moment that this is *television*, and neither are we at home allowed to. So too with concerts, full of adventitious movement: oboe solo—first-violin passage—timpanist for the drumroll—pianist for his entry—general view for the tutti—conductor—pianist's hands—bassoonist's fingers . . . what else can you do, on *television*? The wildlife stuff is marvellous, entertaining to the full, but blessedly not educative to any extent beyond a vague encouragement to agree that some of these birds and beasts are jolly odd in their habits. Programmes about paintings, choreographers, books—arts programmes, in fact—will take a little longer.

Anybody who uses in ordinary conversation the plural of the word 'art' without a sneer or a deprecating grimace is to be regarded with mistrust. 'The arts' is a bureaucrat's phrase, a funding-organiser's phrase, a TV-planner's phrase: for one thing it lumps incompatibles together, for another it reduces the subject to an 'area' like transport or housing. All in all a bad start. Nevertheless it is hard not to be a well-wisher, to give such projects the benefit of the doubt, especially if an interview or a seat on the panel may be on offer. Surely more good than harm is done by any old 'arts' programme. Maybe. But the rigidity of the formats, the contrived debates, the nervous cutting-away to film after a couple of minutes' discussion, the presenters' cheapening summaries, the relentless quiz-show joviality diversified by the occasional homage-to-genius spot, the whole trivialising art-can-be-*fun* approach, perfectly captured in the titles of 'The South Bank Show'—all of it is just what you would expect and will inevitably get from *television*. On this showing, bright people lacking experience of 'the arts'—the very ones aimed at, presumably—could not be blamed for deciding that the entire affair from epic poetry to cartoon films was exactly the load of trendy bullshit they had always taken it for.

It might be thought that the millions are safe with their 'Match of the Day' and 'Coronation Street' and 'Dallas' just because they are millions, and so in a sense they are. But they are also inarticulate and inert. History, especially recent history, shows that change is brought about by vocal and active minorities, pressure groups. This one, the one that wants television to be instructive and uplifting, is supported by all the people—50,000 of them in the whole country? 100,000?—who could be said to take an intelligent interest in 'the medium', as is clear from everything published on the subject: leading articles, think-pieces, letters to the quality papers (not the populars, whose readers generally voice majority opinions here), TV reporting and even more TV previewing. This last, a lowly field but well worth study, shows the common assumptions in a raw state, with deference largely reserved for the foreign, the subversive and the black-and-white, and unedifying stuff blown away either as 'routine' or as 'predictable'—within limits just what the majority want from their evening's viewing.

Television should stick to what the customer pays to see, which unsurprisingly is also what it does best: sport, public occasions, magazine programmes, family and neighbourhood sagas, rock shows (not all of these categories are necessarily very strong with me) and crime and comedy series. Particularly in the last pair, professionalism of a high order is often to be found, though because it effaces rather than obtrudes itself critics will usually miss it. But it gets through to the public, who were on to shows like 'Porridge' and 'Minder' before anybody thought of writing about them. There is a moral in that.

1984

Feminine Complaints

Women, by Naim Attallah, Quartet

This book weighs something like a kilogram and a half, which fact the literary editor of this newspaper omitted to mention when he persuaded me by telephone to agree to review it. Treating it so that it will lie open on desk or lap is impossible to one of normal muscular power. This might matter less if closing it on purpose were not such a constantly attractive option.

Its compiler, Naim Attallah, was born in what was once Palestine. He is a Roman Catholic by religion and is also the head of a successful London publishing group, a director of Asprey's in Bond Street and a producer in the theatre, the cinema and television. He has collected taped interviews with 289 assorted women, which he himself has prefaced with some chapters of historical pretension on women in myth and literature, women in the Middle Ages and the like. The interviews themselves, some 1,000 pages of them, are subdivided under such non-restrictive headings as 'sexuality' and 'relationships'.

The subject of the volume, namely women, is probably not a subject at all, any more than men would be, unless in an anatomical or bio-chemical textbook. Women and African exploration, motor-racing, bathroom-stool design, even politics might just be subjects, however uninviting to a reader. But women, women on women, on being a woman, on not being a man, on men, on having children, on not having children—all that without any direction or incentive to particu-larise, just wittering away as long as the tape lasts—well, it's unlikely.

Nor are the interviewees selected on any principle, neither randomly (ensuring no group was over-represented) nor in a stratified way (ensuring none was under-represented). They are merely women—actresses, journalists, novelists, TV and film people—whom Mr Attal-lah came across as names in the press or in the course of his publishing and producing activities. He could perfectly well have got chatting to Koo Stark, who took the photograph of him on the jacket-flap, and run the list up with her in an hour looking through a copy of *Tatler* and a couple of Sunday mags.

But wherever he got them from he certainly came up with a bumper crop of raging egotists, pompous buffoons and unstoppable talkers, because that is what most of those who would take part in such an enterprise are inevitably going to be, with all humour and power of detachment virtually ruled out. To hear them go on, you would think that no female before them had ever been a child, got a job, met a man, had an affair, got married, had a baby or noticed that women are different from men and often have a different sort of life in certain respects.

Their standard of perception and conversational style, which is remarkably homogeneous, is illustrated in remarks like 'It was a very male-oriented situation' and 'I have an accomplished personal life' and 'My intellectual formation was due to men' and 'The secret of beauty is what you project.' Their ever-fresh astonishment at the ways of the world is well exhibited by the journalist and TV person who recounts in vivid detail, and still spitting with fury, how she found that as a prospective late-night interviewer she was expected to look glamorous, and points out in concrete terms that that would not have happened to a man, with the telling conclusion, 'This is an area of inequality in my view.' I wonder how she would have responded to the experience of an ex-nun and former training consultant with General Motors as described here. On receiving through the post a marble slab carved with the text of a newspaper article about her, the gift of a male colleague, the lady said, 'This is what I call acceptance.' And that's what I call a sportsman.

After sampling this stuff at all thoroughly, the reader perhaps goes back to some of Mr Attallah's introductory material. The male consensus, until very recent times, on the question of female inferiority will come as news to nobody who can read, but the range and diversity of that agreement is easily forgotten. It does no harm to be reminded, or even informed, that a writer in the *Spectator* in 1711 commented, 'When we see a fellow loud and talkative, full of insipid life and laughter, we may venture to pronounce him a female favourite', and it comes in appositely to learn that in Victorian times a lunatic might be allowed to vote in his lucid intervals, a woman never. Mr Attallah thinks we live in 'a sexually healthier age' now. Well, he would, wouldn't he?

Luckily for the rest of us, a few human beings have managed to slip past his selection procedures, though not enough to save the book or make it worth while. Here is Mary Kenny saying what I thought no one was ever going to say about that queen of shams, Simone de Beauvoir:

> She was a big failure as a woman, I think. She refused marriage . . . She refused motherhood. She chose abortion rather than having children . . . She had all the disadvantages of a wife, without the dignity of a wife, and she didn't have the fulfilment of motherhood, and I think her writing shows it.

Here is Rosemary Anne Sisson's recommendation to feminists:

> I think the more you try to assert yourself and be aggressive as a woman, the less respect you will get . . . You know, if you can't manage children and a job, then don't have children or don't have a job, otherwise get on with it and find a way.

And here is Christina Foyle's—let's call it a reminder to men:

> When I was a girl in my father's shop, I'd get all these men always pestering me. I used to get awfully sick of it. I wasn't interested. I don't think a lot of women are. It's very nice if you fall in love with somebody, but I think women have other things they'd rather do.

Sunday Telegraph, 18 October 1987

PART SIX
Education

Pernicious Participation

A student, being (if anything) engaged in the acquiring of knowledge, is not in a position to decide which bits of knowledge it is best for him to acquire, or how his performance in the acquisition of knowledge can most properly be assessed, or who is qualified to help him in this activity. Or other things besides; but the three incapacities I have mentioned correspond to the three main student 'demands' in the academic field: for control over courses, over testing methods, and over the appointment of teaching staff.

As an undergraduate myself—and an unusually well-trained one I was, with excellent and intensive fifth- and sixth-form teaching behind me—I would have made sweeping changes in my course, that of the Oxford English School, if I had had a voice in the matter. My own self-tailored final examination would have consisted of a Shakespeare paper, one or two papers on those writers between about 1500 and 1900 who had most interested me at school, and the remainder on literature since 1900. No Old English, Middle English, history of the language, or any of that. Being a student, I had no way of knowing then what a close study of Spenser, Milton and Wordsworth, pre-eminently but not exclusively, would reveal to me. Nor had I at the outset—again, there was no way whereby I could have had—any but a vague and incomplete idea of what it meant to study an academic subject at the undergraduate level. Without that knowledge which I should never have acquired if I had not been under pressure to do so, I should have been much the poorer for the rest of my life. (I cannot pretend I am glad to have studied *Beowulf*, but I have often wished I had not allowed my dislike for the poem as literature to blind me to the linguistic interest afforded by this part of the course.) My ideas about what an English School should be were mistaken—less mistaken, to be fair to myself, than plenty of contemporary ones—but fortunately I was not consulted on the point.

I must say that all but a very few of today's students are even less qualified to judge of these matters than I was at their age. And this does not only apply to arts subjects; who can understand the importance of Roman law, or anatomy, or calculus, if he has not mastered them? (The word to be on the alert for, in all discussions of the direction in which syllabuses should be reformed, is 'relevance'—to the needs of society, to a developed industrial society, to a bourgeois capitalist society, to the needs of the student, to the interests of the student. The student who is himself looking for relevance is looking for vocational training, a harmless desire in itself, though anti-academic and therefore not to be indulged at a university; the teacher who wants to import it is an enemy of culture. To extend the glossary a little: 'challenging' or 'exciting' courses of study are those in which a non-subject or two, like sociology, social psychology, etc, is thrown to alleviate the burden of concentrating on a real subject; and 'breaking down the rigid, or nineteenth-century, or arbitrary, or irrelevant divisions between disciplines' means offering the student a smattering of several subjects instead of the less inviting task of mastering one.)

The examination system probably needs reform in certain cases, but it is nonsense to say that it does not, even as it stands, provide a good test of knowledge and understanding. Any exam that really tested nothing but memory, a common student complaint, and one which obviously says much more about the student making it than about the exam, would not only be genuine grounds for inquiry in the department concerned, but an academic curiosity too. I myself, in over fourteen years of teaching in Swansea, Cambridge, Princeton and the American South, never came across a student whose examination results were materially at odds with his or her day-to-day performance, though admittedly some nervous candidates did do worse in individual papers than might have been predicted. This sort of minor injustice could easily be, and often is, rectified. The inescapable and unpopular fact is that examinations mean a lot of hard work—and not only on the part of students, either. To call for the abolition of all forms of grading, as the Revolutionary Socialist Students Federation is reported to have done on the day I write this, is of course to call for an end to education. And why not? The dissolution of the universities is, these days, by no means an unattractive project.

There is not much to say about the appointment of staff. Like everybody else who has had anything to do with this, I know how hard it is to determine beforehand whether someone likes his subject, knows it and can teach it, this even if one is qualified in the subject oneself. It might be easier to decide in advance what sort of new appointee would refrain from propagating bourgeois ideology—ie talk Maoism at you—leak examination papers to you—or falsify your progress reports—and go on marches with you.

The reader must forgive the occasional note of asperity. Demands for student participation conceal, or do not conceal, a simple desire to have less studying to do, less of everything that relates in any way to studying. As a consequence of irresponsible expansionism, the universities today are full of students who do not understand what study is about, and who are painfully bewildered by the whole business and purpose of university life; more has meant worse. Student unrest has several causes, but here and now the prime one seems to me to be the presence in our universities of an academically-unfit majority, or large minority. This condition may be beyond cure, but that is no reason for allowing the symptoms to rage unchecked.

The Critical Survey, winter 1969

The Anti-Sex, Croquet-Playing, Statistic-Snubbing, Boyle-Baiting, Black Fascist Paper

(with Robert Conquest)

Our names were referred to to an excessive extent in the discussions on the first *Black Paper*, no doubt because, in a superficial sense, we chanced to be more in the public eye than many contributors more distinguished and experienced in the field than ourselves. This time anyway, while our colleagues provide the formidable structure of evidence and argument, we confine ourselves to the modest and peripheral task of some notes on the treatment of the *Black Paper* in the 'media'.

Of course, there was much support for us there. Julius Gould, reviewing it in the *Observer* (23 March 1969), praised the *Black Paper* warmly and summed up our position: 'What they stress (and I am sure they are right) is that educational "thought" has rested too much upon tendentious, anti-intellectual rubbish and that bad "thought" has driven out good.' John Raymond, in the *Sunday Times* (16 March 1969), made similar comments about our 'blistering home truths'. And there were many others. In general the paper was well received by teachers and educators—but much less well by educationists, educational journalists, and politicians. In some cases, but not many, these were honourable and sensible opponents, who welcomed discussion, and admitted that to call a position unprogressive was not to refute it. We would refer them to the other contributors in the present paper, while we look here at the extraordinary, and to our minds significant, barrage of abuse, misrepresentation and plain falsehood which was the more typical response.

The mere abuse, such as 'prejudices that verge on the hysterical' (applied by the *Times Literary Supplement* to the headmasters' contribution to *Black Paper I*), only deserves the barest reference. The more definite allegations or suggestions are not so lacking in interest. *Teachers World*, for example, suggested among other things that we must oppose mini-skirts, sex and Miss Raquel Welch, and be in favour of cold baths.* The *Evening Standard*, in an editorial written by the editor himself—a man a good deal older than many contributors—called us 'elderly reactionaries'. Mr Christopher Price, MP, in the *New Statesman* (18 April 1969) referred to us as 'educational Powellites'. Mr Anthony Arblaster in *Tribune* thought we stood for universities devoted to port-drinking and croquet-playing. And finally, the Minister of Education himself, Mr Edward Short, associated us with a general 'swing to reaction', to racism, demands for corporal and capital punishment, and the abolition of the welfare state. The smear by association, one used to be told, was a very wicked method of controversy. But the smear by connection with movements and policies with which no one concerned has had any association at all, is surely a new development.

The Minister will have been dealt with elsewhere in the Paper. But it is worth emphasising, as a bad omen, that he aligned himself with those who spoke in terms of yellow political journalism rather than reasoned argument. Admittedly he was offering the teachers a bash at the *Black Paper* in lieu of a pay rise, and a reasoned refutation of us, were such possible, would hardly have been sufficient to the occasion. (Incidentally we *are* in favour of a great increase in teachers' pay—see, eg Amis in *Daily Express*, 9 April 1969.)

In general, the commonest ploy from all these sources was to charge us with a wish to exclude the working class from higher education and to use the educational system as a means of perpetuating the rule of an archaic aristocracy. Such an interpretation could only be supported by ignoring or misreading what we actually said: so that was done.

As to the *Black Paper*'s ideas about teaching methods, there was much talk of a revival of the more brutal type of nineteenth-century schooling. And Mr Stanley Segal (*Daily Telegraph*, 11 March 1969) was only one of those who suggested that we wanted a return to the England of Dickens, of Squeers (though Squeers' system, by which boys combined cleaning the window with learning to spell it W-I-N-D-E-R might be seen on the contrary as a pioneering experiment in

---

* To do *Teachers World* justice, there was no malice in this rubbish, nor in their later quoting, as the educational views of one of us, of an interview in *The Times* on an only remotely related theme. And in the best tradition of non-authoritarian journalism, *Teachers World* invited us, and others from the first *Black Paper*, to contribute to its Personal View Series, which we did.

progressive modernity, both in the method and in the permissive spelling).

But in addition to this sort of thing there were straight falsehoods. The *Guardian* (Miscellany, 10 May 1969) called us 'a tightly-knit group of Righties'. This was simply a lie. We shall speak of the inapplicability of the term 'Right' later, but the fact is simply that no 'group' of any sort, let alone a 'tightly-knit' one, existed or exists. Few of us have met, and fewer still more than briefly. But this sort of attacker was so blinded by prejudice as to have quite lost the faculty of distinguishing between fact and fantasy. The *Guardian* said that Enoch Powell was a contributor. He wasn't. Mr Paul Foot (in *Private Eye*), said that Peregrine Worsthorne was a contributor. He wasn't either.

Mr Foot, who has been described by the *Observer* as the best journalist at this sort of detailed research, made this error in the course of an exposé of the origin of the *Black Paper* which contained no truth at all. The *Black Paper* originated (he claimed) as a plot by the two of us, and Mr Bernard Levin and Mr Peregrine Worsthorne, against Sir Edward Boyle: Lunchtime O'Booze could scarcely have bettered this agreeable tale. But in fact the first either of us heard of any such project was when Professor Cox and Mr Dyson sent Conquest a copy of a draft editorial for their magazine *Critical Quarterly*, to which he had contributed a poem and a couple of essays. When they later decided to turn it into a booklet and solicited essays, Conquest recruited Amis. And Messrs Levin and Worsthorne had nothing whatever to do with it, then or ever.

One of us wrote to *Private Eye* (and the letter was printed) pointing out that its story was a 'complete fabrication'. There can be few journalists who, if so charged, would find it suitable neither to reply, nor, alternatively, to withdraw from their profession. (We should add that *Private Eye* has elsewhere been reasonably benign.)

What seems to emerge in all these cases, is that the self-styled progressive *needs* a Joe McCarthy or an Enoch Powell in every field, both to feed his own self-righteousness and to provide a level of revulsion at which he is not put to the necessity of actual reasoned argument. The *Black Paper* contributors do not fit the bill? Then they must be *made* to fit it. Such is their role in life. And perhaps if the uproar is loud enough, the public will accept the abuse and irrelevance and not bother about the reality. Well, just so long as we know.

Some more moderate opponents—even in the *Guardian* itself—did indeed complain that attempts to smear the motives of the *Black Paper* were a disservice to the debate. If the 'progressive' view had any value, they argued, it must answer other than with authoritarian screams, or mere label-sticking. Not all change is progress and not all reversion is regress. Germany has 'lurched' back from Nazism to the earlier system, and Czechoslovakia attempted a similar 'lurch' back to democracy only last year. When a course of action has proved erroneous, it is rational to abandon it. But all the sort of stuff we have been noting boils down to a mere attempt to pre-empt the weasel words 'progressive', 'democratic', 'egalitarian' and so on—that is, to avoid argument on the merits of the case.

In general, those who condemned the *Black Paper* for 'elitism' are just those who tell us that the students are an elite, well informed, full of political consciousness, social conscience, wonderful young people, and an example to the lower orders. More than that, our critics see *themselves* as an elite, empowered, as we are not, monopolistically to organise the educational system to fit their social and other theories.

It was to be expected that the word 'fascist' should be heard in this uproar. It has been used, after all, of Mr Crosland, so why not of us?—(except that we would regard ourselves as considerably less authoritarian in outlook than he). The meaning of the word 'fascist' has of course been lost in the mists of time, going back as it does several decades. (A phrase common in the mouths of 'radical' 'students' is 'You pathetic fascist'. There are many adjectives, most of them unpleasant, which can legitimately be applied to real fascists, but 'pathetic' is not among them. Nor do we think that the average student would venture to use that adjective if actually confronted with a veteran SS Sturmbannführer. We seem here to have one more little symbol of ignorance either of history, or of the English language, or of both.) But in fact fascism, though hierarchical in its state and social order, was in principle egalitarian from a class point of view in its educational approach, and its promotion system.

One of those who spoke of fascists was Mr Michael Duane. It would be unfair, however, to get the impression (as one might have from *The Times*) that he was one of those who called us fascists pure and simple, though the word did conclude his peroration. (*Teachers World*, 11 July 1969.) What he actually said was that we were either Christians or democrats or fascists—a true enough characterisation. (We are, as it happens, democrats.) Mr Duane had merely misread—or not read— the *Black Paper* before attacking it. He thought that we wished to create an elite with 'leadership, authority and the use of power', and that 'wealth, power and leisure' were the incentives we recommended. He argued that largely owing to 'home background', there is a gross disparity of educational opportunity between the working class and the middle class: he is perfectly right, but far from the *Black Paper* approving of this, it was precisely the contention of many of its contributors (eg Mr Dyson) that the grammar school (or the grammar school type of education) was particularly valuable in providing the working-class schoolboy with the cultural resources often lacking at home, while the flatter style of comprehensive would tend to perpetuate the middle-class advantage.

The commonest argument against the view taken in the *Black Paper* that standards are falling everywhere, was the assertion that statistics proved this to be untrue, so that 'subjective' reports to the contrary— ie eye-witness accounts of actual facts—were false, or irrelevant, or unrepresentative. It need hardly be said that genuine statistics, properly applied, can increase understanding in many fields, including that of education. Nevertheless, this last is a sphere in which one wants to be particularly careful of the alleged objectivity and relevance of statistics, especially when they run against common experience. An American professor of philosophy was once approached by a researcher with the question, 'how many pages of philosophy do your students of various grades have to read each semester?' 'Well,' he replied, 'I suppose I could check that for you. But isn't there a difference between ten pages from a popular handbook and ten pages of Aristotle in the original?' 'That's a matter of *opinion*. The number of pages is a matter of *fact*.'

We could not help being mildly shocked by the widespread infatuation with figures among our critics and opponents. ('Infatuation', with its overtones of imperviousness to reason, seems the appropriate word here, though admittedly it also implies something ephemeral, and there is little sign of the passing of this phase.)

For instance, one of us (Amis) received a staggering rejoinder to an article he had contributed to *Teachers World*. Amis's main point—a simple one—had been that statistics about, say, the number of O-level passes could not, by definition, be used to prove anything about the *quality* of the work shown. A correspondent, a David C. de Massey, LL.B., quoted a table purporting to show the progress made by a number of children at his school during the current year. Now, even granting that progress is measurable, a mere table can convey nothing about criteria, and a single table referring to a single year tells us nothing about progressively rising—or falling—standards. Mr de Massey succeeded only in making the unexceptionable point that some children anywhere make more progress than others, yet he appeared to think, presumably having actually read Amis's piece, that he had thereby refuted its argument.

The latest instance—and a shocking one—of the tendentious use of figures in education is provided by Mr Short himself. As we go to press, he is reported (*Daily Telegraph*, 10 September 1969) to have replaced the old definition of an overcrowded class—more than forty pupils in a primary school class, more than thirty in a secondary school—with a brand-new one, whereby the teacher-pupil ratio *in the school as a whole* becomes the criterion. By this reckoning, overcrowding ceases to exist. Would that all our educational problems could be so effortlessly solved!

To resume—while theorists were giving generalities and statistics, the newspapers were also reproducing, sometimes in the same issue, a good deal of 'subjective material'. As *The Times*, and in particular its education correspondent, made a number of such refutations of our view that standards were falling, its news pages carried such items as 'Boys could not spell own names' (29 March 1969), a report of apprenticeship examinations of fifteen- to seventeen-year-old Dorset secondary schoolboys—(*most* of whom could not spell either 'apprenticeship' or 'secondary', and only twenty per cent of whom got full marks on an arithmetic test in which the most difficult question was to find the cube of two). An instructor remarked that things had 'got progressively worse each year'. Similar glimpses of reality are quoted elsewhere in this paper. Much hard work had to be put in to repress the difficult material, to plug the holes in the dyke of delusion.

The issue of the *Observer* which carried the favourable review of the *Black Paper*, balanced it with a hostile comment from an educational journalist. He asserted that standards of reading and arithmetic have been rising 'so far as standards can be measured accurately'; but reality broke through, and he conceded after all that 'it is equally obvious that far too many children do not learn to read properly'.

These statistical and other attempts designed to prove that academic standards have not fallen at least recognise that such standards need protecting. They are scarcely compatible with the other great arguments—in effect, that if society is abolishing civilised criteria it is the job of universities to abolish them too (or, alternatively, that if society is *not* abolishing them, it is the job of universities to set an example by doing so on their own).

For our opponents justify their educational theories, in part, by the notion that there are established and proven doctrines of psychology, and in particular of sociology, to prove them right. This is, of course, not so. But the worst feature is that, in a situation where pupils are clearly not getting enough of the basics, they crowd these out by what we rightly called 'non-subjects'—that is, in the main, 'sociology' and 'social studies' as they are normally taught at this level.

Our point was very ill received. We had indeed spoken of a genuine sociology—the philosophy of society on the one hand, and the very careful establishment of minor facts on the other. But we had contrasted it with the facile dogmas, or distorted materials, too often presented. It was a professor of sociology (Professor Gould) who warmly agreed (*Observer*, 23 March 1969) with a remark by one of us (Conquest) about the bogus sociology which seeks support for 'preconceived notions, usually of a notably shallow type, from selected or invented material'. The case against sociology as an A-level subject is clearly put in *Sociology* (Vol. 3, No. 2) by Jennifer McArthur; we would add that it is, in general, not a suitable undergraduate subject either, unless preceded or accompanied by other studies more conducive to learning the nature of academic rigour.

It is increasingly taken as the teacher's duty to teach 'Life', to instil moral attitudes in a child—and to integrate his psyche. Bertrand Russell was consciously overstating the point when he wrote, 'It is a bad thing for education and ultimately for character, to let instruction be influenced by moral considerations.' We would surely all agree that it was legitimate for a teacher to inculcate such notions as the undesirability of theft or lying, or snobbery or racism. On the other hand we can presumably demand that teachers should not inculcate partisan viewpoints, political or otherwise. It is not very easy to draw the line, admittedly. But, as Anthony Hartley remarks in his *State of England*, apart from that minimum, this teaching of 'Life' is an intrusion into a sphere 'in which there is not only no consensus of opinion, but also hardly any factual information'. Or as Dr William Pickles has put it, 'We also believe it is wrong to sacrifice intellectual or vocational training to doubtful and untested theories about social training, and that if ever any given social theories are tested and proved right, we shall *still* have to keep a sense of proportion, leaving social training mostly to parents and intellectual and vocational training mostly to teachers.'

Many of those with 'progressive' ideas are often just the teachers with the greatest concern for the good of their pupils. It is not their good will that is in question, but merely their judgement. It must be extraordinarily easy for a teacher who sees a child becoming frustrated or unhappy to turn to every conceivable means to cope with this. But, as Mr David Holbrook has warned recently in the *New Statesman*, this all too often leads to lesson periods for young children developing into a sort of amateur psychotherapy. Even professional psychotherapy is pretty amateur, but attempts by teachers to allay tensions—through various forms of self-expression or otherwise—may be actively harmful or dangerous, particularly among younger children.

On the other side of the coin, some teachers, especially in universities, have even taken the view that particular political attitudes, hostile to the 'bourgeois' order, should be taught. But if it were admitted that any such things were desirable, the consequences envisaged by the pop-revolutionaries would not follow. On the contrary, partisan views taught in a democratic society would have to be those of the majority. We would find a greater, not a lesser, emphasis on patriotism, for example, were the views of either of the great parties in the state to take precedence over those of the Garden Suburb Guevaras now so much in evidence.

And here we can return to our starting point. There is nothing 'Right-wing' about our educational views. They are those which would have been shared by Edmund Burke, John Stuart Mill and Karl Marx, and can be shared by their followers. The preservation of standards is not just a matter for High Tories. Nor can that peculiar section of the 'Left' which wishes to destroy the universities be thrown in the face of the Left as a whole. It is rather a waste of time to blame the avowed enemies of our culture for the conduct natural to them.

Raymond Williams (of course) took the view that the main aim of education was 'disturbed and disturbing argument of a creative kind' (*Times Educational Supplement*, 8 April 1969). He argued that to maintain that education involves passing on the achievements of our civilisation implies an insistence on the acceptance of 'stock ideas'. Now, we are all in favour of developing the critical faculty—and vis à vis stock ideas of the 'left' as much as any. But (as one of us argued) one cannot criticise even stock ideas if one doesn't know what they are. Lenin would have agreed:

> It would be a very serious mistake to suppose that one can become a Communist without making one's own the treasures of human knowledge . . . Communism becomes an empty phrase, a mere facade, and the Communist a mere bluffer, if he has not . . . made his own, and worked over anew, all that was of value in the more than 2,000 years of development of human thought.

Mr Short (on the other hand) attacked the suggestion of one of us (Conquest) that entrance to university should involve a general paper to prevent cultural illiteracy. Short asked how, with such a barrier, could the miner's son from Nottinghamshire or the North East ever get to university? What Conquest had in fact complained of was that some students now were unaware even of the mere names of such figures as Mendel and Verdi, and that this should be corrected. A modest demand, one would have thought, amounting to little more than asking that university students should not be illiterate. Mr Short's unfortunate miner's son is, he seems to forget, at school for a number of years before reaching the university. It is precisely one of the jobs of school to see that students have at least some idea of the riches of our civilisation. Surely there is time for that in all those years, if there is time for so much 'social study' and 'creativity'? Of course the miner's son is at a disadvantage to start with. All the more reason for Mr Short's vast and expensive machine not to leave him in that state, through gross and wanton neglect. Mr Short was one of those who attacked us specifically as standing for 'elitism'. If to urge tests for entry to university is to perpetuate an elite, then Mr Short himself is equally guilty. Our dispute is of course not one about elites at all, but about what should constitute an education. (Another word, and idea, which we hope most people find nauseating is 'meritocracy'.)

In addition to being attacked by Mr Short, we were accused, as noted above, of working to undermine Sir Edward Boyle. No, there was too much to say about the sad results of the present system, and the theories which led to them, for us to be able to cope in addition with the problem of who was to blame. But since the matter has been raised . . . Sir Edward was in the Ministry of Education from 1957, and became its chief in 1962. It was in 1961 that Amis gave his much-misquoted warning that—if pursued by the means then in hand—'more will mean worse' in the universities. It was at that time that we saw, for example, the political pressures by which a quite disastrous expansion was forced on the LSE, as Mr D. C. Watt describes so tellingly in his essay in the first *Black Paper*. Sir Edward's strongest supporter, *The Times*, carried a long column in his defence (17 April 1969). But, apart from insisting that he was a nice chap, the only substantive argument it advanced was that his attitude might win votes. We believe not. But, anyway, this argument would not be regarded as decisive or even reputable in a number of other fields, and in the wholly vital one of education should be even less acceptable. As Mr Watt remarked, 'Both political parties, approaching the 1964 General Election, took up university education as an electoral issue for a brief and disastrous period.'

Sir Edward has recently shown that his attitudes have not changed, or not much. He spoke of an 'ugly backlash from moderate, unfanatical, middle-of-the-road opinion . . .' (*The Times*, 5 March 1969). Unfanatical and moderate, but also ugly and backlashy? That is to say he aligned himself against, and abused, what he recognised to be reasonable people. But his worst disservice seems to have been his typically futile attitude on Circular 10/65. Lacking parliamentary sanction, it 'requested' local authorities to prepare forthwith for complete comprehensivisation. He announced that while the Conservatives would not themselves have launched such a scheme, he would not recommend them to withdraw it when they came to power. This really is a case of limping behind the hare and losing the trail with the hounds.

For, once again, it is not a question of Left and Right. There is a Conservative tradition of novel schemes for the improvement of the deserving poor. Sir Edward, and the rich ladies and others who support his line, should read Chesterton's 'It shall not be forgiven you'. The virtuousness of their intentions is not an adequate defence.

But if there are disastrous Conservatives, there are also, as we have suggested, sensible men on the political Left. Even the *Tribune* reviewer, while condemning our supposed squirearchical attitudes, said we were right to insist that learning cannot be all fun. There are Communists, even, who agree with Lenin (and with us), that the culture of the past should be absorbed to the maximum possible degree. Many of the contributors to the first *Black Paper* have in fact been loyal Labour voters. Others have taken part in various 'liberal' campaigns on social and international issues. Labour and Conservative, Right and Left alike, are perfectly capable of extricating themselves from the Sargasso into which they have been lured by pilots with more confidence than competence.

For our part, we believe in giving everyone all the education which he can take: we only wish it to be education, not eyewash. And as we have said we oppose much in present-day trends precisely because they fail to bring the necessary compensation to the student from the more culturally deprived home backgrounds; by failing to educate they leave the advantage with the already privileged.

We do not automatically associate ourselves with everything that has been written in this *Black Paper*, partly because we do not associate ourselves automatically with anything. But we think we have shown the not inconsiderable extent to which the views urged against us rest on plain prejudice and on unproven assumptions. If these are cleared away, together with any similar faults on our own side—we are far from claiming immaculateness for ourselves and our colleagues—the issues can perhaps be debated next time round with the seriousness and care they deserve.

The Critical Survey, autumn 1969

A Short Educational Dictionary
(With apologies to the Sunday supplements)

(*with Robert Conquest*)

Academic. 1) (Pejorative) Used of knowledge difficult to master, irrelevant (qv) to contemporary reality and deriving from dead or elderly 'authorities'.

2) Used of qualifications for university posts: eg 'Having beaten up the Vice-Chancellor's office in the course of a relevant protest, he is academically qualified for a post as Lecturer in Sociology.'

Alphabet. A set of arbitrary (qv) signs which children are still often compelled to learn by rote* (qv); usually taught, moreover, in an arbitrary order. For the (equally arbitrary) methods long prescribed in joining these signs, *see* Spelling.

Arbitrary. Prescribed by bourgeois tradition and consensus, as: 'The arbitrary divisions between subjects'; 'the arbitrary exclusion of illiterates from university entrance', etc.

Better. Divisive term. As applied to one pupil rather than another, or one examination script rather than another: reproducing bourgeois ideology and/or irrelevant facts with greater servility. Contrast Underachieving.

Bourgeois. Conventional, unpleasant, fascist. Used of opinions and attitudes held by the working class in particular, and, more generally, by all supporters of the Conservative, Labour, Liberal and (sometimes) Communist parties, the more backward clergymen, most members of the Caucasian races etc.

Bourgeois objectivity. Concern with facts even when these are irrelevant, unexciting etc; more especially, the deducing of opinions from facts and not, as if preferable, vice versa.

By rote. Applied to acquiring (irrelevant) knowledge in such a fashion

---

* A common malpractice: children forming a capital 'A' will tend creatively to leave the upward strokes vertical, and not joined at the top. Instead of this being encouraged, they are forced, often with considerable suffering, to learn to reproduce the accepted, but not thereby superior, form.

as to remember it, as 'Learning multiplication tables by rote', 'being taught the provisions of the Reform Bill by rote', etc.

Capitalism. System on the point of collapse owing to its creation of mass poverty; is also reprehensible on the grounds of corrupting the masses with too many consumer goods. Its role in education is to finance institutions and studies directed towards its overthrow.

Challenging. Of immediate interest to a student; lacking in pedantic precision; readily discussable in terms of this dictionary.

Classics. Dead languages, formerly the basis of education. Objectionable because a) irrelevant, b) difficult.

Continuous assessment. The method whereby teachers can ensure that their favourites are accepted for further education without arbitrary or irrelevant tests.

Creative, creativity. Used a) of activity resembling the plastic or literary arts, while unrestricted to established and arbitrary techniques. In content, challenging, revolutionary, etc, b) of activity not resembling those arts.

Creative play. The assembly, or dispersal, of materials defined as artistic—eg paint, plasticine, string.

Counter-culture. 1) Socially: living off bourgeois society without paying literal or metaphorical taxes to it. 2) Artistically: creativity (qv) which, whether using bourgeois materials (words, pigments etc) or other materials or none, does not admit of the elitist (qv) application of divisive criteria showing one work to be 'better' (qv) than another.

Concern. (Also Conscience) The holding and propagating of left-wing or revolutionary views on politics and other matters. It is improper to speak of a right-wing or moderate 'concern' for anything, even if the bourgeois in question has spent his whole life, expended his whole fortune, or been killed in connection with the issue in question. Concern is best felt about issues arising in far-off continents, on which information has been provided by concerned foreign political organisations and has not been confused or polluted by a student's immediate experience. The depth of concern is determined by the amount of noise (or, if possible, violence) expended in expressing one's views.

Demands. Wishes. Normally described as 'non-negotiable'.

Democracy. 1) The system prevailing in North Vietnam, China, Cuba etc. 2) The running of a university on the basis of suitably revolutionary students having a decisive voice in all matters. Participatory democracy implies conducting a state, a university, or any other organisation not by the mass vote of the apathetic and bourgeois majority, but by the conscientious, concerned minority.

Dialectic. 1) Word of no particular meaning, conveying intellectual high-mindedness and serious concern (*See* Polysyllables). 2) Word used to provide status to an argument otherwise subject to analysis by narrow, formalist minds as self-contradictory.

Dialogue. (meaningful). A dialogue between students and staff can only be said to be meaningful if a) it consists of demands (qv) from the students, and b) the points expressed by the authorities are ignored or (better) shouted down. (*See* Freedom of Speech).

Discipline (arbitrary: there is no other form of discipline). It involves requiring students or schoolchildren to do things which they may not feel like doing. It includes attempts to prevent confrontation, etc. And it may also imply requiring students to do things at arbitrary times. (*See* Fascism).

Educationist, Educationalist. Theoretician; his main duty is to improve the theses developed in this dictionary. Actual teaching experience, with its narrowing, ossifying consequences, is a disqualification for such employment.

Elitism. The theory that some people are better at some things than others are. In education, specifically the idea that children of high 'intelligence' who have 'learnt' a lot should have a higher claim to further education than those lacking in or actively resistant to, these qualities. Politically, the purpose of elitism is to perpetuate the rule of ignorant capitalists (*See* Dialectic). It is improper to speak of elitism in connection with the right of a concerned etc minority of teachers, students etc to assert its superiority, and that of its views, and to establish control of any educational, political or other system.

Establishment. 1) The rulers, or system of rule, in reactionary, bourgeois society only. It is improper, for example, to speak of a Cuban 'establishment'. 2) The ruling body or organisation in a reactionary, bourgeois university or school. 3) (Uniting these) A fascist conspiracy.

Examination. An irrelevant, external test purporting to check a student's knowledge by a set of written questions often repugnant to his personality, and failing to take into account the distractions inevitable in a concerned life. (*See* fascist).

Exciting. Giving pleasure by an easily mastered repetition of themes the student has heard very often before, so long as these are progressive (qv) (*See* Challenging).

Fascist. 1) Anyone in authority (except in Cuba, etc), *especially* the head/members of any elected Western government. (To have fought against the Nazis is an aggravating circumstance). 2) Any member or supporter of the Conservative, Labour or other bourgeois parties. 3) Any policeman. 4) Any university authority or teacher who does not accede, and promptly, to non-negotiable demands. Also, any university authority or teacher.

Grammar. Supposed rules covering the structure of a language, especially English. The teaching of grammar inhibits creativity.

Grant. Money provided to students, as of right, by bourgeois, fascist society.

History. Ancient, Medieval, Byzantine etc: obsolescent, irrelevant study. Modern: as 'taught', an agglomeration of irrelevant 'facts' and bourgeois propaganda incompatible with the principles of sociology (2) (qv).

Identity. One of the main concerns of education, and the main concern of concerned students, is to seek, establish etc their identity. Methods include a) becoming unconscious through hallucinatory drugs; b) joining an organisation all of whose members accept identical opinions, etc. At an earlier age children may be taught their identity, or one better suited to them than the original, by progressive and concerned teachers.

Interdisciplinary. Descriptive of a method of gaining some acquaintance with two or more 'subjects' without being held up by the unexciting, or unchallenging, or irrelevant detail of either or any.

Irrelevant. 1) Referring to some event two or more years in the past. 2) Used of any argument or idea put forward by university authorities, members of any Western government, or the representatives of the Right, Centre and non-extreme Left. 3) Not in accord with sociology (2) (qv).

Layabout. Bourgeois expletive, showing indifference or hostility, applied to students who do not uncritically accept the tenets of the university power structure.

Lazy. (Obsolete) Divisive bourgeois label for those with a low motivation to accept 'teaching' (qv). (*See* Stupid).

Literate. *See* Elitist.

Moderate. A moderate student is one who 1) Politically favours revolutionary social change, but has certain reservations about the tactics advisable, and is often 'non-violent' (qv). It is improper to speak of a Conservative or Social-democratic student as a moderate. 2) In the university context, makes the same demands as the 'extremist', but secures acceptance of them by threats about what the extremist will do if they are refused. If extremists are 'victimised' (qv), the role of the moderate is to secure the maximum student participation in disrupting the fascist etc power structure responsible.

Marcuse. Expression, mainly Irish, Brooklyn etc, meaning 'Attend to what I am about to say.'

Non-conforming. Accepting without question the ideas of certain foreign politicians and British, American, French and German academics and student leaders.

Non-violent. Fairly violent.

Obscenity. Bourgeois usage for a) an art-form. b) a mode of addressing teachers, fascists etc.

Police State. State with police (excluding China etc).

Political Persecution. 1) A method of rule in Greece, Rhodesia, South Africa, Portugal, Spain etc. 2) Preventing students from legitimately and conscientiously breaking bourgeois law, and 'victimising' them afterwards. (*See* Victimise).

Polysyllables. The main object of higher education is to teach the student a working vocabulary of some twenty to thirty of these— (many of them covered in this dictionary).

Progressive. 1) Concerned, creative, polysyllabic, relevant, self-expressive etc. (qqv), 2) In politics: left-wing (including Communist,

Maoist, Castroite, etc etc). 3) In education, favouring non-academic criteria, against examinations, classics, history, arbitrary discipline, learning by rote, teaching, etc etc. (qqv).

Provocation. In principle, any action by educational or governmental authorities.

Punctuation. Arbitrary system of dividing written words (obsolescent).

Relevant. Applied to a university course: 1) Meeting the demands of concerned students. 2) Designed to turn unconcerned students into concerned students. 3) Undistracted by historical experience.

Repression. Less than instant accession to student demands (qv).

Rights (students'). Students' wishes. (*See* Demands).

Self-expression. One of the chief aims of education. Achieved by writing down, drawing etc, whatever may drift into the mind without reference to arbitrary etc concepts of intelligibility etc, or arbitrary techniques of grammar, punctuation (qqv) etc, in preference to being 'taught'. (*See* Teach).

Sentence, savage. Any penalty, academic or legal, meted out to those alleged to have contravened some aspect of the authoritarian academic or legal structure.

Social responsibility. The main concern of education. It involves the structuring, restructuring etc of the educational system a) to prevent elitism (qv) b) to eliminate bourgeois concepts from the curricula.

Sociology. 1) an academic, bourgeois, irrelevant (qqv) study of society and its institutions now largely outmoded by 2) a polysyllabic briefing on the decadence of Western society and the means to overthrow it.

Speech, Freedom of. 1 (Pejorative). An aspect of bourgeois repressive tolerance, acting as a safety valve for progressive energies. Often interpreted, in addition, to deny adequate free speech to progressives, when they wish to speak, shout etc, singly or in unison, in debating time arbitrarily allotted to others. The term is also misused to excuse fascist etc speech. 2) The right of progressive students to speak etc on all occasions. 3) In a progressive society (China, Cuba etc today, England, America etc tomorrow) the unrestricted expression of correct opinion by all deserving and qualified cadres.

Spelling. A bourgeois pseudo-accomplishment designed to inhibit creativity, self-expression, etc.

Standards. Irrelevant academic concept designed to exclude, or penalise, students distinguished for *either* concern *or* creativity *or* both.

Structure (especially power structure). The existing fascist system of government, university organisation, etc.

Structured. Applied to the future: exciting, challenging system of intercourse between minds in the new community of self-realisation.

Student. 1) A young man or woman studying an academic subject under the guidance of more 'senior' men/women. 2) A person under thirty-five supported by the State at or near a seat of learning while following his or her own inclinations at it, near it, or at any distance from it.

Student Power. The rule of concerned (qv) students.

Stupid (obsolescent). Divisive bourgeois label for those with low motivation to accept 'teaching' (qv). (*See* Lazy).

Teach. Impose irrelevant facts and bourgeois indoctrination upon.

Totalitarianism. 1) A political and social system in which a) life continues, food reaches the consumer, the laws are enforced, recreation is available, etc as in the USA, Venezuela, Israel, Luxembourg, etc; b) concerned students etc are not permitted to control society. 2) Applied to any idea, phenomenon or person repugnant to progressive opinion — eg examinations, Anthony Crosland etc etc. (*See* Fascist).

Under-achieving. Coming out near the bottom in tests designed to measure a child's ability to memorise irrelevant facts and accept bourgeois indoctrination, ie to be taught. (*See* Teach, Better).

Union, Students (The apostrophe is always omitted). 1) A building in which the law of the land does not run. 2) An organisation existing to impose the wishes of concerned (qv) students upon unconcerned students and university authorities.

Victimisation. The inflicting of any penalty upon concerned (qv) students violently or non-violently (qv) contravening an arbitrary regulation of the university or state.

Youth. 1) Young people (obsolescent). 2) Those under thirty-five (or, in certain contexts, about forty-five) who seek financial support from the State while they a) contribute nothing to its resources b) work for its destruction.

The Critical Survey, winter 1970

ILEA Confidential

(edited with Robert Conquest)

The following is a transcript of a tape-recording which appears to have been made inadvertently, and which has come into our hands in a way which cannot at present be disclosed. While we are as yet unable to vouch unreservedly for its authenticity, it does cast a more plausible light on recent educational decisions in London than most current explanations.

We have arbitrarily labelled the voices (apart from that of the obvious chairman-figure) with letters of the alphabet.

CHAIRMAN. Today, no doubt owing to the flu epidemic, we have the pleasant situation that, though there is a quorum, none of the human members of staff of the ILEA are with us. We can therefore relax—to the extent even, I suggest, of resuming our natural forms. [*A slithering noise*]

CHAIRMAN. [*an approximation only. All such transcriptions herein are approximate.*] Xtll p'bmorrra zan zannu . . .

VOICE A. As most of us have spent decades on this planet, and are perhaps a little rusty in the Imperial High Speech, I move that we proceed in English.

VOICE B. I second that. And, moreover, *Eye-elleeyay*, a collocation of syllables we can hardly avoid, is a subversive obscenity in the High Speech.

VOICE C. It is in English too!

[*A series of rapid clicks and rumbles—? laughter*]

CHAIRMAN. I agree. I put it to the vote . . . Thank you—carried by a show of pseudopods. Nevertheless, let us begin proceedings with a formal obeisance to the Holy Emperor. Our Mother Star, Betelgeuse, is now on the eastern horizon. If all will turn in that direction . . . Anzz anzz upollolla na rrumu . . .

ALL. Na rrumu.

[*We here omit 2 mins 53 secs of similar exchanges*]

CHAIRMAN. In the circumstances, we will not bother with the Agenda: I will compose suitable Minutes later. This is, however, a useful opportunity for me to address you in my Imperial capacity, as Political Officer.

I think some of us tend to regard our task on this planet as tedious and unimportant compared with what is being done elsewhere to extend the Empire. But we must remember—

VOICE D. Tedious is right! When we are going to see some action? I'm sick of all these Resolutions and Directives!

[*Some buzzing sounds, perhaps indicating agreement*]

VOICE A. If I may . . . My dear Tormentor-General, we all know of your magnificent performance on Rigel II—what was it, eighteen billion intelligent beings incinerated?—but you must bear in mind that our objective on Earth is quite different.

VOICE B. I think too that the General underestimates our difficulties here, what with the loss of most of our Expeditionary Force in transit.

CHAIRMAN. It was that factor, you recall, General, that led us to try to extend our activities through the use of synthetic creatures or androids. It is most lamentable that the experimental model was so lacking in verisimilitude, particularly as regards the facial movements, and could not be rationally controlled. Nevertheless, now it's been turned loose, it does seem to be helping to cause confusion in a small way in other circles, under the name Toniben.

VOICE C. Great Pdahrg! On television recently it insisted it was human twice in the same minute. At that rate of over-compensation I don't see it lasting long.

CHAIRMAN. No doubt. As I was saying, our task may seem slow, but, when it is finished, Earth will have become a luscious farm and mankind a self-renewing herd of high-protein meat-animals sufficient to feed half the Empire. We know that essential work to this end is being done by our fellow servants of the Holy Emperor in the political leaderships on other parts of the planet. Yet the destruction of Western civilisation, so called, is the key to final success. And our own share of that undertaking here in London ranks high.

I will not rehearse all our achievements. Still, who would have believed, even a few years ago, that we could have got away with such triumphs as diverting money and teachers into special centres where truants can devote themselves to—I quote our spokesman—'impromptu music, dancing, dressing up, cinema, lighting fires, painting and playing games'!

[*Clicks and rumbles*]

CHAIRMAN. That is one of *this* year's accomplishments. For two or three years now we have been getting the public accustomed to, for example, schoolchildren's strikes and demonstrations. And here I want to emphasise an important point . . .

VOICE E. [*slow and clumsy in tone*] What were they . . . demonstrating about?

CHAIRMAN. Well, things like victimisation.

VOICE E. What's that?

VOICES. Punishment!

VOICE E. Well, if they can get away with it, you can't blame them. I . . . suffered just the first of the Eighteen Punishments once, and my pseudopods have never—

VOICE C. Look, we know all about your brain injury on landing, but surely—

CHAIRMAN. Order, please. In this case, punishment means being kept in for half an hour or something of that sort. However, to continue. Our chief education officer issued a statement on the strikes and other encouraging activities, saying that it was important to give 'due consideration to legitimate views of pupils, some of whom may have been involved in recent events': and this was in rebuking two headmasters who proposed taking action against their charges!

The point here is that we aren't simply in the business of destroying London's educational system. Of course we are proud of the fact that reading ages in our area are already ten months behind the national average. Naturally we are delighted with the bad blood and general trouble caused by transferring children to and fro between schools, particularly when this is contrary to their parents' wishes. Naturally, too . . . Have you a point?

VOICE B. I was merely anxious not to leave uncommemorated the current plan to create a comprehensive from two schools separated by the most dangerous crossroads in London.

CHAIRMAN. Well taken—an outstanding case of getting everything right. I was going on to express our pleasure at truancy and indiscipline. What a heartening report that was the other day about a formerly 'good' school where the number of chairs smashed per annum is two and a half per child!

VOICE A. Agreed, Mr Chairman, but we have no cause for complacency. Can we in London match the record of the eleven-year-old Bradford schoolboy who committed fifty-one burglaries and other thefts in a month? And the Empire has only a single Psychotechnical Sergeant there!

VOICE D. Splendid fellow! Deserves a decoration!

CHAIRMAN. Er, yes. Let me turn now to teachers. Alongside the presence of desirables who claim that violence in schools is caused by the presence of authority and of pressure to learn, we have the highly satisfactory and steadily growing shortage of teachers willing to work in our system.

VOICE A. What about getting rid of 'good' ones who persist in actually trying to teach and keep order?

CHAIRMAN. There are ways, and we have our allies. Look at the abrupt dismissal from his headmastership of the miscreant Rhodes Boyson upon his election to Parliament. There's no such hurry to be rid of progressives, you may be sure.

VOICE E. Sorry, er . . . progressives?

VOICE C. For Pdahrg's sake!

CHAIRMAN. Order, order. A progressive teacher is one of ours, of course. Now: above all, I draw your attention to the remarks made in our name, which I was quoting a few minutes ago. We are not only producing illiteracy and animal conduct among children. We are getting the population as a whole quite accustomed to hearing meaningless bleats instead of their rational language. Another excellent example came at the time when we suppressed the yearly carol-singing festival. The explanation, you may remember, was that the children should 'have a more liberated style of folk-song'. Again, 'self-expression', that sturdy old standby, continues to serve us well.

VOICE A. Won't someone notice some time that a lot of people—their Kipling, for instance—were exposing that one sixty years ago?

VOICE C. They would have to be able to read to find that out!
[Clicks and rumbles]

CHAIRMAN. At any rate, we now have it accepted that an allegedly adult body, as well as acting anti-socially, can *talk* in this way too.

I think we can all be particularly proud of a remark made in *The Evening News* of Tuesday, 11 June 1974 by its columnist Miss Angela Ince. She noted a number of what I think we may call our cleverest ploys, and concluded with the following remarkable words: 'ILEA's grasp of logic is comparable to that of a labrador puppy.' And that, my fellow servants of the Holy Emperor, is precisely the level to which we are working to bring—and over the decades laid down in the Imperial Plan will succeed in bringing—the entire human race. I should add that she specifies a '*six-month-old* labrador puppy'.

[*Clicks and rumbles*]

CHAIRMAN. I propose, with your approval, to include this testimony to our endeavours in a Special Despatch to the Emperor's Secretariat. [*Buzzing sounds*]

VOICE B. Mr Chairman, urgent: my psychoprobe indicates the approach of a human, speed 2.9 kph, distance thirty-seven metres and closing.

CHAIRMAN. All present, please resume your human forms.

[*A slithering noise*]

CHAIRMAN. A useful discussion, I think, ladies and gentlemen. A fruitful exchange of views. I look forward to the fulfilment of—

[*Sound of door opening and closing*]

CHAIRMAN. Ah, good morning [*name unintelligible*]. I trust your influenza has relaxed its grip?

VOICE F. Er? Yer, I'm a bit better now, thanks, Bert, I mean Fred. You boys been up to anything?

CHAIRMAN. Ha, ha, nothing out of the way.

VOICE F. Er, well, I got something out of the way, in a manner of speaking. I was on the phone to the Ministry just now, and according to what I heard, the grammar schools are going to be—

[*The tape breaks off at this point*]

The Critical Survey, 1975

PART SEVEN
Language

What's in a Word?

A *Supplement to the Oxford English Dictionary Volume I—A-G*, edited by
R. W. Burchfield, Oxford University Press

When, with the appearance of its third and final volume in 1977,
this *Supplement* is completed, it will run to something like a
quarter of the size of the original OED, which came out piecemeal
between 1894 and 1928, with a first *Supplement* in 1928. So have we,
since that period, really been coining new words and usages ten times
as fast as in the previous three-quarters of a millennium, or is this
publication rather fatter than it ought to be?

Well, yes and yes, I suspect. Some of the extra bulk comes from
sensible broadenings of approach. First, 'we' no longer means 'chiefly
those in Great Britain and Ireland, plus a thin scattering in North
America'—it now includes North America in depth, Australia, New
Zealand, South Africa, India, Pakistan. The large growth of scientific
and other technical terms is properly reflected. I am less wholehearted
about the decision to include widely used proper names: *Dracula, Dra-
mamine, Drambuie*. Handy, true, but should a dictionary be an encyclopedia as well, even if Webster and subsequent Americans have thought
it should?

A fourth source of expansion, quantitatively minor but qualitatively
striking, has been the policy of putting in, with full (verbal) illustrations, sexual and excretory terms eschewed by the *OED*; not totally
eschewed, by the way, for whereas *fuck* was of course missing, *wind-
fucker*—'1. A name for the kestrel; 2. *fig.* as a term of opprobrium'—
quaintly slipped in. Good for the compilers of the *Supplement*, if only
in that reading through the articles on all these words, their usages
and transferred meanings set out with the solemnly conscientious
thoroughness appropriate to their learned context, breaks new ground
in hilarity. By the way, again, delicacy or ignorance has seen to it that
some sexual applications, for instance *bush* and *gobble*, are omitted.

The same sort of incompleteness marks the wholesale injection of
the vocabulary of the pot-and-pop scene: *acid* (LSD) and *acid-head*,
surely current for ten years or so, *downer* for a relaxant pill, and no
doubt many of the hundred-odd synonyms for marijuana listed in

Eugene E. Landy's recent *Underground Dictionary*, find no place here. Nor, probably, should they; my objection is not to the failure to be complete, but to the evidently earnest, and foredoomed desire to be complete. Many of these terms will have become obsolete or obsolescent before ever having found their way into these pages, even before attaining any sort of general currency. It is doubtful whether such transients should find hospitality outside ephemeral lexicons of specialised slang.

Here, and not only here, there arises the problem of authority, of prescriptiveness. The entry of the Dictionary under *dictionary* lays claim to nothing more than the recording of a word's origin, history and usage. And everyone will agree that the language must continue to change and develop as it has always done, is going to continue to do regardless. Phrases like 'he has authored a dozen books' or 'the project is sound moneywise' cannot but cause irritation here and there, but they have evolved by the traditional processes of using noun as verb and tagging on a space-saving suffix. Other novelties may be less tolerable, and any such that appear in this *Supplement* will receive the licence for future use that the *OED* inevitably confers.

The editors of the *Supplement* are intermittently aware that what has been written and what can properly be written are not always the same. Under *agenda* as a singular—as regular readers will know, the *Observer* helped to blaze the trail here on 1 July 1928—one compiler remarks, 'a use now increasingly found but avoided by careful writers'. That is the fact. But *data* as a singular is silently lumped in with *data* as a plural, and *alright* is merely, or worse than merely, labelled 'a frequent spelling of *all right*'. Where? By what sort of hand? Permissive grammarians should ask themselves, not just whether they would pass undisturbed over that frequent spelling in the work of another, but whether they would ever use it in their own, and if not, why not.

The dilemma, propriety and usage, keeps coming up in this book. '*Erron[eously]*', '*illiterate*', '*affected*', '*in trivial use*', '*journalese*' are bandied about. But uncensored barbarities are everywhere; *fraught* used absolutely ('don't look so fraught'), *cohort* for 'supporter' (first offender, M. McCarthy), *demyth* (verb), *disambiguate* and other revolting *de-* and *dis-* compounds, *elisionable* (once in G. M. Hopkins—what about just forgetting it?), *fund* as verb, going back as far as 1900, incidentally, and in the *Westminster Gazette* at that.

It would be easy to take off at this point with jolly stuff about *camp*, in the 'extravagantly affected' sense, having been first recorded in 1909, and *berdache* being a term for a transvestite North American Indian, and *aprosexia* not meaning anything like what it might, just 'abnormal inability to concentrate'. But all dictionaries have that sort of thing, and this is part of a very special one. I commend the enterprise and industry of the compilers in having read so widely, as far afield, in different directions, as *It, The New Zealand Journal of Agriculture, Melody Maker, The Village Voice* and *Carpet Review*. And yet I wish they had more consistently faced the fact that they can do their duty as recorders of usage without abandoning their other duty of indicating what usages they, in common with other educated people, see as mistaken, ugly, harmful rather than helpful to the language.

In practical terms, I wish I thought that, in 1975, we shall read, alongside *hopefully*, not '*also*: it is to be hoped', but something like '*also, in loose political rhetoric*: with luck'; alongside *protagonist*, not just '*also*: proponent' but '*also, improperly*:proponent'. And, in 1977, let us be told that *ransack* (which means 'search' or 'rob') is '*illiterate*' for *sack*, that *scarify* (which means 'wound') is '*erron.*' for *scare thoroughly*. But I expect to be disappointed.

I was going to end by remarking, in hangdog fashion, that by the latter date we shall be needing another Supplement explaining what *illiterate* and *erron.* used to mean. On reflection, however, I doubt whether that stage will be reached before about 1990, perhaps even later, so I sign off on a more cheerful note: I have never come across any kind of lexical work with so many references to drinks as this one contains. Quite uplifting.

Observer, 15 October 1972

A Word in Edgeways

A Supplement to the Oxford English Dictionary Volume II — H–N, edited by R. W. Burchfield, Oxford University Press

The rate of growth of our language continues to increase. When, four years ago, I reviewed in these pages the first volume of this supplement, I noted in some wonder that, over the preceding forty-odd years, we had evidently been coining new words and usages ten times as fast as in any previous period. Now, a year later than foreseen, Volume II turns up as the next of the four—not, as foreseen, three—thought to be needed to complete the enterprise. The *OED* itself devoted nearly twice as much space to the letters A to G as it did to H to N. Will they ever finish?

The compilers have read at least as widely as before: *The Good Food Guide, Analog Science Fact/Fiction,* the *Sunday Advocate-News* (Barbados), the *Observer*, M. Drabble, N. Mailer, G. Greer, D. Francis and many others constituting what seems now and then a rather eccentric choice, but no matter; very little poetry, at least very little is quoted, and I think I can see why. As before, again, there are hundreds of new scientific and technological terms and combinations—well and good; proper names of places and peoples in the Third World—fairly well and good; proprietary names—I have doubts. Is this the place to be told of *Lastex, Also lastex* and *nylon. Also Nylon*?

The other great area of expansion is colloquialism in the broadest sense, including the full range of obscenities. I missed what had been one of the star attractions of Volume I—a basic bawdry followed in each case by a sweeping, sonorous litany of instances—and suffered brief puzzlement before realising that of the initial letters that English favours for such words, B, C and F had already gone, and P, S and T were yet to come. What had not changed was the mass of faded slang. Surely, if *hepcat* and *jitterbug* have to go in, they should be accompanied by an *Obs[olete]*, or possibly a *Hist[orical]*.

I was a little severe last time about how easy it is to go on about the funny things you keep coming across, but propose now to relax. The ancient lineage of what one could have sworn had turned up yesterday is a perpetual surprise. *Halitosis* appeared in 1874: had halitosis itself recently appeared? Change in eating habits? The first *he-man* showed his hairy chest not in 1932 but in 1832. The first *hooker* [whore], though not of course the first hooker, came out in 1845. *Hip* ['with it'] dates from 1904, *juvenile delinquency*, attacked in the 1930s as a barbarous innovation, from 1816, *iron curtain* from 1920, and *[public] image* from 1908—in the works of Chesterton! On a different tack, try 'Mr Chamberlain literally bubbled over with gratitude', and '. . . with his eyes he literally scoured the corners of the cell', the latter coming from V. Nabokov, of course.

This supplement has already attracted a great deal of praise, most of it fully justified, so I hope not to be thought unsporting if I start to carp a little at this stage. There are one or two definitions which a minute's more effort would have improved a great deal: an *Immelmann turn* was indeed 'an evasive manoeuvre in the air', but specifically it was a half-loop followed by a half-roll. It is true that *Herr* is the German equivalent of *Mr*, but to cite '*Herrgott*, he was tired' here is an error. The word means 'Lord God,' not, as is implied, 'Mr God' (which is what would be meant by *Herr Gott*).

Slipping another of my hats on over my present one ('hat, *sb*. Add: 3. a. An office, position, occupation'), I must throw doubt on the provenance of *Martini* (cocktail) suggested here. 'f [rom] the name of *Martini* and Rossi, Italian wine-makers'. I used to accept that too, but recent research (see John Doxat, *Stirred, not Shaken*, 1976) has undermined it by establishing pretty firmly that whenever it was that the cocktail appeared 'there are printed references to it ante-dating the Supplement's earliest citation of 1894. Martini and Rossi vermouth had not yet become available in the United States. The inventor of the

Dry Martini may well have been a certain bartender at the Knicker-bocker Hotel, New York, especially since his name was Martini di Arma di Taggia, but he seems not to have come on the scene until about 1910.

The article on *jazz* makes one historical slip and one omission. For 'originating among American Negroes' I would read 'originating among the American proletariat, both black and white'. And I would add as sense 1. c. 'Any old meaningless, tuneless, rhythmless rubbish played on jazz and other instruments by idiots or charlatans who used to play jazz, in sense 1. a.' In rather similar vein I would add, after the definition of *Marxist* adj., 'Also, as in "Marxist guerrilla, Marxist forces", of any very horrible person or group without the slightest interest in what Marx wrote or even knowledge of who he was but operating or fighting in the interest of international communism.' OK?

So at last to 'hopefully' in the sense of 'let us hope', or, political use, 'with luck', first recorded 1932. '(Avoided by many writers)' is as far as the editor will go. He does once condemn a usage as 'improper', (*literally* as shown above), and calls *media* 'erron[eous]' when used as a singular, but elsewhere it is only misspellings, like *longeur* for 'longu-eur', that he finds erron. The sign ¶, described in the prefatory list of such as denoting 'catachrestic [misapplied—OED] and erroneous uses', he reserves for harmless bits of facetiousness like *larf* for 'laugh', though *nerts* (for 'nuts') escapes.

'Hopefully' for 'let us hope' is ¶. The argument against saying so is that language is always changing, that today's misuse is tomorrow's accepted use, etc. The most important way in which our language is changing at the moment is that fewer and fewer people pay any attention to how they use it. Some former misuses, like *reliable* fiercely attacked in the mid-nineteenth century as an ungrammatical and unwanted synonym for 'trustworthy', have turned out to be needed. This is rare. After all, too, decline is a very well known form of change.

It must, of course, be said that, like the *OED* itself, its Supplement is indispensable to anyone interested in words. This volume appears at a time when, rather contradicting my view that the appeal of the subject is in decline, dictionaries are coming out in droves. Among them, *Webster's Third New International Dictionary* (Merriam/Longman) could fairly be called indispensable too. Its encyclopaedic rather than strictly lexical approach makes it the ideal adjunct to the *OED*. One thing that is less than ideal about it is the size: it has 2,662 pages and registers nearly 13 lb, on my admittedly most unreliable bathroom scales. Not one for the bedside.

Observer, 21 November 1976

Up to Our Neck

The Survival of English: essays in criticism of language, by Ian Robinson, Cambridge University Press

The title and subtitle of this excellent book may mislead the general reader. It is not a work on popular illiteracies, but a series of polemical tracts about literature (in the broadest sense) and society. More precisely, as the author puts it in a knotty introduction, it discusses some 'different examples of the interplay between language and life'.

The first essay contains a vigorous, closely argued attack on the New English Bible (1961 and 1970) and other modernised versions of scripture and liturgy. What is revealed here made me rub my eyes. No satirist would have dared to invent the real title of the (American) English translation of the Roman Catholic services: the New English Missalette. And one would have to try hard, suppressing all humour, all sense of style and all reverence, to achieve some of the ineptitudes of the NEB. A single example must suffice: the King James Bible has 'Save me, O God, for the waters have come in unto my soul'; in the NEB, 'the waters have risen up to my neck!' (Exclamation mark in text.) The rhythms of the new version make it move about three times as fast as the old. It would go best gabbled on television over trendy shots of religious art, or perhaps film-clips from Biblical epics; anything really religious would make it inaudible. As Mr Robinson says, it is journalistic, though not as good as good journalism. It turns the faith it professes to embody into something literally unbelievable; it is indeed 'the Atheists' Bible' in what I think is intended here as a single sense: the Bible for atheists, but can well be extended to suggest the Bible by atheists, however they might describe themselves.

There is more in all this than an appalling failure of taste. If people are to talk seriously about religion, even to think about it as what it is, they must have a language in which to do so. Mr Robinson's case is that the effect of these novelties and novelisations is to erode the language of belief, just as 'religious instruction' at schools, in which the 'facts' of Christianity are recounted by a non-believer and/or in a non-believing tone, help to erode it. The time is coming when a child will just have no way of acquiring belief.

That will be a bad time. I must make it clear that I am not, any more than Mr Robinson is, a believer. Nevertheless, our civilisation, like all others, rests on its history, and the greater part of our history is involved with religion. All our literature, to look no further, requires us to understand, which means having a real chance to share, that religion. A society in which it was no longer possible to be a Christian would be as nasty as one in which nobody could be a poet. (Work is being done on that, too.)

In the second essay, another language, that of politics, is shown in decline. It is true that shabby men will speak a shabby language, forging a new one if need be; but language reflects back on men. The shifts in the word 'unthinkable' are instructive. Thirty-five years ago ('in the unthinkable event of another war') it meant 'horrible to think about'; more recently ('the unthinkable policy of using armed force against civilians') it came to mean 'immoral to think about'; now ('military resistance to Soviet expansion is unthinkable') it nearly means 'unthinkable') Mr Robinson sees our politicians with the clarity of a fresh approach, finding men who seem unable to talk about anything but production, growth, structure. He might have added that one of the factors in Enoch Powell's appeal is that he seems to talk another, older language, one in which the Dunkirk spirit would not be evoked unless it was appropriate to do so. The echoes Mr Powell arouses may be tinny ones; his style may be at the service of wrong ends; but a style it clearly is.

The language of journalism, as exemplified in what has happened to *The Times*, comes under fire in a third essay. There is now a style in which it is impossible to discuss anything seriously. I have seldom seen a better-organised assault on this front, nor ever a phrase that better sums up the prevailing tone of newspaper comment than 'a directionless irony that gives nothing but the writer's superiority to what he describes'. Other pieces treat pornography and sex education (a hostile diagnosis of both, remarkably clear and cogent), the present state of the language of love as found, or not found, in the poetry of the day, and . . .

And a celebration of criticism as the supreme literary form of our time, with Dr Leavis as its supreme exponent, now that—forty-three years after—D. H. Lawrence is dead. There I . . . let us say dissent. But Mr Robinson has written a frightening account of some of the ills of our time, one that cuts deep and is funny as well.

Observer, 6 August 1973

Langham Diary

It's going to be sort of language again, I'm afraid. I sometimes feel I have shifted a good way to the right in this matter (as in others) over the years, but I feel no less often that (as in other matters) I have stayed more or less where I was while nearly everybody else has shifted to the left. These days I run the risk of being confused with those elderly pedants who write to the papers denouncing some harmless, even useful, not very recent coinage like 'spin-off'—better that, though than not mind or notice if someone says 'perpetrate' when he means 'perpetuate', as on Radio 3 the other day. In 1950, say, before they started demolishing our educational system, it was easy to be a linguistic egalitarian, scorning the idea of rules (but not, be it noted, the rules themselves), regarding usage as sole and sufficient authority. That was all right at a time when, for instance, you would have been astonished to hear a Prime Minister say 'flaunt' when he meant 'flout', a double puzzling case, in that Mr Heath was thereby forgoing a chance of making his favourite 'eou' noise. When that sort of thing starts happening, you have to turn a bit reactionary and elitist. We cannot, at least without a fight, allow solecisms to pass into the language simply because they happen to have been uttered in public. Even to talk of solecisms in the 1970s is to swim against the stream, the only direction worth swimming if you like swimming.

Illiteracies over the meaning of words, such as good old 'disinterested' for 'uninterested', have attracted quite a lot of attention recently, though without, of course, any perceptible reduction in their incidence; those who don't notice what they say or write don't notice what they read either. One department much less often remarked is that of punctuation. When I was a lad, it was illegal to hitch two sentences together with a comma: 'The dog barked, I threw a bottle at him.' More than two could be so hitched, on some unargued view, probably, that the writer was setting out a kind of list. But not two: that was sloppy, lazy etc. And it still is to me, and also to the press, which has become—who would have thought it?—a custodian of our language on this point and some others. The chief and particularly heinous offenders are writers of fiction. A widely-acclaimed, indeed award-winning, novel of a couple of years ago was full from end to end of 'I looked out of the window, rain was falling.' If challenged, and if able to understand the challenge, the author would most likely have retorted that it was academic to go on about a thing like that, and/or that it was liberating to do away with arbitrary conventions. ('Arbitrary', by the way, has become a favourite lefty term of abuse, emphatic and inexpressive at the same time, as is the way with such terms: 'The police made an arbitrary search of his house' doesn't imply 'without a warrant' but means just 'The police bloody well searched his house.') Well, it's sad and rather worrying to find, in the forefront of the assault on our language, some of the very people who ought to be most concerned to defend it. I mean novelists; poets have long ago opted out of the struggle, and even some quite good ones would as soon think of wasting their energy on stuff like commas as of rhyming or using metre.

Those hyphens a few sentences back remind me of another now-forgotten law of my youth. It said that, in phrases consisting of a . . . No, I'd better just give examples. You wrote of 'science fiction' but 'a science-fiction fan', 'the novel was widely acclaimed' but 'a widely-acclaimed novel'. Nowadays we read all the time of science-fiction (when we don't read of scific, a trendy abortion guaranteed to nauseate anyone who knows anything about science fiction or SF or sf) and of widely acclaimed novels. Cases in the second category are often not the fault of the writer; sub-editor or printer will have invoked the 'house style' and whipped away that useful and untroublesome hyphen. The posh reason for such removals is a supposedly aesthetic one: modern design has decreed that hyphens just look ugly, you see. Do they? Why, 'science-fiction', then? Why not 'sub editor'? 'Man eating tiger'? The real reason, I should guess, is the severely practical one that, especially in the columns of a newspaper, dropping the hyphen makes a line easier to justify. No excuse, though.

'Modern design reasons' (nifty transition again) are also at work on that equally handy and harmless speck of notation, the apostrophe. A few years ago I had some dealings with an organ called *Teachers World*, and remarked in a letter to it that, since it must have *something* to do with reading and writing, it might consider putting an apostrophe in its name, tricky as it no doubt was to decide just where. I was told loftily, though not at all unamiably, that çela had all been *changé*, because of modern design reasons. Good boy for owning up. You rightly expect Students Union, but Teachers World makes me frown. So, in a rather different way, does Visitor's London at the head of brochures and notices; perhaps it's all right; I'm not sure. The truth is that that little mark, or the possibility of inserting it, sets up uneasiness in the user. The less learned will over-react and offer to sell us Fresh Lettuce's, or will write in their examination paper of Keat's poems — and pass regardless. But is it Keats' or Keats's? This is often felt to be a matter of choice; I come out for Keats's. After all, nearly everyone nearly always *says* 'keetsiz', not 'keets'. What constantly trips up even the literate minority is that family we all try to keep up with. If you never get it wrong yourself, you will not believe how many people write of them as the Jones's instead of the Joneses, and would be gravely daunted if asked to put in the engagement diary a party at the Joneses'. But such knots will be cut any year now, if not by those crappy modern design reasons then by EEC cultural harmonisation, and, German-fashion, we shall be reading Hardys poems and Conrads novels without turning a hair.

The question-mark is going too. This is seen mainly at the end of long or longish sentences, the writer presumably having forgotten he kicked off with a 'why' or a 'if may I point out'. It means you have to plod back to the beginning to check your impression that the thing did start off as a question, which really is irritating. But short questions are beginning to be affected too. When the voice rises at the end, usually in yes-or-no questions like 'Are you coming to the film?', it would take a real moron not to mark it as a question. It seems to be all to natural, however, with supplement-questions that take the voice down at the end, to round off with a full stop—'Hey you, what's the time.' I ask you where will it all end. Eh.

Commas and hyphens and apostrophes and question-marks may not matter much, though I and a few others will despise and perhaps not employ you, or review your book unfavourably, if you act on that view. What I think really does matter, without knowing quite how, is the declining interest in language as spoken in the media. Clearly, a large number of actors and actresses are either too stupid to understand their lines or too lazy to bother to, and the director isn't listening: he's making sure it all 'looks right'. Our audio-visual age is a bloody sight more visual than it is audio. So, the other week on television, one young man turned to another and said curtly, 'How's your cousin, Bernadette?'—he had been calling him Fred or something a moment before. He meant, I divined, 'How's your cousin Bernadette?' This is not new. Years and years ago, in the terrible film of Graham Greene's *Confidential Agent*, Lauren Bacall said to Charles Boyer, 'I could have had any man I wanted. Why did I have to *fall* for you?' I wanted to scream, 'Fall for *you*! Fall for *you*!' and more besides. The theatre and the radio, where directors and such do listen, sin much less often in this way, though it was on radio, Alun Owen once told me, that the chap who didn't want to use guns at the forthcoming bank robbery was asked sneeringly by the gang leader, 'What's the matter with you, Scruples?' (There are no Scrupleses in the London telephone directory.)

Announcers are doing it all the time too. Recently, a girl on Radio 3 said—I quote from memory, not having known she was going to say it until she'd said it—'We come now to Schumann's Fourth *Symphony* in D minor. Despite its number it's actually his second *symphony*, written soon after his First *Symphony* and before the one we know as the Second *Symphony*. Since Schumann revised the D minor *symphony* after completing his Third *Symphony*, it's always referred to as his Fourth *Symphony*.' Well, at least she didn't talk about Pur-cell or Bate-hoven or Elgah or Me-yoh [Milhaud] or Phil-harmonic.

The Listener, 21 February 1974

Getting It Wrong

The *Concise Oxford Dictionary* (COD) defines malaprop(ism) as, 'Ludicrous misuse of word, esp. in mistake for one resembling it', and gives the example *derangement of epitaphs* for 'arrangement of epithets'. A glance at Sheridan's play *The Rivals* reveals this and comparable misuses, but a second glance shows there to be others present of a rather different kind. For instance, immediately upon her first entrance, Mrs Malaprop says of her daughter Lydia, 'There, Sir Anthony, there sits the deliberate simpleton who wants to disgrace her family, and *lavish* herself on a fellow not worth a shilling.' (I will italicize malapropisms throughout, hoping to save my readers' time without insulting their intelligence.) In the fourth act, the lady commends Captain Absolute for being full of *alacrity* and *adulation*. A distinction is soon stated. *Derangement* is nothing more or less than the wrong word, and the right one very readily suggests itself. The other three are nearly the right words, but not quite. Thus 'lavish' means not 'bestow' but 'bestow liberally'; 'alacrity' can be used of somebody's demeanour at a given moment ('he followed with alacrity') but not of his settled state; 'adulation' likewise refers to what is shown a second party, not what is possessed as a characteristic, and in any case carries an inappropriate suggestion of obsequiousness. Nevertheless, the closeness to the target each time is such as to let us feel the wind of the shot, and might prompt us to say that the speaker has not so much used the wrong word as used a word in the wrong sense. Anyway, in what follows I have kept apart Wrong Word malapropisms and Wrong Sense ones, more for convenience than to suggest any deep division of principle. Note that all citations are genuine, though many are immaterially shortened or changed to save space or confusion; paraphrases, of something heard in talk, on radio, etc, or seen without possibility of copying or clipping, are prefixed *P*.

In *Modern English Usage* (1926), Fowler devotes a little over a column to 'Malaprops' and a little more again to 'Pairs and Snares', words often confused with each other through similar sound and appearance, like affect/effect, alternative/alternate. If he were writing today he would surely devote several pages at least to such topics. Till quite recently, perhaps about 1960, it was comparatively rare to find misuse of words in the writings of the supposedly educated, among whom I include journalists and those who get their letters printed in the newspapers. But now, five minutes' reading almost anywhere will turn one up. No research was needed for this article, just the energy to record the examples that passed by me in the ordinary way of business over some weeks. I collected a dozen times more material than I could use.

The meaning of this sudden abundance I will consider when I have displayed my collection.

To start with, then, Wrong Word malapropisms at the shallow end, simple pairs and snares. Someone *alternatively* sulks in his tent and issues out to make statements, does not wish to *distract* from another's fine sporting performance, will not *detract* from any part of his planned speech and descends vigorously on all punctuation sins—however *venal*. An actor is *derisory* about Ernest Hemingway, last week some demonstrators *laid* down in front of a police vehicle, a mixture of acting styles didn't wholly lend *credulity* to a hugely enjoyable film, an epidemic of moderation has *inflicted* ('infected' plus 'afflicted') some West European communists and certain factors *mitigate* against success-ful treatment. A new snare-setting pair, flaunt/flout (show off/mock, insult), has arrived; it is hardly a pair any more, because one element has killed the other and taken its place. As far as I know, no one uses 'flout' for 'flaunt', but there is plenty of this kind of thing:

> We might call the recent performance of sterling 'obscene', not to suggest that it is lewd or indelicate [ah, but whether he likes it or not that is just what he is absurdly suggesting], but because it *flaunts* every rational calculation of British currency.

More shortly: 'French Communists *Flaunting* Party' (those communists again). But the word confusingly survives in its old sense, as I heard on the radio since starting this paragraph (*P* Beethoven doesn't allow the pianist to flaunt his virtuosity). Perpetrate/perpetuate is another old pair, similar in that they often write *perpetrate* for 'perpetuate', but not, or not often, the other way round: 'Small neo-Nazi and German-American groups picketed NBC in protest against the film, claiming that the holocaust was a hoax and that the television series *perpetrated* that lie.'

Quite often a Wrong Word seems little more than a spelling mistake, resulting from telephoned copy or bad luck at the printers', but we must reflect that someone thought it was right. Thus a question *illicits* a reply, an unfortunate has a *fiercesome* appearance and there is the *martialling* of evidence. There is even a concert audience in a state of *psychophantic* respect. Often, too, the writer seems just to be choosing a till-then unrecorded variant of a familiar word, either perversely or in the grip of a desire to find a form of higher cultural standing than the one ordinary people use, a very common motive behind solecisms of most sorts. Thus:

> The Kremlin has been *appraised* of the President's interest.

> We *unreservably* apologise.

> I believe the pamphlet to be *inimicable* to the essential idea of a university.

> *P* The school-book was full of violence and *depravation*.

In roughly ascending order, an anthology of getting it wrong (alert readers will have to forgive me for jogging the memories of others):

The sonatas are just the *anecdote* to a gloomy summer day. ('antidote')

A wind-machine is used to *emulate* breathing at the start and finish of the work. ('simulate')

The food and surroundings were very poor value for money and in *inexorable* taste. ('execrable')

Even those apparently *simultaneous* gestures that inspired his men were the result of careful planning. ('spontaneous')

The Council is not a *paradigm* of virtue. ('paragon' – nice example of a Wrong Word that is also what Fowler would have called a vogue-word)

Marriage was ordained for the *procuration* of children. ('procreation', but one of the actual meanings of 'procuration' is 'obtaining for immoral purposes')

Alice B. Toklas and Gertrude Stein, both American *ex-patriots*. ('expatriates'—after a moment's thought)

Anthony and Cleopatra, by *roisterous* William Shakespeare. ('roister' and 'boisterous' run into one)

We have so *emaciated* our laws that the young hooligan is almost immune from punishment. ('emasculated' eventually suggests itself)

It was a rather elderly, staid, condescending but solicitous aunt gathering her *voluptuous* skirts. ('voluminous'—presumably)

The actress had to run the *gamut* of protesters. ('gauntlet', influenced by phrases like 'run up and down the gamut')

In our course of study we covered the whole *gambit* of banking, *cashiering*, current accounts, deposits. (Two misses in four words. 'Gamut', of course, and 'cashing', I suppose, influenced by words like 'pioneering' and by 'cashiering' itself, which means only 'discharging [from armed forces, etc] with ignominy'.)

Many of these young refugees may eventually *pass muster* as guerrillas. ('be mustered'—UK or 'muster in'—US; influenced by 'pass muster' meaning 'be pronounced adequate', even perhaps partly intended)

For anyone who wants to know about the Victorian theatre this book will be a *minefield*. ('gold mine' or 'mine of information', with some influence from phrases like 'rich field of study'; writer not being sarcastic)

P The Americans really have a free press; it's *incarcerated* in their constitution. ('incorporated', certainly, but only after a long struggle to establish beyond reasonable doubt that no ironical or other nuance is to be found, and perhaps the recognition of a faint influence from 'enshrine' where it comes nearest to 'enclose')

He brought to his job a style and verve which were refreshing and *enervating*. ('energising' and 'elevating' in as near equal proportions as could be, with what 'enervating' actually means— 'causing weakness'—forgotten or never known)

She is supposed to have most trust of all in the *implacable* screen of her senior adviser. (No certain meaning. How any kind of screen could ever be placated, appeased, conciliated it is impossible to say. Some influence from 'impassable', 'impassive', 'impenetrable', 'impermeable', 'impregnable', etc)

There's a lot of *ethos* about living in poor London [ie, poor parts of London] these days. (No certain meaning. 'Ethos', somebody's or some group's set of beliefs, was not what the writer meant; 'kudos', glory, prestige, possibly was. Or could he have reasoned that as 'pathos' is to patheticness so 'ethos' is to ethnicness? He must have meant something like that. Last guess: ethnic kudos.)

His speech would not prevent an unprecedented and possibly *volatile* White backlash. (No certain meaning further than that it is gloomy or otherwise unfavourable. All the meanings of 'volatile', *viz* 'evaporating quickly, gay, transient', are ruled out by the context or 'and'. Influenced by 'violent', or conceivably 'versatile' thought to mean something like 'mercurial'.)

Students of Russian and Chinese subversive activities have noted that *esurient* revolutionary movements in most parts of the non-communist world have been receiving less support from Moscow and Peking than formerly. ('Esurient', noted in *COD* as a jocular or archaic synonym for 'hungry' or greedy', out of use for almost a century, is impossibly fanciful for the businesslike flatness of the context. The word confounded itself in the writer's mind with 'emergent' or 'existent' or something or other.)

As far as I know, the above anthology consists entirely of novelties, of nonce-uses. For some mysterious but fortunate reason, Wrong Word malapropisms don't catch on, except for wrong members of pairs like *flaunt*. Those apart, no harm is done beyond some momentary bafflement or irritation among readers and possibly an outburst of editorial rage, and here and there amusement may be caused—no direct harm, that is. Whether it is the hankering after an up-market synonym or an over-hasty search of the memory or both that brings such a solecism to consciousness, what gets it down on paper is a lazy or defiant refusal to think twice, let alone check. No need to get it right (I imagine them mumbling), not very near is near enough, and what does it matter? That isn't harmless.

Wrong Sense malapropisms are more of a mixed bag. Some, not always the most obviously useful, take a one-way trip into the language, others vanish from sight after a single showing. In nearly every case, their appearance is the third stage of a process which may never be as clear-cut and as conscious as I show it here.

STAGE I: A writes (let us say): He was a voracious reader, doing little else but work and sleep. (A knows that 'voracious' means 'greedy'; it seems a legitimate metaphor, like 'devouring' books.)

STAGE II: B reads A's sentence and takes 'voracious' for a learned-looking synonym of 'keen, enthusiastic, constant'.

STAGE III: In due time, B writes (in actual fact): This *voracious* contributor of letters to the correspondence columns of the press . . . (We should think ourselves lucky he didn't write *veracious*, which I once saw used in such a context: Wrong Word piled on Wrong Sense.)

Exactly the same thing has happened to 'avid', producing someone 'who believes *avidly* that everybody needs love' and someone else who is 'an *avid* pilot'. Well, those who don't know or who fail to remember what the words mean elsewhere aren't going to mind, and the rest will tend to smile rather than scowl.

The effects of Wrong Sense can be much more inappropriate than that, as follows. We have a Stage I involving 'pantheon', not in the root meaning of a temple to all the gods but, figuratively, of a group of admired characters as in, say, 'When he was a boy his pantheon included Plato, Shakespeare, Buffalo Bill and his headmaster.' In Stage II, B thinks it refers to one's favourite personification or symbols, and in Stage III writes (in actual fact): 'Democratic Campuchea, as the country is renamed, occupies in the *pantheon* of the Right the same places [sic] as does Chile in that of the Left.' It is always something of a feat to come up with the least apt word in the language. The existence of 'pandemonium', abode of all demons, should have warned B, but of course he would never have heard of that. No such excuse serves the writer of the next Stage III: 'The report [of alleged sightings of unidentified flying objects] is unlikely to shake hardened sceptics, but on those who already believe in such phenomena the effect will be *devastating*.' Undeflected by knowing—as he must surely have known—what is meant by utterances like 'The hurricane caused great devastation', he managed to say exactly the opposite of what he intended. Perhaps he thought cloudily that the participle and the noun were unconnected.

Briefly noted:

He stiffened in alarm, but the look-out remained *oblivious* to his presence. (To be oblivious to something is not to be unaware of it but to be no longer aware of it.)

P Many children leave school altogether *bereft* of mathematical skills. (To be bereft of something is not to be without it but to be deprived of it. This extract from an editorial in the London *Times*—on falling educational standards—comically suggests that many children, possessed of mathematical skills, have them taken away from them. Not even British schools of the late 1970s could do that to more than comparatively few children.)

The sound of the car rose to a *crescendo*. (A crescendo is not a loud noise but is itself a noise that rises, from soft or not-loud to loud.)

Compared to the 'Save Our Children' campaign, the campaign waged by the anti-repeal forces was *pristine* clean. (A pristine thing is not spotless but primeval, as in, say, 'the pristine innocence of America before the white man came'. Not that I admire that phrase much either.)

P Courage is often thought of as a virtue we should try to *emulate*. (To emulate someone is to try to equal him. Trying to try to equal a quality brings nothing very definite to mind. The speaker was a professor of philosophy in a television series called 'Dilemmas'. These were questions like the nature of virtue. A dilemma is not a question but specifically a situation posing a choice between two equally unattractive courses, as it might be lying to save your skin and telling the truth to save your soul.)

A universal *panacea* from a mixture of sulphur, lime and water. (A panacea is already, so to speak, a universal remedy.)

New York City is *paranoid*—with reason—about rising crime . . .

Enough. The result of such misuses is no more than to make us change our use of the language, each small in itself. We will perhaps go extra carefully with 'avid' and 'voracious', we can afford to go on using 'pantheon' and 'devastating' on the confident assumption that they will not lose their old meanings, but in other cases those old meanings have been extinguished or are being driven out. If we want to be sure of being completely understood, a concern that takes priority over any notions of elegance, let alone correctness, we must stop saying and writing 'oblivious' and make it 'no longer aware' instead, substitute something about louder and louder for 'crescendo' except in musical circles, abandon 'panacea' and fasten on to 'cure-all', etc. At the same time, when another uses these words in an ambiguous context we must try to establish, if unavoidable by asking a question, whether he is ignorantly and trendily applying the new meaning or obstinately and uselessly sticking to the old. Or that is what we would do if we were inhumanly energetic and logical.

Let me produce my three final exhibits. The first only gets in because it is my favourite solecism of all time; it is that because of its ludicrous history, more complex than the shift from avid reader to avid pilot. To be sure, this is a reconstruction, but I regard it as certain.

STAGE I: A writes (let us say): His arguments are unoriginal and jejune. (A knows that 'jejune' means 'thin, unsatisfying', a rare word, admittedly, but one with a nice ring to it.)

STAGE II: B notices the nice ring. He doesn't know what the word means and of course doesn't consult the dictionary—you would be as likely to find him consulting the Doomsday Book. There is something French as well as nice about the ring to 'jejune'; in fact now he comes to think of it it reminds him of 'jeune', which he knows means 'young'. Peering at the context, he sees that 'jejune' could mean, if not exactly 'young', then something like 'un-grown-up, immature, callow'. Hooray!—he's always needing words for that, and here is a new one, one of superior quality, too.

STAGE III: B starts writing stuff like 'Much of the dialogue is *jejune*, in fact downright childish'. With the latest edition of *COD* giving 'puerile' as a sense of 'jejune', the story might be thought to be over, but there is one further stage.

STAGE IV: Having 'jeune' in their heads, people who have never seen the word in print start pronouncing 'jejune' not 'dj*idjoon*' but 'zher*zhern*' (*r's* silent), in the apparent belief that Frenchmen always give a tiny stutter when they say 'jeune'. (I have heard 'zher*zhern*' several times in the last few years.) Finally C takes the inevitable step of writing *jejeune* (I have seen several examples), or even, just that much better: 'Although the actual arguments are a little *jéjeune*, the staging of the mass scenes are [*sic*] impressive.' Italics in original!—which with the acute accent sets the seal on the deportation of an English word into French, surely a unique event.

(For the interested, 'jejune' is indeed connected with a French word, but it is 'jeûne' with distinguishing circumflex. Both derive from the Latin '[dies] ieiuna' or 'jejuna', a 'fast [day]'. Hence the familiar 'déjeuner', to de-fast as we break-fast. 'Jejune' then first meant 'fast-like, scanty, Lenten'—like the entertainment which Rosencrantz feared the players would receive from Hamlet.)

My last two examples can be considered more briefly. In the first example (*hopefully* the new product will reach bars and liquor-stores by the end of next month) it is not of course the product that is hopeful but the writer. Floating *hopefully*, once German, then become English in the US, is now establishing itself in the UK. Its misuse in the way illustrated is a matter of function rather than of meaning.

P Is it true that you've abused your powers as President?
I *refute* that totally and categorically. [end of interview]

(A popular misuse: I have a dozen other examples.) To refute is not to deny or to repudiate but to disprove, to overturn with facts or argument or both. A refutation on the scale required might take a millennium, involving as it would a demonstration that everything said and done by the President during his presidency was a nonabuse. He should have said 'deny', but after decades of authoritarian governments denying things, and indicted criminals denying similar things, the word is irredeemably tarnished. 'Refute' has both the feel of quality and the valuable covert suggestion that somehow something more than a mere denial is going on, which is what makes it a politician's word. That is the unarguable objection to floating *hopefully*. The fellow can't say 'I hope' because that would imply he has surrendered control of events; he can't really use J. F. Kennedy's favourite, 'I am hopeful that', without being J. F. Kennedy; he can't say 'with luck' which is all he means; so he says 'hopefully' and basks in a fraudulent glow of confidence.

I promised near the start to say what I thought had happened. That won't take long. Various changes, not all of them educational, have seen to it that most of the men and women who use words in public don't care any more which words they are, apart from a feeble hankering after the seemingly stylish. The concept of finding the right word, which used to be a strong influence on that of finding a good word, is being lost. How such people keep awake while they write is beyond me. Anyway, their handiwork, or handi-idleness, is all about: growing imprecision as words without a synonym, like 'disinterested', become synonyms of other, less exact words; quite commonly ambiguity or sheer nonsense; and everywhere awkwardnesses that force the reader to pause without profit, even if only for an instant. This is decline.

I know, or at least am constantly being told, about languages having to change if they are not to die, though it seems to be often forgotten that death is a very important form of change. Not that I see this as imminent in the case of our language now: the biggest recent change in it—the immense expansion of its vocabulary since 1945—seems successful enough. And in one way of course there's nothing you can do about it. Floating *hopefully* was the most widely and loudly denounced import to the UK in living memory until Japanese motorcars came along, and now it and they are everywhere. People who use floating *hopefully* aren't the ones who read articles on good and bad English. But there is something you can do, or someone can do, as follows.

In the introduction to *COD* the editor explains what he calls his usage labels, which appear in the main body of the dictionary between a word and its definition; for instance, '(joc.): jocular, used only in humorous or playful style; (vulg.): vulgar, used only by those who have no wish to be thought either polite or educated' (this eccentric and anachronistic gloss appears, not as I originally supposed in the first edition of *COD* in 1911, but in that of 1976). What about '(illit.): illiterate, used only by those who have no wish to write accurately or vigorously'? The principle could be extended. A dictionary records usage impartially, agreed, but whatever anybody says or does (here come some italics that don't signal a malapropism) *when consulted it is taken as prescriptive too* by almost everybody who is not either a lexicographer or a linguist, and prescription is partiality. It seems harsh to deny guidance to the lonely and diminishing minority who may genuinely need and want it.

From *The State of the Language*, (ed.) Leonard Michaels and Christopher Ricks, University of California Press, 1980

Usage and Non-usage

Longman Dictionary of the English Language, Longman

As the schoolchildren of the 1960s take up writing jobs in Fleet Street and the provinces, and illiteracy spreads through the public print, new dictionaries go on appearing. The latest one has of course no more chance of starting to slow the trend than any of the others, though like them it does draw attention to some usages that some people dislike. That is about as far as it can bring itself to go in reprehension; indeed it turns a trifle lofty on the people who dislike the use of *aggravate* to mean 'irritate' and *epithet* to mean 'term of abuse'. But at least the wink is tipped to the diminishing few who may actually want guidance.

The guidance given here on such matters is patchy. I checked out thirty popular catachreses, usages that are actually destroying useful words by making them ambiguous. In twelve of these cases *Longman* is what I will call sound, in that, however fastidiously, it indicates that some of that old dislike is felt. So *crescendo* (sloppily used to mean 'climax', as in 'it rose to a crescendo'), *dilemma* ('problem'), *fulsome* ('lavish'), *pristine* ('clean'), etc, have tasteful warning signs attached.

That leaves eighteen. Longman is unsound on seven of these, in that it lists the sloppy alongside the proper without turning a hair. So *brutalise* ('maltreat'), *fissiparous* ('fissile', as in 'the Labour Party's fissiparous state') and *forensic* ('technical', as in 'the Yard's forensic squad') are passed as fit. Of the remaining eleven, which make no appearance here at all, some though seemingly established have no doubt not been around long enough to qualify, like *infamous* ('quaint'), *quixotic* ('absurd') and *peremptory* ('sudden', as in 'the car came to a peremptory halt'). But others, like *panacea* ('cure', as in 'a universal panacea'), *bonus* ('goody', as in 'an added bonus') and *schizophrenic* ('divided', as in 'any patriot is bound to be schizophrenic over the Falklands') seem to me to be real omissions.

Well. Another thing about *Longman* is that it weighs a lot, 5 lb. as compared with 3½ lb. for the *Collins English Dictionary* of 1979, 4 lb. plus for the great *American College Dictionary* of 1947, and 12½ lb. for the giant *Webster's Third New International Dictionary*. All these, including *Longman*, are encyclopaedic dictionaries. This means among other things that they tell you rather more about plants and animals and suchlike than you strictly need, but much less than you want if you are really interested in the subject. For example:

> *horseradish 1* a tall coarse white-flowered plant (*Armoracia rusticana*), of the cabbage family cultivated for its white pungent root; *also* the root of this plant *2* a pungent condiment prepared from the grated root of horseradish.

Not enough for the botanically-minded inquirer, whereas an ordinary one will be just as well off with the entry in the *Concise Oxford Dictionary* (*COD*) of 1982:

> plant whose pungent root is scraped or grated as condiment, often made into sauce

—which actually adds a point omitted by *Longman*.

Not all the bulk of this book is put on by giving largely unwanted information about things like the cabbage family or what the Douay Version is. It also sets out, as observed earlier, to be a guide to usage, not stopping at some-people-dislike labels but handing out advice on how to deal with *every* and how to pronounce *patent* in different senses. The advice is sound enough but, again, it is bound to be much less than full; for instance, the usage note in the entry on *and* says nothing more than that it can be legitimately and effectively used to begin a sentence. (But then many times that space would be needed to describe fully the legitimate uses of that uniquely difficult English word.)

The style of the usage notes is often discursive, wordy in fact, however funny a term that may be to apply to a dictionary. The same, or similar, applies to a third addition, or dilution, the bits of thesaurus, of synonym and antonym, appended to some words. Then there are the preludial pages, which include an eye-confounding explanatory chart, and the—many more—postludial ones.

These include short essays on style, which turns out to mean punctuation and related matters, and on vexed points of grammar like the dangling participle and the split infinitive, where the tone is somewhat firmer than in the body of the dictionary. Next comes a catalogue of about 5,000 notables like Homer, Al Capone and Elton John, useful chiefly for dates but affording the pleasure of seeing who is there—and not there. Finally, such Webster-type items as the periodic table of elements, cardinal and ordinal numbers, and badges of rank in the British and US forces. It is interesting that while those of the respective armies are altogether different, those of the navies are all but identical, right down to the thin middle stripes on the lieutenant-commanders' cuffs. Little article there?

If you want a dictionary as a bedside book, *Longman* is probably as good as any, full, entertaining and as far as I can tell not parasitic on any other dictionary. Its etymologies in particular are remarkably exhaustive for a work of this size, where it is unexpected to find the Irish Gaelic as well as the Scottish root of *whisk(e)y*, or in the *vodka* entry not only the Russian root-word *voda* ('water') but also the cognate Old English *waeter*. (The article on *gin* made my hair stand on end a bit: too accurate by half.) If on the other hand you want something designed for what might be called a quick in and out, then you will stick to *COD*, which weighs in at just a spot over 2 lb. Not that it is only useful: the clipped elegance of its definitions is a joy—eg *far from*, more nearly the opposite of than the same as. It will stay on my desk, but *Longman* gets a place on my shelf.

Observer, 19 September 1982

Use and Abuse

The Oxford Guide to English Usage, compiled by E. S. C. Weiner, Oxford University Press

This book is founded on a principle taken for granted by most writers and readers since time immemorial: that there is a right way of using words and constructing sentences, and plenty of wrong ways. Until very recently this was denied by linguists and lexicographers, who would have returned a hearty No to the question asked in the title of a scholarly paper of 1964, 'Can Native Speakers of a Language Make Mistakes?' Or was it so hearty? In the course of giving their followers leave to spatter their talk and prose with any old illiteracy or howler that took their fancy, such people were always noticeably careful to make no 'mistakes' themselves, like a parson grimly preserving his own chastity while recommending adultery to his parishioners.

Anyway, after years of permissiveness the OUP signalled a clear change of front in 1979, when their new Paperback Dictionary categorised some misuses as 'unacceptable' and other expressions, thought to be less heinous but still dodgy, as 'informal'. The 1982 edition of the Concise Dictionary introduced a symbol, a D in bold type, signifying a 'disputed' usage, and various persistent offenders like *disinterested* for 'uninterested' and *anticipate* for 'expect' received this mild stigma, though others like *aggravate* for 'exasperate' scraped by as colloquial and yet others, *jejune* for 'puerile' among them, got off scot-free. The compiler of the present volume remarks that what interests him is 'the degree of acceptability in standard English of a particular use' rather than any 'dogmatic' question of right and wrong, but after thus touching his hat to linguistic egalitarianism he settles briskly down to telling us what to do and what not to do, and quite right.

Not that the book sets out merely to correct common errors: it comprehensively justifies its title. The first of four main chapters concerns word formation, such matters as the -able and -ible suffixes, the use of capital or lower-case initial letters (herculean labours but Homeric conflict, french chalk but French vermouth), the apostrophe and the differences between British and American spelling. This closes with a useful list of words often misspelt or wrongly arranged, though I could have done with a few more examples of horrible would-be terse joinings like *anymore, worthwhile* ('you will find it worthwhile') and *under-way* ('a movement is underway').

The second chapter is about pronunciation, with the treatment based on RP or Received Pronunciation, that of 'educated speakers in southern England'—OED Supplement. 'This is not to suggest that other varieties are inferior.' Good heavens no—what an idea! Will nobody ever suggest that the merit of RP is that, however offensive to some ears, it is intelligible in Land's End, John O'Groats and perhaps Newcastle too?

Well, among others there are good things here on accentuation and the sounding of the R between words. On the second point I again feel I could have done with more, more than a mere passing reference to the epidemic introduction from about 1950 of a glottal stop before initial vowels and even inside words. The intrusive R in *lawr and order* and *Shahr of Iran* may be an ugly noise, but at least it is an English noise. The catch in the breath that more and more speakers are inserting instead, even between the syllables of *fore/arm* and *over/all* and *Queen Juli/ana* is an American noise I first heard in the Thirties and, beyond that, a German noise—*Deutschland über alles*. But here at least resistance is vain. Every newscaster uses it.

It is in the third chapter, on vocabulary, that most of the distinctions are made and warnings delivered. Plenty of what Fowler called pairs and snares are identified, from the veteran *imply/infer* to comparative newcomers like *fortunate/fortuitous*. Modish wince-producers also come in for a drubbing: *in excess of* for 'more than', *parameter* for limit', *refute* for 'deny' in politician's language.

The book ends with a chapter on grammar (sound treatment of the subjunctive) and appendices on punctuation, clichés (all too short) and English overseas. Its rulings are judicious and vigorously urged throughout and the information it offers makes it indispensable. The foolish and the wicked who lack respect for the language will not take the slightest notice of it.

In a way this is not to be regretted. Nothing gives bad people away like what they say and write. So if somebody talks about 'this moment in time' without trying to be funny I know at once I have a pompous buffoon to deal with. 'That shirt is pristine' (clean) betokens a novelty-hunter who also lacks genuine curiosity. And (here it comes at last) 'delivery hopefully in the spring' marks a victim of appalling herd-instinct. One such person, by the way, is at large somewhere in the OUP. The jacket blurb of this book calls it 'an exciting new work of reference'. Naughty, naughty. Exciting books have murders and car-chases in them, not stuff about genders and gerunds.

Observer, 19 February 1984

Word Perfect

The English Language, by Robert Burchfield, Oxford University Press

Dr Burchfield is the editor of the Supplements (three volumes so far out of a promised four) to the *Oxford English Dictionary* (*OED*). The present book is not a grammar nor a survey of usage but a description of the English language at its various historical stages. Another good thing it is not is a theoretical work on the mysteries of communication. 'The origin of language is unknown and all theories about this problem are spurious,' the author says roundly on page two, and we are away.

We begin at the beginning with the origins of the language of the Anglo-Saxons, the runic and Latin alphabets and the infiltrations into the vocabulary of words from Latin (early forms of *wine*), Scandinavian (*husband, law*) and Norman French (*parliament, people, pauper* and an untold number more). And so on, from the time of Caxton in the 1470s to 1776, not just a political date but a good marker for the point or stage at which English ceased to be solely the language of the inhabitants of the United Kingdom and became also that of autonomous speech-communities round the world.

All this is fine, distinguished by clarity, compression and a sure nose for the appropriate and interesting example. My approval dips slightly when Dr Burchfield divulges some of his literary preferences: Sterne, Hopkins, Virginia Woolf, by implication the Joyce of *Finnegans Wake*. It is most legitimate that he should be attracted by dictional, syntactical and other linguistic interestingness, but I think he is in danger of relating this to artistic merit; somewhere he describes Aelfric (*ob. c.* 1020) as a great writer. Oh well—but there is a great return to form with an erudite and dismayed account of the new Bible and liturgy. The old language was woven into English literature through the centuries, the new versions can never enrich it in the future, and 'the loss for society as a whole—not so much of particular words as of the way they are put together—is grievous beyond all knowing'.

The discussion of dictionaries which follows can hardly help bringing up the old differentiation, or row, between the prescriptive breed of lexicographer, who knows that some usages are better than others and says which they are, and his descriptive fellow, who indifferently records what he hears and sees. In what must be a mildly thorny situation for him Dr Burchfield acquits himself with fairness and poise, acknowledging the futility of opposing linguistic change while stoutly continuing to call this or that usage erroneous or unacceptable.

He will not mind if I throw in here a word for my party, the libertarian-prescriptives, and plead that it is not innovation as such that we may dislike. For example, our objection to *refute* in the sense of 'deny' is not that it is new (or newish) but that it is destructive, verbicidal, forcing us to say or write 'overturn with facts or arguments' where once upon a time 'refute' would have been enough. Any unnecessary proliferation of words must be a weakening.

In the course of his discussion Dr Burchfield tilts at a number of linguistic or stylistic myths. Some of these are hardly worth standing up for: the idea that short words are better than long ones, that words of mixed ancestry, like *television*, are bad, that Saxon-derived words are better than non-native ones (though any decent writer will keep an eye on nouns ending in -*tion* and verbs in -*ise* or -*ize*). Other 'myths' disposed of here are more in the nature of piquant pieces of information that I in my diffident way had got into the habit of dispensing round the place, among them the notion that in early times in what is now England speakers respectively of Anglo-Saxon dialects and of Scandinavian ones each dropped the inflected endings of their words to improve mutual understanding. This was not, it appears, what happened, but I can let that one go without fretting.

Another such case is perhaps more generally interesting. Myth: the Normans introduced the names for cooked and eaten meats (*beef, pork*) as distinct from those of the supplying animals (*ox, pig*). Fact: the Norman names came in all right, but for a long time they referred to the animals as well as the meats. Until the Eighteenth Century *mutton* referred impartially to what you saw in the field and what you found on your plate. It was only after that that the present differentiation became established. So be it.

I will fight a little over a third one. Myth: contemporary US spoken English is closer in important respects to seventeenth-century UK spoken English than contemporary UK spoken English is. Fact, or proffered fact: not so, there are instances that point the opposite way, both varieties have drifted though in opposite directions. But of the four major respects in which the contemporary accents differ from each other Dr Burchfield mentions only one, the retention in the US of the R-sound in words like *port* and *more* and the dropping of it over most parts of the UK.

The other obvious three are the unrounding of the O-sound in the US, so that the vowel in words like *from* somewhat resembles the UK vowel in words like *palm*; the US vowel in *glass* is close to the UK vowel in *lass*; and, most striking and baffling of all to UK ears, the US vowel in *talk* quite closely resembled the UK vowel in *palm*. There is evidence that all three of these contemporary US vowels were to be heard in the same positions in seventeenth-century UK speech. Perhaps it is evidence that will not stand up: nevertheless if Dr Burchfield had taken time off to knock it over I for one feel he would have carried his argument more conclusively.

Intensive search has failed to reveal any substantial ground for finding fault with this valuable and vigorous book, but here are a couple of unsubstantial ones. The author seems to want us to abandon the apostrophe; apart from unloosing a flood of ambiguity the step would be a gross concession to the weaker brethren—clot-coddling in other words. Again, you do not just eke out an existence in the sense of managing to support it; you supplement what you have, you eke out your pension *with* consultation fees, and the first usage, if not unacceptable, is certainly erroneous. Finally, Dr Burchfield seems unaware that the traditional pronunciation of *centenary* was with the stress on the first syllable. I may be wrong, but if so the *OED* is too.

Observer, 27 January 1985

Hopefully up to Date

Winged Words, by Philip Howard, Hamish Hamilton

Philip Howard is the tireless literary editor of *The Times*. Not content with the onerous duties of the post, he has for years written a regular column in that newspaper on the subject of words, new words, new usages, good and not-so-good ones. He has even recently started a rare words quiz next to the crossword puzzle, 'a daily safari through the language jungle' as somebody (not he, surely) has captioned it. Now here comes what seems to be his sixth book on the subject, every line of which proclaims his enthusiasm and his knowledge.

Most of its short chapters evidently began as *Times* articles but then most of the material, the author indicates, is specially written. Anyway, we have a couple of dozen pieces on new words and expressions and about as many on new usages, though the distinction is lightly enforced. Mr Howard is unfailingly interesting on the origins of linguistic novelties in trade jargon, technology or slang and in the frequent vulgarisations and misunderstandings of these, and his persistent curiosity in tracking them down is rare and much needed.

His discussion of *state-of-the-art*, for instance, a recent example of what Fowler would have called a popularised technicality, is a model of its kind. Mr Howard shows neatly how from meaning 'up to date, at the frontier of scientific knowledge and development' it has become a mere tatty-glossy synonym for 'the latest' among people like the trendies who write British Telecom advertisements, while shifting into something like the opposite sense, 'established, approaching obsolescence' for the engineers and others who brought the phrase to birth. The confusion and ambiguity these misuses bring about are more important than any amount of groan-eliciting violence they may do to anyone's aesthetic sense.

Barbarisms in language, like more serious barbarisms in moral conduct, may become familiar, even stereotyped, but they are not thereby superseded or made of no account, certainly not while they continue. The use of *hopefully* in a floating position, to mean 'it is to be hoped', has often been excoriated, but not often enough, and never more thoroughly than here. And yet in the end Mr Howard shrinks from coming out and condemning the usage. He will go no further than register his personal avoidance: 'if you don't like it', he concludes, 'you don't have to use it. I don't.'

This is unsatisfactory. To discharge your duty to animals, say, it is not enough not to shoot or kick any yourself, and should you see something vile on television you have not done all that is required of you by turning off your set. The author of this book knows perfectly well that every time we use a word we do something to our language, and he is self-contradictory as well as wrong when he says that 'each man is an island entire of his idiolect' (the sum of his own usages).

Mr Howard is infinitely willing and able to show that English is in a constant state of change and never more so than now. What he will not do is go any of the way with those who say, and even try to demonstrate occasionally, that some of this change is for the worse. He will not admit that in certain fields (not, to be sure, astrophysics or microbiology) it has become harder in recent years to express oneself clearly and unambiguously, nor that to do so has become less highly regarded. For Mr Howard, everybody who thinks like that is worse than any Disgusted of Tunbridge Wells; such a creature has a problem not with language but with the male menopause.

This intemperate lurch into Auberon Waugh's repertory throws light on Philip Howard's problem. By temperament and training he is a linguistic elitist, acutely and continuously aware of what makes the difference between proper educated usage and the base, lazy or flashy vernacular. Some other motives warn him of the frightful danger of being thought snooty, uppity, anything but one of the boys as seen here in his elaborately off-duty jacket photograph. The division in him is nicely shown in the title of *Winged Words*: for the hoi polloi, the wings are merely those of modern communications, but the upper crust of classical scholars like himself will catch the tacit Homeric reference (*Iliad* I, 121 *et passim*).

Not only does Mr Howard regularly denounce fancied (or real) snobberies in attitudes to language, he shoves little disclaimers into every other sentence in the form of bits of slang, catch phrases, digs of all sorts. Okay, chaps, he says chummily, let it all hang out, give it the old heave-ho, up to a point Lord Copper, that's enough daft academic words—Ed. Fragments of trite quotations swim into view and out again: 'through a glass, darkly'—'puzzling, but not beyond all conjecture'—'would not stay for an answer'—'nasty, brutish and short' (twice), only recognisable or intelligible to the cognoscenti. And there are more puns than you have had hot dinners, ha ha ha.

The introduction to this book carries a warning of frivolity in what is to follow: 'it is possible to be serious without being solemn: there are jokes'. Indeed there are, and there are jokes and jokes too, and it is at least as possible to be whimsical and facetious as either serious or solemn. Mr Howard works too hard at brightening up this rather difficult linguistic stuff of his for the common reader, keeping him entertained while he feeds him information, like a popular-science presenter on TV. But the sad truth is that only quite a small minority are actually interested in questions of language however treated, and such people will follow considerable parts of what Mr Howard has to tell them with their teeth gritted, and the others will not follow any of it at all.

Sunday Telegraph, 10 July 1988

PART EIGHT
Films

Spectacular Manifestation at Trieste

The cinema ought to be an ideal medium in which to render science fiction. The most characteristic writers have always gone in for action, movement, suspense and the kinds of visual effect that the large screen is equipped, technically and financially, to handle. With a bare half-dozen exceptions, actual science-fiction films have given less satisfaction than imagined ones. No other cinematic category betrays more grossly that almost universal fallacy of entertainment manufacturers, the persistent undervaluing of what the public is intellectually and emotionally prepared to take. Costs must be recovered, the argument seems to run, so we'll pack 'em in with gore and monsters (giant wasps, giant sea-snails, giant pterodactyls, giant anything) and keep the budget down by hiring lousy actors—and doing the special effects on the cheap. How else explain the lack of technical advance whereby King Kong, after thirty-odd years, remains about the least unconvincing beast one has seen?

'King Kong', in fact, dubbed in Italian, was arguably the best effort of its kind to be seen in Trieste during the recent First International Festival of the Science-Fiction Film. But 'Kong' wasn't part of the Festival, it just happened to be showing in the town: the entries were evidently restricted to stuff that hadn't appeared in Italy before and hadn't already been booked for circulation there; the Federation of International Film-Producer Associations withheld its official recognition from the Festival. The result, or at any rate what we got, engendered for the most part trance-like boredom relieved by moments of weary outrage.

That was while the films were showing: Trieste itself was all right, the afternoon discussions (held in a chamber that curiously recalled the Nuremberg Trials) gave a glimpse of the seething world of Italian science-fiction politics, and the outdoor cinema, in a castle on top of a hill, was an impressive locale, especially on the first night when a partial eclipse of the moon weirdly—but very easily—distracted attention from the screen.

Some of the expected kinds of badness were richly represented: no giant praying mantises or such, but an abundance of vulgarity and sheer naked ineptitude. 'X—the Man with the X-Ray Eyes' (American) scored high on both counts, with poor Ray Milland giving as much as he has to a theme that nibbled feebly at comic possibilities before plunging into repulsiveness. 'If thine eye offend thee', an evangelist advised him in the final sequence, 'pluck it out—and by George he did. 'The Attack of the Puppet People' (American, and years old) featured a chap with a machine that shrunk you. Once shrunk, you entertained him by jitterbugging on a tabletop, having parties with champagne served in dolls' glasses, etc. The atmosphere of French intellectualism that pervaded the Festival induced me to see in all this an allegory of the degradation of the worker under capitalism, but my English-speaking colleagues couldn't go any of the way with me there.

The British entries are best passed over: that not-short-enough cartoon short, 'The Little Island', which is whimsy anyway, not science fiction; and a so-called feature, 'Masters of Venus', which turned out to be a glued-together six-part Saturday-morning children's cinema serial. [Sociological note: nice Venusians speak Standard English, nasty ones have Central European accents.]

The Communist countries had much more to offer. 'The Cybernetic Grandmother' (Czech), a puppet-and-model colour short, was a piece of impressive technical virtuosity that had a lot to say about the horror to be associated with automata that behave in quasi-human ways, recalling Freud's observation on the uncanny, that it derives from uncertainty about whether something is alive or not.

A Czech feature, 'Icarus XB 1', displayed at length the familiar fault of Iron Curtain science fiction, a built-in lack of conflict and drama deriving pretty recognisably from ideological preconceptions: the future must be socialist, and socialists are all by definition unselfish and loyal and dedicated, so that opposition to the common good can come only (as here) from the momentarily deluded. Space-sickness may take its toll, unfamiliar radiations cause concern, but People's Science will soon look after everything. However, the space-ship interiors were splendidly imagined and executed, the first ones I have seen on film which seemed commensurate with the subject, and there was a party on board with twenty-first-century drinks and music and dancing that one could believe in.

Much against my expectation, it was a Russian film which won my own private award. 'The Amphibious Man' earned some disapproval from the more rigorous observers at the Festival—ie those ignorant enough to believe that science fiction must be engaged in some heavy way with science, or at least be scientifically respectable—for being nothing more than fantasy. In fact, though neither the Russian soundtrack nor the thunderous Italian commentary afforded me any detailed guidance, there was certainly enough opportunity for the half-minute of double-talk necessary to establish the intended plausibility of the hero's adaptation by surgery into one who can extract oxygen from water as well as from air. The setting, all of it beautifully photographed and rendered by a colour process more pastel in tendency than those we are familiar with, was supposedly South American. I suspected Cuba, until knowledgeably informed that it was all done on the shores of the Black Sea really, with Tartars and such brought in to do the Indian types.

The whole thing made unassisted sense to one who could understand not one word of the dialogue—an important virtue. It was a lyrical fable about a youth enabled to grow up in a subaqueous Arcadian solitude who finds life on land exciting and horrific and finally unendurable. A tour of the waterfront, ushered in and given definition by the devastating shot of a steer struggling in a net being hoisted aboard a steamer, ends in a scene of alarm and flight, for which someone had evidently strapped a camera to his chest and run like hell up and down the right sort of fishing-port alleys. The emotional climax comes when the boy visualises himself in the depths, gambolling like a dolphin round the girl who can never in reality share his world. There was a jail-break and shooting later, too late to impair the passionate conviction of the whole.

When the Highly Qualified International Jury met to make its awards I voted hard for 'The Amphibious Man', but what could I, and a solitary American ally, do against two Frenchmen and two Italians? The palm went to a piece of French *avant-garde* kitsch, the title of which I will not advertise. It consisted entirely of stills. One of the Frenchmen, the one who kept saying we lived in a science-fiction world these days, explained that this severe self-limitation was excitingly experimental. Like having your leg broken before running a mile. I wish I'd thought of saying.

Observer, 11 August 1963

Tapping Feet of One-take Temple

Shirley Temple: American Princess, by Anne Edwards, Collins

This is an agreeably written but not very necessary publication. The child star Shirley Temple, born 1928 and so named on her birth certificate, appeared in over fifty films in all. The first was a ten-minute short made when she was not quite four years old and the last was produced in 1949, but the time of her greatest celebrity and success was comparatively brief, perhaps no more than 1934–7. The latter date is reached less than a third of the way through *Shirley Temple: American Princess*.

The story of the decline of Shirley's film career and of the failure of her first marriage is mildly distressing and rather overlong as told here, and there is inevitably a great deal of information about her mother.

Later in life, as Mrs Shirley Temple Black, she pursued an effective political career, first as a campaigner for Richard Nixon, subsequently as a holder of diplomatic posts at the UN and elsewhere and US ambassador to Ghana in 1974–6. To use an overworked adjective perhaps justly, it is ironical that the final event in the personal chronology given here should be her presentation with a full-sized Oscar trophy—she had received a miniature one in 1934.

As seen and heard in my vivid recollection, Shirley was no great eyeful or singer. Her face was not far from puddingy and her expression in repose was doleful and discontented, with little hint of her strong good looks in maturity. In her songs she sometimes strayed in pitch, her delivery was disfigured by 'cute' mannerisms ('On the goo-oo-ood ship Lollipop') and, to a British ear, her American accent could be obtrusive ('And there you *ore*, happy layanding on a choc-o-late bore'). Nor did her speaking voice endear her to me. Where she really scored was in her tap-dancing. That whole style is a historical curiosity now but in its day Shirley Temple was one of its greatest exponents.

It would have been fun of a kind to see her partnering Fred Astaire, with whom she never appeared, though she came somewhere near it in *Dimples* (1936), where according to this book she performed a number with a full-sized male doll painted to look like him strapped to her toes—an occasion worth missing, like her imitation in the same film of Al Jolson singing 'Mammy'. Incidentally in the following year Shirley was paid over $300,000 by Twentieth Century Fox to Astaire's $260,000 plus by RKO.

In the fashion of the time these dances entailed most complicated routines incorporating flights of stairs, pieces of furniture and whatnot. Shirley always got them right, and first time too, being known around the studio as (no doubt among other things) One-take Temple. And, whatever the deficiencies of her singing, she mastered tongue-twisting lyrics with apparent ease. Her IQ was measured at 155.

It was, I submit, the spectacle of a rather ordinary-looking little girl being so amazingly nimble and professional that constituted her main attraction, with, of course, some satisfying sassiness to grown-ups thrown in. I remember feeling quite sorry as well as embarrassed for Victor McLaglen and C. Aubrey Smith as the sergeant and colonel in *Wee Willie Winkie* (1937).

Sex is notoriously hard to rule out as a motive in human likes and dislikes, and critics have not been slow to impute morbid, paedophilic interest to some of Shirley's admirers. One of the fastest of all was our own Graham Greene, whose notorious *Night and Day* review of *Wee Willie Winkie*, together with the transcript of the High Court proceedings awarding substantial damages against the magazine, is reprinted here, and very silly-clever film-critic stuff it looks now.

Not only that. If a group of normal schoolboys sees nothing sexual in something, it is as safe as it can ever be to say there is nothing sexual to see, and my pals and I found Shirley about as on-turning as a dodgem car. Those slavering 'middle-aged men and clergymen' of Graham Greene's article seem like the products of a distorted imagination, or more probably of the same impish sense of fun that led him, in an essay of about that time, to produce a Freudian analysis of the works of Beatrix Potter.

Sunday Telegraph, 11 December 1988

PART NINE
Amis Abroad

Amis Abroad

It can hardly be more than twenty years ago that the social conditions governing travel writing in these islands changed quite abruptly. What had been the domain of the few became that of the many. I can remember my mild surprise when about 1960 a friend of mine, the headmistress of a Swansea girls' school and admittedly an enterprising person, told me that the Costa Brava (a newish expression in those days) was getting too crowded for her and that she proposed to holiday in Morocco. In Portugal only five years before, temporarily deported by the conditions of my Somerset Maugham Award, I had found British tourists honking their horns and waving excitedly at the sight of another GB plate on the road, and an upper-class couple encountered in Estoril (I had popped in for a rich drink at the Hotel Edward VII) were amazed by my not knowing any of the people they had thought I must have seen at Ascot or Henley; in fact they could not make out what I was doing in the country at all. By the mid-Sixties, as is known, large parts of the entire peninsula were being seasonally colonised from all over Western Europe. Other places soon underwent the same fate.

That fate, with the money and freedom it brought the locals, was nothing so terrible, one might have thought. Nor was that of the millions fetched to the sun and exotic sights for the first time in their lives, even if the sights had often to be peered for between the ranks of new hotels (nor, to take another view of the matter, need any concern be spared for those who enjoy or endure lying on beaches). Nevertheless the process is here and there spoken of as if it were somehow a bad thing, and there will be talk of spoiling, at which my progressive nature automatically revolts. The complaint is in effect that the inhabitants should have been left unmaterialistic, ie poor, to suit the odd visitor's more or less crappy notions of picturesqueness and authenticity. The point about the spoiling of places is rather more difficult; even so, when it comes to it there cannot be many who would not barter a traditional flower ceremony or fish auction for boldly innovative plumbing, pharmacies, dentists etc. As for my Estoril acquaintances and their like (not that anyone cares) they will always find somewhere unspoiled, or spoiled more lavishly and longer ago.

One unqualified casualty of these barbarian invasions, as he could

hardly have been blamed for calling them, was the old-fashioned travel-
ler or travel writer, the sort who for decades had been getting away
with calling Spain a harsh, bitter land or, if queer, sometimes when
demonstrably not, going on about the civilisation of the delicate olive
at the other end of the Mediterranean. The distinction of this kind of
thing had been its exclusiveness or, if you prefer, its snobbery. The
fellow knew the place in question, and 'intimately' was the word for
how he knew it, an intimacy achieved by means of money, a superior
education and, above all, a lot of spare time. Now and then, it might
be noted in passing, the last attribute would serve on its own; a sub-
section of the genre celebrated the adventures of those who had simply
turned their backs on the rat-race and bummed their way round Bulga-
ria with their bagpipe. But most of the time the old intimacy had
results like this in the works of Norman Douglas:

> As to that secluded grove of pines—what an inspiring place to
> spend the evening of one's days! One of many attractions was its
> inaccessibility. And yet, I thought, once a path has been con-
> structed across that wilderness of boulders and through a rocky
> spur of the hill, where a gate should be placed, you are within a
> few minutes' walk of the piazza, the centre of such life as there
> is. Go to that centre, if you wish to see fellow-creatures; lock
> your gate, and wall up that fissure in the rock higher up, and only
> a bird can reach you. An aerial situation; you are poised between
> earth and sky. Here, if anywhere, one might still find peace from
> the world; here one might gather together the wrecks of one's
> belongings and dream away the hours, drinking the heady per-
> fume of the pines and listening to that Theocritean melody of
> theirs, which is not truly a whisper, but an almost inaudible
> breathing: summer music. Here, if anywhere, one might—

His fade, not mine. Or, more shortly:

> My favourite resort was the catacombs, a ghostly and solitary
> region, a labyrinth of dark recesses hewn laterally into the rock
> below the surface of the ground, yet open to the sky for the most
> part . . . Day after day I sat somewhere in that enchanted hollow,
> thinking of the next chapter or two, and listening to the liquid
> croaking note of the bee-eaters which skimmed over my head. The
> boy Achmet, meanwhile, played about gleefully and devoured the
> dessert I had pocketed for him at luncheon; later on, towards
> evening . . .

My fade, but only in fun. Anyway, wherever the place in question
might be you had never been there, except possibly, to point the
contrast, on a one-day school excursion or a one-night stay in furtherance of commerce. This effective monopoly of information and so of
response proved vulnerable to the results of increased wages in other
lands. It would have become hard to go on with intimacies about Paros

when the tours started arriving there three times a day. And shifting
to Antiparos across the strait would be no more than a delaying action.

Considerations rather like these, at least, must be the reason for the
virtual demise of the travel-book or the get-there-and-stay-there-book
as written by Douglas or D. H. Lawrence. (This pairing reminds me
to say that I have nothing against Douglas, a shrewd, observant and
funny writer whose gifts were never better displayed than in his
account of Lawrence's varied meannesses.) As holidays abroad have
expanded, then exploded, so a literature of sorts has grown to fit their
needs, telling you where and how to go, where to stay, what if
anything to see, all that and very little more; most useful. At the same
time anything at all exploratory or far-ranging, from a rare butterfly
in Borneo to what might be a tomb in Chad, has come to demand
the incomparably more immediate and vivid images of the television
camera. No kind of successor to Peter Fleming's marvellous *Brazilian
Adventure* of 1933, travel-book and skit-on-travel-book in one, could
be contemplated now. Over the shoulder of every such adventurer in
the Eighties there looms for good or ill a PanAm jet going his way.

At a time when everything has been done before, new feats are
forced into being by adjusting the rules and records. You have no hope
at all of being the first person to swim the Hellespont, but how about
being the first Comanche or gynaecological endocrinologist to do so?
More to the point, now that any fool can cross the High Andes in
whatever may be the conventional style and write about it, cross them
on a polo pony and write about that. Books about the Sahara are two
a penny; jump in with one about honeymooning there. Be the first to
chronicle a journey following Tamerlane's 1386 campaign through
Central Asia against the Golden Horde. No whimsical invention here;
a British writer, John Ure, has done all three—Andes, Sahara, Asia.
And some years ago, of course, there were those two chaps who redid
Johnson's and Boswell's Scottish tour.

I hope I have not allowed any uncharacteristic touch of malice or
ill-nature to seem to colour these remarks. The desire to visit remote
parts of the planet, even those very mildly remote and no matter
how many other people have done so or are there now, is evidently
ineradicable. And, like other human activities, travel—terrible word,
but there is no other—is going to go on getting written and read about.
The advantage of it as a stimulus to creation is that it smartens up the
eye and the mind. You look at that old Spanish church longer than at
St Swithin's down the road and you think more about it and—vital
supplement—about other things too. It would be something to be able
to look at England as if it were Patagonia. Only Graham Greene,
himself an excellent travel writer of the old school, has managed that,
and the England he sees is rather like one that used to exist thirty years
ago but not very like. Interesting, all the same.

Anyway, having agreed to go abroad for the first time for five years,
perhaps a bit tepidly as will appear, I thought it might be fun to keep

a notebook of the trip and later see whether its contents would write up into some piece or other. (You may care to know that I drafted this part while staying with friends in the Dordogne, just like an old wanker trying to work up a travel piece for *The Nineteenth Century* before the war.) Jane and I went on a fortnight's voyage, much diversified by sightseeing, round the north-west coast of France, Spain, Portugal and Spain again, ending up at Nice. Not quite the Limpopo, you may think, but be advised that our company was a 200–strong gang of oldsters diversified by some unwary younger couples and a few defeated children, these latter groups between them keeping the overall average age down to something under sixty-five. So intrepidity had its role. And it was a Greek ship.

A novelist had better be careful about what sort of situations he likes showing his characters in. Life certainly came up with a spot of art-imitation that hot afternoon at the end of July when, just about understandably misled by a passage in the travel documents, Jane and I began the urgent task of discovering where, in the whole of Southampton docks, our ship, M.T.S. *Orpheus*, might be. I kept a great deal to myself for the next half-hour, at the end of which we proceeded on board under the eyes, it seemed, of all passengers and crew. We were perceptibly ahead of an American couple called Jones, who arrived by London taxi five minutes before the ship finally sailed. Their view had been that 1300 hrs meant 3 pm.

Art-imitation, well yes, but of course we all suffer something like that or worse sooner or later and are daunted. I brooded, then and later, on travel angst, a topic worth some study. I get it a lot, but I suspect that everybody gets it at least a bit, gets, that is, more discomfort than the situation warrants. A missed boat is a bit of a bugger, granted, but this one at least could have been caught at its next port of call (though I shuddered when I thought of what that would involve), and a missed anything-else can usually be retrieved in a couple of hours, and if not, sort of what of it? But more is or seems to be at stake at such times than inconvenience or loss of money or even making a fool of yourself. One factor might be that to make a complete voluntary departure from home and group is a very recent piece of behaviour and when it goes wrong the poor old naked ape is likely to feel naked indeed. Territory and all that, I mused as I was led off to the Coffee Veranda for tea.

This was no veranda in any sense I had met before, but a dark, airless cubby-hole off the main lounge, a strong contender for the position of hottest place on that smouldering vessel. Heat and humidity between them at once established themselves as one of the major themes of the tour. In palace and art-gallery, café and theoretically air-conditioned coach, even in cathedral, the passengers constantly collapsed into little groaning, dabbing, fanning heaps, their attention sadly distracted from whatever it was they were supposed to be appreciating. Poor old things. And that, of course, was the other great theme. You could not go up or down anywhere, even along anywhere, bus aisle, crypt staircase, gangway, cloister, without finding yourself stuck behind a great globe of fat or a character with one leg and a swinger or a plain fucking old fool who had forgotten which way was straight on. And welcome! In this company I was a youngster again.

What with that reflection, relief at not after all having to be winched down to the sun-deck of the *Orpheus* from a helicopter and self-approval for not ballocking Jane—she it was who had screwed the time-table—I was in a good state to be told that she had taken out insurance against my calling off the trip at the last minute. But I never do things like that, I said.

The food on the ship was what I will call consistently unappetising. Everything for the two weeks had clearly been brought aboard and stuck in the freezer at Southampton. It takes a certain firmness of mind to slouch unheeding past Iberian fruit and vegetables, but our kitchen managed it because it was so definitely easier for them to open a tin and face the risk of shortening my life by calling the contents fresh whatever-it-was. Fuel and water might come aboard when we docked, of food not a sausage except, late on, a few bunches of nearly-ripe grapes. The bread rolls were little balls of instant dough, each and every one clearly the product of a single vast primordial baking process. The meat varied, but not much.

The drinks were better, as drinks so often are. I had given up hope years before of finding any sort of tolerable Greek red wine, let alone a very decent one at a modest price, but the Naoussa 1978, shipped by Boutari and Sons, was pitched somewhere vague but quite liveable between claret and Beaujolais. The St Helena 1975 (Achaia Wine Co.) was just a nice Greek dry white wine, like retsina minus that resin. I drank freely of both without ill effects, short-term ones, that is. Bar drinks began with large ouzos at the stiffish price (for on shipboard) of 36p, and often finished there. Oh yes, it was possible to lead a modestly alcoholomorphous life on that boat. But it was a dark moment, as charged with significance as seeing the lights of Scilly fade, when I quaffed the last drops of The Macallan ten-year-old from my travelling-flask.

The touring part of the tour began with a vengeance the next morning, early, earlier even than it seemed because they had made us put our watches on an extra hour. Immediately upon rising and breakfasting we were to disembark and get into buses. Then and on subsequent mornings the question of timing and achieving one's shit came up in a potentially acute form, acute to some degree for all, of course, but several times over more so for those I will call the elderly. The reader will forgive me if I pass over the likely reasons for this and observe only that here is the starting-point of a great deal of oldsters' fussiness, dislike of change, cleaving to routine, etc, or alternatively that if you really want to put the wind up Grandad, thrusting him into any sort of public eye at dawn has a lot to be said for it and no mistake.

Moist about the brows and armpits even so early and so comparatively far north (this was Brest), we got into the buses, some with prolonged effort, others cursing them or the occasion *sotto voce*. All tour buses are the same tour bus, quite comfortable but for the tendency of the chap behind to push his knees into the small of your back and of the chap in front to complain of your doing this to him. But there were never any real problems of this sort; you played it docile, not to say ingratiating, piling up points for the moment when you would have lost your boarding-card or left your spectacles in the sacristy. Also you really must like sitting in buses for hour after hour or you would hardly have come on such a venture, let alone come for the dozenth time as plenty had.

That Friday we drove for about an hour across rather pretty wooded hills, noticing huge unattended collections of cylinders and pipes and flat-faced houses with dingy shutters. Here and there the front door was half a story from the ground, recalling the era when the livestock were driven into the basement during the winter to keep the household warm. Personnel-management trainees lived there now, I could tell.

We stopped at Guimiliau church, one famous for its Calvary, in other words a carved three-dimensional tableau fancifully representing the events there and others from the life of Christ and including a couple of hundred small stone figures, in general appearance very strange and not very reassuring otherworlders—like from Aldebaran IV, I mean, rather than Purgatory or any of those. What Christianity has allowed in over the centuries is remarkable.

'Where's Jane?'

'In the charnel-house buying postcards.'

Bearing *rhum*, or rum, and that sad exile from the UK, Johnny Walker Red Label, we made our way back to the buses. A strong, momentarily unidentifiable odour touched my sense; I knew at once that years ago it had been of daily familiarity, now long since removed, breathing of home and history, everything natural and innocent. It was horse-shit, I realised.

That evening we and others were invited to the captain's table. The low ceiling, the humidity and my own hardness of hearing made conversation effortful. On my right I had a very attractive dental surgeon from Brazil who had seen a fair amount of service in Botswana and other parts of black Africa. Some of her experiences there, she said, had reversed her formerly friendly attitude to Soviet communism, which she had once considered a possible remedy for her country's ills.

'Oh? What happened?' I asked, and strained to catch her reply from among the tumult.

'Well, there aren't many dentists in those parts, and I was called in quite a few times to attend to Russian diplomats and advisers and so forth. And honestly, what I saw there . . .'

I recalled an expression of my own dentist's and crossed my fingers as I spoke. 'Would you say that Soviet mouths were terrible?' I said, by now practically auscultating my neighbour.

'*Terrible*,' confirmed the lovely creature, her eyes flashing with remembered professional disgust. 'The workmanship was not all that bad, but the materials were appalling. Some of that cement wouldn't have lasted more than a year. Well, the conclusion was obvious . . .'

It would never have been obvious to some people, I reflected. Truly, there are many paths from the Devil.

The next day, at Nantes, we had the alternative of going along up the Loire to Angers, there to look at St Maurice's cathedral, or visiting a Muscadet vineyard and sampling its products. After careful deliberation the choice fell on the trip to Muscadet. Yes, indeed it is the name of a grape, but surely by now it has become the name of a place too.

The Angers lot left early because they had further to go. We sat about on deck in uncertain sunshine while all possible sorts of cloud at once, like an illustration in an encyclopedia, passed over our heads. That was all that was worth a second glance. I tried to winkle something quintessentially Breton, then after a few seconds anything vaguely French, out of my surroundings. Difficult. Like Hoboken, New Jersey, like Newport, Monmouth (sod Gwent), Nantes from the water is a matter of corroded machinery, huge piles of rubbish, floating debris, oil, tar, soot and a very ugly skyline. I picked up my book.

It was Len Deighton's splendid and, as it at once proved to be, absorbing para-historical novel *SS-GB*. (They came here in 1941.) With its honour and barbarity, schoolboy's-fantasy uniforms and outlandishly-named ranks, it has always struck me as the most fascinating of all iniquitous organisations. Until Mr Deighton told me I had no idea that you could be a member of the Gestapo as well as of the SS and still not be a member of the Party. The whole Nazi structure or lack of structure, that farrago of *sui generis* hierarchies and autonomies which nevertheless held together well enough till it ceased to exist under overwhelming outside stress, seems unbelievable as the work of only twelve years, six of them at war, unbelievably advanced along its alien path.

To return: *SS-GB* is distinguished also by a skill I have never seen so highly developed elsewhere. A large part of the dialogue naturally consists of what is supposedly German presented in English. Any self-respecting author in that position faces the difficulty of keeping his readers reminded that this is indeed the case, that the characters are not simply talking English. The comic-strip or 'Mein Gott!' solution is often to be found a surprising distance up the market. It has the disadvantage, among others, of suggesting that the speaker is talking English after all most of the time, but keeps slipping back into German when confronted by the simple expressions he must have come across at the start of learning the language. 'How you say?' is the other usual recourse, occasional lapses into literal translations of German phrases. Neither of these will do at all, obviously, for characters whose mother-tongue is English.

Mr Deighton solves the problem triumphantly by writing fully idiomatic English but now and then deviating into an expression which is just a little wrong for the speaker or the situation, thus evoking in a flash the conscientious 'translator' grappling manfully with a refractory German colloquialism. It must have been fun to write those passages and they are certainly a joy to read.

This excellence and others notwithstanding, SS-GB remains an example of what we usually understand by escape fiction; it grips the reader far too firmly and uninterruptably for a straight novel. I will have you know that I took not one example of the latter away with me, and this out of nothing more than good sense. Consider that to write about human relations as such, without benefit of gun-fight or car-chase, is a most hazardous enterprise that nearly always fails, most often miserably. Whereas of course when it succeeds it is more fascinating than any thriller. It is? Of course? My heart goes out to all those youngsters sitting in Minorca or Mykonos trying to read War and Peace and wishing they had the guts to go through the hotel bookshelf for some old Mickey Spillanes. Until quite recently I was a bit like that myself.

Across the aisle of the bus a woman was explaining that Muscadet was a dry white wine with a flinty taste. We drove through fields of cabbages, then vines, to a long low building with thousands of empty Muscadet bottles outside. Here an unexplained twenty-minute delay supervened; well, it was 3.15 pm on a Sunday. Then several Frenchmen arrived and led us through gloomy, acid-smelling sheds of uncertain specific purpose. Bit by bit it emerged that they were not the vineyard, which was shut. What we were looking at was a bottling-plant, which was not shut, just not working. No account of how a bottling-plant operates is necessary when it is working, and I doubt whether any would have been adequate as things were. Since none of the Frenchmen spoke any English we should presumably have had to make do with mime and grunts only, had an interpreter not been present, and it was a near go, that, for as I saw that evening he was one of the passengers.

As the promised tasting approached my hopes of it sank more and more, but then, instead of the ten minutes' standing in a sudorific shack I had been counting on, we were shown into a pleasant building with stained-glass windows, evidently a reconstructed barn, seated at a long table and poured a succession of three wines. The first was a Gros Plant du Pays Nantais, and it was white, and dry, and rather thin, but not bad. The second was a Muscadet. I forgot to note whether it was a Muscadet de Sèvre et Maine or a Muscadet du Coteaux de la

Loire or just a Muscadet. No matter; as expected, it was a sour little potation, flooding the mouth with saliva at each sip. Finally we had some rosé or other from somewhere else, and it had most of what a rosé can have, such as it is. We had a good time, though. The stuff came in large glasses filled most of the way up and there was no nonsense about rolling it round your mouth, let alone spitting any of it out; you swigged it and they topped you up. There were giggles and little shrieks as we climbed aboard the buses and considerable babbling and dozing on the way back to the ship. But I wonder what the winery got out of it.

Later we sailed down the Loire towards the setting sun. That much is all that remains of what was going to be a rather fine descriptive paragraph. I just could not prevent it from going either sugary or self-consciously austere (worse). I suppose I am used to doing descriptions in novels, which are not really descriptions but extensions of mood and drama by other means. If your travel-piece, unlike this one, is full of mood and drama, then the kind of set-piece description I am think-ing of would probably work. Well, anyway.

The following morning we landed near La Rochelle and were taken to it and allowed to wander about unguided for a bit. The chain-saw noise of the motor bikes was enough to make you yell, far worse than at home. I noted with satisfaction the offensiveness of the post-war housing, again even worse than at home. Paul, who has lived for longish periods in France, told me that French snobbery was incompar-ably worse than British or American.

'You have to admit they come out into the open about it,' he said. 'A place will be advertised as a *Résidence de Grand Standing*.'

'They live in the Rue de Shagbag so that'll give you some idea of what kind of people they are.'

While Paul thought this over I reflected how much conversation was carried on in invented quotations from imagined persons, and how difficult it was to transfer this to the page in a way that seemed natural. Then Paul spoke again, frowning.

'Not *some* idea,' he said in his emphatic way. '*The whole* idea.'

We came up with the buses. I recognised that I was quite relieved to see them and the tour representatives standing by them. The latter took a good deal of the dread out of moving about abroad; in particular, once put into words, your sudden need of a toilet became transfigured into theirs.

Some of us were already aboard the bus when a Frenchman came by leading a small tiger, or tigress as it proved to be, name of Sonia, five and a half months. I wanted to know what he was doing there and why he saw fit to have a tiger at all, but no one else did. Twittering like schoolgirls, nearly everybody, including most of those who had been on the buses, including too a lot of persons easily old enough to know better, rushed over to the creature and stared at and clucked over and took photographs of it. Wonderful they all thought it was, or marvellous. It certainly looked amiable enough, but I mean really . . .

'Couldn't happen in England,' said Neil.

'Thank God.' I at once realised that I should have said, 'I wish I agreed with you.' There could hardly be a better example of what I think should not be encouraged than a fellow taking a tiger along a street on purpose.

This time we drove through flat fields with cows in them. Leaving nothing to chance, the local guide explained that they produced milk and butter. After a time there were no more cows and the fields had sunflowers in them. They produced sunflower-seed oil.

We arrived at Surgères and looked at what must be the dullest church in Western Europe, forgettably carved outside and almost completely bare within, as if completed yesterday afternoon. I was wearing my hat that day, a rather controversial effort in a grey plastic somewhat resembling straw that I had picked up in a sale at Moss Bros. I forgot it was there until we had almost reached the chancel, when I snatched it off, naming aloud the Son of the church's dedicatee.

Neil had been gazing at me. 'You don't look Jewish,' he said.

It was better across the road in the Ronsard (he used to visit the local château) Restaurant, where we started with celeriac, beetroot, cauliflower, tomatoes, spam, clams and rice, went on to roast veal, chips, green beans and flageolets and finished with apple tart followed by coffee. Except slightly for the veal, which was between warm and lukewarm in the French style, everything was delicious and the wines were unsensational but went jolly well with the food. I was slightly dismayed to reflect that what was an occasion for us was nothing out of the way for the locals. Then I remembered the French character and brightened a little. Considering they are as they are on food like that, the mind shrinks from what they would be like on our muck. Bloody hell, they would cut your throat if you asked them the time. Yes, all is for the best, really.

In the afternoon we visited another unaccoutred frowsty barn, St Pierre's at Aulnay. The south (was it?) door is supposed to be interesting, and so it is, and yet it was dull. Then we went to the Domaine de la Roche Courbon, a sort of château with a formal garden. We looked at the garden first, in my case from a distance. It consists of a smallish area of smooth gravel picked out with even littler strips of mown grass, conical shrubs (box, Jane said) and a few geometrical patches of flowers. The house is a long narrow museum full of junk bought since the place last changed hands in 1920 and, in August 1980 at least, tremendously hot. After a few minutes a couple of us went and drank glasses of Kanterbräu, a sweet gassy beer. And to think that we could have gone on the other excursion, the one to Cognac!

The next day, after three spent or partly spent sightseeing, was passed at sea, crossing the Bay of Biscay to La Coruña. We slept on a bit in the morning, sat about the deck, took it easy. It dawned on me that I was enjoying myself—I, who had hated holidays for years, the orthodox hotel-and-beach sort, anyway. The trouble with a holiday in that sense is that you get no free time; there are no changes of gear from what must be done to what need not be done, no moment when you can relax and put your feet up and have a drink—you have been able to do that all day. A man who marries his mistress is in something of the same position (admittedly for longer than most holidays). Once, he could enjoy planning to go, then going, over to her place, look forward to a nice bit of his life that was quite different from the rest, cut off from it; now, here she is week in, week out.

The tour thing we were on is not a bit like that. The military comparison is not hard to make: reveillé at 0700 (really 0500) or some earlier time, anyway in the dark, and in due course on parade with full equipment, namely (in my case) both pairs of glasses, passport, money, cheroots, lighter, pen, notebook, hat and Lomotil (not known to all—a minute pill obtainable on prescription, which will stop any ordinary case of trots dead in its tracks). 'On parade' of course meant on deck ready to disembark. When on the first couple of mornings Jane and I turned up on the dot, at the first minute of the ten-minute-period specified in Part I Orders (the daily programme), we found a couple of dozen people already there. If challenged, they would no doubt have said truthfully that they intended to make sure of a seat in the bus that carried the best tour guide. But the expressions on their faces as they noted our arrival told of more than that; nothing military, rather the downcast eyes and slightly pursed lips of consciously good children proclaiming by their presence that *they* were not going to keep anyone waiting. Old people spend a lot of their time trying to be good like that. But then on reflection there is plenty of childishness in the army, and not only in the obviously derogatory sense.

Other similarities could be noted, among them the phenomenon of the sudden unexplained delay, as at the Muscadet joint. But a more straightforward analogy would be simply with work. After an hour or two in the bus and a good couple of hours trudging round sights and sites and from one to the next you are ready for your lunch, and after more bus and more trudging and yet more bus back to the ship you can put your feet up and relax and have a drink and *feel you have earned it*. A very British arrangement.

On the way to Santiago de Compostela it was all lighting effects. A thick mist at first hid even the position of the sun, which successively gave a diffused glow above long stretches of pine trees, showed its almost-white disc, broke through and was covered again, the mist in a matter of seconds vanishing and re-forming. It had altogether cleared by the time we entered a featureless twentieth-century town and then quite suddenly, with no preliminary view from the bus, were in the square in front of the huge, supremely elaborate cathedral. Under our feet among the cobbles were draincovers with the Chalice and Host depicted on them.

Catholics will not need to be told that this is the third Christian shrine in the world, after Rome and Jerusalem. The Iago or James in question is likewise the apostle of that name, believed at one time to have preached in Spain. According to tradition his coffin or tomb was conveyed there from Palestine and lost for a thousand years, after which period it was semi-miraculously rediscovered and the present cathedral begun on the site. It does seem more likely that the shrine was set up with the calculated purpose of heartening in various ways the Christian forces who, having held out for so long in that corner of Spain against the Moorish invader, were about that time beginning the reconquest of the peninsula. St Iago certainly seems to have had a big thing about the Moors, on one occasion long before his rediscovery appearing in the flesh, they say or said, to lead a body of Christian troops against them.

And yet one would not envy a man who, whether eagerly or automatically, accepted without hesitation or afterthought the second, materialistic explanation of the origin of Santiago as entirely adequate. Quite likely this kind of instant rationalist has a label unknown to me, but the word 'scepticaster' suggests itself. C. S. Lewis must have a passage somewhere on those who are unfortunate enough never to run any risk of having been born yesterday.

I tried to expel from my mind all traces of scepticaster's sentiments, along with a more tenacious distraction, an anti-graven-image principle handed down by my Chapel ancestors. In due course our party filed through one of the doorways. The interior was of course enormous, also crowded, though the distracting effect of this was small, which surprised me mildly till I remembered that it had been built to accommodate crowds. There was something going on, not too momentous, a choir of French Boy Scouts singing various pieces, presumably of a pious tendency, singing them annoyingly well, I thought. Ecclesiastics were in attendance. The whole thing was impressive—how not?—but I had no feeling of being in a hallowed place before I reached the crypt, and to me the most striking object was not in the cathedral at all but in one of the minor churches nearby, a seventeenth-century painting of Our Lady of Expectation, the Virgin in pregnancy, an aspect new to me then, though I was to see another portrayal, almost as appealing, the very next day in the cloisters of the cathedral at Oporto.

The highlight of the morning was provided by the *botafumeiro* in a performance specially laid on for our party. This is a huge, dustbin-sized censer suspended on a rope and swung in ever-increasing arcs till it reached almost to the ceiling. I readily believed the tale that it had once slipped its moorings and gone flying out of the round window a couple of hundred feet above our heads, and was glad I was not, as some of us were, directly under the path of that bloody great chunk of metal full of burning incense. The local guide explained that the ceremony, which took about ten minutes, had no religious significance, only a hygienic one, the original object having been to fumigate the church against vermin deposited there by pilgrims. Nice, but I could not drive out the image of Father Brown saying to me, 'Oh yes, Catholics are very practical people. It's you pagans who are full of empty superstition', blinking mildly at me until I sent him sprawling with a backhander across the chops. No, just my fun, really.

We bumbled out into the Plaza de España and over to the Hostal de los Reyes Católicos, a modern hotel inside the structure of a sixteenth-century hostel for pilgrims. I say we bumbled; well, most of us bumbled while Neil and I made smartly for the bar. Soon afterwards we made nearly as smartly for the dining-room. Lunch began with turnip-top soup, a local dish, and not bad it was. Next, *coquille St Jacques* — St James's shell, you see, that of the scallop being an emblem of the saint and the medieval pilgrim's badge. The contents of this particular shell were very nasty. Uneatable beef and good potatoes followed. Two wines were offered, the house white like dilute cider and a Rioja red that was about as bad as any that have come my way, which is saying quite a bit; I noticed that everyone else left most of it undrunk. Why the Riojas are so much admired in England I cannot discover. A choc ice came last, and it was all right.

The problem that had faced the organisers at this stage was that of keeping the passengers occupied while their ship did some more of the hundred-odd-mile trip from La Coruña to the re-embarkation point at Vigo. At 14.30 hrs there was a Folklore performance in a courtyard of the Hostal. I had thought I would try it — at least one was sitting down — but as soon as the lads and lasses capered in in their traditional costumes and began to leap about to the skirl and groan of the authentic musettes, I took myself off (to wander fruitlessly round the torrid streets). Surely the point of all communal music-making or dancing, from madrigal-singing (especially that) onwards, is that you are supposed to take part, not listen or watch, or if you are a spectator you have some connection with the performers as relatives, fellow-villagers, etc. Anyway, I had not had a folk-dancing father-in-law for nothing.

At Oporto, or rather Leixões three miles from it, we sat in the coaches for twenty minutes with the doors shut and the engines running and ourselves pouring with sweat despite the overcast sky. Then, duly softened up, we were carried into the dingy, dusty, rubbish-laden city with its slums and political graffiti, more thickly strewn, these last, than anywhere else I have ever been (except Lisbon the next day). A sleek, petite *apparatchik* harangued us over the bus's PA system.

As units of Party 'A' (Coach Two) we went first to the Moorish Hall in the Stock Exchange. Everyone was quite open about the whole thing having been done in the Nineteenth Century. It was colourful, but if you could somehow have been handed the impression that it was actually Paul Getty's card-room, you would have called it irremediably vulgar. When we had seen it we trooped out to walk a short way to our next objective. I mentioned to Paul the state of the streets, which would have shamed even London. He said it had been just like that on his last visit three years ago but then, according to the locals, they had been too busy having revolutions to clean the place up.

The church of St Francis was mostly rebuilt in the Eighteenth Century and is smallish, richly gilded, and no longer in use. I knew that last fact as soon as I entered, not that any special sensitivity was needed. The impression was of a provincial museum incompetently kept and seldom visited. The *apparatchik* told us things about the building in her unmodulated voice and it was hard to want to listen. You cannot demand that a person doing her job should share the beliefs of the men who made the church, but such a person might do the better for finding those beliefs—what? Respectable? Interesting? Human? Well, at least nearer home than Micronesia.

First halting to allow the passage of a lorry-load of smashed bicycles, we came to the house of Prince Henry the Navigator, and were invited to look at a replica of his and his wife's tomb (the real one is somewhere else altogether). Next, the cathedral, once described as 'infamously restored', though I thought it was all right. Next, up a great hill, the Sierra do Pilar, to look down on the city and along the Douro valley. Close below us were a couple of the little sailing-boats of the type that used to bring the unprocessed port down the river; they are used for advertising purposes nowadays, and the wine arrives by truck. It was quite moving to stand there and read the names off the signboards— Taylor, Ramos Pinto, Croft and, among others, Sandeman. Here was our last stop of the morning. Daily orders had mentioned 'an opportunity' for port tasting. H'm.

Seeing all those sights had rather taken the edge off the curiosity of most of us, and we gazed without ardour at this cask and that vat while information was dispensed about blending and maturing. But then we were shown into a large low room with lots of glasses and enough bottles in it, and everyone started to take notice again. There was a white port, Clipper, and a ruby, Partner's, and both were most enjoyable. The fellows let you smoke, too; in fact, looking through their house publication, I see Sandeman *recommend* a cigar or cigarette with a glass of port. Christ, and in an era of pandemic anti-smoking frenzy too.

On the return journey some of us were perhaps a little drowsy, certainly indifferent to the proferred commentary on the interest of what was to be seen out of the windows. It was raining. Juddering on the cobbles, the bus took us past the horrible Sixties memorial to Portugal's overseas discoveries and through a spectacular shanty-town hung with ragged clothing and blankets, horrible in a different way. Here and there stood small forts of one or other bygone time, some adapted for modern purposes, most in ruins. In ten minutes we were safely back on the ship, freshening up, wondering about a gin and tonic after all that port, moving in to lunch in the Dionysos Restaurant or the Jason Taverna.

It was decided to go independent at Lisbon, since Paul and Betty knew the place, and so the four of us avoided the sightsee of the Belém Tower and the trip to Queluz and Sintra. We got another terrible monument to those discoveries, though; at least we passed it and I walked over to check the date—1961, yes. What was the *matter* with all the people who commissioned that and designed it and made it and let it be erected and refrained from blowing it up? We made an unedifying visit to another empty church, built in the Sixteenth Century to commemorate a discovery of Vasco da Gama's and once accounted the finest in Portugal. Then we went shopping. I got a pair of shoes. Paul and I tried and failed to buy jackets, inevitably, he said; Portuguese jackets were made to fit Portuguese men, not us. Our wives astonishingly turned out to want to go on shopping when we had had enough, so we went and drank beer outside at a café in one of the main squares. The outlook was not as unlovely as what I had seen in Oporto, but I could find nothing of the Lisbon I remembered from previous visits, a sparkling town, shiny white in the sun. Perhaps we were in the wrong part; everything seemed faded, stained or parched. There were more people in the streets than I would have believed possible, short of the emptying of a couple of football stadiums in the next block. Most of them strolled or halted conversationally as if lacking any special goal. In a short time I noticed several cripples and blind persons.

We had lunch at one of the seafood restaurants for which Lisbon is famous, and very bad it was, I thought, one dish bereft of all flavour, the next dangerously off, with nothing in between except some clams. But the other three loved it, picking and scrabbling at the shells without rest in a way that told of long experience and yielded almost nothing in the way of actual meat, robustly devouring the more obviously inedible and toxic portions, telling me truly that I would rather have been having fishfingers. They went on fiddling for hours. We drank vinho verde, 'green' ie immature, unripe wine, an excellent description of the puny, paltry, unenjoyable stuff set before us. I resolved never to touch it again, being perhaps well placed to then. When it was time I called for brandy, specifying Antiqua. The first swig was rather like something out of a yawl's binnacle, but the subsequent ones improved and so did my general outlook.

In the afternoon we visited the Museu de Calouste Gulbenkian. I enjoyed it very much and advise anyone who gets within a hundred miles of it not to miss it on any account. That seems a little bald, but one hesitates to go on. It seems very hard to write sensibly about works of art, visual art that is, hard if not (what a glance at practising writers in the field might well suggest) impossible. Perhaps the thing is to get through it quickly.

I passed and pass over various pieces of Egyptian and Persian forgettability, wondering only why people bother with ridiculously remote stuff like that when so much Western art is difficult enough. A lot of furniture and knick-knacks generally is displayed too for some reason, clocks, pots of different sorts, milk-jugs, ashtrays probably, sofas and carpets. Having stumbled over the edge of one of these I walked a few semi-involuntary paces on it and was shouted at by an attendant to bloody well get off it sharp in Portuguese. Anyway, never mind; there was nothing to show that Gulbenkian thought carpets and milk-jugs were somehow like pictures.

Among a small collection of sculpture I noticed a terracotta bust of Molière by a certain J.-J. Callieri. Whoever he was he produced a masterpiece on this occasion: he makes the subject look a good chap, and funny. Also handsome, which I suppose he might really have been.

With the paintings, no attempt had been made to be comprehensive in any sense; a few Dutch, a few Flemish, a few English, but all of them, from what I could tell, first-rate. Just two Turners, one of them, 'Shipwreck of the *Minotaur* on the sandbanks of Haar', perhaps sufficiently characterised by its title, the artist at his most vertiginous, evoking a sympathetic groan for the wretched mariners. One or two of Monet, one or two of Degas, including a self-portrait which I recognised at once. But how could I have done? I must just have recognised it as what it was.

Gulbenkian had his favourites too, to judge by quantity. So quite a few of the jolly eighteenth-century scenic painter Hubert Robert, and more than a couple of Fantin-Latour. One of the latter has stuck in my mind, 'The Reading', two girls, the attention caught by the one listening, the pretty one, then passing to the one reading, the beautiful one. Perhaps it is rather a writer's painting, but I give it my personal first prize all the same. My runner-up: 'Fight between a peacock and a cockerel' by the seventeenth-century Flemish artist Paul De Vos, a strange and terrible picture.

A quick look at a nice Burne-Jones and we were away. I reflected that Monet (b. 1840) and Degas (b. 1834) were the only two Impressionists represented. There is virtually nothing of the Twentieth Century at all, no Post-Impressionists, no Dadaists, no Cubists, no Futurists, no Surrealists, no . . . And how did that come about? Because Gulbenkian was any or all of too tough, too conceited, too independent-minded, too schizophrenic, too intelligent, too rich to care what anybody else thought about whatever works of art he might buy. He says in a note that in assembling his collection he was always and exclusively guided by his personal taste, and I believe him. How many of us would dare to be that, always and exclusively? Put it another way: which pictures would *you* take to a desert island if you had a completely free choice and nobody was ever going to see or hear from you again? Faced with (say) a Raeburn or a Braque, which would you take? Really?

When I was there twenty-five years ago there were two hotels in Portimão—well, more like boarding-houses than hotels. Whereas now . . . Between them and me—the ship was anchored off the beach—there stretched an irregular band of colour mottled with fawn and medium brown, betokening sand and bodies; ten thousand saw I at a glance. Lying in the sun, just lying in the sun and no more, strikes me as a terrible thing to do. I am baffled and alarmed to think that, for instance, an intelligent woman like Jane enjoys it, travels great distances for it, says she has to have it. She wants the sun, you see. Clearly, but what for?

I had gone along with the business until 1971. That summer I was on a beach near Albufeira, just a few miles up the coast from Portimão, not as prelude or postlude to bathing, which I had had the belated sense to give up years before that, nor please God to sunbathe, but merely to be of the party. I was trying with little good-humour to find a comfortable posture in which to read my paperback when Jane said helpfully that there was a bar of sorts further along where surely there would be chairs as well as beer. So it proved. Five minutes later I was sitting quite contentedly in the shade when it hit me. I realised in a blinding flash that I could have had all that in a superior version at home and stayed in pocket, not to mention not had to stroll a couple of thousand miles. I think the whole thing is got up by the women. All holidays are. And not only . . . Sorry, where was I?

The Alcazar at Seville is rather boring, no doubt because it contains so many tapestries; how could anybody ever have thought that they were a good idea when there were paintings about, and have they all got to be lifeless or was that put in on purpose, and why are they always the same two dull colours, and what is this lot doing there, tapestry-weaving being a Spanish rather than a Moorish thing (I find) and much later anyway? The cathedral is immense, the most extensive in the world and so larger than Santiago, but not as grand, indeed almost showy, like a boutique precinct. The park of Maria Luisa makes it abundantly clear that one lemon tree or orange tree is much like another. But the restaurant where we had lunch is delightful, tucked away in a picturesque alley, decorated with some quaint ironwork and boasting a fine chandelier. We relaxed there with a grateful sigh.

The meal was of course filthy. It began with glazed seafood and continued with ridiculously tough veal or something, the whole washed down with vile wine. Spanish food and drink were never up to much in my experience, but you used to be able to depend on simplicities like tomatoes, onions, olives, oranges and the local red. Not now. The bread has gone too. The only things that are always all right are potatoes, tinned fruit, ice cream and sherry. And Coca Cola, I dare say.

Pondering on this, I thought for a moment I had discovered a straightforward inverse correlation between nations and their food-and-drink. Spanish, like English, nice people, nasty food; French, nasty people, nice food. Oh yes, and Greeks, nice people, *terrifying* food. But then, Italians, nice people, nice food. Danes too. Surely there must be . . . Got it: Germans, nasty people, nasty food (drink better, but beer overrated, wine no good with food, schnappses often delicious but not enough on their own). Also Belgians—Walloons anyway. So no little article there.

The expedition to Granada began propitiously enough. Jane and I got up as planned at 05.45 (04.45 British time) in pitch darkness. We made it to breakfast at 06.15, and felt a keen sense of achievement at being the first pair to arrive. We lost some ground by being only in the first couple of dozen passengers assembled gasping in the pyrogenic entrance-hall before disembarking, but attained the vital objective of seats in Coach Two with the best guide, and had there been an award for the Tourist Couple of the Day, as there cruelly was not, we should have been well in the running for it.

Then the coach took us to Granada through fairly impressive upland scenery, but the outskirts of the city turned out to be rather ugly, partly because there was a great deal of building going on, though the Royal Chapel, where Ferdinand and Isabella are entombed, is very fine, the cathedral rather less so, the Alhambra fine in a different way, being Moorish, if not as Moorish as it was before the Spanish rebuilders set about it, and a must for people who like climbing a lot of steps not very slowly in the sun with the humidity chasing a record. There! I promise you that the Chapel really *is* fine and that I was interested in everything I saw, but to write of such matters in any kind of favourable terms is difficult without turning either leadenly informative or self-congratulatorily sensitive in the old wanker's mode. Or is it just that *I* find it difficult, am only comfortable describing discomfort?—witness the tiny twitch of life in the style when I came to the Alhambra there. Well, never mind.

I expected something up my street from lunch at the Hotel Alhambra Palace, but the décor there is inoffensive, even rather pleasantly and mildly Moorish, and the meal was almost adequate, the wine even quite tolerable. It was white and called just viño de mesa. (If you happen to be reading this out to your young children, better remind them that 'mesa' means simply 'table'.) Now at that lunch I heard an old shag sitting near by explain to another that Mesa was a small region near Rioja. If we had all been thirty years younger I should of course have gone up and demanded to know if he was taking the piss, or at least tried to tease more out of him by asking him what type of grape they favoured in that part of the world, etc. But as things were, no. Oldsters hate shocks, anything requiring them to regroup mentally at short notice. Or perhaps it is their hard luck that people think they do.

Part of the afternoon was crappy enough to satisfy any but the most exigent. We were turned out of the hotel and, after a short bus ride, into the garden of a place bemusingly called the Generalife, in fact a Moorish summer palace. You might have thought that a large part of the point of a thing like that, situated not much more than fifty miles from Africa, would have had to do with keeping cool. Maybe indoors was. That afternoon at any rate the garden would have served at a pinch as an early-to-intermediate stage of an acclimatisation centre preparing a team for a hot-side crossing of the planet Mercury. There was a tour of it, I think; nobody I saw took part. The lucky ones instantly folded on to the scanty benches and chairs; the others, including Muggins, tried to find a place under the trees to lie down. Impossible. I sat with my back against some cypress or cedar and tried to read. No good, but I got an idea for my next novel to do with (the idea, not the novel) a drunken ventriloquist, and staunchly entered it in my notebook, where I found it just now.

There was nothing to see at Alicante, where we called because, I imagine, we had to call somewhere between Motril (the port for Granada) and Barcelona, where we shopped for things like handbags and whisky, and where I had my profoundest emotional experience of the whole trip—standing for a whole five minutes in front of the great air-conditioner in the wallet shop. But at Barcelona there was enough to see and to spare. We began well and enjoyably with the cathedral and its especially good cloisters, but things took a profound turn for the worse at our next stop, the so-called Museo Picasso, once presumably a residence of the artist.

I first came across this man's work before the Second World War, when the Tate Gallery acquired three or four samples of it. One of them, often reproduced, has perhaps for that reason stuck in my mind: 'Seated Woman in a Chemise' (1923). I disliked it on sight and was also baffled: I could not see why the likeness of the woman was so ugly when, being obviously not a close likeness of anyone, it had no need to be. Other pictures of his flouted my good sense by showing faces with both eyes on the same side of the nose. Of course I dared not admit any of this, even to myself; Picasso was much too famous and well regarded. Years went by before I felt secure enough to let my true feelings about him come to the surface. I was probably helped by the way people were starting to say out loud something else I had long thought but kept to myself, that Ezra Pound was no good.

The temperature that day was 90°F, the humidity 100 per cent. I was perhaps not in the ideal frame of mind to see what was to be seen, but along I trudged. You begin with some rather stiff drawings and undistinguished paintings of heads and figures from the period 1895–7, when Picasso was in his teens; I doubt if anyone would give them a second glance unless he had known who they were by. Upstairs, I viewed some unappealing aquatints of 1966, some really vile 'portraits' of 1957—the most unsightly objects in the entire place—and some grotesque, decadent drawings of 1970. I was embarrassed throughout, but these last puzzled me too: why had he bothered? Surely he had enough cash by 1970, and no one could have got an ounce of satisfaction out of doing them.

By a lucky chance I had seen not many months before the Salvador Dali exhibition at the Tate Gallery—and while the subject under discussion is Picasso let nobody try to tell me Dali is a gimmick man. I was able, then, to make a comparison, which is rather hard on Picasso because it points to shortage of natural talent as his gravest weakness; he has only to put half a dozen lines together to reveal a duffer's hand. This is not to forget that, as Dali did with his much greater endowment, he abused what talent he had, breaking new ground, forging a personal style, developing and other self-destructive nonsense of that kind. Still, that was to give him something; before visiting the museum I would not have conceded him any talent at all.

I put my revised view, rather experimentally I admit, to Tony, who said with some warmth, 'Oh, he had plenty of talent, no doubt about that; he just got talking to the *wrong people*.'

After Picasso we were taken, all unsuspecting in my case, to see that evidently major attraction of Barcelona, the Church of the Holy Family, or what little there is of it, just one end really. The architect, Antonio Gaudi, began work on the church in 1883, but had done only that much by 1926, when he was fatally knocked down by a tram; perhaps he lost interest. The fragment has been left as it was ever since, though the local guide told us with a grave face that the government (or the municipality) were beginning to evacuate people from the buildings where other parts of the church would stand. The existing part unites, or rather separably has, Gothic, Moorish and *art nouveau* elements, and its overall style is generally considered to be flamboyant, in other words self-aggrandising and self-indulgent. The spirit of Catalonia must come into all this somewhere. The fact that another awful man, Joan Miró, is of it, was born right there in Barcelona, is surely thrown in to show that more than chance is at work. (What we are to make of another fact, that Dali was born not far away, is less clear.)

We, a dozen or so of us, avoided the Spanish Village, an all-balls permanent exhibition of Spanish art through the ages, and went instead to the museum of Catalan art—I had not at that stage reached any conclusions about Gaudi and the others. The main attraction of the museum is church frescoes of the Romanesque period transferred by some unimaginable process on to specially-shaped bits of wall. Parts of some of them are worn away, but the colours, being made from natural earths, are unfaded. They are striking pieces, and particularly after old Pablo; their piety is of the totally unself-regarding sort that disappeared for good at the Renaissance. Dear God, that ever I should find anything but vulgar abuse to apply to the Middle Ages! Not having had to read Chaucer and Langland all these years has probably mellowed me no end.

The next morning we arrived at Nice and suddenly, in a moment long foreseen but still suddenly, the cruise was over and a small brief sense of community gone. I had grown into the routine; I was going to miss waking up to a completely new sight through the porthole, the bustle of getting off and into the bus, the sightsee, the lunch, however shitty the food, the final sense of duty done and of course the plunge back into the grateful bosom of the ship. Altogether it was as pleasant a way of dealing with abroad—by not really leaving England—as I can imagine.

We now felt, as people do in our situation, that we had been away from home for a couple of years, not a mere couple of weeks, and were to feel when we reached home, again as people do, that the period of absence had been just a few days. I take these two mild illusions to be the remnants of powerful evolutionary instincts in primitive man at the stage when staying with the group was very important to survival. Thus, through an access of curiosity or sheer chance, Ug would become momentarily separated from his fellows and almost at once would feel he had been absent for an immeasurably long time; the resulting uneasiness would send him shambling back to them before they could move out of sight. On his return it would seem to him that he had merely stepped aside for a moment, which would limit any harmful effects of shock or fear. A familiar spatial variant of the same illusion causes any outward journey through unfamiliar territory to seem longer in distance than the return to the starting-point.

I have greatly enjoyed writing this small essay. Readers usually sense that kind of thing and respond to it, so good. I set against that my slight suspicion that in one way the job has been a bit too easy: selecting from what actually happened is less exigent than making it all up, or ought to be. But then again that selection suffers constraints from outside. For instance I wanted to put in something about our very comely local guide on the Granada trip and her marvellous English, on which she set the seal by keeping up her impeccable accent even for the Spanish words. But I thought I had better not, because when that or about that had been said of her she was going to disappear, and having heard so much and no more a lot of readers would dimly expect her to come in again, as she would in a novel. Our familiarity with fiction, indeed our wired-in responsiveness to it, leads us to look for bits of plot-and-character development and the like in any account of events. The travel writer, then, had better try to avoid arousing such expectations, a requirement that puts him under severe strain. The reader's interest must be directed exclusively to what is happening at any given moment. Every page must justify itself in full, every sight seen must be fascinating or unspeakable, everything, every observation, every sentence must be *good*.

This necessity is especially trying when it comes to the repeatable stories, funny remarks and accounts of awful moments that some books of this sort contain. The wretched travel writer is in a cruelly exposed position. Whatever he attempts in this line must be *good*, because there it is, planked down on the page, quite beyond being passed off as anything but what it is. The novelist is protected by his plot, by the cumulative element in what he is doing. If the anecdote strikes some people as flat, it never was an anecdote, just essential or at least interesting information about X's history; if the funny remark turns out to be unfunny, that was the whole point—it shows you the kind of thing Y, who utters it, thinks is funny; if the awful moment fails to chill, well then, how naïve or neurotic or pitiful of Z to be chilled by it. There are of course novelists who neglect these obvious precautions. One alone has no need of them: P. G. Wodehouse.

All in all, we can hardly wonder if a travel writer improves on reality. But he must do so only with extreme care and self-restraint; one obvious fabrication and the reader's confidence is destroyed. Making things up is for novelists. To plead that editing personal experience is as much as a lot of novelists are doing would be accurate enough but irrelevant. Our man has little enough to tie him down, to rescue him from the inducement to improvisation and whim that is inherent in his venture—for however much information he may dispense, whatever insight we may gain or seem to have gained into this place or that people, his only real subject is himself. So he is a bit of a fraud at best, and that best cannot emerge unless before he starts he subscribes in spirit to the following:

CLAIMER

No event in the following narrative is in any way fictitious, and any resemblance to real persons is entirely intentional.

Sunday Times, 26 July 1981

Something Does Not Work with My Car

I was often told at school that to have your intellect and your emotions working together in close harmony meant you had a unified sensibility, like Donne's, and that this was very good for you. Since Donne's time, the story went on, people's sensibilities had got more and more dissociated. My own sensibility is very dissociated indeed. Thus while experiencing the events I am about to describe I felt awful, a total emotional ruin, comforted in no way whatsoever by any equally total intellectual conviction that the moment it was all over I should start laughing at it. Perhaps to enjoy comedy fully, to identify yourself with the characters, you need a dissociated sensibility.

It began at Barcelona. The boat from Majorca nosed past the mole in what I had worked out was good time. Then it cruised at two knots all over that extensive harbour, evidently looking for a place to tie up. By the time it found one and we got off, we were three-quarters of an hour late. But we still had six hours to drive the 165–odd miles to Narbonne, where everything was fixed for us to put the car on a train and get carried with it almost to Calais.

For the next hour we watched vehicles of all sizes, makes and nationalities being craned off the deck in nets or bursting thunderously out on to the ramp leading from the hold. Ours was not among them. Eventually they seemed to run out of cars altogether, and I wondered very much if ours was on board at all. Had anybody seen it during the voyage? No. After a time someone found another source of cars—down in the keel, I expect—and ours appeared. There was a rewarding moment, or rather five minutes, when I thought I had lost the document that proved it was ours. We drove away finally with just over four and a half hours to go before train-time. Quite possible, with a reliable car and no delays.

Of the car's reliability we had no doubt. We thought it was clever of us to have hired it in London instead of bringing our own, which is feeling its age. Our faith had remained unimpaired when, on the island, the car had tried to slide off a minor precipice and then run out of petrol with the gauge at about one-third full. Might happen to anyone, we said.

There was an hour and forty minutes' delay at the French frontier. As we crawled up the steep slope away from the Customs I said to my wife:

'You can relax now. Even if you drove at sixty all the way we'd still miss the train.'

'What are we going to do?' the children asked.

'Oh, we'll manage,' I said confidently. 'We've got money.'

Just then the car started bellowing loudly.

'What's the matter?' I asked. 'Put it into gear.'

'It's in gear,' my wife said.

I said something the children shouldn't have heard. In the next few hours I worked it out that the car could hardly be blamed for everything. What had happened was clearly that the Duty Officer at Bastards' HQ, having arranged the necessary delays to make us miss the train, had then got drunk, forgotten all about it, and fixed things up a second time by a different method. Or perhaps he had merely organised the delays and gone off shift without remembering to leave a note for his relief. One or the other. With me and my sons pushing, plus an occasional shove in the rear from a Dutchman in a Volkswagen, we made it to the top and began to coast. That felt good, though the road could hardly be expected to go downhill as far as Calais.

After ten miles we came to a slight upward slope. That was that. We were in a small town called Le Boulou, a name I shall never be able to see on a map (which is as close as I ever intend to get to the place again) without horror. I dislike addressing strangers even in English, but I had addressed plenty in what I will call French before we found a garage that said it did repairs.

'Something does not work,' I told the proprietor, 'with my car. The clutch,' I added, turning a page of the phrase-book, 'does not function.'

On request I told him the make of the car. He screamed.

After a preliminary examination, he put his hands together, laid his head on them and snored. 'Schlaffen ici,' he said.

'He say sleep here,' another man said.

'I know, I know,' I said. 'Is there a good hotel?'

He said there was. It was fairly good, though not as good, the children reported later, as any of the others in the town—just good enough for the garage proprietor to spend a fair amount of his time serving behind the bar of. When I saw him there I began to wonder. But what could I do about it, except go on wondering?

The car was promised for noon, after lunch, tonight, tomorrow morning, later today, at five o'clock. I don't quite know how we got through those two days. I played liar dice with my sons, read science fiction, squirted the flies in the bedroom, watched French television in the bar. The food was good. So I kept saying, anyway.

At last the car was pronounced ready. I understood the garage proprietor to say that, having vainly scoured south-east France for a clutch of the right make, he'd sort of made a clutch himself. Just as good as the real thing, he said, and took £17 off me. The hotel took £31 off me and we drove into the night. Only 760 miles to Calais, I announced.

The car knocked off 200 of those miles without a tremor. Then, to my amazement, something started going wrong with it—the clutch,

actually. At the time we were mounting a kind of Alp. It was 3 am.
We must have gone twenty miles farther, jumping out, pushing until
the car woke up, hurling ourselves back in. Somewhere near the snow-
line, I imagine, we came to a slope too steep for the combined efforts
of both adults and all four children. That was that again.

'What are we going to do now?' they all asked.

Perhaps I said something. Certainly I took a swig of brandy.

At 6 am we made a car stop. At seven I was saying to a garage
proprietor: 'I am an English tourist. Something does not work with
my car.' I left the clutch out of it, having decided to give this man the
car and let the hire company get it off him later if they could. 'Are
you willing to go and retrieve it? It is perhaps ten kilometres from
here . . .' He listened intently, nodding, taking everything in. When I
had finished he shook his head. 'My comrade has injured his knee,' he
said, seizing his own in both hands. 'Impossible.' Then he told me
more about his comrade's knee.

The only other garage had a proprietor who, under a couple of days'
beard, looked just like a distinguished American literary critic I know.
'Something,' I told him thickly, 'does not work with my car.' He
towed it in. We entrained for Paris and fresh horrors, such as a good
hour when a night in the park was looming up. Another story, all
that—but it felt like exactly the same story then, believe me. We'd
finished with the car, though. I hope the critic's twin had the sense to
break it up for scrap.

'Perhaps you'll fly next time' is the standard reaction.

'Good idea,' I say. 'Because if the plane goes wrong in mid-air, it's
their responsibility, isn't it?'

Spectator, 23 November 1962

PART TEN
Eating and Drinking

Sluicing and Browsing

Wine with Food, by Cyril and Elizabeth Ray, Sidgwick & Jackson
The Whiskies of Scotland, by R. J. S. McDowall, John Murray

Somebody should do a book of gastronomic horror stories. Accounts of just amazingly vile dishes would of course find their place in it, but, at the festive season, the intrusion of drink suggests itself. The material falls into two classes: terrible combinations of food and drink. Examples: Queen Victoria used to top her claret up with Scotch, seemingly to the disquiet of Mr Gladstone, and a nameless couple from the North of England on holiday in Majorca, finding Spanish Sauternes too dry to go with their sea-bass, called for Crème de Menthe. The importance of having a famous person in the story is interestingly unclear: take the Queen out of the first of those two and it collapses; put her into the second and it becomes only marginally more frightening.

One notable subdivision of the genre concerns the peculiar vindictiveness with which people punish the drinks of their own country or region. Aalborg aquavit drunk neat and ice-cold, and with or without a beer chaser, is one of the greatest of all spirits; the Danes do what no non-Dane would dare to do and liven it up with bitter lemon, *and the makers recommend it*. The Portuguese put lumps of ice in their red wine. (It tastes better like that, actually, though I intend no slur on the wine, which is usually very decent in the un-iced state.)

Those who above all others should know better can be the most heinous offenders. The Rays' book tells the tale of how they were once offered — and had to accept — an outstanding vintage of Château d'Yquem, by common consent the most marvellous sweet wine in the world, to wash down roast mutton; this at the house of a noted Sauternes winemaker. Another time, in Bordeaux, they were given a first-growth Graves with curried prawns, and enjoyed it. Really? Well, the fact that the locals do it doesn't make it right, and although the French admittedly make the best wines of all, you can never quite trust a nation that also makes stuff like Byrrh, Chambéryzette and dry vermouth. The latter should never be seen outside a Martini cocktail, and then dimly.

On record here too is Thackeray's fondness for burgundy with bouillabaisse: anything to take his mind off what he was eating, I suppose. But what *Wine with Food* says most about is, not surprisingly, what you should drink with what. No, not 'should', rather 'might like to'; the Rays are refreshingly undogmatic. Cyril talks about the wines in their various categories and Elizabeth gives recipes that usually include a sauce or flavouring made with the wine concerned. Some of these stress the wine component pretty hard. A potato-egg-and-bean salad would no doubt be made a good deal more interesting by having half a bottle of champagne and a glass of brandy thrown over it, and I was greatly taken with Coq au Beaujolais, where you brown a chicken, add bacon and other garnishings, and pour a whole bottle of the wine on top. That one reminded me of Stephen Leacock's Chicken au Whisky, only there you strain off the chicken before bringing the dish to table.

Elizabeth must forgive me if, being no sort of cook, I pass over her contribution with just one pat on the back: I never thought I should see the day when someone would have the sense and taste to call Crêpes Suzettes a crashing bore. As for Cyril, he passes what amounts to a litmus-paper test by speaking up for Asti Spumante. To sneer at it is like sneering at the music of, say, Meyerbeer: neither is the greatest in its sphere, but contempt for them shows a basic berkishness in each case.

Cyril Ray is the rarest of writers on drink, one who can make us share his enjoyment. He knows all about the dangers of the purple-patch style (of which he includes some splendid examples, including one that compares a Pichon-Longueville 1899 to Cyrano de Bergerac) without ever yielding to the other temptation of plain-man bluffness. His common sense leads him to raise a cheer for the wines of Tunisia, Morocco, Algeria, Chile and Yugoslavia, which are still much under-valued. Surprisingly, he omits Australia here.

He is, of course, a fearful old Lefty besides. He admits that he once enjoyed a South African brandy in South Africa, hastily apologises by calling the place an unhappy country, and promising never to go there again, then at once tells us about a brandy he drank in Soviet Georgia without a word about how nasty it is *there*. What is perhaps more serious is that he differs with me over Tavel, which he pronounces the most 'important' (uncharacteristic ill phrase) of all rosés, and which I find the dullest wine on earth, though he does come half a step towards the proper view with the concession that he prefers other rosés from somewhere else.

Let that go. This is a charmingly written and very useful book. It includes an excellent chapter on cold and hot punches, with due stress on ease of preparation, and practical advice on glasses and decanters. Some pretty drawings from Paris in the 1870s embellish the text. A splendid Christmas buy.

The Whiskies of Scotland briefly delineates all the distilleries at which publicly available malts are made and many of the blending houses. It also describes fully how Scotch is prepared. I was glad to see that the learned author endorses my practice of cheering up a blended whisky with a little malt. He treads the brink of what, rightly regarded, is horror-story terrain when he deplores the addition of ice, ginger ale, etc—only water will do for good whisky—and crosses right over with his tale of the Highland hotel where everybody was mixing his Scotch with lemonade supplied free by the management. Will no one tell them what they drink?

Observer, 21 December 1975

Drunk in This Way

The World Book of Whisky, by Brian Murphy, Collins

Books on booze tend to shift from—as a librarian might say—terms of high extension and low intension to the opposite way round. In other and less horrible words, where you used to get encyclopedias of wine with maps of every vineyard in the world and bartenders' guides that told how to do everything from mixing a Hot Pants on the Rocks (vodka, Maraschino and Angostura) to dealing with drunks and cheats, you now get treatises on individual regions and types of drink. The most highly-intensive tipple-tract I know is John Doxat's *Stirred—Not Shaken*, nearly 200 packed pages on a mixture of one spirit and one wine, the Dry Martini.

It would be hazardous to emulate Doxat's virtuosic feat; whisky is a more comfortably-sized subject. Brian Murphy fills it out a little by succumbing to a perennial temptation of the alcoholographer and tracing everything back to its starting point. Thus 'primitive man' may have done his first toping out of pools full of rotting fruit or barley-containers in which rainwater had accumulated. Indeed he may; we are on surer ground with the introduction of distilling into Spain by the Moors about the year 1200. But there is a question here.

Like most other commentators, the author credits the Moors, or rather the Arabs, with inventing as well as disseminating the process. It is quite true that 'alcohol' and 'alembic' (part of a type of pot still that is used to this day for the making of cognac and armagnac) are

Arabic-derived words, though, *pace* Mr Murphy, 'alcohol' isn't quite 'al' (= 'the') plus 'kohl' (= 'Eastern eye-make-up'); there was an earlier stage when it meant something like 'sublimate' or 'essence'. Anyway, another school of thought declares there to be no hard evidence of actual invention by the Arabs, who on this view merely handed on what they had learnt from Byzantine or even Chinese originators. And 'Strongbow', Earl of Pembroke, is said to have noticed that the Irish were already drinking whiskey when he invaded them in 1170. Most probably, like the human race, the stuff turned up independently in more than one place in the same eon or so.

Neither Mr Murphy's book nor whisky itself stands or falls over this matter of origins. The history of the drink given here—technological, financial, economic, social—is thorough and also pleasantly digressive. The literary section starts with Holinshed, who must have been stoned on vodka when he wrote in 1578 that *uisage beatha* (the ancestor of Scotch) 'keepeth and preserveth the head from whirling . . . the tongue from lisping . . . the hands from shivering', though he adds truly enough that it also keepeth the guts from rumbling. Johnson's commendation of it as strong but not pungent, and 'preferable to any English malt brandy', whatever dreadful thing that might have been, is quoted here, but not his further remark on the same occasion that he had no chance of asking how it was made, 'nor do I wish to improve the art of making poison pleasant'. He must have been in one of his off-the-drink spells.

Mr Murphy rightly stresses the supreme importance of barley in the making of Scotch, observing that present-day distillers go far afield for this material, as far as Australia and India; 'ancient Scottish barley did not produce as rich a malt [the treated cereal, not the liquor] as modern imported barley'. This is made to sound like a gain, but I wonder. Professor R. J. S. McDowell, an authority Mr Murphy has a proper respect for, suggests the reverse in *The Whiskies of Scotland*, Highland barley being poor in starch and so yielding less alcohol per corn, but giving the result more flavour with its higher fat and protein content. Oh, well, we'd need a time-machine to get any further along those lines.

A Scotch is also formed by the local water, the peat used in kilning (Islay peat has a lot of seaweed in it, which some say they can taste in Laphroaig and other malts from that island), the shape of the still and the method of heating it, the proportion and composition of 'impurities' admitted by the stillman, the humidity of the warehouse in which ageing takes place, the size and type of cask, and here and there less obvious agencies: the proprietor of Linkwood, a Speyside malt admired by Professor McDowell, once declined to have spiders' webs removed from his distillery lest quality suffer. Mr Murphy lets this fall in the course of a general survey of malts and blends. Of the latter he remarks that, the classier kinds like Chivas Regal excepted, they are much of a muchness. Well said; so too, in effect, that Scotch is not really suitable for mixing with anything but water. The other day I tried it on purpose with lemonade, the favourite additive of the Scots themselves, who often get it free in bars, and was quite struck by how revolting the result was.

The last third of the book treats of the rest of the whisky world, starting with the American product. There are good stories not only of Prohibition (a recipe for hooch made my hair stand on end) but of the less-studied Whiskey War of 1794, settled in the nick of time by George Washington, who turns out to have been among other things a commercial distiller of rye. Irish comes third, perhaps surprisingly in view of the author's name. Even more surprisingly, he has never tasted the illicit version, potheen, not for the lack of trying, he says. Well, I once got a glass of it in the office of the editor of a leading national newspaper without any trouble at all; I could tell it was pretty sexy, kind of like directors' potheen, and I found it quite smooth but so alarming that I left it unfinished, which I hope is saying something.

After Canada, whose inhabitants have achieved the expected impossible by contriving a boring whisky, come strange sources like Bolivia (with the highest distillery in the world at 12,000 feet), the USSR (which used to make a brand called Pollynnaia, flavoured with wormwood) and Thailand (Red Cock is out in front). Japan of course is in the ascendant. Mr Murphy, who writes vigorously throughout but not everywhere with due care and attention, says of its products that 'they do not imitate Scotch but are whiskies very much in their own right. Drunk in this way, you will discover their true excellence.' I'm sure it's as good a way as any.

New Statesman, 1 December 1978

Drink—and Stay Merry

Like the search for God, with which it has other things in common, the search for the infallible and instantaneous hangover cure will never be done. But although there is always something new to say on the topic, it would be wrong of me not to glance at some of the more established truths. Let me begin all the way back, with the night before the morning after.

Some sound work has been done on hangover avoidance. (Hangover evasion, in other words not drinking much or even at all, is unworthy to be discussed in a reputable journal.) The findings are easily summarised—I pass over obvious precepts like having a decent meal, smoking as little as possible and spacing your drinks, especially the first couple. If you do not follow these already, no words of mine will make you.

So: point one is do not drink coffee. Alcohol makes you sleepy; coffee keeps you awake, lengthens your evening, increases your input. If you are dining out, you will have to face a lot of irritating surprise and curiosity from hosts and fellow guests. Face it. Say firmly, 'I'm not allowed coffee', and let them think what they please.

The myth that mixing your drinks is bad dies hard. What gives you a hangover is (1) fatigue (2) alcohol (3) harmful concomitant substances popularly known as congeners. The commonest one is fusel oil, from a German word meaning 'bad brandy', and indeed brandy is rich in congeners. So is bourbon whiskey. Fortified wines, especially port, and sweet liqueurs are also to be treated with care. The myth arose because any chap who ends his evening with a lot of port and brandy will probably have begun it with a lot of vodka, sherry, Scotch and continued it with a lot of wine. It is not the mixture itself, but the quantity of alcohol and congeners *in* the mixture that will have done the mischief. If you do not believe me spend an evening on nothing but port and see how you feel the next day.

Some people dose themselves with aspirin, digestive powders and so on before going to bed and claim that they make them feel all right in the morning. I doubt this; I mean I think that what makes them feel all right is having drunk so comparatively little as to have been able to remember to take the pills and where to find them. But I always keep several bottles of mineral water beside my bed—always, so I don't have to do any special remembering—and can start working on my dehydration as soon as I wake up.

Very well, the patient is awake. What follows is largely dependent on how much time he has before he must go to work or otherwise function. If he is free for the day or until the late morning, his only problem is forcing himself to stay in bed for an extra couple of hours, and if he is a lazy sod that should not be hard. I am far from being a human dynamo, but I hate lying about in bed; nevertheless on evil mornings I stick it, telling myself what is true, that rest is actually the quickest way to get on top of a hangover and the nearest thing to a certain cure.

Now to the patient's ablutions. He will avoid a cold shower, which in his present enfeebled state will only do him further damage. Hot shower, good; hot bath, good; both, even better. Washing hair is recommended. It is a refreshing exercise, it helps to remove the general feeling of grubbiness which goes with so many hangovers, and it is the kind of undemanding activity that takes the mind off its troubles without strain. The same goes for shaving, which must be attempted unless the shakes are really extreme.

As far as internal treatment is concerned, the ideal opener is half a litre of chilled Vichy water; few such things are more worth the trouble than keeping two or three bottles in the refrigerator at all times. Failing Vichy water, take soda water or water, then coffee and/or milk: black coffee, milky coffee, straight milk. What not to go for, I have decided after much testing and re-testing, is the chilled-fruit-juice idea: just too acid. Eats should be very light: nothing cooked—even a boiled egg does an upset stomach no good—and certainly nothing fried. Yoghurt, cereal or toast should do it.

So much for natural remedies. Unnatural ones are of two main kinds, digestion-adjusters and headache-removers. It may sound unfeeling, but the first are better left alone. Pouring a lot of alkaline in is as dodgy as adding a lot of acid. The insides will recover quite quickly on their own if they are treated sensibly; in other words, when lunch-time comes eat in moderation and avoid anything rich, greasy, creamy or served with an elaborate sauce, also anything that makes the tum work hard, from lobster and pigeon to suet pudding. Advice on drinks comes later.

Headache-removers I allow, but I have one tip for you here. Some of them, perhaps all, affect the state of the mind as well as of the skull. This can be disagreeable: for years I would hesitate before taking the brand in our bathroom cupboard because, although it cured the headache all right, it also made me feel twitchy. At last I realised that different brands have different effects on different people because they are made to different formulas, and shopped around. On my second try I found a brand, not on prescription, which gave me relief from pain plus a very slight, harmlessly slight, lift. I won't name either brand because, as I say, what is right or wrong for me may not be the same for you.

When physical discomfort has been removed or perhaps has not been felt at all, there is often a mental or emotional condition that is at least as unpleasant: call it anxiety, tension, restlessness, what you will, seasoned drinkers will know what I mean. This condition can be greatly alleviated, even dispersed altogether, in a few minutes without the use of drugs. What you do is administer relaxation therapy to yourself. I must emphasise here that I am not trying to be funny or fanciful; I use it and it works. (It is helpful too with anything that could be described as stage-fright.)

The subject makes himself really comfortable and starts taking deep, slow breaths, one every five or six seconds. He then consciously and deliberately relaxes every part of his body a bit at a time: feet, ankles, calves, knees, thighs, hips, belly, chest, and so on, not forgetting neck and face. If you try that in the chair you are now sitting in, soon you will be amazed to find how tense your posture has been. Physical relaxation mysteriously brings mental relaxation and the effect lasts for hours. If you do not do it properly, by the way, all that happens is that you feel only a little better instead of a lot.

The trouble with the technique is that it is bloody boring. What I do is to provide myself with something mildly pleasant to look at (out of the window) or listen to (Radio 3 or 4) and take it a piece at a time. I tell myself I will do six breaths and stop; then I try another six, and another. Five minutes is really refreshing; even two helps.

I promised some advice on hangover drinks. I used to be great on those horrible potions like Fernet Branca and Underberg whose horribleness guaranteed, in an oddly British way, that they were good for you. No doubt they are—I just find I do not use them (nobody could be said to *drink* them) any more.

What I do have is one serious shot of Scotch and water before lunch and a glass or two of wine or beer with the meal. In painful cases some authorities recommend a Corpse-Reviver, brandy and dry ginger, better drunk without ice (if you can face that) to get the alcoholic message to you that much faster. So be it. The notion that the Bloody Mary is good for hangovers belongs to folklore. The vodka in it will help on the hair-of-the-dog principle, but the tomato juice, and even more the lemon juice which is essential to a well-made Bloody Mary, will not help your ailing digestive system. A splendid drink, agreed, but best kept for non-hungover occasions.

One word of warning. However grave your state, do not take any alcohol on mornings-after until 12.30 pm at the earliest. Those whom the gods wish to destroy they first persuade to reach for the bottle at breakfast-time.

Sunday Telegraph Magazine, 18 December 1977

In Pursuit of the Edible

The British at Table 1940–1980, by Christopher Driver, Chatto & Windus/Hogarth Press

The author was once Features Editor of the *Guardian* and more recently editor of *The Good Food Guide*, and these facts would be worth bearing in mind if his book did not incessantly proclaim them in one way or another. Like *Guardian* and *Guide*, it is addressed in the first place to an eccentric minority; perhaps not so much like them, it also has a more general appeal and significance.

The first and shorter half consists of a dietetic and culinary history of Great Britain in the period 1940–55, with preludial accounts of the Frenchifying of genteel cooking in the last century (worse luck) and of how badly the working classes ate in the period up to 1914 and to some extent up to 1939. The working-class part is seen here as more a matter of malnutrition than of under-feeding—a 1935 document shows the family of a part-time East End docker doing by no means badly for protein, though not so well for fresh vegetables. The food Orwell says he was given in his Wigan digs is depressing beyond measure, unhealthy and barely eatable, but he was always improving on reality about this sort of thing, and it seems safer to get one's bearings from a Royal Institution lecture of 1940 which demonstrated that laboratory rats given an Indian village diet thrived, while another group given generic, British working-class food (white bread and marge, tinned meat, tea, sugar, etc) became diseased, distressed and finally cannibalistic.

The reality behind this, and much they began to put right, not very predictably, by government rationing during and after the war. To me, the history of those years is the most interesting part of this book, and even readers who lived through none of them may feel the same. The putting into effect of food rationing, and its subsequent course, were among the very few uniformly successful British operations of that era. For once we were ready—rather creepily so in retrospect, since it seems the department that grew into the Ministry of Food had got permission to print ration-books in July 1937, over a year before the Munich agreement.

As Christopher Driver's account makes clear, the Ministry's policies in outline and detail were largely the work of two men, a gourmet nutritional biochemist and a reforming shopkeeper. The scientist was Jack Drummond, early on fetched in by some sharp fellow to advise the Ministry, not known to many until in 1952 he achieved sad and terrible fame by being murdered, along with his wife and daughter, by a crazed farmer in Provence. The tradesman was or soon became Lord Woolton, Minister from April 1940, set on using his powers to stamp out the nutritional diseases he had seen among Liverpool children. So the British were given the high-extraction National Loaf, kept short of fats, starved of sugar both as such and in jam and sweets, encouraged both by deprivation and in broadcasts and advertisements to make soups and use green vegetables cooked and in salads. So far from going short, the nation ate more healthily than ever before, or as Driver phrases it on a subsequent page, stoutly putting truth before trend, the Ministry of Food 'did more for British popular nutrition than the Left Book Club ever contemplated'.

The Ministry, and the wartime experience of keeping the family fed, did more yet. Shortage of familiar materials and flavourings, and the frequent presence of unfamiliar unrationed ones, encouraged a bit of experiment in household recipes and menus, though it may be doubted whether any lasting impression was made by the availability in the late 1940s of whalemeat and snoek (tinned barracouta from South Africa). The need to use up leftovers and scraps had the same emboldening effect. When normal supplies finally returned a few years later, the stage was set for the enormous success of Elizabeth David's books on Mediterranean food, French country cooking and Italian food. The return from France and Italy of thousands of servicemen newly accustomed to a daily intake of wine no doubt helped to make a kind of middle-class hobby or craze out of food and drink.

Even committed cooks need nights off, but what these would have found in the restaurant or café round the corner was mostly miserable in both aim and performance—no gastronomic revolutions there. But elsewhere there was stir and movement. This was the period of Raymond Postgate, the Good Food Club, its *Guide* and, to concentrate much into one name, the Bell Inn at Aston Clinton in Buckinghamshire. The first object of the Guiders was given by Postgate as 'to raise the standard of cooking in Britain', but of course he didn't mean in general, he meant in posh places, the kind of places he and other prosperous socialists felt at home in. Heedless and unheeded, the masses went back to their beloved white bread, sugar, sweets, biscuits, cold ham, baked beans, pickles, crisps and the rest as soon as they could, and straight on when the time came to fish fingers, chicken in the bag, frozen peas, TV dinners and Black Forest gâteau. There was no other way, and I have nothing against elites, but there are elites and elites, a point worth returning to.

The second half of the book offers half-a-dozen essays on more recent developments, beginning with something on the various foreign cookeries, Cypriot, Italian, Korean, etc, now established in Britain. Here I part company a little from the author, and even demur once or twice. Were Chinese and Indian restaurants outside London really so uncommon in the 1950s as he says? Ah, but in the *Guide* they were. He (later) approvingly quotes a reference to Chinese cuisine. Surely 'Chinese cuisine' has about as much precise meaning as 'European cuisine'? And I think chop suey originated in America, not China. Never mind. My quarrel is about authenticity. Driver keeps scolding us for normalising or Anglicising exotic dishes and not putting up with genuinely ethnic ones. Pfui! Authenticity has never done anything for me; I go to a restaurant for a meal, not a history lesson. What we take from others we inevitably and rightly assimilate to what we have already. I wonder if Driver (who likes musical analogies) enjoys authentic gypsy music more than what Kálmán and Johann Strauss made of it.

And yet frozen chicken does taste of nothing very much, and real Cheddar is much better than whatever it is they try to give us instead, and out at lunch yesterday I was issued with a roll whose 'crust' must literally have been painted on, because its texture was no different from that of the crumb. The chapter on food technology, all about 'plant milk' and TVP—texturised vegetable protein taken from cotton-seed or groundnut and got up as steak or smoked salmon—is no fun to read. Before very long the Guiders may be as far out on the fringe as Morris dancers or collectors of Nazi gear, only working longer hours with all that livestock to look after.

They are some way out already, if Driver is a fair sample. An elite, even a benign, post-entry one, is often in danger of forgetting the public. 'Mary Douglas's work "on deciphering a meal" is well known', we hear. Not where I am it isn't. But anyway, here is an extract from an extract from her essay on food 'as a system of communication', commissioned by the DHSS:

> One of the structural rules of this food system is progressive desiccation and geometrification of forms through the day. . . . This progressive desiccation allows of the shift from forks and spoons to fingers. The British biscuit . . .
> In the very simplicity and economy of the working-class dietary system we are able to see at work universal principles of recognition and stable structuring . . . Each significant unit . . .

But perhaps Driver just thinks we should take note of that sort of thing for our own good. No, he says himself of cooking in Hong Kong that 'in its technical accomplishment and imaginative innovation it is itself a medium of communication'. Now if all this were no more than a silly, pompous way of saying that a good cook concentrates on the customer, makes sure he gets through to him, etc, then the best of luck to everyone. But a dozen pages later Driver is saying, incidentally contradicting himself. 'A Hong Kong meal . . . is a statement to which customers are secondary.' I know that sort of meal, and the statement is Fuck You, and you haven't got to go to Hong Kong for it. Soho is far enough.

What does this talk of communication and geometrication, structuring and significance remind one of? Pseuds' Corner, certainly, also of introductions to catalogues at one-man shows and reviews of works of literary criticism; art talk, in fact. No harm in that, you may say, nothing new either; people have always gone on about the art of cookery. There is the point that if you call a cook an artist, you are stuck with having to find a new word to describe Delibes and Offen-bach, never mind Schubert and Brahms. Still, as long as no more is meant than that a first-rate meal is a splendid experience and a first-rate chef a fine fellow, then again all right. The trouble is that Driver means far more than that. Cookery to him pretends to be not just an art but a contemporary art, progressive, innovative, challenging, self-aware and cut off from the public like contemporary music. His kind of meal is a transaction between specialists. Hence his attitude to authenticity—leave the seaweed and the strychnine in the anaconda soup for him and Mary Douglas and forget the rest of us. As far as I know he has not yet applied for a restaurant to be given an Arts Council grant, but wait till an Eskimo eatery opens in Camden Town.

Not so much an elite, more a coterie. One day we may find ourselves faced with the choice of Driver's anaconda soup and synthetic turkey made from soya bean. In the meantime, I wish he and Mary Douglas would use some of their influence on that old thing about raising the standard of cooking in Britain. *That* is the need. If tomorrow every restaurant and club in the land were to cook exactly what it cooked today, *but properly*, the job would be three-quarters done. Take a case— although poached salmon is a favourite dish of mine, I hardly ever order it these days because of the number of times it has arrived so overcooked that I have had quite literally to wash it down. Let some energy be put into getting that sort of thing put right. If I can have a last musical analogy, I should like to see our food upgraded from somewhere around Sterndale Bennett to Elgar, not transmogrified into Villa-Lobos or Khachaturian, let alone Stockhausen.

It must be added that when Driver is not being tiresome about communications systems or chiding 'the British' for their taste in food, he has some very interesting things to say. He is good on prices, on taste-measurement, on the strictly limited convenience of convenience foods and particularly on how 'the British' run their catering industry. Like—dare I say it?—an expert chef, he balances his ingredients of narrative, background, fact, figure, illustration and anecdote with a sure hand. Consequently he is able to convey a great deal of information in a most readable form. I found his book thoroughly enjoyable.

But he really should not go moaning on about the absence of a successor to the reports on national food habits compiled by the marketing division of W. S. Crawford Ltd and published in 1938 and 1958, valuable as these no doubt were. Why on earth could he not perform or at least organise such an investigation himself? That can be his next job.

Times Literary Supplement, 15 July 1983

Christmas

I have long thought it a pity that Scrooge, like so many people in Dickens, spoilt his case by overstatement. To dismiss the Christmas spirit as humbug will not quite do as it stands, but it gets close. Although the reason for celebrating Christmas is very far from humbug, nearly everything else about it merits that name or a stronger one. All those presents, ingenious devices for taking money off you for things other people don't want in return for things you don't want yourself, in fact you often don't just not want them, you find them positively offensive. So that's the kind of book/tie/bottle of booze/ gadget they think I'd appreciate, you mutter aggrievedly. Then there's the points-for-trouble-taken system used by wives on your present to them, whereby a diamond necklace scores zero if ordered by telephone and paid for through the post, with something like a maximum score for a Cannibal Island nose-ring obtained on the spot in person, though in practice they'll usually settle for quite a humble object provided you get it after a couple of days' trudging round town.

I can see the attractions of stopping work for a couple of weeks. The British in general don't mind not being able to get anything done for that time. This is due to their tolerance, which means you cheerfully put up with the very bad service you get from the other fellow because of the very bad service he gets from you. This is only right while the country's prosperous, but don't let's go into that. I can't say I like working much, but I like not working even less. I always try to get in half an hour on Christmas Day. The glow of righteousness lasts until evening drinks.

Talking of which I have something which makes it all bearable, the presents, the in-laws, other people's children, your own children, the games, the noise, the mess, the ridiculous meals. It consists of one part French cooking brandy, one part Irish whiskey and four parts fresh milk. The hard part is remembering to have put milk instead of water into one of your ice trays the previous night. Drink the mixture immediately on rising, while the others are having breakfast or throwing up behind the snowman.

Written for a charity publication, 1985

Restaurants

LA TANTE CLAIRE

They used to advise extreme caution in approaching a French restaurant in London, especially the sort that gives itself airs. They used to argue that the proprietors and chefs of such establishments are there only because they have failed to make the grade in Paris or even in a French provincial city where the competition is much stiffer. They used to allege that London-French places will coast fraudulently on the deserved reputation of French-French cuisine. And by golly they got it right all along the line.

Rather unhandily far from the centre for a restaurant of such metropolitan pretension, La Tante Claire (who she?) has the distinction of being the only one ever recommended to me in person by a world-famous expert on food and drink. I suppose it ought to have sounded a warning. A whole book could be written (I might even write it myself one of these days) about the way various arts and skills and techniques have in this century come to be practised not for the benefit of the customer, of the general public, but to appeal to the colleagues and experts. Contemporary poetry is written to impress other poets or would-be poets, not to please the ordinary reader. Buildings and other public works are notoriously intended to strike a response from architects, not to be good to live or work in or even look at. And restaurant catering is designed less and less for those who simply want a good meal somewhere nice and more and more for food specialists of various kinds. And snobs, of course.

I was last chez la Tante Claire some years ago at a do organised by the German wine trade. A nobleman of vast stature, in fact the biggest count I have ever seen, introduced some of his country's wines to a group of food-and-drink writers and delivered a harangue on their merits as accompaniments to food. (He just made me long for a decent French red, but that is by the way). Much, including the whole physical shape and layout of the premises, has changed since those days, but the tradition of serving bad pretentious food has been faithfully kept up.

If you happen to have the luck to get a seat on one of the pair of sofas at the back of the room you can have a pre-meal drink there, otherwise this must take place at the table. It must be said that the dining-room is an extremely pleasant place to eat, light, airy, uncrowded, its general style reminding one of us of the restaurant at some up-market furniture emporium of thirty years ago. The clientèle was familial, unbusinessy and (always a gain) unarty. It included an old fellow who had done his fair share of eating in the past (or so he looked) lunching by himself—normally a good sign.

Our pre-meal drinks included a so-so Dry Martini, a tomato-juice served with vodka in error and a glass of Kir, my choice in deference to the prevailing Frenchness. The Kir, named after a mayor of Dijon, is a mixture of Cassis (blackcurrant liqueur) and (inferior) white Burgundy. I had forgotten what a sour, paltry little mix it was, or so it was on this occasion. There was nothing wrong with the condition of the serving of the wines, which were not even much overpriced. To nobody's surprise or indignation the list was entirely French.

The menu, too, was French, also written in that language, and advanced-level into the bargain. I suppose there must be some English people who like this affectation. The head waiter translated it all for us, not too fast and with perfect good-humour, but after listening to 500 words or so of close culinary description one's powers of recall and choice, even of staying fully awake, are likely to be past their best. That, I assume, was why written menus were invented in the first place.

The general level of starters rose as high as being patchy. The cold paté de foie gras was as palatable as that dish normally gets; the *frivolités de mer*, a curious fish hors d'oeuvre, was one of those dishes you have no particular objection to eating, but would never have ordered if you had known what you were going to get; the langoustines wrapped in pasta, though pleasant, would have been much tastier plain with a couple of slices of lemon. That was the good news. The hot paté de foie overdid the grease; the pigeon salad needed a large spoonful of Branston pickle to revive it; the coquilles St Jacques, quite tasteless, came in a sauce that looked like Bovril but tasted like bland soy sauce.

Now main courses in telegraphese, all they were fit for: lobster— flabby, tasteless, dubious sauce; pig's trotter—sort of mince under totally uncrisp skin, sweet greasy sauce; duck—quite eatable in a way but unidentifiable as duck, greasy sauce; lamb—looked fine but completely tasteless; rabbit stuffed with langoustines—bizarre, unidentifiable as rabbit; Dover sole—tasted of what thin strips of leather may well taste of. It was failed designer food, the very antithesis of genuine French cooking, that makes (or was still making when I was last there) marvellous dishes out of simple, left-alone materials.

Nothing bad lasts for ever, though admittedly it sometimes seems to be doing so. The last courses we sampled, the fruit, the sorbets, the cheese, were all good. The bread was good, the sensible large wine-glasses were good, the service was good, though the French are perhaps too independent-minded (putting it very politely) to make really top-notch waiters. But nearly everything else was bad, so bad, and bad in such a way that we wondered once or twice where the stuff was actually prepared. And it was ferociously expensive. Perhaps nobody would go if it were not.

Illustrated London News, 1987

LE GAVRÔCHE

According to my Webster's, a *gavrôche* is a street urchin, and this must explain the presence of the unappealing little figure on this restaurant's ashtrays, paper napkins and, in wraithlike form, menu and wine list. The point of the name and the emblem rather escapes me. I gather that of the brothers Roux who run the place, touches like that are more typical of Albert's than Michel's sense of humour. Such bits of information often come the way of the seasoned food-writer, and I offer this one for what it may be worth.

After a pair of catastrophes at La Tante Claire a year or two back, I promised myself to steer clear in future of French restaurants outside France, and held out against Le Gavrôche as long as I could. But it kept winning prizes and citations and being generally agreed to serve the best food in London, so, having done no more in the past than eat there a couple of times, not very enjoyable but at someone else's (considerable) expense, I caved in. Alas!—or rather *hélas*!

Drinks before the meal are served at a few tables on the ground floor and at rather more below stairs at one end of the dining-room. The furniture here is not much to look at nor good to sit on, rather crowded together in a take-it-or-leave-it spirit. You can get a not-very-cold Dry Martini or, among other serious drinks, a glass of The Macallan 1967 malt whisky, though not the better and cheaper ten-year-old. Or you can fill in a form securing you one of 250 copies of the English edition of *The Roux Brothers on Pâtisserie* (£40 inc p&p in GB). The tables in the dining-room are farther apart than in what they call their lounge, but the curved banquettes are badly built, so that you either have to sit with only half your back against the upholstery or eat with your plate at an angle instead of squarely in front of you. Whatever your choice, you are surrounded with dreadful pictures of every age and clime. This basement room as a whole offers no comfort to eye or body. I took the message to be that all that counted here was the food and drink.

The importance of both is certainly rubbed in by the way they are served. As soon as your course is ready an imperceptible signal is given and a group with something of the air of a Soviet colour-party at the Berlin Wall advances on your table, bearing plates of food under silver domes. When the senior ministrant has pronounced a brief ritual formula in French the domes are simultaneously snatched off and eating may perhaps begin.

This sort of thing makes me nervous. I sat for a minute or two looking at my lamb cutlets and waiting. 'Are you sure it's all right to start?' I muttered to my guest. 'He hasn't said "*bon appétit*" yet.'

'Yes he has, and you said "*merci*" back.'

'That was before the first course.'

'Yes, but it counts for the whole meal. Now eat up while it's hot.'

Just in case you might start to settle down and relax, another fellow bustles up every other minute to top up your glass, whether it needs it or not. Anything like a connected conversation becomes difficult. The service of both food and wine at Le Gavrôche is excessive in quantity and deficient in quality. Except from the pleasant girl who took our orders at dinner, any hint of humour or warmth or ordinary easiness of manner was lacking. Things cheered up only when we showed signs of leaving. The thing is that the French are not really cut out to be waiters; the temporary but real power it gives encourages them to indulge their sense of superiority. The British, with their laziness and cockiness, are not much better. In my experience the Italians and the Greeks are the best.

After all that, what about the food? *The Good Food Guide* treats it with the respect due to somebody like Beethoven, not only great in itself but the foundation on which half of what we love and revere has since been built. Can the editors be talking about the same restaurant? In 1986 they remarked of the cuisine: 'There are no tricks . . . there are no frills.' *Mon chapeau!* 'Tricks and frills' would be an excellent description of what you get three-quarters of the time: meat or fish smothered in sauces that make it virtually unrecognisable and are in themselves too rich for comfort, dustbin lid-sized plates, sweets wittily made to look like slices of liver paté and cream cheese . . . But then the same fellows found the service 'unobtrusive'.

The best dish either of us had was a starter consisting of oysters something-or-other. The sauce they came with was a *nonpareil*, luscious without being over the top, a combination of nuances I could not and was not meant to anatomise. And then, so to speak, there were the oysters. I could identify them, mainly by the texture, but then I was expecting them, and I think you could have fooled me with the right sort of mushroom or half-a-dozen other materials. An instructive comparison came my way a couple of days later when, at Hilaire in Old Brompton Road, I sampled a kind of oyster *à la Gauloise*, with laver bread and a touch of cheese, and there the addition was again most agreeable, but the oyster came first. Surely that must be to get things the right way round. The wine list at Le Gavrôche is naturally most extensive, reaching 533 numbered bottles and a couple of dozen halves, with eight pages of clarets. I stayed in the foothills of the price range, but there are peaks at £300–500 if you can scale them. All in all it costs a lot to eat and drink there. Which, of course, is an attraction to some people.

Illustrated London News, 17 February 1988

RULES RESTAURANT

Through the written word, Rules Restaurant in Maiden Lane, Covent Garden makes an interesting impression: oysters, George III, porter, Dickens, steak and kidney pudding, Thackeray (though they call him William Makepeace Thackeray now), tripe and onions, the-Prince-of-Wales-and-Lily-Langtry, vintage port . . . Well, a strong impression. I am probably alone in thinking Teddy the most boring figure in our national life since Rules opened in 1798, not excepting his grandson Edward VIII, allegedly another *habitué*.

The menu, too, reads well: English delicacies like whitebait and potted shrimps, red cabbage, boiled mutton and caper sauce, grouse, partridge and pheasant between stated dates, East End eels, mashed potatoes and peas, and if that 'East End' sounds a bit of a false note, one must try to think that it will be a romantic note for visitors. Value-free dishes like sea trout and escalope of veal are also on offer.

Spirits had fallen a little on arrival in a rather cramped and overheated place where there turned out to be only a fifty-fifty chance of getting a seat in the drinks-before-food area. In our case at least these drinks were well made and quickly served, but on my second visit the waiter tried—in vain, actually—to put me right on the orthodox recipe for the Old-Fashioned Cocktail. Part at least of the reason for this venture was that, as further observation soon showed, some sort of quarrel was evidently going on among the staff. Well, no comment, except that in these matters slackness at the top is to be looked for.

On this occasion the move to the table brought a further lowering of morale. The semi-circular banquette in a booth looked inviting but turned out to be too narrow from back edge to accommodate a standard bottom in any comfort. How the heavy-weight Americans across the aisle made out I cannot imagine. The technique had perhaps been borrowed from those hamburger joints where the disagreeable seating is designed to get the customer out and away as soon as possible. Any such intention here would have been more than adequately fulfilled by the quality of the food.

It must be said at once that the wine was outstanding value and impeccably stored and served. The coffee was excellent, though the Irish coffee was not hot enough. The veal escalope was perfectly adequate. The whitebait was fairly good but a bit soft. Everything else was disgraceful. I pass over a woolly tomato salad, tasteless asparagus, dull chewy mushrooms and devils on horseback with disastrously underdone bacon. The venison, evoking thoughts of pemmican or biltong rather than a dish seriously offered a diner-out, was as dry and void of flavour as anything I have ever tried to swallow, but it is a notoriously difficult meat and it too I leave on one side in favour of an account of what Rules did to three traditional English dishes that it presumably prides itself on serving.

Sausages, onions and mash. (I have been known to prepare this myself and so was in a position to apply that valuable test: is the restaurant's version at least as good as mine? Because if not . . .) Sausages, English sausages, are easy enough to cook but they need some attention to see that they are done all over. I fixed on one of the several supervisory-looking chaps who were standing about and directed him to see to this, and sure enough when they arrived an hour later the things were so raw the meat had to be dragged out of them with a fork. Unless care is taken, again, cooked onions tend to go to nothing and this lot certainly had. The mash was no good either—see below. And this with a dish the place prepares as a 'special' every Monday lunch-time and evening of its life.

Tripe, onions and mash. Tripe, described by Katharine Whitehorn as boiled knitting, is more literally part of the stomach of the ox, a fact which the Rules treatment does nothing to help you forget. It has little flavour of its own and none was given or suggested on this occasion. Pieces the size of A4 envelopes came in a thick over-buttered sauce instead of the milky mixture required by tradition. There might once have been onions present but none was apparent to my senses by the time the plate was set in front of me. As regards the mash—well, all I had better say is that if anyone can produce a more lifelike imitation of instant potato from real potatoes then I should like to hear from him.

Steak and kidney pudding. This looked well enough when it arrived, though rather stiff and invulnerable. When the outside of this sort of pudding is pierced with the knife, gravy should *gush* out. Not this time, very much not, in fact the whole thing was forbiddingly, impossibly dry, the steak too dry to cut properly. There was too little kidney, but of course only home cooks put in enough. The taste, far from overwhelming, was hard to pin down. Like the smell of turkey *Whiskas* was the nearest my guest could get—unexpectedly toothsome, in fact. Failure here is the more reprehensible in view of the admirable pop-in-the-steamer portions supplied by Marks and Spencer. All main dishes sampled at Rules were served not much better than lukewarm on a plate with the chill barely taken off it and supported by undercooked vegetables.

There are cheaper eating-places than Rules where the atmosphere and service are so pleasant that they drive out other impressions. Far from the case here; but then I find it hard to imagine an establishment Elysian enough to dispel the memory of two of the most disgusting full-dress meals I have ever tried to eat in my life. They would have stood out even in—where? Wigan? Nijni Novgorod? It seems that this hogwash-counter was a few years ago narrowly saved from the bulldozer. Pity. Let us hope that before too long a decent doner-kebab joint or Albanian takeaway may arise on its ruins.

Illustrated London News, 1988

LANGAN'S BRASSERIE

Michael Caine is pursuing me, not in the body but in pictured shape. A photograph of the well-known actor gazed at me from the wall of the Caprice the other week, and I found what I took to be a drawing of him, looking rather pale, at the top of the menu at Langan's Brasserie, in which I have heard he has an interest. Here, even more than at the Caprice, showbiz is the order of the day, with many customers wearing the uniform of the profession: jacket, white shirt, no tie.

The part where you have drinks resembles the tea-room of a station hotel given over to part of an amateur art exhibition. Terrible paintings hang there, not all in a modernist style, though one such—or rather two, one roughly tacked across part of the other—disfigured the down-stairs dining-room where I lunched. Along the far end of this room there are shelves randomly stacked with very second-hand books like Chapman's plays and the poems of William Edmonstoune Aytoun, the latter of which I should really have tried to buy or perhaps, more appropriately, stolen.

The upstairs dining-room, where I dined, is called Venetian something and a half-hearted attempt is made to evoke that city with some of the décor. Elsewhere a sort of student-cum-artist Parisian feel is aimed at, the most authentically Parisian touch being the bossiness and rudeness of the pre-meals service, though this is heftily backed up with an ineptitude and inefficiency all too characteristic of our own capital. On both my visits the performance was effortlessly the worst I have come across since starting to write this column.

Arrival at 12.30 pm with a table booked for one o'clock should, most people would feel, guarantee ample time for drinks before lunch. Not at Langan's Brasserie. At 12.45, jolly early, I thought, in fact before my guest and I had finished our first round, we were asked not at all tentatively to go to our table. I said we would like another drink first. 'Oh, they want another drink first!' somebody cried, and when the general amazement had died down we were duly brought more drinks but, perhaps because the waiter knew very little English, they turned out to be the same as the first round, which we had not asked for and did not want. We were no more than half way into the replacements when we were again asked, even less tentatively, to go to the table, and tamely let ourselves be driven from the not-nearly-full drinks room to the almost-empty dining-room at 12.55. Only when we had sat down did it sink in that, although we had been allowed to see menus, we had not been asked for our orders, in which case . . . I determined to improve on this.

When we turned up for dinner a couple of days later we made a better start, in that the fellow who had played the piano too loudly and in too concert-platform a style at lunch-time was now giving it a miss. This was made up for by the serving of a Dry Martini on the rocks instead of, as asked for, straight up—an internationally understood term for *not* on the rocks, plain. When a pert little creature tried for the second time in ten minutes to hustle us to our table and stood over us, I said we would like to order first.

'We don't take orders in the bar,' she said unapologetically.

Instead of asking her then what the hell, etc, I said in what I still think was a fairly neutral tone for the situation, 'We'd like to finish our drinks first.'

'I asked nicely,' she said untruthfully.

By this time we were quite ready to move, not least because arrival at the table at lunch-time had brought us into a different world, of smiles and eager service and efficiency. It was the same when we reached the (again almost empty) upstairs dining-room, though here the waiters became overworked, while remaining polite, as the place filled up. If we had thought we were in for more of the same as in the bar I think we would have walked out.

Had we done so we would have missed a treat, or rather two treats. We started off none too favourably with boring bread rolls, usually the sign of more boredom to come, and well-boiled instead of lightly-boiled quail's eggs. Everywhere else we saw the other side of the Parisian coin with food as delicious as I expect to be given anywhere, though not selected or deployed after any Parisian fashion one would normally think of. The starters were excellent, including gigantic succulent Mediterranean prawns and an artichoke heart stuffed with mushroom mousse that would have drawn a smile from a newly disqualified driver. All was well with the finishers too.

But it was the middle courses that, not at all as usual, brought the real resplendence. From an uncommonly varied and eclectic menu I chose for lunch black pudding with apple and onions and was transported: surely it was never as good as this on the banks of the Irwell, nor came with such generous trimmings. In the evening I opted with some trepidation for bratwurst and mash, mindful of what a highbrow sausage can be like, but this was thoroughly cooked despite being much less browned than I usually care for, and had been beautifully made. My guest enjoyed a roast partridge that was both tender and retentive of every scrap of flavour and a roast duck fully worthy of that dish at its very rare best.

Writing and remembering has made me want to go again. But I won't. Like all human institutions, restaurants tend to do what they can get away with, and having got away with murder in the bar they may try a spot of massacre in the dining-room. Not worth the risk, even for a glimpse of Michael Caine in the flesh.

Illustrated London News, 18 November 1987

PART ELEVEN
Music

All the Boys in All the Bands

The New Grove Dictionary of Jazz, edited by Barry Kronfield, Macmillan
Jazz Giants: A Visual Retrospective, compiled by K. Abé, Columbus Books

From the outside the *Grove* dictionary looks expensive all right, if not quite up to what is surely a lot of money for something under 1,400 pages long, much of it—I have not measured how much—reprinted material. It also looks kind of cheap, with gold and black lettering thrown around a bit on scarlet. (It reached me without dust-jackets.) Well, I suppose a touch of showbiz feel is to be welcomed when it comes to a form of entertainment that sixty years ago, certainly, you would have called an art only if you were French or trying to be funny or clever, and now has over 3,000 courses on it running in music schools and university arts departments. (I think it is 3,000 but I may be mixing it up with the number of available courses in science fiction, to which something very similar, and nearly as awful, has happened.)

Anyone writing a jazz piece for the non-specialist press had better nail his colours to the mast, or at least declare an uninterest, early on. I seem to have done so already. To me, an element of entertainment, of enjoyment, is inseparable from art, and I find it especially appropriate that it was the aestheticising Rossetti of all people who should once have insisted on the duty of poetry, as of all art, to be as *amusing* as any other human activity.

Most listeners to jazz (or the ones I speak to) found the entertainment beginning to depart from the music as it developed some time in the later 1930s. The first record I heard which sounded to me in parts disagreeable, as opposed to merely boring, was Fletcher Henderson's purposefully-titled 'Queer Notions' (1937, I think, though I cannot trace it in *Grove*). The first 'serious' book on the subject we heard about, Wilder Hobson's *American Jazz Music*, appeared in 1939. The explosion of 'modern jazz', associated with the names of Charlie Parker and Dizzy Gillespie, after which nothing was ever the same again, is usually traced to 1941. Meanwhile, a world war had started.

These and other dates, events, names, and many a learned musical exposition have been shifted around far too often for anything but a flat assertion here. For whatever reasons, whatever else had gone in, entertainment had gone out. Jazz had stopped being a naïve American form like science fiction or Westerns; it had stopped sounding pleasant and enjoyable because it had begun to lose its links with dancing and singing, the heart of all music. Being so much less complex, it had run through in only twenty-five years what it had taken serious Western music centuries to use up, or become afraid of being about to use up. But then it—jazz—had had technology to speed its decline, the LP record to break the connection with the three-minute dance-number, film and television for the anti-musical percussion exhibition. (No one with normal hearing will need reminding that mere links with dance and song, with mere beat, with mere pitch, are not enough on their own for anything.)

I doubt whether many people are capable of surveying a survey of such a balkanised, indeed mosaicised, field as 'jazz' has become. I at least am not. All I can do is look at a couple of the bits I think I know about, see how they do them and leave the reader to surmise how, for instance, the expert Bert Noglik manages with such 'neglected' (neglected!) East German masters as Gunter Sommer and Ulrich Gumpert.

Fats Waller shall be first. He is the jazzman as entertainer par excellence, comic hats and all, everything they hate, guying the words, chitchatting during the other fellows' solos (and his own), being funny, capable of being very unfunny too. His numbers are not so much jazz performances as tiny cabaret turns with his Rhythm, a tight little group that understood him perfectly. Nearly half a century after his death his records are constantly requested on radio: they divide significantly into Fats and his Rhythm and the Thirties and Forties oldies on Radio 2, and Thomas 'Fats' Waller and his more august Buddies or on solo piano or pipe organ or at least not singing on Radio 3. *Grove* inevitably stresses the solos, calls him a 'significant' organist—I hear him there as a master of the marcando style drowning in treacle. It (*Grove*) relegates a far livelier swinging organist, Milt Herth, to a couple of references found in entries on other people.

Significances, influences, importances, developments, schools, breakaways are inevitably the stuff of encyclopedias, academic courses, manuals, and not, just as inevitably, the stuff of art, or entertainment either for that matter. *Interestingness* is, must be, their overriding interest. This can be seen in detail in the disgracefully offhand entry *Grove* gives Sidney Bechet. See, he travelled too much to develop a popular following. He had too little competition. He was too solitary to exert direct influences. In closer detail: the two sides recommended here from the Noble Sissle 1938 session are 'Blackstick' and 'Southern Sunset'. Now, they are probably more 'interesting' than the other two, 'Sweet Patootie' and 'Viper Mad'. But anybody who thinks they are *better*, better entertainment, better art, must be tone-deaf, or a fool, or a musicologist.

K. Abé's photograph album, again a little pricey for its size, has 350 photographs, some in colour, of jazz people, mostly in action, mostly from the period 1940–60. The most famous pair has Louis Armstrong in 1944 opposite Dizzy Gillespie in the same year. Louis shown in vaudeville garb, coloured derby, waistcoat with brass buttons, check pants, Dizzy in beret, suit, hornrims. Louis is America, entertainment; Dizzy is the world, art. K. Abé sees all this, of course, and no doubt more, but I wonder whether he finds it as sad and final as I do.

Spectator, 11 February 1989

Mister Jelly Roll

J azz is often claimed to be the characteristic music of the Twentieth Century, and not only by those who have been professionally concerned with it. Some would go further and call it the most interesting or the most enjoyable. Well, there's not a lot of competition. The century's concert music, or classical music, or whatever we are to call it, is only now showing signs of coming back out of the wasteland it entered eighty years ago. Rock, the degenerate offspring of jazz, is the other possible contender, and jazz-lovers must face the unpalatable fact that that stuff is no less universally spread over the globe and much more popular than jazz ever was. But more interesting? Not to any number who have tried jazz too, surely. Characteristic of our century? All I can say is I hope not.

For many years and for millions of people over those years, first in America, then in the other Western countries, then in Latin America and further afield, jazz was the music that mattered, not only contemporary, happening all the time, but immediately attractive, no sooner heard than delightedly responded to. It was the music of youth, part of growing up, and as such unofficial, unwelcome to authority, a piece of underground culture long before the phrase was coined. It was Our music and They could only disapprove, deliver lectures (if anyone was listening) about its limited harmonies, formal unadventurousness, etc, or most often simply pay no attention. Which was fine with Us.

I was one of those—there were quite a few in the days of the Second World War and after—who became fascinated enough with the music to want to know something about its history, its ancestry, the places it had come from, almost anything, in fact, that would make the men who played it into something more than names on the label of a gramophone record. Books on jazz were thin on the ground then and what there were tended to be written by Frenchmen. Nevertheless it proved quite easy to establish that jazz had been born in New Orleans in Louisiana, half a world away on the Gulf of Mexico. The Crescent City (a name we soon learnt) quickly to take on for us the aura of a holy city, arousing the kind of feelings of awe and veneration that Christians of the Middle Ages must have felt towards Rome: somewhere wonderful, the fountain of blessedness, but of course to be visited in the flesh only by a rare and privileged few.

Fortunately there turned out to be someone to take us to the land of dreams, as 'Basin Street Blues' had called it, by way of the printed word. Alan Lomax had produced a book, revolutionary then, extraordinary still, that evoked in unbelievable detail and vividness the city with its sights and sounds and smells, the unique mixture of races and classes and languages, the semi-legendary individuals that brought jazz into being. And we who had welcomed jazz as displeasing to the establishment found it had been just as disreputable in its origins. But *Mister Jelly Roll* is such a rich portrayal of a society at a particular stage of its development that it ought by rights to appeal to anyone—anyone with an interest in human behaviour as it has been in the last hundred years, or longer. Most of the action is seen through the eyes of an appropriately remarkable and very egotistical man who proclaimed, loudly enough to be heard on this side of the Atlantic even before Lomax came along, that he invented jazz.

Jelly Roll Morton's own words in this book show how untrue that is and at the same time how large is the grain of truth within it. His piano improvisations are perhaps too much of their period; most of them were already beginning to sound dated less than twenty years after being recorded. But his contribution as an arranger is incalculable. Others besides accredited jazz-lovers will find the most fascinating of these pages those where Jelly Roll gets his chosen men together and takes them painstakingly through rehearsal and recording. 'He was exact with us,' the great clarinettist Omer Simeon remembers, and nobody ever drank at his dates. Sure, jazz is spontaneity, feel, improvisation, but it must be sober brainwork too, and for all his flamboyance and love of high living Jelly Roll never forgot that.

The music he helped to develop is of course dead, or can be said to live only in its corrupt descendants. It is sadly appropriate that he died in the very year, 1941, that saw the beginning of its irreversible decline. The old New Orleans is gone too, utterly; almost as I write I see the last dance-hall in the city, the San Jaquinto, has been turned into—what? An arts centre! But we still have some of the music, and this book.

First published as Introduction to re-issue of
Mr Jelly Roll, by Alan Lomax, Columbus Books, 1988

The 1982 Proms

I was delighted when the BBC asked me to write this article. I enjoy writing about music and am seldom given the chance; perhaps the reader will be able to see why by the time he gets to the end. My enthusiasm waned slightly when I came to read through the actual programmes in the series of Prom concerts. So many of them turned out to contain works that strike my ears and mind as of modern or modernist tendency and therefore to be avoided. I use the terms in a far from purely chronological sense, to include plenty of pieces written well before I was born sixty years ago—so it cannot be their newness that I find objectionable. Some people's tastes are different, I know, but I think the Corporation might be surprised to find how many hearts sink at the sight of certain well-known names and, even more, at the phrase 'first performance'. But I must pass on.

My brief was to indicate which concerts I intend to listen to, not merely which individual works. There are plenty of the latter, but there have turned out to be dismayingly few of the former. Take Prom 2. I am always glad to be able to hear a new performance of César Franck's miraculous Symphony in D minor, the finale of which is just beginning to make sense to me after all this time. But then, think of sitting through Dukas's *Sorcerer's Apprentice* yet once more and trying not to think of Mickey Mouse (in *Fantasia*) and enduring Ravel's *Pavane*— not mournful or elegiac, simply cheerless. And by all means let there be a Saint-Saëns piano concerto, but let it not be No. 2, though I can see why pianists like it: no rubbish about the orchestra being an equal partner.

It is not till Prom 38 that we reach a concert I mean to attend, so to speak, rather than just drop in on. Even now I have to arrive late, or metaphorically stay in the bar while Debussy's *Ibéria* is played, not a modern work exactly but sparing of those elements that make earlier music pleasant to listen to. But then!—Mozart's Piano Concerto No. 23, one of the great five that crown his work in this form, and if, as many believe, Mozart's piano concertos as a whole are his finest achievement, where are we to find anything fit to compare with these five, anywhere? I first heard No. 23 on records borrowed from the school library (I forget who was playing, but I have never been able to care much about such matters). Before then I had not known that music could be, yes, pleasant, celestially pleasant and deeply moving at the same time. It is what gives this concerto its special excellence.

Brahms's Symphony No. 1 also happens to have school associations for me. Our music master, the splendid Mr Taylor, gave a series of musical appreciation classes after school in which he explained, with illustrations on blackboard and on piano, the structure of this most elaborate of symphonies. Is this kind of thing still done? Or is it thought to be 'academic' or something? To this day I understand the Brahms 1 better than any comparable work. But I wish I could ask Mr Taylor something that never came up then. Would he agree that to call the speed-up at the end of the last movement 'unconvincing' is to miss the point? Brahms was unconvinced himself; he was bravely putting on a show of good spirits to hide his awareness that pain and sorrow do not go away. Or is that too elaborate in another sense?

Prom 42. Finding something new to say about the merits of Schubert's *Unfinished* Symphony is beyond most people, certainly me. The same may well be true of the reason for its unfinished state, but I will bash on regardless. It is surely not that Schubert knew he had a masterpiece in what he had already written—no composer with his training would have thought that—but that going on would have been uncongenial to him. He was not cut out for the substantial scherzo and massive Beethovenian finale needed to balance the first two movements, as he proved when he gritted his teeth the second time round and finished his C major symphony, which collapses at that very point.

Prom 43 opens with one of the least unacceptable of Stravinsky's works, *Pulcinella*. In fact, he did not compose it in the proper sense, merely adapted a number of pieces by Pergolesi; anyone less self-promulgatory would have settled for a credit as arranger. For good or ill it was always so with Stravinsky, the lifelong warmer-up of other men's creations, the great media modernist. How sadly inevitable it seems that he should have finished up semi-deified in America.

No carping at Beethoven's Piano Concerto No 1. I like the story of his having written the last movement on the day of the concert, with successive pages of manuscript passed under or round the door to the waiting copyists. It is certainly the best movement, and has the added distinction of being the only movement of a concerto by Beethoven referred to (though not named) in *Lucky Jim* (see Chapter Eight). The pianist Andor Foldes succeeded in working this out from the text. Nobody else ever has. Or is the fact too universally known to be worth remarking?

As I feel at the moment I will not be taking the risk of Berg's *Seven Early Songs* being early enough to be tolerable (anyway I am getting a bit old to tolerate music that is no better than tolerable) but I shall be in my seat for the Beethoven Symphony No. 8. Antony Hopkins has shown how Beethoven's symphonies constantly refer to and throw light on one another, and even I can hear echoes or rather anticipations of the Ninth in the Eighth, in its first and last movements at least. But of course differences remain, and there are preferences too, and the Tenth, had it ever been written, would surely have moved on from the Eighth, not the Ninth; we know it was to have no choir. With Purcell, Mozart, Weber, Schubert in our minds it is easy to forget how much we have lost by Beethoven's death at the not-very-old age of fifty-six. Had he lived even to sixty-five, nobody can imagine the consequences to music.

Prom 48. Except perhaps for J. S. Bach, Haydn was the laziest of the great composers, though like him a very productive one. With decades of drowsy symphony-simulation behind him he suddenly produced a masterpiece, No. 92, the so-called *Oxford*. It was first performed on the occasion of his being given an honorary degree there, and I used to think he had roused himself to meet the occasion, but apparently he had had the thing lying around for two or three years beforehand. The impulse had come from the usual place, nowhere in particular. (Afterwards he relapsed, stirring again briefly for parts of No. 100.)

Any kind of Haydn (d. 1809) is well followed by Liszt (b. 1811), who takes off into the very empyrean of brashness with his First Piano Concerto and *La Campanella* fantasy—all very fine, though concentrated on the performer in a new and unhealthy way. After the interval, Sibelius, before he reconstructed himself in the name of progress.

Prom 52. We easily fall into thinking that an artist's last work is his last word, that *The Tempest* is Shakespeare's farewell to something instead of just happening to come at the end of his full-time career. Tchaikovsky's Symphony No. 6 is about as much like a farewell as such a thing could be: literally his last production, completed and first performed only days before his suicide, the whole of it written to sum up his life and final destruction. And yet it points forward, full of new ideas, a new kind of music he must have longed to go on writing and developing. As it is, I suppose the nearest to a Tchaikovsky Seventh is Sibelius's First, parts of which have some connection with what is to be heard in No. 6, in that amazing and harrowing passage in the first movement immediately before the last return of the second subject and again and again in the last movement. This great piece of music has had less exalted descendants too. The soundtracks of a thousand Westerns, I always feel, come straight out of the coda of its first movement, where you can almost hear the jingle of the harness and see the sunset.

The Prom concerts before the Second World War in the old Queen's Hall were designed to appeal to a wide public and to attract new listeners, especially among the young; they attracted me. That policy meant that in the course of one season you would expect to be able to hear all the Beethoven and Brahms symphonies, a dozen or two popular nineteenth-century concertos, and so on. Things are different now, and in 1982 we are to hear appreciably more works written in this century than in the last. Well, audiences do change. Or perhaps it has been decided that there are quite enough people in this country listening to music already, and any new recruits would just be a nuisance.

I foresee no real or lasting success for the present policy, in the sense of creating a mass audience that would genuinely just as soon listen to Boulez as to Berlioz, to Stockhausen as to Schumann. For better or worse, twentieth-century music is like paedophilia. No matter how persuasively and persistently its champions urge their cause, it will never be accepted by the public at large, who will continue to regard it with incomprehension, outrage and repugnance.

The Listener, 6 May 1982

Rondo for My Funeral

I open my exposition with a short *mezzo piano* passage outlining some of my disqualifications for writing about music at all. I play no instrument, not even badly. Although capable of learning things from a score, I flounder if ever I try to follow a piece in one as soon as the tempo bucks up. I can hear something of what happens in the bass and inner parts, but any remotely subtle harmonic effect is lost on me. On the other hand, I have a good ear for pitch and, having been a chorister in my youth, might still be able to sight-read my way through one of the simpler Anglican hymns, especially if standing next to somebody who knew his business. And I listen a lot, occasionally at concerts, often to the wireless, usually on a hi-fi apparatus that, as far as I know, has no superior anywhere.

But, again, I admit to further limitations. The sound of a choir, unless I am one of it, offends me: sonic wool roughened with sibilants. The sound of a small body of strings, unless helped out by wind instruments or a keyboard, strikes me as meagre, half-starved: good taste with the gloves off. I might warm towards a string quartet whose leader opened the proceedings with the announcement, 'I'm sorry about the breakdown of the bus with the other chaps in it—we'll do what we can to give you a sort of rough charcoal-sketch version of what it ought to sound like.'

As some readers may have guessed, I also (*più forte*) object to certain composers and works. Here I ask the indulgence of any musicians who have not already turned to the sports pages. If I declare that Mahler lacks talent even more spectacularly than he lacks genius, or that the choral theme in Beethoven's Ninth Symphony is the most boring great theme in the world, it is useless to scold me for ignorance, lack of understanding, narrowness and shallowness of perception—useless because I already know I suffer from these failings among others. All amateurs must be philistines part of the time. *Must* be: a greater sin is to be coerced into showing respect when little or none is felt.

After this brief but very likely premature bout of in-fighting, I should state that, since starting to find it in my early teens, music has given me more pleasure, and more intense pleasure, than any other art. (For reasons I will touch on later, literature comes second for me here, and any sort of visual thing, from a cameo to a cathedral, just about comes nowhere at all.) Further yet: only a world without love strikes me as instantly and decisively more terrible than one without music. Yes, friendship would beat music too, but not instantly.

My kind of music starts at or about the beginning of the Eighteenth Century. But I have a grave Bach problem. From, say, the last movement of the Flute Suite — no point in steering clear of well-known examples — even these cloth ears can hear how energetic he was: from the Fourth Brandenburg Concerto, that amazing violin concerto that is really a concerto for violin and two flutes (or recorders) but actually a violin concerto after all, ditto how supremely clever he was, and more. Still . . . dare I say I find him abstract, indifferent to his audience to a degree unapproached until the advent of 'modern' jazz in the 1940s, indifferent to his medium in the sense that, as Basil Lane emphasised some ten years ago, the same material turns up in versions written for totally diverse, one would have thought quite irreconcilable, instrumental forces?

Probably not. Musicians would tear me apart in depth. They love playing his works, and that ought to be that. All the same, let me offer non-musicians, amateurs, listeners, a nasty little tip: look twice at composers or works that performers particularly enjoy performing. Much of the enjoyment generated may end with them. Mozart's last piano concerto, K. 595, is very popular with pianists. Is it as popular with audiences? I only asked.

Handel, I find — the whole of this article is what I find, so I will prune such pseudo-humilities from now on — Handel is a different pair of shoes. All right, he too plagiarised himself, but out of laziness or haste, not philosophy. The hallmark of his music is a superb masculinity, all over, for instance, the first movement of the Organ Concerto in F major, usually known as No. 4 — oh, if only one could behave like that! His anthem *Zadok the Priest* would fire a tone-deaf republican (it was written for the coronation of George II) and soars over my prejudice against choirs. Handel can even lead me some distance through the not very lush pastures of pre-classical opera.

The first half or most of the Eighteenth Century is crowded with composers of whom I can honestly say I enjoy everything of theirs that I have heard. They deserve better than being put in a list, but my space compels it. So — Sammartini, Albinoni, Quantz, Nardini, Tartini, Geminiani, Leclair . . . And of course Vivaldi, with those nuggets of oddity and asymmetry among the four-square blocks. And of course Pergolesi, whose death at twenty-six is a loss comparable to that of

Keats at a few months younger. And of course Telemann—I can do no more or better than beg anyone who has not already got it to rush out and buy his Violin Concerto in G as finely recorded under Neville Marriner: what utterly undull music.

Now for a giant, one I am particularly attached to through having discovered him for myself. True, Carl Philipp Emanuel Bach, third son of old JS—the latter being known in my household, or at least to me, as Bach's father—is hardly a figure of remote legend, and these days one hears a lot of him. But, twelve years ago, to an amateur, he turned up chiefly in musicology and, now and then, on the air with the odd organ piece. Then I saw a record called *Music in Potsdam* that offered a symphony by Frederick the Great, a Quantz flute concerto and a CPE harpsichord concerto: hard to resist. King and flautist were variously jolly; Bach made me forget to pick up my drink. Those switchback melodies, full of leaps and plunges and interspersed with sudden silences and murmurs, those agitated rhythms seized me at once. They conveyed passion of an intensity never found before in music of the pre-Beethoven era, and this was (said the sleeve) 1748. What sort of passion it might be—anger? grief? exultation?—I am still far from identifying, but passion it is. I was fascinated to learn of CPE's reported remark that nobody will be moved by the composer's material unless he is himself moved by it.

Mozart's more famous remark, that he owed everything to CPE, is informative, also generous, if less than generous to CPE's younger brother, Johann Christian, and to his own father. Now: to defer for a little the fearful task of trying to say what I find in Mozart's music, I will explain a small personal point. Many years ago, a character in a novel of mine was irritated to hear somebody singing something by 'filthy Mozart'. He had a hangover at the time, and the singer was an enemy of his, and authors are allowed to dramatise attitudes they do not share, and anything on the lines of 'filthy Pavel Josef Vejvanovsky' would lack bite, but some people have been dull enough to think that that was *my* sentiment. Aargh! *Obviously*, in such a context, you invoke the artist you most admire.

Other composers can make me feel their joy, sorrow, fury, high spirits; Mozart affects me rather differently. What he offers is something more purely musical, in a sense less human, a series of glimpses of a state of perfect order. I cannot tell why this should give any pleasure at all, let alone such keen pleasure, especially given the state of disorder of most other things, inside and outside the self; indeed, to shed tears at Mozart's music could be a symptom of pain at the recognition of inadequacy. But I will not shamble further along a path that has landed many better-equipped explorers in the mire. Certainly, one approaches his works very much as in expectation of pleasure, and feels uplifted at the close—if, again, that is characteristic of pleasure.

If all of Mozart except one category were to be blotted out, which would I keep? It must be the piano concertos. Here I follow the

admirable Arthur Hutchings, who has helped me to feel I can see quite
a lot of what the composer is doing in them. His book (*A Companion
to Mozart's Piano Concertos*, Oxford University Press), has taught me
more about music than any other. To particularise among the concertos, no interesting general statements about them being possible,
means either trying and failing to write a short book of my own or
baldly reciting K numbers, so—449, 450, 453, 466, 467, 482, 488, 491.
Which of those? 482. I think.

I am afraid I can be little better than annoying about Haydn. As
soon as the man on Radio 3 says, 'We now present the eighty-ninth
in a series of 300 programmes devoted to Haydn's chamber music', I
start muttering paranoiac stuff about conspiracies and blackmail. When
he took his finger out, as in the Oxford Symphony (full of that rarest
of musical qualities, humour), he was splendid; most of the time he
left it in. Still, I like his spurious works: there is a very decent flute
concerto falsely attributed to him, and 'his' Second Horn Concerto is
most odd and rousing. I keep hearing CPE in it, but a title-page
bearing so famous a name can hardly have got lost; perhaps a pupil.

About the end of the Eighteenth Century, something untoward
happened to music-according-to-me: it went difficult, or more obviously difficult. This means that, with a single exception to be noted
later, I turn to liking works rather than composers. Beethoven is
and must be the great case in point. His Second Symphony I enjoy
thoroughly; I cannot tell whether, apart from all the other things he
was doing, he meant to demonstrate how enormously much can be
done melodically with ideas rather than tunes, but that is one of the
ways the piece strikes me. By the time of the Third Symphony I start
losing him, and most of his chamber music is out of sight. If old age
should bring me wisdom and humility (no sign of either at the
moment), and leave my ears more or less unimpaired, mature
Beethoven is my target.

A good deal of what remains must, I am afraid, be a matter of
stealing at a smart pace through the classics. No bad thing, that pace:
what man in my position would dare to try to say anything remotely
new about Schubert's Unfinished Symphony, Mendelssohn's Italian
Symphony, Brahms's Third Symphony, Rachmaninov's Second Symphony?—not to speak of all those concertos and operas and polonaises.
The best I can do is to be unmitigatedly personal and/or hope to
mention a work or two that not everyone will know by heart already.

So: be good enough to arrange to have Weber's headless bassoon
concerto, the Andante and Hungarian Rondo, played at my funeral:
the Rondo is the most gallant (not *galant*) music I have ever heard, as
well as being buoyant and humorous and touching—not bad for half
a dozen minutes. I look to a higher Power to lay on a performance of
Schubert's Trout Quintet when, afterwards, I take Jackson's Earl Grey
tea and cucumber sandwiches in the Elysian Palm Court.

I was delighted to hear Raymond Leppard say on TV a few weeks ago that the French were an unmusical nation. I had always thought so, what with how dull Berlioz is to listen to rather than think about, and how silly that more recent crowd are: Satie, Milhaud, Ibert; how disrespectful, too, being Gallicly witty about, poking leaden sly fun at, the circus and bandstand music they grabbed at when they ran out of ideas. But Saint-Saëns' Third Symphony and parts of his piano concertos are better than all right, good, solid, pompous, vulgar, driving stuff. And Vincent d'Indy's *Symphony on a French Mountaineer's Song*, in fact nearly a piano concerto, marvellously blends lyricism, sentimentality, humour and what in 1887 must have been 'modern' shock tactics. (And César Franck was Belgian-German.) Puccini, *si!*, Verdi, *possibilmente?* Wagner, *nachdruecklich nein!*

Music-according-to-me started to die before the First World War, with Schoenberg, the James Joyce of music, a comparison I mean as precise, in that each, of set intellectual purpose, systematically undid his great natural gifts to the general detriment of the art he practised. I still cling to parts of Sibelius, Rachmaninov, Richard Strauss. But, with Stravinsky, the Ezra Pound of music, also at work, the end was bound to come. And, so far as I can, I know what I am talking about: if I had a quid for every 'contemporary' work I have listened to the first couple of minutes of . . .

I have kept until nearly the end the solitary post-classical figure I swallow whole: Tchaikovsky. Mozart is for me the greatest composer, greatest artist. Tchaikovsky is my favourite composer. He idolised Mozart, and by no coincidence: both, in whatever different ways, have the capacity to administer sharp jolts to the emotional solar plexus while ostensibly being nothing more than gay, airy, pretty. Yes, Tchaikovsky bears down much harder at other times; his music has a palpable design on me; he wants me to participate in his forebodings, his passions, his bouts of wild energy, his despairs, and I do, wholeheartedly.

As good a test, and differentiation, as any is the famous tune, and its varying appendages, in the first movement of the Pathetic Symphony. Anyone who fails to be moved by it all has no feeling for music; but anyone who feels that there can be no finer music in the world has not looked hard enough elsewhere. Tchaikovsky saw this with perfect clarity, remarking that Mozart was tragic while he himself was no more than pathetic. But it would be worth testing the second half of that pronouncement after a good performance of the whole of the symphony referred to, with its last movement fresh in the ears.

I said near the start that, as a source of pleasure, music takes precedence for me over literature. That is the priceless recompense of my amateur status. I know enough about literature to be able to tell when a work takes a wrong or unfortunate turn. To mention a favourite poet, Housman, highly apposite in a Tchaikovsky context for several reasons: one of his very best poems, 'Fancy's Knell', uplifts me all the way until the final four lines, which let me down, not hard but unmistakably. Nothing so definite can happen to me with music I respond to. A musician friend commented, when I was extolling the son of Bach's father, that he was indeed a most interesting composer, but that his bass line often left something to be desired. It will never, I think, leave much to be desired by me.

Ignorance is always deplorable, and I am often nettled, to put it no more strongly, to reflect that I cannot hear the same symphony as my friend and his colleagues can, that I know just enough to know how much I miss. But it is a great blessing to be able to catch glimpses of the world of mysterious, ideal beauty that music offers, even though I cannot truly enter it.

Sunday Times, 1 July 1973

Index

All references to individual works are grouped together under the entry for their author, except that where the author is not mentioned in the text a work is listed in alphabetical sequence; the works of Kingsley Amis are treated similarly.